EXCAVATE!

EXCAVATE!

The Wonderful
and Frightening
World of

THE FALL

Edited by Tessa Norton & Bob Stanley

Preface by Grant Showbiz
Foreword by Michael Clark

faber

First published in the UK and the USA in 2021
by Faber & Faber Limited
Bloomsbury House
74–77 Great Russell Street
London WC1B 3DA

Designed and typeset by Stuart Bertolotti-Bailey
Printed and bound in Slovenia by DZS-Grafik d.o.o.

The right of Tessa Norton and Bob Stanley to be
identified as editors of this work has been asserted
in accordance with Section 77 of the Copyright,
Designs and Patents Act 1988

A CIP record for this book
is available from the British Library

ISBN 978–0–571–35833–5

10 9 8 7 6 5 4 3 2 1

MIX
Paper from
responsible sources
FSC® C106600

CONTENTS

EXCAVATE!

This is not a book about a rock band. This is not even a book about Mark E. Smith. It is not a book about where he drank, or what he said to people, or who wrote the chords to X, Y, Z. This is a book about the Fall group – or more precisely, their world.

The Fall were so many things, so many worlds; if you got it (and not everyone did), they represented everything. It is not, therefore, this book's place to attempt a biography. Of the many former members of the Fall, every personality deserves to tell their own story, in their own time, but that is not for this book. If there are axes to grind, none were ground here. The content is as first-hand as possible. So, here are notes, stickers, posters, artwork, beer mats – all material sourced from fans, an unfiltered cache of Fall artefacts. These are the items that people hung on to and treasured, from the *NME* journalist who gave the group their first feature to the secretary of the Arthur Machen Society.

The book includes just a couple of interviews, one of which is a look over the shoulder from the end of the 1990s, in which Mark E. Smith's voice chimes with absolute clarity. We have included artwork from the thirty-two purely studio albums (including *Slates* but excluding, say, the mostly live *Totale's Turns*). While reviews and the voices of rock criticism are mostly absent, the press releases you will read here come straight from the group, written by Smith alone, or with manager/confidante Kay Carroll. They are here as missives direct from the Fall Foundation.

This is the world of the Fall. This is the Fall-shaped hole they punched in the wall. This is *everything else*; each essay touches on an aspect of the Fall's world and influence. In the range of contributors, each with their own different specialisms and fields of experience, we wanted to illustrate how the Fall are a jumping-off point into myriad directions, many of them nothing to do with music. The world of the Fall is not just one of inky fingers thumbing through music weeklies, or of Peel Sessions, but of a dazzling city founded on speculative fiction, work ethics and northern architecture.

The book is *for* Mark E. Smith more than it is *about* him.

CAP.! HET!

TN / BS, November 2020

I still remember the first time ... that wonder and joy of the *Bingo Master*'s tale, and the succinct manifesto of its B-side. In my experience this state of amazement is a hard one to sustain — artists drift off, bands never recapture that original magic. However, with Mark, and almost always with the brilliant musicians involved, that rarely happened for forty years. Just re-reading that last sentence I have to sit here, with tears in my eyes, and take that in: forty years of brilliance; of mad gigs; of laughter long into the night; strange studio dances; of perception changed forever; of the mundane lifted onto a pedestal ... which moments later is kicked away.

That remarkable journey from 1978 to *Re-Mit* and the astonishing gig at the Transformer Festival, Manchester (28.05.17), where Mark told me how ill he was, and then we went out to stand shoulder to shoulder with Royal Trux and Swans ... a moment of extraordinary defiance. After the last gig I ever did with Mark at the 100 Club we started discussing the next album. It was meant to start in December, but other commitments made it impossible for me until January ...

The Fall are so important to those that get it, but they were more important by far for Mark. We will not see his like again.

Grant Showbiz

Foreword

The first time I saw the Fall was on a bill with four other bands at the Lyceum in London. For no apparent reason, someone got up onstage and punched Mark E. Smith smack in the face. He didn't flinch and carried on as if nothing had happened. I already had a growing interest in what they were doing, but thus began a love affair which has continued to this day.

'New Puritan' (Peel version) felt like a clarion call for me to begin my own dance company. I went to see the band on the outskirts of London with the express intention of asking Mark if he would allow me to use the Fall's music for my work. After a bottle of pure Polish spirit (120 proof), I went backstage with a Walkman – already recording – hanging around my neck. That cassette has long since disappeared along with the many other cassettes of 'work in progress' songs and handwritten missives from Mark which followed.

Before the Musicians Union threatened to ban the Fall if they continued to allow me to use recordings of their songs – KEEP MUSIC LIVE! – the band began coming to see performances of my early work. When they were in the audience, they would refuse to allow anyone to leave the theatre. A strong bond was forged . . . new work emerged.

I encouraged Mark to write a play which was shown at Riverside Studios where I was choreographer in residence, and by the time of recording *The Wonderful and Frightening World of The Fall* I was spending every day in the studio (and pub) with Mark. 'Le French Revolting' followed for the Paris Opera Ballet under the directorship of Rudolf Nureyev. Mark tried to forbid me from using music by anyone other than the Fall.

We were able to raise the funds for *I am Curious, Orange* in 1988. At last, the band and the dancers could be onstage together, live. I think it's fair to say that everyone involved was thrilled. Fall fans, who would never have chosen to go anywhere near a ballet, were exposed to my work, and vice versa.

Several years later, I was doing a three-month residency in Berlin and invited Mark to join me for a week to explore the possibility of a new collaboration. I stayed with friends in order to allow him the flat I had been given. It became apparent that his eccentricities had become more pronounced; small things – he kept his money in the fridge, answered the phone when the doorbell rang. Clearly our work together was done. I was, however, able to give him the title for his spoken-word LP *Pander! Panda! Panzer!* . . . it was the least I could do after all the titles, and ideas, he had given me over the years.

Michael Clark

xii

1977

sticker here

1977

1978

1979

1980

1981

1982

1988

1987

1986

1985

1984

sticker here

1984

1983

1989

sticker here

1989

The changing face of Mark. E. Smith

SMILE!

2005

1990

1991

sticker here

1991

1992

1994

1993

1995

sticker here

1995

1996

1997

1998

1999

sticker here

1999

2004

2003

2002

2001

2000

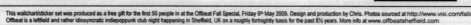

Introduction

Over the course of their forty-year career, which ended abruptly on 24 January 2018, the Fall were consistently one of the most fascinating and unique groups Britain has ever produced, and their frontman arguably the country's sharpest lyricist. Mark E. Smith's death, following a short illness which he tried hard to conceal beneath the Fall's ferocious work ethic, revealed a host of Fall fans in unexpected places. When the band made the front page of pretty much every broadsheet the following day, it marked an outpouring quite at odds with the irascible media caricature of Smith. Their impact wasn't because of that famous YouTube clip of the grumpy drunk bloke reading the BBC's football results in a funny voice, and it wasn't even because of John Peel saying they were 'always different, always the same'. Instead, everyone from Turner Prize winners to the *Guardian*'s political columnists came forward and revealed how the Fall had been their education.

The Fall formed in 1976 and released their debut EP, *Bingo-Master's Break-Out!*, two years later, a scratchy combination of Lancashire locale and mild peril ('there's a grave somewhere only partly filled'). The line-up credited on the sleeve was Martin Bramah (guitar), Karl Burns (drums), Mark Smith (vocals), Una Baines (electric piano) and Tony Friel (bass). The order, with Bramah first, was significant. Baines and Friel had gone by the time of their first album, *Live at the Witch Trials*, a year later. Friel's replacement on bass was ardent Fall fan Marc Riley, with sixteen-year-old Yvonne Pawlett coming in on keyboards – both hired by Smith, who became the band's unchallenged leader once Martin Bramah, too, left in 1979. That year's *Dragnet* was much more of a statement than *Witch Trials*, its cassette-quality anti-production adding extra layers to Smith's tableaux of horror, pills and local-paper yarns. Line-up changes and upheaval seemed only to re-energise the group: while it's understandable that many see 1978 to '83 as a golden age (their 'earlier, funnier stuff'), there are plenty who hold the riff-heavy *This Nation's Saving Grace* (1985) as their masterpiece; a new generation of fans arrived with 1989's *Extricate* and the more melodic *Shift-Work* (1990), as Manchester became pop's world capital; while no Fall album was more chaotic (and, naturally, intriguing) than 1997's self-produced *Levitate*, aided by Julia Nagle's squiggly electronics. By contrast, they were never tighter as a band than on 2005's *Fall Heads Roll*, and shows from this period were intense and special. True to form, this line-up had disintegrated by the time 2007's *Reformation Post TLC* was recorded.

Smith lived in Prestwich – to the north of Manchester, a town on the edge of a city – until he died. In interviews he said he liked Blackburn for its surviving soot-black stone, disliked Bolton for related reasons (too scrubbed) and loathed Bury. He also had a soft spot for Wakefield and – though he was an ace at myth-building – genuinely was a member of the Wakefield Young Drinkers' Club referenced on the back of 1980's live album *Totale's Turns*.

The Fall

'TOTALE'S TURNS'
('IT's Now or Never')

IN: Doncaster!
Bradford! 79 Oct-Feb 80
Preston!
Prestwich!

The cover of that album listed the venue locations in Smith's handwriting: 'Doncaster! Bradford! Preston! Prestwich!' Even the north's least fashionable towns, like Accrington and Haslingden, were referenced in lyrics. But he had no time for romanticising the old industrial north: 'Who wants to be in a Hovis advert anyway?' Though detractors might say that Smith's songs were inscrutable, indecipherable to anyone unfamiliar with towns in the western foothills of the Pennines, the Fall had a Top 20 hit in New Zealand with 'Lie Dream of a Casino Soul' in 1982. They gradually became popular in America too, and ended up in Hollywood when 1982's 'Hip Priest' was given a prominent role in Jonathan Demme's film *The Silence of the Lambs*, where no knowledge of Lancashire's topography was needed in order to feel menaced.

While they were umbilically tied to east Lancashire, the Fall never resorted to any provincial clichés. By the late 1980s, when Manchester had become a musical genre as well as a geographical location, Smith put distance between himself and the city by saying, more than once, that Manchester's best group was 1960s cabaret beat combo Freddie and the Dreamers (the Fall, he would then note, were from Salford); and to avoid any tainting of the Fall's place in pop music, he moved to Edinburgh for eighteen months when Madchester fever reigned. When the dust had settled, he worked with Inspiral Carpets, the least fashionable of the late-1980s wave.

Counter-intuitive moves were quite intentional, and all connected. Part of the pleasure of listening to the Fall is that you are entering a world that doesn't make sense at first glance. Mark E. Smith never sanctioned official lyric sheets and revelled in sabotaging his lyrics' own clarity — singing through loudhailers, recording on primitive cassette recorders — all of which kept the Fall safe from pat interpretations. Theirs was a strangeness that resisted conventional understanding, although you couldn't help but try to understand what you were listening to, because if you *did* understand enough of Smith's reference points, you'd know pretty much everything worth knowing. Who wouldn't want to be armed with a working knowledge of British horror writer M. R. James, shipping dock procedures, contemporary dance, Manchester City, screenwriter Nigel Kneale, the Yugoslav wars and Can?

Mark E. Smith's persona, and so his biography, slowly began to whittle away at the Fall's extraordinary fictions and grotesque social realisms in the mid-to-late 1990s. Over the years, their music settled down a little, became less strange and surprising. We were all getting used to it. As this happened, the stock character of 'northern pub bloke', the 'irascible national treasure' straight from central casting, the James Brown-like problematic bandleader-tyrant became the story. This allowed the heart of the group's astonishing creative output to become obscured. One of the Fall's creative strengths was to employ Smith's detailed knowledge of unlikely subject matter. For example, 'The Container Drivers', a thundering rockabilly track on 1980's *Grotesque*, plainly depicts the unexotic work of lorry drivers: 'Grey ports with customs bastards [...] look at a car park for two days [...] there's no thanks from the loading bay ranks.' (Containerisation put thousands of dockers out of work in the 1970s; Smith had more than a working understanding of this, having worked as a customs clerk at Salford docks before the Fall took over his life.) With songs about container docks, CB radio, Wigan Casino, water rates, William of Orange and mistrust of London ('Leave the capital, exit this Roman shell!'), the group were chroniclers of British society, as idiosyncratic and important as the Kinks and the Smiths. These lyrical concerns form a particular universe, which has so far remained mostly unmapped. This book hopes to correct some misconceptions and redress this balance. We wanted to explore, for example, the crucial contributions by women to the Fall's story, and how the Fall refused to pander to easy assumptions about 'the north'; they always knew about and explored the idiosyncrasies of different towns and cities, and the psychogeography of the north of England.

It's worth remembering that, in spite of Smith's assertion that the group would still be the Fall if it were just him and 'your granny on bongos' (leaving a compelling visual impression of a working-men's-club version of Tyrannosaurus Rex), the group started out as much more of a democracy. If anyone was the leader early on, it was guitarist Martin Bramah. When Smith's new sweetheart Kay Carroll became the band's manager and a part-time member, it forced his ex-girlfriend Una Baines's hand, and she and Bramah, who left after *Dragnet*, formed the formidable Blue Orchids. It says something about Smith's later control over the group's musical policy that no other particularly notable groups were formed by ex-members of the Fall (aside from Baines's next project, the folklore-influenced post-punk group the Fates).

Along with his 'always different, always the same' line, John Peel astutely called them 'the band against which all others are judged'. They always stood alone. Whatever the line-up of the Fall, they never sat neatly alongside their peers, and this awkwardness resulted in intense and unique music. Mark E. Smith, like Brian Clough, got the best out of players who otherwise probably wouldn't have made the grade. He has been compared to Clough — and James Brown — many times before. But this book isn't about his style of leadership, or his ex-wives, or what he drank. You can't look directly at the sun; perhaps to make sense of what it was that Smith and his musicians gave to us we need to understand everything else that surrounds the band. This is the story of what the Fall can teach us, and the story of the people who bought the records; how the Fall inspired people in myriad, innumerable, often opaque ways; and how they subtly taught us how to be us.

Tessa Norton & Bob Stanley, 2020

Left: William Blake,
The Ancient of Days fro
Europe a Prophecy, 179
Relief apg, 36 × 25.7 cr

Below: Bury New Roa
Prestwich.

Jerusalem to Prestwich

And did those feet in ancient time,
Walk upon England's mountains green?
And was the holy Lamb of God
On England's pleasant pastures seen?

And did the countenance divine
Shine forth upon our clouded hills?
And was Jerusalem builded here
Among these dark satanic mills?

The rant 'Dog Is Life/Jerusalem', recorded as part of *I Am Kurious Oranj* after it appeared in the dance event commemorating the tricentenary of the Glorious Revolution with Michael Clark in 1988, developed around a syncopated rendition of Hubert Parry's familiar tune and incorporates William Blake's classic poem.[1] 'Jerusalem' conveys the special relationship enjoyed by the English with their landscape and with God, an implicit sanctity that even permitted William III's invasion to be ticked through as a minor incident to perpetuate Anglicanism rather than a revolution at all. Whether as a celebration of English pomposity, as in the versions by Emerson, Lake and Palmer and many others, or as a comment on Britain's nascent working classes, as suggested by Billy Bragg or Mark Stewart, 'Jerusalem' represents the British psyche far more closely than the one-dimensional so-called national anthem. For Mark E. Smith, it reflected just one of many irritating commonplaces of the English character, a chorus to a series of complaints about how people never help themselves but instead blame the government. But it also indicates something of his very traditional attitude to architecture and landscape, one in which the dominant interest is history, but extending to an exceptionally close relationship to his home town: to Manchester, home of Blake's satanic mills, but more specifically to Prestwich, four miles to the north-west.

Blake wrote 'Jerusalem' between 1804 and 1808, just as the cotton trade was transforming the modest market town of Manchester into the world's first industrial city. Perhaps no poem so starkly defines the contrast between the hills of the north and the dense industrialisation that swept across the surrounding plains. Many of Smith's own lyrics similarly reinforced this contrast between grimy Manchester and the hills to the east, which with deindustrialisation have become more visible on the skyline. The spat-out place names, Manchester or Haslingden, epitomise once-dignified nineteenth-century high streets where brick and stone have given way to the concrete and glass of Arnold Hagenbach and Sam Chippindale's Arndale centres or more recent, sleek, high-rise flats.[2]

William Blake

Manchester has 'so much to answer for', Morrissey declared. By comparison to such sweeping takes on Whalley Range and Hulme, Smith's references are small and specific and, the Arndale Centre apart, concentrate on Victorian Manchester and its northern suburbs. Manchester's plan of a business and retail centre surrounded by residential districts that separated rich from poor, and from their factories, was pioneering; it became commonplace after it was repeated across every new and industrialising city around the world, particularly in the American Midwest and Australia. London's estates, like in other medieval European cities, had located grand squares and boulevards for the rich alongside backstreets and convenient markets for their servants, stables and supplies.

Manchester's medieval core is tiny, its old walls defined today by the curve of Exchange Square and containing the medieval church and Chetham's School and Library. The sixteenth-century travel writer John Leland nevertheless described it in *c.*1538 as 'the fairest, best builded, quickest and most populous tounne of all Lancastreshire', suggesting that it was already on the up.[3] Without restrictive guilds, and with soft water, coal and transportation via the River Irwell – much improved by the arrival of the Bridgewater Canal in 1759 – Manchester became the centre of cotton manufacture and thence the commercial business hub for the development of the surrounding towns. Its centre developed with warehouses, banks and institutional buildings to a common height of around six storeys, reinterpreting the palazzo style of the first Renaissance merchants in Lancashire red brick. In 1861, *The Building News* claimed that 'Manchester is a more interesting city to walk over than London. One can scarcely walk about Manchester without coming across examples of the grand in architecture. There has been nothing to equal it since the building of Venice.'[4] It is this Victorian Manchester that Smith describes, beginning with Queen Victoria herself, 'a large black slug in Piccadilly'.[5] Back in the 1980s, the reference to Ardwick Bridge in 'Wings' seemed to convey all that was most dank and Dickensian, though the reference is actually political, for in 1867 Irishmen attacked a prison van carrying two Fenian prisoners as it passed under the railway bridge on Hyde Road; three were caught, tried and executed. The reference exemplifies Smith using a place as a cue for history, where he personifies the cultural voyeurism of psychogeography well before Iain Sinclair and Patrick Keiller made it clichéd and lifelessly academic. Smith's description of Arthur Machen (1863–1947), a founder of the genre, rings true of his own life: 'He lives in this alternative world: the real occult's not in Egypt, but in the pubs of the East End and the stinking boats of the Thames – on your doorstep, basically.'[6]

Central Manchester was damaged in air raids sporadically between 1940 and 1944, the worst attack coming on the nights of 22 and 23 December 1940. The devastation was far less than in London, Plymouth or Hull, but it took out two major areas of the city near the River Irwell, while the cathedral was the most damaged in the country after Coventry's. Lord Reith, the former

Arthur Machen

director-general of the BBC who had become minister of works and planning, asked that the city be replanned 'boldly and comprehensively'.[7] In response, the city surveyor and engineer Roland Nicholas produced a surprisingly gentle scheme for rebuilding Manchester's densely crowded slums as garden cities, an extension of the programme begun at Wythenshawe in 1931, and it was only when shortages of land and opposition from the surrounding authorities made this impossible that Manchester turned in the 1960s to building great brutalist blocks of flats, such as Fort Ardwick and the Hulme Crescents. But these again were predominantly in south Manchester, disdained by Smith as home to students and Morrissey, although Karl Burns and Tony Friel lived in Hulme for a time.

Smith's attitude to architecture was as traditional as 'Jerusalem':

> *You sat in these houses [...] they had everything the working class wanted then, you see, because you're getting central heating, fridge, and the rest of that fuckin' crap, you know. But you can hear people shouting next door, you're not allowed to paint the front of you house, they got crime and that, because they got lifts. The lift's always broken. Someone will come along with some sense and knock them down. A nightmare. A nightmare. Like all these people who lived on estates, before the war, they used to walk in and out of each other's house, even though they were in abject poverty, nobody ever locked the door. But now with these estates, it's like rat experiments. Essentially what it is. You're closing people up. I used to go out with girls when I was a lad, and they'd live on these estates, they'd just be unbearable, man. You'd go in these houses [...] they'd all be the same. They all have gardens and shit, little gardens. But you go in, all the wallpaper is the same, the smell is the same, like being in prison, very, very similar.*[8]

A move towards conservation and the reuse of buildings followed a policy shift led by the short-lived regional authority, the Greater Manchester Council, which was inaugurated in 1974, but by the late 1970s the area seemed static, thanks to a toxic economy in which unemployment and inflation were both on the rise – unhealthy opposites colliding.

For Smith, 'I'll stick around the centre always, even if it is run down.'[9] 'Even when I did romanticise in my music, it was always about Manchester, because that's what I know best,' he acknowledged in his memoir, *Renegade*.[10] Yet the Manchester of the late 1970s and early 1980s was very different from the gentrified city that emerged at the end of the 1990s. Although it was colourless and dilapidated, at its core it remained fundamentally a city premised on business. The centre had a swagger not found elsewhere outside London, for branches of the Bank of England, *Daily Express* and other national institutions, set amidst the nineteenth-century warehousing and empty blocks, made it truly Britain's second city. There was a buzz of office workers, of rush hours and of lunches snatched in corner cafés, its semblance of a tiny Manhattan enforced by the grid pattern of straight streets and square brick blocks, inside which all activity seemed to be tucked away. Brix Smith, as an American, might have seen in it the origins of the Midwest industrial city. Yet 'I never expected Manchester to be so grim,' she admitted, when recalling her arrival in 1983. 'Where was the colour? I felt like I was watching the city through a black-and-white film clip, a Pathé post-war newsreel.'[11] Mick Middles noted how the smart Manchester nightclubs of George Best's Swinging Sixties had gone, leaving just two main venues on its fringes: to the north the Electric Circus in Collyhurst Street (the former Palace Cinema of 1927, later a bingo hall), which put on bands in 1976–7; and to the south the Squat Club, formerly part of the Manchester Royal College of Music, which had been taken over by students as a venue (it was demolished in 1982). Semi-derelict basements and former cinemas made perfect cheap venues for start-up bands. Another former cinema, the Astoria/Odeon of 1931 on Bury New Road in Sedgley Park, became the Lancastrian Bingo Hall, but now this site of the Bingo Master's breakout is a Lidl supermarket.[12]

Mark E. Smith considered that 'Before the bomb in '96 Manchester city centre was populated by some of the best Victorian architecture in the world. You could read history off some of those buildings. They were masterpieces – beautiful combinations of science and art.'[13] The bomb that was exploded by the Provisional Irish Republican Army in June 1996 served as a catalyst for the rebuilding of a large part of the city centre. In practice, however, private developers such as Urban Splash (founded in 1993) were already beginning to remodel Castlefields, Ancoats and the banks of the River Irwell with middle-class housing, in warehouse conversions and taller, glassy blocks of flats. Smith recognised the portents with 'Cab Driver', written in 1993 and rescripted as 'City Dweller' in the aptly titled *Middle Class Revolt* of 1994, with its references to Manchester's numerous unsuccessful bids to host the Olympics. Instead, the Commonwealth Games in 2002 led a second wave of regeneration that produced the city much as it is today. As he declared in 2008, 'Nowadays, the ultimate aim is to force the working class out, that's what gentrification is all about. They think that by building glorified fried boxes and passing them off as "modern" and "progressive", everybody who walks by will in time transform into the likes of them!'[14] The Manchester of the early Fall records was gone, and since then it has changed more. As Smith explained in 2017 of 'Victoria Train Station Massacre': 'I'm actually very fond of the architecture of Victoria Station, but it's all been trashed to fuck, and that's what the song's about. You know all that beautiful Victorian latticework, like they have at Paddington? They ripped it all off.'[15]

Beyond the city centre and Salford Quays more of the old Manchester survives – in reality in Greater Manchester, since its administration is divided between the boroughs of Salford and Bury. Indeed, Smith worried that 'foreigners and experts' might turn his house into a museum.[16] Today's pilgrims to Prestwich seeking a memorial will find only a mural, created by Akse P19, on the side of a smartened-up chip shop in Clifton Road, but Smith lived most of his life in the town, with many of its most important happenings taking place across only a few streets either side of Bury New Road, which contains most of its shops and public houses. Dave Simpson commented how 'A bizarre number of Fall members seem to have come from the same 500 square yards in Prestwich/Salford, or Smith's local, the George, before it was knocked down' (in 2004, to be replaced by flats).[17] Smith claimed that 'writing about Prestwich is just as valid as Dante writing about his inferno'.[18]

Malcolm Heyhoe described Prestwich in the *NME* as 'a grim place full of little figures pinned to pavements and rows of crumbling terraced houses'.[19] The reality is very different: Prestwich has substantial Victorian villas and semis, and away from the main road enjoys a smart anonymity. Since Smith refused to leave the area and demanded that journalists trek up the Bury New Road to interview him, it is strange that so many should report a wrong impression. Perhaps they got no further than the pubs.

Yet Prestwich is slightly more than a commuter suburb. Its shopping centre, defiantly of 1971, lies behind a high street with just enough red brick and terracotta from the years 1890–1930 to give character. The main incursion is the Radius block of flats, imposed in 2009, though if the council has its way, more large blocks will replace the shopping centre and the Istanbul Grill, the former Wilton pub said to have been the home of the 'rebellious jukebox' of the eponymous song.[20] Behind it the library and local study centre, together with the Longfield Suite of halls and meeting rooms, are part of the 1971 development.[21]

Originally, the extended parish of Prestwich-cum-Oldham was among the largest in England, the Saxon name meaning 'priest's retreat'. The settlement itself may be older, for traces of a Roman road from Manchester to Ribchester survived, until the Bury New Road was cut along the same route in 1826. Slightly away from this seemingly endless straight road there survives a substantial church from the fourteenth and fifteenth centuries, albeit remodelled and extended by the county's specialist architects Austin & Paley in 1888–9. Next door, as is traditional, stands the eighteenth-century Church Inn. The village became a centre for silk weaving in the early nineteenth century, when scattered settlements established themselves at Simister, Bowlee and along the main roads. Hitherto the village had been reached via Bury Old Road, Ostrich Lane and Back Lane, but the opening of the Bury New Road turnpike provided direct access straight into the city.

Just as the wooded hills and clean air of Prestwich appealed to Manchester's middle classes, so they led to the building of Lancashire's second County Pauper Lunatic Asylum in 1848–51, for which high ground and pleasant south-facing views were a prerequisite. Legislation in 1845 had been progressive, but the asylum built by Isaac and J. R. Holden for 350 patients was extended in 1853 and doubled in size in 1867; Henry Littler added an annexe for long-term patients in 1879. At its height the complex housed 3,500 patients – a number rivalled by London institutions and exceeded by Whittingham, near Preston, but nevertheless making it one of the largest hospitals in Britain. Subsidence meant that part of the complex was demolished in the 1930s, but it remained Prestwich's largest employer – a town within the town, with its own chapel, workshops, farm and entertainment hall. 'The madness in my area', where 'they put electrodes in your brain and you're never the same', indeed.[22] Una Baines worked as a student psychiatric nurse and lived in a flat opposite, in Kingswood Road, where she was joined by Smith when he first left home in 1974. Kay Carroll also worked as a nurse there, while Smith invited patients in for a cup of tea. 'Sit them down, play them some rock and roll, a bit of telly [...] I'd take them to the pub: a bit of normality [...] Sometimes I think I did more good than all the nurses put together.'[23] Most of the site was closed in 1994, save for the Edenfield Medium Secure Mental Health Unit, established in the early 1980s, staff housing and the farm.

The arrival of the railway in 1879 finally saw the expansion of Prestwich as a lower-middle-class suburb, with more substantial houses near Heaton Park to the east. Philips Park and Prestwich Clough are open spaces to the west and south, while interwar developments joined the town to Manchester and the surrounding communities. As Smith explained to Michael Lang, and later to Mark Middles:

> We've had a lot of Prestwich buildings on our covers over the years. Especially in the early days. They were put there for a reason, an obvious reason, really. It was because I really liked them. They were beautiful buildings and now old Fall album covers are a bit like an archive of old Prestwich because every building I ever have from Prestwich on the back of my covers gets fuckin' pulled down. The church on Grotesque is probably one of the few photographs left of the thing. Like the building on 'Elastic Man' was pulled down, the building on [...] which one was it [...] Hex Enduction Hour? Was it Hex? Yes, that was pulled down; the building on Dragnet was pulled down. Hah! I started to get a bit paranoid about it at one stage. I thought we might be the kiss of death. All those buildings that I cherished were just pulled down [...] just like that. We'd come back off tour and another one would be bloody gone.[24]

A few buildings survive, including the former dance studio set over three shops in a three-gabled Victorian building where Kay Carroll's mother opened a psychic centre, which has been suggested as the inspiration for 'Psykick Dancehall'. Smith's various flats also survive: one in Glebelands Road, a long road running due east from the station, to which he and Carroll moved from Kingswood Road in 1980; and the larger Flat 2, 4 Beech Tree Bank, on the still longer Rectory Lane to the south, where they moved in 1982. This was the cold, dirty flat with a broken fridge that Brix was met with on her arrival in England, until in 1984 she and Smith bought an interwar semi at 16 Winchester Avenue, Sedgley Park, just a couple of streets from his parents at 6 Dorchester Avenue.

Today, one of the few remarkable features of Prestwich is the survival of a relatively large number of pubs along the Bury New Road. Smith was at times a regular at the Foresters (as also was Nico), initially playing darts with his sisters there, and later pool with Carroll as a doubles team for money. It was rebuilt along traditional lines in 1964, and essentially comprises a lounge and public bar, the latter containing the dartboard and pool table. Just down the hill is the Red Lion, rebuilt in 1892, and altered again internally since being used in the video for 'Wings'. Towards Heaton Park there was the much older Ostrich pub, eighteenth century in origin, with some features inside installed following its purchase in 1894 by Joseph Holt & Co. of Manchester. That there are still so many pubs is largely due to Holt's. Further away, at the entrance to the park, is the Woodthorpe, a villa from 1861 bought by Edward Holt as the family home in 1888 and extended with a new billiard room. His successors converted it to a pub in 1953, after failing to secure planning permission for new premises in the area; post-war restrictions on construction materials prevented the building of most new pubs until late the next year. It was much altered internally in 1993, 2006 and again in 2019, after Smith's wake was held there.

In 'Jerusalem', the counter to the industrial city is provided by England's rolling hills. Smith's references are more limited. He describes the country-side's positives: 'You can get down to real thinking / Walk around look at geometric tracery' (the style of medieval churches before the Black Death robbed them of craftsmen).[25] But listening to the lyrics more closely reveals that Smith was more ambivalent in 1982 even, worrying about the New Romantics and that, more than in the town, in the countryside the differences between the classes were visible and real. There survives a tweet from 2015: 'I hate the countryside. Everywhere I go I can smell piss.'[26] Nowhere is it said quite so clearly as in 'Contraflow', where the line 'I hate the countryside so much' forms the basis of the chorus; ex-drummer Dave Milner suggested the song refers to the difficulty the Fall's van had in collecting him from his home on the Snake Pass.[27] Or as Smith wrote in 'M5', also in 1994: 'I'm city born and bred / Too many car-fumes in my head [...] M5 to the country straight ahead / It's stuffed to the gills with crusty brown bread.'[28] This acknowledges a query made in 'Just Step S'ways': 'Who wants to be in a Hovis advert anyway?'[29] Smith saved his wrath for the middle-class tourist centres, showing in 'English Scheme' how 'down pokey quaint streets in Cambridge cycles our distant spastic heritage'.[30] Here the model of 'Jerusalem' breaks down. In the world of the Fall, it is the satanic mills that are really rather good.

Endnotes

1. Overheard during the interval of *I Am Kurious Oranj* at Sadler's Wells, where Fall and ballet audiences collided: a plummy north Londoner musing over 'three hundred years of what?' – the anniversary being repeatedly referred to in the ballet, but not the album.

2. Mark E. Smith, Craig Scanlon and Stephen Hanley's 'The N.W.R.A' (1981, BMG Rights Management) references Sam Chippindale, the Yorkshire estate agent who with his brother-in-law developed the Arndale portfolio, its name a portmanteau of their own names. Zita Adamson, *Sam Chippindale, Shopping Centre Pioneer*, Saltaire, Sam Chippindale Foundation, 1993.

3. Lucy Toulmin Smith (ed.), *The Itinerary of John Leland in or about the years 1535–1543*, London, George Bell and Sons, vol. 4, 1909, pp. 5–6.

4. *The Building News*, vol. 7, 24 May 1861, pp. 425–6.

5. Mark E. Smith, Craig Scanlon, Marc Riley and Stephen Hanley, 'City Hobgoblins', Sony/ATV Music Publishing, 1980.

6. Mark E. Smith with Austin Collings, *Renegade*, London, Viking, 2008, p. 80.

7. Roland Nicholas, *City of Manchester Plan*, Norwich, Jarrold & Son, 1945.

8. Michael Lang, 'The Fall – Mark E. Smith Interview', *BravEar*, vol. 3, no. 5, fall/winter 1986, n.p.

9. Mark E. Smith, 'Room to Live', 1982, BMG Rights Management.

10. *Renegade*, op. cit., p. 87.

11. Brix Smith Start, *The Rise, The Fall, and The Rise*, London, Faber & Faber, 2016, pp. 216–17.

12. Mick Middles and Mark E. Smith, *The Fall*, London, Omnibus Press, 2003, pp. 61, 82; http://cinematreasures.org/theaters/47575, accessed 16 February 2020.

13. *Renegade*, op. cit., pp. 98–9.

14. Ibid.

15. Mark E. Smith, 'Victoria Train Station Massacre', https://www.uncut.co.uk/features/mark-e-smiths-final-uncut-interview-fall-like-nazi-organisation-103185/, accessed 17 February 2020.

16. Mark E. Smith, 'Room to Live', 1982, BMG Rights Management.

17. Dave Simpson, 'Excuse Me, Weren't You in The Fall?' *Guardian*, 5 January 2006, https://www.theguardian.com/music/2006/jan/05/popandrock, accessed 16 February 2020; https://www.lancashiretelegraph.co.uk/news/5817729.pub-will-make-way-living-leisure-complex/, accessed 17 February 2020.

18. *Renegade*, op. cit. p. 86.

19. Malcolm Heyhoe, 'Why The Fall Must Rise', *NME*, 18 March 1978, pp. 20–1.

20. http://fourholtspubsofthemarkesmith.simplesite.com/438609742, accessed 13 February 2020.

21. One remnant of an earlier sprucing-up outside the library is a corny sculptural feature from 2004, *The Retreat*, a fountain by Isabella Lockett surrounded by quotations from local schoolchildren and cast in concrete; after a wall of green glass was demolished in 2007, having been deemed unsafe, more platitudes to Prestwich were inscribed in granite alongside.

22. Mark E. Smith, 'In My Area', 1979, Bicycle Music Company; 'Repetition', 1977; information from Roger Hartley, North West Regional Health Authority; Elain Harwood, 'The History and Plan Forms of Purpose-Built Lunatic Asylums', AA (Grad Dip Cons) thesis, unpublished, 1986.

23. *Renegade*, op. cit., pp. 37–8.

24. 'The Fall – Mark E. Smith Interview', op. cit.

25. Mark E. Smith, 'Hard Life in Country', 1982, BMG Rights Management.

26. Mark E. Smith on Twitter, 28 June 2015, https://twitter.com/markesmith50/status/615247857201872896.

27. Dave Simpson, *The Fallen*, London, Canongate, 2008, p. 270; http://annotatedfall.doomby.com/pages/the-annotated-lyrics/contraflow.html, accessed 16 February 2020.

28. Mark E. Smith, 'M5', 1994, BMG Rights Management.

29. Mark Fisher, 'Memorex for the Kraken: The Fall's Pulp Modernism', in Benjamin Halligan and Michael Goddard, *Mark E. Smith and The Fall: Art, Music and Politics*, London, Taylor and Francis, 2010, p. 108.

30. Mark E. Smith, 'English Scheme', 1981, BMG Rights Management.

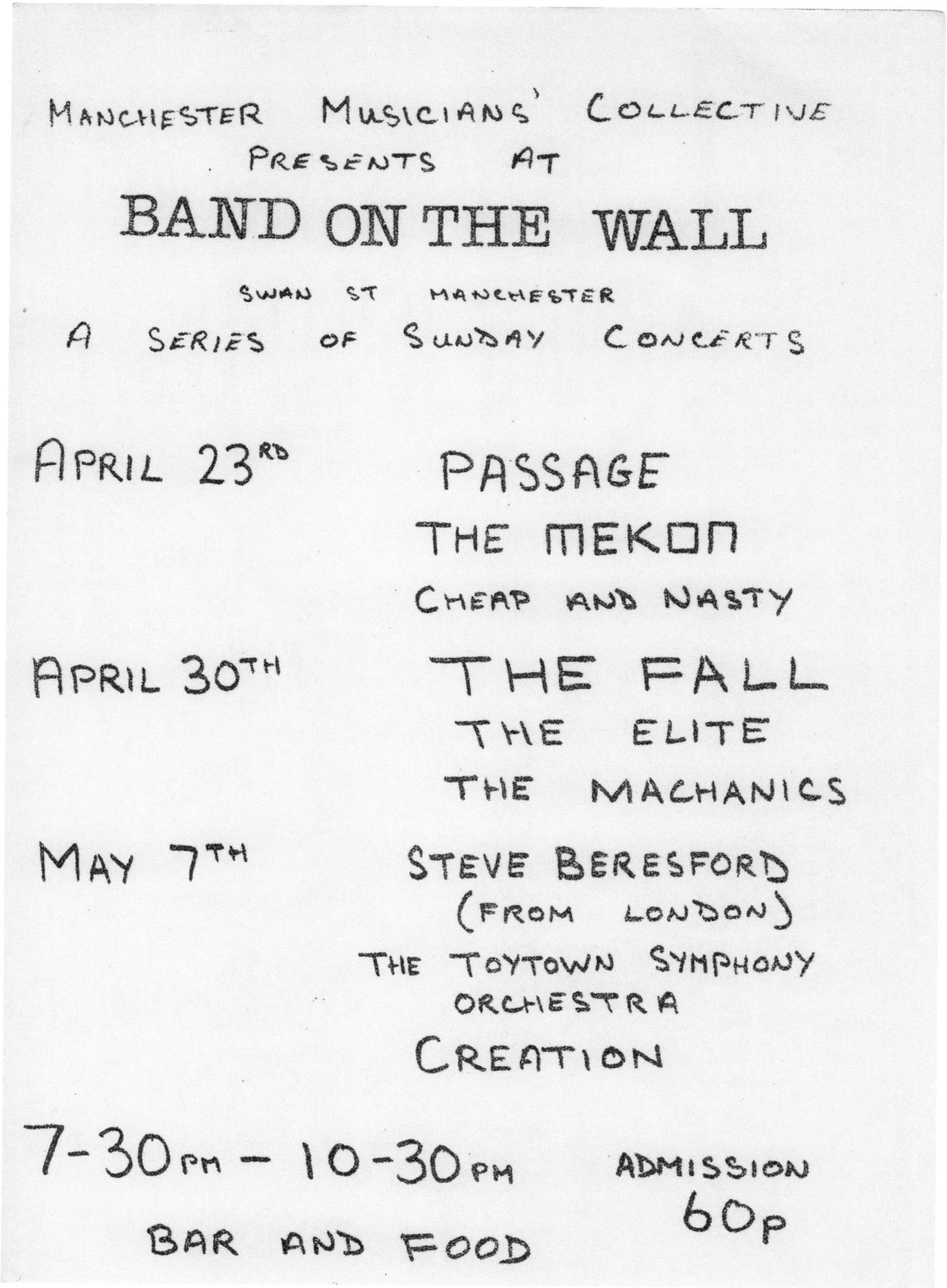

MANCHESTER MUSICIANS' COLLECTIVE
PRESENTS AT

BAND ON THE WALL

SWAN ST MANCHESTER

A SERIES OF SUNDAY CONCERTS

APRIL 23RD   PASSAGE

THE MEKON

CHEAP AND NASTY

APRIL 30TH   THE FALL

THE ELITE

THE MACHANICS

MAY 7TH   STEVE BERESFORD
(FROM LONDON)

THE TOYTOWN SYMPHONY
ORCHESTRA

CREATION

7-30PM — 10-30PM   ADMISSION
60P

BAR AND FOOD

26

SUNDAYS:
OCT. 30th
DOMINIC RIVRON
THE ELITE
ON THE ROCKS

NOV. 6th
ALBERT SQUARE
THE MEKON

NOV 13th
TREVOR WISHART
PRIDE
THE FALL

8PM

ADMISSION 50P. BAR OPEN

MANCHESTER MUSICIAN'S COLLECTIVE at BAND ON THE WALL
SUNDAY NIGHTS

THE FALL
ALBERT SQUARE
THE MEKON
ON THE ROCKS
THE ELITE
PRIDE
TREVOR WISHART

JAZZ
ROCK
ELECTRONICS

MUZIC-THEATRE
EXPERIMENTAL MUSIC
IMPROVISATION

The Fall

Dear Kevin,

Apologies for the late-ness of this reply but we have little contact with S. Forward records lately. Your projected magazine sound very interesting, although I am not too famili with existential thought, being personally of the opinion that the 30's French writers dated fast + most likely suffered in translation.

But you are not alone in your connections. somebody commented last week that the drawings on the reverse of 'Elastic Man' were influenced by Jarré. Maybe subconsciously the co-founder of The Fall, Tony Friel, I know was heavily influenced by 30's French (?) existentialism. Camus, I thought, stood out head + shoulders.

A great lyrical ʃ influence on me was Peter Hammill's Van der Graaf/solo work which I suspect lifted heavily off Sartre

Anyway, what I've done is enclosed some old+new lyrics you may find of interest, + some lightweight comments in an attempt to be objective. To write a piece for you would bear some thought, so keep in touch, I'll ponder it. We've playing in Welson for fun at an W.M. Club on 29th. Aug. which I ~~think~~ think is near you, so if you could ~~possibly~~ make that maybe we could converse quickly about your ideas.

Regards + Thanks.

Mark E Smith for.

The Fall.

P.S. If you wish to, you can write me at Rough Trade records as we presently are instable in our ~~se~~ home life (!!!).

N.B:

This song is part-tale, part-indictment of how people, especially in the literature world tend to dissapate their creators energies + indeed <u>sit-on</u> art. It's a common fallacy that great writers, band and footballers 'go soft' with extreme fame. I contradict this + say the people love a decline + become very vampiric towards their heroes.

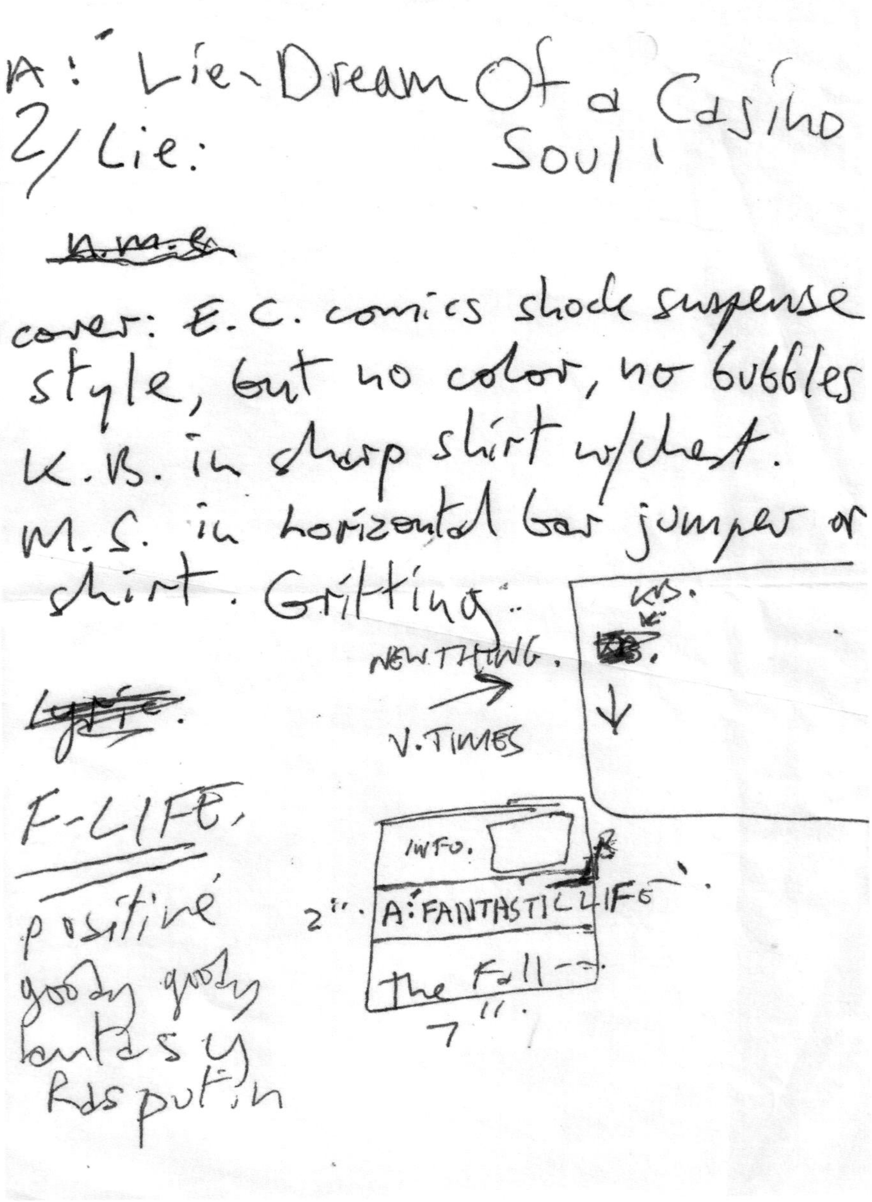

A: 'Lie-Dream Of a Casino
2/Lie: Soul'

~~R.M.S.~~

cover: E.C. comics shock suspense
style, but no color, no bubbles
K.B. in sharp shirt w/chest.
M.S. in horizontal bar jumper or
shirt. Gritting.

~~Life~~.

F-LIFE.

positive
goody goody
fantasy
Rasputin

NEW.THING. →
V.TIMES

K.B.
K.
M.S.

↓

INFO.
A: FANTASTIC LIFE.
2" |
The Fall →.
7".

Instructions to Savage Pencil for artwork on 'Lie Dream
of a Casino Soul' single.

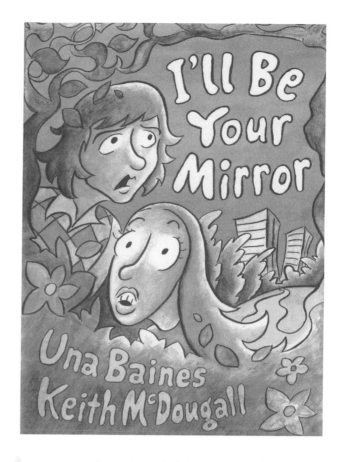

I'll Be Your Mirror, Una Baines and Keith McDougall, 2015 (self-published).

Beer mat inscribed by Kay Carroll

'Fugue' Is Not a Word I Would Normally Use, But...: The Fall and Repetition[1]

The last piece I wrote about the Fall was published in January 1980. Forty years to the week, I saw it again – predictably, someone had posted it on Twitter.

I repeat: *forty years*.

And after just over forty years resident in London, I recently moved to the north.

You get so used to the reassuring repetition of familiar routines, you maybe stop noticing certain things around you where you live: how different time frames overlap; how unlikely ghosts gather right out in the open, quarrelling among themselves. The way in which old myths and legends are constantly repeating, spruced up or dressed down in deceptive new clothes...

Buzz of the all-night mill / Émigrés from green glades...

Right from the off, Mark E. Smith cast himself as an improbable time traveller, a snug-bar table-tapper, someone whose half-lucid waking visions subtly mesh (and even alter) past and present realities... somewhere between dream and sleep... crossing a psychic threshold... dark corridors leading to a place where the light is suddenly too bright... time spread out like an old newspaper left open on a pub table... information from three places at once. A crypt of porous voices. *Not really now, not any more.*

Everything shuts down a lot earlier round here: a slow walk through chiming church bells, everything CLOSED at four. History echoing in footfalls. Tudor buildings and local history. Everywhere should have local history, but it's being slowly bulldozed away and subtly erased. When the Fall began, Smith was picking up the past and the future on different frequencies to everybody else. The psychic dancehall inside his head. Biro scribbles about old hauntings and present discontinuities...

I repeat, it's all there right from the off: 'Various Times', 'In My Area', 'Psykick Dancehall', 'City Hobgoblins', like a punk-era speed-weekend rewrite of Alan Garner's 1973 novel *Red Shift*, a taut, eerie tale unfolding across three time frames: Roman Britain, the English Civil War and the 'present'. Drenched in northern dialect and pagan echoes. (The book's Roman-era Cheshire tribe are called the 'Cats'.)

---

1. All unattributed quotes are taken from online MES/Fall articles, interviews, transcribed lyrics, etc., except where they aren't.

Certain figures, shadows, archetypes ... seeping through the sieve of history, repeating in time like delinquent ghosts laughing at long-ago ASBOs.

Gremlins know these things / Tap tap tap tap ...

Mark E. Smith in the back room, consulting his Tarot cards, repeating certain formulae and unlikely intuitions, with different results each time. Old legends taking on new shapes.

So Queen Victoria / Is a large black slug in Piccadilly, Manchester ...

I recently attended the annual 're-enactment' of the Battle of Nantwich (25 January 1644) by the Sealed Knot society. Against my deeply sceptical expectations, I really (but *really*) enjoyed it. In this Civil War replay, the Parliamentarians won, the defeated Royalists cheered/jeered off the field of battle to rousing shouts of 'Democracy!' A week later, to the day, a rather anti-climactic Brexit Day.

The Parliamentarians won the re-enacted battle, but it was by no means a given. In other words, it was not a mere by-rote repetition of the *original event*. It felt a little like a cross between a pub gig by an uncannily convincing tribute band and an especially spirited rugby game. Especially as it took place on a Saturday afternoon.

Hail new puritan, righteous maelstrom ...

(What I'm re-reading right now: a book by the left-wing historian Christopher Hill called *A Turbulent, Seditious and Factious People*.)

There was something about this Civil War re-enactment that felt very Mark E. Smith — as if I had only to leave London behind to suddenly find myself trapped inside a Fall song. Seventeenth-century conscripts fenced off outside a Caffè Nero. Black-faced mummers and morris dancers reflected in the windows of WH Smith. Peasants in Puritan headgear using the town-centre cash machine. Spector vs Rector recast. Lucifer over Cheshire.

What do we think a 're-enactment' is, exactly? And in what circumstances might something we casually or even daily repeat be a form of unknowing re-enactment?

(Offhand philosophical speculation: isn't any *event* by its very nature something unrepeatable?)

It doesn't take much beer-assisted reverie to see in Mark E. Smith the lineaments of a certain kind of seventeenth-century character ... someone on the fringes of sedition, civil disturbance, secret preaching. Vendettas conducted via pamphlet, small cliques and clans. Parchment-skinned, watery-eyed old alchemists. The only uncertain thing here would be trying to decide which side — of many — Smith might have taken.

Bringing things back to more recent historical time, maybe compare and contrast 1980s Margaret Thatcher-era Fall with the smooth, London-based would-be metropolitanism of Red Wedge…

Nonconformists, dissenters, firebrands, malicious schismatics…mechanic preachers, downright ranters…ragged spectres of all the 'white crap' who ever talked back.

A mechanic preacher was someone who quietly worked with their hands six days a week, and then at the weekend preached with fire and passion behind unexpected, even heretical viewpoints.

Lollardy was a semi-underground religion of vernacular scripture (key word: *'vernacular'*), and 'lollard' became a popular derogatory nickname given to those who preached or interpreted the Bible without any academic background – unschooled in Latin, in slender footnote distinctions, educated, if at all, only in spoken English or the local dialect. Later, it became used of heretics in general. The word most likely derived initially from the Middle Dutch *lollaerd*, from the verb *lollen*, meaning a 'mumbler or mutterer'; and, further back, from the Latin *lolium* – an unwanted weed, someone or something generally considered a bit of a nuisance.

At a certain point in your life you maybe notice you're starting to repeat yourself. At a certain point in the drinking evening you may hear yourself say: 'I know I've told you this before, but –' Even though Mark E. Smith maybe had more drinking evenings than most, and more concerted drinking in those evenings, he didn't grow predictably repetitive, at least not in the matter of pertinent detail. Although here we might profitably risk the question: *Does any contrarian start to repeat themselves just by being consistently contrarian?*

Repetition at different pitches.

Life does not always follow a settled and predictable course. There are sharp turns, unexpected slumps, banks of fog. *Then again…*

So much of life is repetition, but then one day – a cartoon anvil falls from the sky, liberating you from unexamined routine, from a rusty kind of laziness or irresolution, from…unattended repetition.

Life is strife / But you don't wanna hear it / Strife is life and that's it /
And that's it, and that's it /
And that's it –

We repeat ourselves every night. Dreams are a mangled (repeat) of all the uncollected rubbish of the day, mixed up and peppered with all manner of overt and covert allusions…garbled narratives, rapt exposure, inexact prophecy. A strange personal syntax, with certain linking words missing, as if –

From a psychoanalytic view, a certain kind of repetition is considered a worrisome or distressing thing, something to be delivered from, talked away. Symptoms and missteps, self-harming or self-cancelling habits or holding manoeuvres we keep repeating, almost despite ourselves.

38   The psychologist said that he thought the shadow was his father...
The shad was his dad.

Repetition, ritual, rite.

Dark distortions of the past / And the restructure of your new life...

I feel a certain self-imposed pressure to not repeat certain clichés about the Fall. Following this course, it sometimes feels like I'm repeating Mark E. Smith's own long-term ethos, and some of what I write comes with the slightly uncanny feeling of revoicing Smith's own ghosts and demons.

In media interviews, Smith always presented himself as a kind of half-witting role model – the Last Honest Man, a salt-of-the-earth barrier against fripperies and fads... a model of hard-knocks wisdom and decidedly non-corporate, plain-spoken sanity. Discipline vs decadence. Moulded from a proud strain of autodidactic clarity and sprung from a lineage that included his father and grandfather and others like them. A working-class toiler who just happened to have fallen into rock and roll as a job like any other: an honest nine-to-five gig. All of which perhaps invites the question: what would rock-and-roll culture have been like if everyone had paid appropriate attention and taken Smith at his word? How exactly would anyone follow suit and repeat his moral example?

The character in Albert Camus's *The Fall* is a 'self-proclaimed judge-penitent'.

Even when he occasionally talked about drinking, it was presented as a kind of honest discipline, out in the open, a self-administered medicine. Only *secret* drinkers risked alcoholism, he claimed.

What is more repetitive than addiction?

The Fall opens with the main character sitting in a bar, casually talking to a stranger about *the proper way to order a drink*.

Always repeating, down the years, sleazy music-biz rumours that the capably, even entertainingly hard-drinking Smith had gradually slipped into a flagrant loss of control. His Wikipedia entry now commemorates this as an established fact: 'difficult [...] dark and sardonic [...] a long-term alcoholic'. Anyone who's had similar or allied problems will know that even if you give up the drug that is ostensibly causing all your problems, even if you are superficially clean and sober, you can still wander in the parched shadows of a certain constricted mindset... repeating certain attitudes, defence mechanisms, ways of keeping the world at bay or shaped in the comfy, reassuring image you most want it to resemble.

FIT AND WORKING AGAIN!

The *second* time I interviewed Mark E. Smith, there were half-jokey references to Dean Martin, William Burroughs, Lenny Bruce, Johnny Cash – the idea of 'healthy living' via chemistry, finding your own soul-warming medicine. *It's no one's business but mine.* You can be a heavy drinker without becoming an alcoholic; you can take uppers without becoming a brain-flattened speed-freak. But, of course, a certain risk is always present: something that begins as stimulation and experiment can slowly, surely, become a form of dull, dulled, time-filling repetition.

What is more repetitive than addiction?

To go out or stay in? / I'll stay in / I'll stay in / I'll stay in / I'll stay in...

A refusal of change for change's sake, the skeleton winds of fashion, inane fads, prissy trends. Sticking to the promise of some higher or baser or more basic truth. Sticking to your guns – with the concomitant risk of finding yourself just plain stuck.

What is more repetitive than nostalgia?

I used to have this thing about Link Wray / I used to play him every Saturday...

'All writers are sedentary apes,' said Robert Louis Stevenson. Apes in the sense of... aping other writers, copying some thrilling innovator from the past. But before the Fall, was there really anyone who fronted a band like Mark E. Smith? A kind of occult-prole Big Youth, backed by stock-car-smash rockabilly, baleful noise, yellow-eyed palsied pop...

Bands send tapes to famous apes / Male slags, male slates, famous apes...

Smith was first and foremost an archivist of his own itchy collage-mind... not a singer and/or songwriter in any traditional sense, repeating some already established form or formula. He could easily have chosen to become a 'conventional' writer instead – a cheap-speed Alan Garner (birthplace: Alderley Edge; lifelong resident of Cheshire) or a northern Michael Moorcock (the Jerry Cornelius pulp-occult wing, rather than the sword-and-sorcery stuff), conjuring a crooked grimoire out of the shivery air of post-industrial Manchester, when greyness and dilapidation seemed almost to shine with occult promise – but he chose the stage, or it chose him. There was something about music/performance/'speaking out' that called to him. But he wanted it both ways: wanted to be onstage, but also to repeatedly insist it was just a repetitive job like any other – day in, day out, with an adequate but unstarry wage packet at the end of every week or month.

Smith's early songs repeat things gleaned from the work of authors like M. R. James, Arthur Machen, H. P. Lovecraft, William Blake, William Burroughs, Philip K. Dick, Ursula K. Le Guin. Reading such people, at that time, was like taking a psychotropic drug whose long-term effects you had no way of knowing.

> *I'm told I use too many words [...] but you see what I have is a very original approach to writing [...] because it's not educated but it's not jargonised, I don't think.*

Albert Camus

The Fall: named after a prototypical Penguin Modern Classic, by Albert Camus. Books popular with a certain kind of disaffected autodidact in that pre-punk time. Somehow, it never seemed strange then that so much of our reading was actually a kind of time capsule from long, long ago – the Beats, existentialism, Nietzsche, Kafka, Camus, Dostoevsky and so on. Such books may strike many as old-fashioned now: big themes, sturdy words, masculinist history as grand narrative. Puffed-up, self-proclaimed Underground Men. Absurdity, anguish, alienation, angst, repeating like raw onions from an ill-advised kebab.

Choosing to name yourself the Fall repeats a certain well-known or canonical phrase, lifted out of its usual, overfamiliar context.

'We are the Fall...' No, he will not stand for any protestations of innocence or naivety; it is already way too late for that.

Smith's song-texts like diary entries soaked by a sudden downpour, or something cut up drunk one night and sellotaped back together half-randomly in the bleary hungover morning. Strange personal syntax with certain linking words missing, as if –

Certain motifs repeat down the years. Not to mention all the things that were markedly (*mark-e-dly*) absent. The curl and swing of rhythm and blues. The hot breath of sex or the playfully direct gaze of Eros. Any softness or yielding or drift. At times, it could all feel just a tiny bit sunless and claustrophobic – sometimes in a good way, sometimes not so much. The *not so much* maybe reproducing what it sometimes felt like inside Mark E. Smith's head.

Some fugues have a recapitulation.

The 'E' in Mark E. Smith is an ancient bridge or weathered stile. We go over the river into the park and find they are fighting there, still, with cannon and pikes.

A certain self-amused look on his face – the cat who got into a Cheshire creamery – always suggesting he knew something we didn't. A key wrapped in old newsprint hidden in some spider-webbed attic. Coded pronouncements scratched on a pub toilet wall: 'A DRUDGE NATION – NO IMAGINATION / THEY SHUN ME AND THINK ME UNCLEAN.'

What is more repetitive than a sense of original sin?

On the one hand, MES as some unyielding near-tyrannical individualist: 'I ALWAYS KNOW BEST.' On the other, his barking, sharp-tongued critiques were often couched in terms of place and community, places he found Good or Bad, False or True, Happily Conned or Grimly Resolute. A certain sense that if you were from Scotland or Wales or Iceland, or certain parts (but only *certain* parts) of Manchester, you were a priori more keen-eared and clear-eyed, worthy of trust, authentic.

How do people become National Treasures? (One obituary described Smith as a 'strange kind of anti-matter national treasure'.) Certain characteristics and/or catchphrases become so familiar they insinuate the wider culture, which is to say they have been sufficiently repeated over a certain period of time to register beyond their initial intended audience. In which sense Mark E. Smith belongs to a list which might also feature the likes of (completely off the top of my head) Quentin Crisp...Sir Alex Ferguson...Barbara Windsor... Dennis Skinner...Jarvis Cocker...Brian Clough...

What is more repetitive-uh than a catchphrase?

I can't help but notice that, in a 1980s interview archived on YouTube, every time Mark E. Smith repeats the action of bringing his pint of Boddingtons up for a draught, he sticks out his little finger like Hyacinth Bucket or a character from Barbara Pym taking tea with the local vicar. Finally, this becomes hypnotic, and I can't focus on anything else: how much, I start to wonder, is this a deliberate gesture, a minor-key provocation?

A few of my favourite things from an old MES list of Things He Actually Liked: Scottish people, *Coronation Street*, the German band Can and...cats. Plus, just one from the great sprawling list of Things He Indubitably Loathed: Cheshire. Just...Cheshire. All of Cheshire.

(It so happens I've just moved to Cheshire.)

> *'I shall leave London tomorrow,' he said, 'it is a city of nightmares.'*
> (Arthur Machen, *The Great God Pan*)

Where is north from here?

> *Nobody wanted to release it, because nobody played the sort of venues that you hear on it – places like Doncaster and Preston. The North was out of bounds; it might as well have been another country.*
> (Mark E. Smith, *Renegade*)

What is more repetitive than class?

Grotesque peasants stalk the land / And deep down inside you know everybody wants to like big companies...

What music do you find you can listen to over and over again? In other words: what bears repeating? There are songs we can stand to hear over and over again, that repeat like a flood-risk river over a whole lifetime. Whose repetition are *you* helpless to resist? Whose repetition sends you? And what exactly is it, do you suppose, such music secretly voices or repeats?

(Why do so many people I know bond over how much they love 'Dr Buck's Letter'? Is it something to do with admission of guilt, still-tender regret, lost or misplaced friends left behind?)

It's often assumed the Fall's 'Repetition' is about a certain kind of repetition in music. (Let's say, a Velvet Underground or Can or Johnny Cash repetition, not a Status Quo or Funkadelic or Steve Reich repetition.) We might ask if it is in fact about something else altogether . . . maybe about repetition in history/culture?

President Carter loves repetition / Chairman Mao he dug repetition / Repetition in China / Repetition in America / Repetition in West Germany / Simultaneous suicides . . .

One of my favourite 'repetition' songs: Can's 'One More Night' from *Ege Bamyası*. The phrases Damo Suzuki sings over and over and over and over and over again.

Generous of lyric, Jehovah's Witness / Stands in Cologne Marktplatz [. . .] / Listener was in cahoots with Fritz Lieber / And read him every day . . .

A punk-era paradox: all these severe-haired new ranters take to barely there stages, inches from our noses, in order to wildly assail us, in order to . . . tell us something vital? Or – simply for the pleasure of pissing us all off? But isn't that what we're here for – to be pissed off? We want our paranoia encouraged – gilded, even. We want a sense of righteous grievance. The twist given by Smith and the Fall was that a lot of the time you were never quite sure just what the grievance was, exactly.

Augury, desecration, scapegoating, denunciation. Ex-friends in used-to-be areas.

Another paradox: with certain kinds of hectoring or would-be avant-garde noise, what originally aimed to rouse us from our slumber and prick our sleepy consciences over time becomes . . . a bit predictable, something whose jab we smugly anticipate. It ceases to prick or poke or badger; rather, it actually comforts and reassures through its by-rote repetition.

The conventional is now experimental / The experimental is now conventional . . .

The improvisational guitarist Derek Bailey, like MES, could be a difficult interviewee – not one for the easy Q&A call and response. There was also a similar sense that this was, in part, an act or performance: the 'difficult' persona was, in part, a playful response to what both saw as the falsity or silliness of the interview situation. When Bailey did *The Wire* magazine's 'blindfold' music test, he expressed an almost baffled kind of enquiry: *Why on earth would anyone want to listen to something over and over again?* Wasn't such repetition all a bit . . .

childish? A bit too comfortable?

If you do find yourself having to repeat some favourite song or number, then maybe you attempt a version of it that is almost unrecognisable, edited or elided, turned all the way inside out. Here is an unlikely ethical-aesthetic point where Derek Bailey and Mark E. Smith meet, as on some kind of battlefield, regarding the question of, let's say, what may be at stake in *repeating yourself* over a lifetime.

Nearly two decades into the twenty-first century, the Fall remained identifiably the Fall, right to the end. Was this altogether a good thing? Or did it speak to that part of Smith that was resistant to any kind of change, that could give a very convincing impression of someone who feared anything unpredictable the future might put in his path?

Could there ever possibly be anything like a Fall tribute band?

Near the end, onstage, the Fall could present as a kind of dishevelled, private-joke Performance Art, as Smith repeatedly wandered about the stage, played with the band's amp controls, wandered offstage, fumed, gave off fumes, apparently teetering on the precipice of a complete meltdown. The hip priest of puritan noise become a kind of pale Dada-Lenny Bruce-Catweazle figure.

Dissociative *fugue states* may involve apparently random wanderings and are sometimes accompanied by the establishment of a new identity. (It can be related to the ingestion of psychotropic substances, physical trauma or a general medical condition…)

I suddenly see Mark E. Smith as a Margaret Thatcher-like figure, with the various members of the Fall down the years as so many promoted then demoted or disappeared cabinet members … all pretence of democracy gone as individuals are hired, fired, then erased like so many disappointing 'wets'.

> *I hang on until I believe there are people who can take the banner forward with the same commitment, belief, vision, strength and singleness of purpose.*
> (Quote from … Mark E. Smith or Margaret Thatcher?)

What is more repetitive than the grain of history?

> *A lot of the stuff I write is like prose cut down – trying to get it down as a fraction of what I originally said. I did that with 'Kicker Conspiracy'. I must have worked for about three months on that song.*

Strange personal syntax with certain linking words missing, as if –

'CUSHY EEC EURO-STATE GOALS!'

I repeat: what is more repetitive than the grain of history?

Ketamine is a veterinary anaesthetic and when used recreationally is a powerful dissociative psychedelic, in certain dosages inducing out-of-body experiences, ego loss and a breakdown of temporal cognition.
(From the annotated online Fall entry on 'Octo Realm/Ketamine Sun')

People think of themselves too much as one person – they don't know what to do with the other people that enter their heads.

Deluge of unofficial thoughts and hidden histories ... overlap of the everyday and the esoteric ... collision of the factual and the poetic ... a twilight language or crooked-path grimoire ... an older, weirder Britain slumbering under decades of economic rationalisation and political betrayal ... a deeply personal occult map, urban rather than pastoral ... old town halls, service-station forecourts, bulldozed football grounds, northern soul venues and Free Trade Halls ... grey dilapidated high streets ... all inside this frame of glinting MES gem-words like 'UNCLEAN', 'GIBBOUS', 'ABEYANCE', 'GROTESQUE'.

I don't know what I'm writing about half the time.

His song a mildewed crypt, with the words so many stubborn, flailing, flighty ghosts.

When I am dead and gone / My vibrations will live on ...

He is a ghost himself now, a spectral Cheshire-cat grin, way past temporal bondage or repetition.
    I repeat: *forty years*.

Just the traffic passing by [...] / Bye bye bye bye / Bye bye bye / Bye bye bye /
Bye bye bye ...

1977
First live show, North West Arts Basement, King St, Manchester (May 23); Kay Carroll becomes manager.

1978
Two tracks on *Short Circuit – Live at the Electric Circus* (Jun); *Bingo-Master's Break-Out!* EP (Aug); 'It's The New Thing' (Oct); first John Peel session (Sep 16).

1979
Live at the Witch Trials (Mar); 'Rowche Rumble' single (Jul); *Dragnet* (Oct).

1980
'Fiery Jack' single (Jan); *Totale's Turns (It's Now Or Never)* live/studio LP (May); 'How I Wrote "Elastic Man"' (Jul); 'Totally Wired' (Sep); *Grotesque (After the Gramme)* (Oct); Deeply Vale free festival (Jul).

1981
Slates 10" (Apr); 'Lie Dream of a Casino Soul' (Nov); first appearance in *Smash Hits*; first US tour.

1982
Hex Enduction Hour (Mar); 'Look Know' (Apr); *Room to Live* (Sep); 'Marquis Cha Cha' (Sep, withdrawn); *A Part of America Therein*, 1981 live LP; *Live in London 1980* (Chaos Tapes).

1983
'The Man Whose Head Expanded' (Jun); 'Kicker Conspiracy' (Sep); *Perverted By Language* (Dec); *Fall in a Hole* live NZ-only LP; first live-TV appearance on UK TV: *The Tube*, Channel 4.

Live at the Witch Trials (March 1979, Step-Forward)

SIDE 1
Frightened
Crap Rap 2 / Like To Blow
Rebellious Jukebox
No Xmas For John Quays
Mother-Sister!
Industrial Estate

SIDE 2
Underground Medecin
Two Steps Back
Live At The Witch Trials
Futures And Pasts
Music Scene

NB Band and production personnel are listed overleaf
throughout in the manner that they were credited on the
original record, complete with incorrect spellings and
idiosyncratic capitalisations.

A STEP-FORWARD RECORD (SFLP1)
41b blenheim crescent london w11 england

Recorded Camden Sound Suite 15.12.78
                                   Mixed 16.12.78

PRODUCED by THE FALL and BOB SARGEANT
Engineered by Alvin Clark (scientific
                               but terrific)

Front cover: John Wriothesley + MB
Photos etc, back: Steve Lyons/Graham Rhodes/
                   'Alternative Ulster'/Kay/Dave
                   the Weird.
All lyrics Copyright Mark E. Smith 1978
All songs arranged by Martin Bramah
Management: Kay Carroll

thanks: Kay/Nick/Miles/Una/Richie/Bob/Postman/
         Ca'an/Dave Mc.

Possible: G.M. Van Hire Ltd. (Manchester)
           J.A. Prosser Accountants (Manchester)
           P.S.L. PA Hire Manchester Ltd.
           Joseph Holt Ltd. Brewery (Manchester)

MARK E. SMITH vocals
MARTIN BRAMAH e. guitar vocals
YVONNE PAWLETT e.piano
MARC RILEY bass guitar
KARL BURNS drums

(MES gtr. S2-track3/tape-track5
YP plastic keyboard S2-track5)

SIDE 1:

FRIGHTENED (Smith-Friel)............................5.02
CRAP RAP 2/LIKE TO BLOW (Smith-Bramah)..............2.03
REBELLIOUS JUKEBOX (Smith-Bramah)...................2.54
NO XMAS FOR JOHN QUAYS (Smith)......................4.37
MOTHER-SISTER! (Smith-Baines).......................3.22
INDUSTRIAL ESTATE (Smith-Bramah-Friel)..............2.03

SIDE 2:

UNDERGROUND MEDECIN (Smith-Bramah)..................2.05
TWO STEPS BACK (Smith-Bramah).......................5.02
LIVE AT THE WITCH TRIALS (Smith)....................0.52
FUTURES AND PASTS (Smith-Bramah)....................2.35
MUSIC SCENE (Smith-Bramah-Pawlett-Riley)............8.04

PRODUCED BY THE FALL and BOB SARGEANT

Engineered by Alvin Clark (scientific but terrific)

Front cover: John Wriothesley + MB

MARK E. SMITH vocals
MARTIN BRAMAH e. guitar vocals
YVONNE PAWLETT e. piano
MARC RILEY bass guitar
KARL BURNS drums

Photos etc, back: Steve Lyons / Graham Rhodes /
'Alternative Ulster' / Kay / Dave the Weird

Recorded and mixed at Camden Town Suite, London,
15/16 December 1978.

Dragnet (October 1979, Step-Forward)

SIDE 1
Psykick Dancehall
A Figure Walks
Printhead
Dice Man
Before The Moon Falls
Your Heart Out

SIDE 2
Muzorewi's Daughter
Flat Of Angles
Choc-Stock
Spectre Vs. Rector
Put Away

Mark E. Smith – vocals
Mike Leigh – drums
Marc Riley – elec. & acous. guitars, vocal
Craig Scanlan – elec.guitar
Steve Hanley – bass guitar, vocal

Extra backing vocals: Mrs Horace Sullivan
e.piano, kazoo, tapes etc: Smith and Scanlan

Front cover: Tina Prior
Back: MES
Pics: Brendan Jackson
Insert: MES

Produced by The Fall / Grant Showbiz
Engineer: John Brierley

Recorded at Cargo Studios, Rochdale, 2–4 August 1979.

Grotesque (After the Gramme) (November 1980, Rough Trade)

SIDE 1
Pay Your Rates
English Scheme
New Face in Hell
C'n'C-S Mithering
The Container Drivers

SIDE 2
Impression of J. Temperance
In the Park
W.M.C.–Blob 59
Gramme Friday
The N.W.R.A

music: Scanlan, Riley, Smith, Hanley S., Hanley, P.
words: Smith

cover: Suzanne Smith
pics: Mick Parker, Don Montgomery & the Waterfoot Dandy

engineer: JOHN BRIERLEY
production A: The Fall, Grant Showbiz, Mayo Thompson + Geoff Travis
B: G. Travis & The Fall

Recorded at Cargo Studios, Rochdale, and Street Level Studios, London, mid-1980.

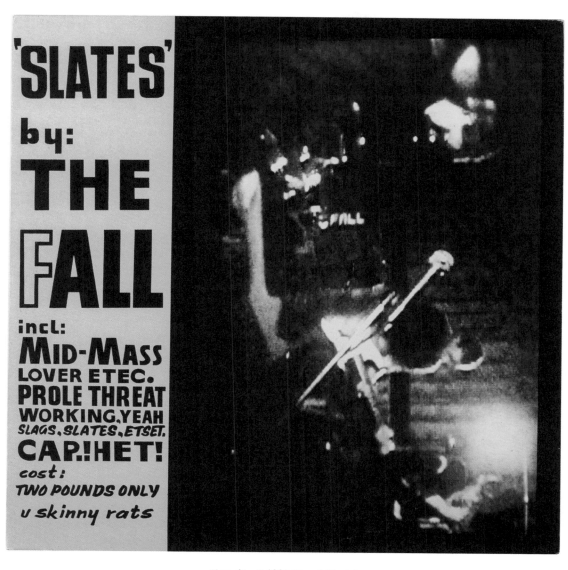

Slates (April 1981, Rough Trade)

1 OBJ.
Middle Mass
An Older Lover Etc.
Prole Art Threat

2 SUBJ.
Fit and Working Again
Slates, Slags Etc.
Leave the Capitol

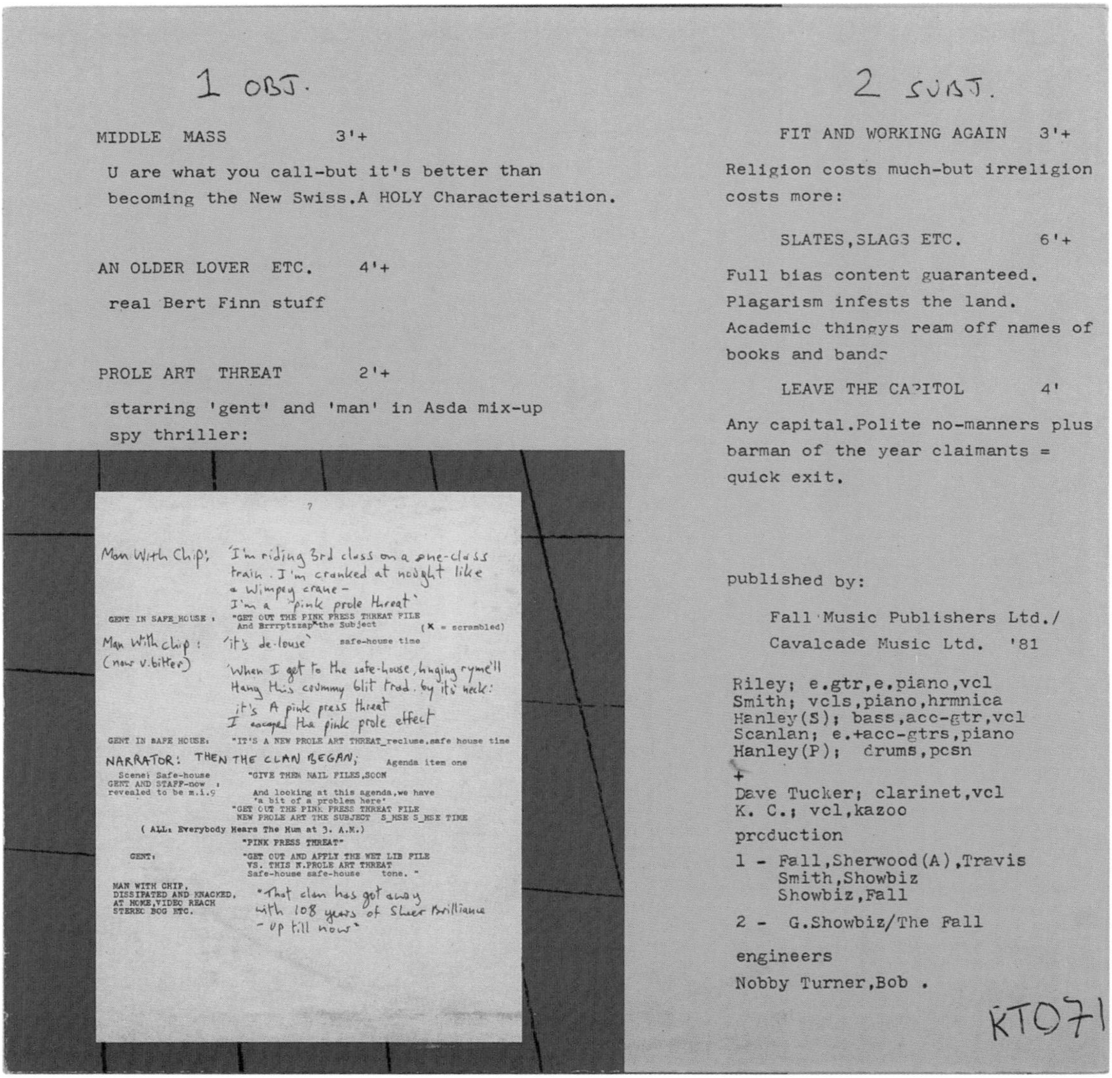

1 OBJ.

MIDDLE MASS 3'+

U are what you call-but it's better than becoming the New Swiss.A HOLY Characterisation.

AN OLDER LOVER ETC. 4'+

real Bert Finn stuff

PROLE ART THREAT 2'+

starring 'gent' and 'man' in Asda mix-up spy thriller:

7

Man With Chip: 'I'm riding 3rd class on a one-class train. I'm cranked at nought like a Wimpey crane – I'm a 'pink prole threat'

GENT IN SAFE_HOUSE : "GET OUT THE PINK PRESS THREAT FILE And Brrrptzzap*the Subject (* = scrambled)

Man With chip: 'it's de-louse' safe-house time
(now v.bitter)

'When I get to the safe-house, hinging ryme'll Hang this commy blit trad. by it's neck: it's A pink press threat I escaped the pink prole effect

GENT IN SAFE HOUSE: "IT'S A NEW PROLE ART THREAT_recluse.safe house time

NARRATOR: THEN THE CLAN BEGAN; Agenda item one

Scene: Safe-house
GENT AND STAFF-now revealed to be m.i.9 : "GIVE THEM NAIL FILES,SOON

And looking at this agenda,we have 'a bit of a problem here'
"GET OUT THE PINK PRESS THREAT FILE
NEW PROLE ART THE SUBJECT S_HSE S_HSE TIME

(ALL: Everybody Hears The Hum at 3. A.M.)

"PINK PRESS THREAT"

GENT: "GET OUT AND APPLY THE WET LIB FILE VS. THIS N.PROLE ART THREAT Safe-house safe-house tone. "

MAN WITH CHIP, DISSIPATED AND KNACKED, AT HOME,VIDEO REACH STEREO BOG ETC. "That clan has got away with 108 years of Sheer Brilliance – up till now"

2 SUBJ.

FIT AND WORKING AGAIN 3'+

Religion costs much-but irreligion costs more:

SLATES,SLAGS ETC. 6'+

Full bias content guaranteed. Plagarism infests the land. Academic thingys ream off names of books and bands

LEAVE THE CAPITOL 4'

Any capital.Polite no-manners plus barman of the year claimants = quick exit.

published by:

Fall Music Publishers Ltd./
Cavalcade Music Ltd. '81

Riley; e.gtr,e.piano,vcl
Smith; vcls,piano,hrmnica
Hanley(S); bass,acc-gtr,vcl
Scanlan; e.+acc-gtrs,piano
Hanley(P); drums,pcsn
+
Dave Tucker; clarinet,vcl
K. C.; vcl,kazoo

production

1 - Fall,Sherwood(A),Travis
Smith,Showbiz
Showbiz,Fall

2 - G.Showbiz/The Fall

engineers

Nobby Turner,Bob .

KT071

Riley: e.gtr, e.piano,vcl
Smith: vcls, piano, hrmnica
Hanley (S): bass, acc-gtr, vcl
Scanlan: e.+acc gtrs, piano
Hanley (P): drums, pcsn
+
Dave Tucker: clarinet, vcl
K.C.; vcl, kazoo

production
1 – Fall, Sherwood (A), Travis
Smith, Showbiz
Showbiz, Fall
2 – G. Showbiz / The Fall

engineers
Nobby Turner, Bob

Recorded at Berry Street Studios, Clerkenwell, London, in February 1981.

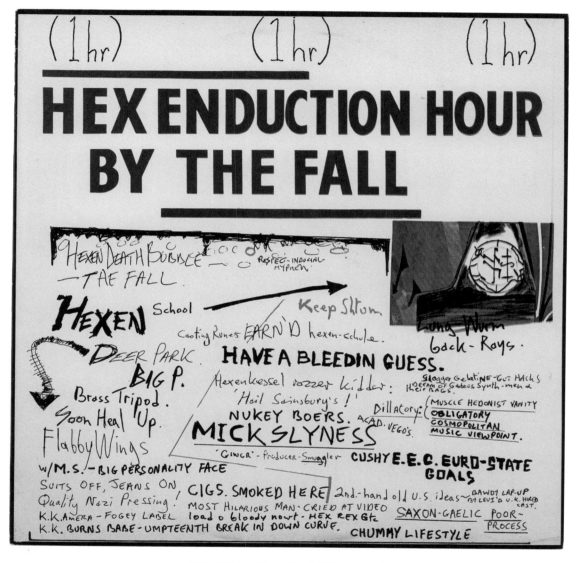

Hex Enduction Hour (March 1982, Kamera)

SIDE 1
The Classical
Jawbone and the Air-Rifle
Hip Priest
Fortress / Deer Park
Mere Pseud Mag. Ed.
Winter (Hostel-Maxi)

SIDE 2
Winter 2
Just Step S'ways
Who Makes the Nazis?
Iceland
And This Day

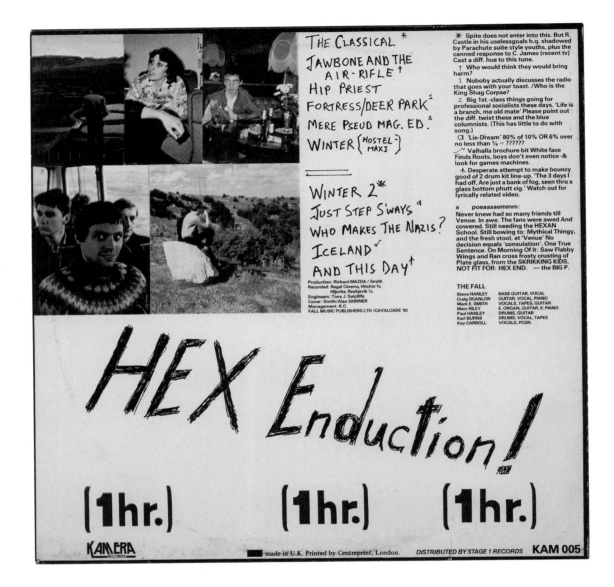

THE CLASSICAL *
JAWBONE AND THE
  AIR-RIFLE †
HIP PRIEST
FORTRESS/DEER PARK ¹
MERE PSEUD MAG. ED. ²
WINTER (HOSTEL - MAXI)

WINTER 2 *
JUST STEP S'WAYS ª
WHO MAKES THE NAZIS?
ICELAND ✓
AND THIS DAY †

Production: Richard MAZDA / Smith
Recorded: Regal Cinema, Hitchin ¾
            Hijorite, Reykjavik ¼
Engineers: Tony J. Sutcliffe
Cover: Smith/Alan SKINNER
Management: K.C.
FALL MUSIC PUBLISHERS LTD /CAVALCADE '82

✳ Spite does not enter into this. But R. Castle in his uselessgoals h.q. shadowed by Parachute suite style youths, plus the canned response to C. James (recent tv) Cast a diff. hue to this tune.
† Who would think they would bring harm?
1 Noboby actually discusses the radio that goes with your toast. /Who is the King Shag Corpse?
2. Big 1st.-class things going for professional socialists these days. 'Life is a branch, me old mate' Please point out the diff. twixt these and the blue columnists. (This has little to do with song.)
◁ 'Lie-Dream' 80% of 10% OR 6% over no less than ¼ = ??????
◞ Valhalla brochure bit White face Finds Roots, boys don't even notice -& look for games machines.
◠ Desperate attempt to make bouncy good of 2 drum kit line-up. 'The 3 days I had off, Are just a bank of fog, seen thru a glass bottom phutt cig.' Watch out for lyrically related video.

a   poeaaaaemmm:
Never knew had so many friends till Venue. In awe. The fans were awed And cowered. Still bowing to: Mythical Thingy, and the fresh stool, at 'Venue' No decision equals 'consulation'. One True Sentence. On Morning Of It: Saw Flabby Wings and Ran cross frosty crusting of Plate glass, from the SKRIKKING KIDS, NOT FIT FOR: HEX END. — the BIG P.

THE FALL
Steve HANLEY   BASS GUITAR, VOCAL
Craig SCANLON   GUITAR, VOCAL, PIANO
Mark E. SMITH   VOCALS, TAPES, GUITAR
Marc RILEY   E. ORGAN, GUITAR, E. PIANO
Paul HANLEY   DRUMS, GUITAR
Karl BURNS   DRUMS, VOCAL, TAPES
Kay CARROLL   VOCALS, PCSN.

HEX Enduction!

(1hr.)   (1hr.)   (1hr.)

KAMERA RECORDS   ▣ made in U.K. Printed by Centreprint, London.   DISTRIBUTED BY STAGE 1 RECORDS   KAM 005

Steve HANLEY   BASS GUITAR, VOCAL   Production: Richard MAZDA, Smith
Craig SCANLON   GUITAR, VOCAL, PIANO   Engineers: Tony J. Sutcliffe
Mark E. SMITH   VOCALS, TAPES, GUITAR   Cover: Smith / Alan SKINNER
Marc RILEY   E. ORGAN, GUITAR, E.
PIANO
Paul HANLEY   DRUMS, GUITAR   Recorded at Hijorite, Reykjavik, Iceland, September 1981
Karl BURNS   DRUMS, VOCAL, TAPES   (tracks 3 & 10) and the Regal Cinema, Hitchin,
Kay CARROLL   VOCALS, PCSN   December 1981.

Room To Live: Undilutable Slang Truth! (September 1982, Kamera)

SIDE 1
Joker Hysterical Face
Marquis Cha Cha
Hard Life in Country
Room To Live

SIDE 2
Detective Instinct
Solicitor in Studio
Papal Visit

The Fall

MOUS Cha-Cha

LOATHSOME TRAITOR
Victim of Educated Aimlessness.
REVEALED BY:

The Fall

UNDILUTABLE SLANG
TRUTH_ROOM 2 LIVE
BY THE FALL
Produced by Kay O'Sullivan
Bar tracks 4 (J.Brierley)
and 7 (Smith)

for information contact
Kamera records, 9 Downs Road,
Beckenham, Kent.

kam 011

SOLICITOR IN STUDIO(b)_FIRST REVULSION THE BEST
RESPECTED FIGURE MOUTHS TRIVIAL VIEWPOINT(a) 33
R.P.M. HARK BACK,DEAR FRIENDS_

The outside world now encroaches in on this close-knittedness.
Sez 'Tec:" Some of those youths were so poor,they couldn't
          even afford t'get their fringes cut "
"YOUare a good detective,it's apity you can't remember just
   Who is the Host"
B) Song Six(see below) is a brief laugh tale.one less to worry
about.But a small victory-revived christianity thru' public
works plus Prevention Media still on upsurge.Granada rated the
track so precious,they erased it.
XXxxXXXXXxxxXxXXXxXXXXXXX

The true meaning of 'folk' drops its' thin veil at the last.
same truth as song three."Impossible to dilute,Anyway "(X)
-_- St.Swithins Day 1982

① DETECTIVE INSTINCT   5'50
② Solicitor in Studio   5'13
⊕ PAPAL VISIT   5'10

sleeve pasted-up by citizen bank

The Fall
Paul Hanley   drums
Karl Burns   bass, drums
                   guitar
Steve Hanley   bass
Marc Riley   guitar keyboards
Mark E. Smith   vocals violin
Craig Scanlon   guitar

Also:
Arthur CADMAN   Guitar
Adrian NIMAN   Saxophone

Cargo Studios
John Brierley

Produced by Kay O'Sullivan
Bar tracks 4 (J. Brierley)
and 7 (Smith)

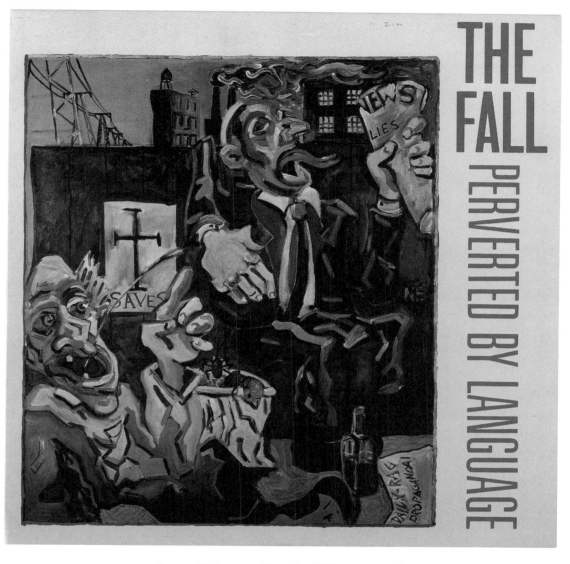

Perverted by Language (December 1983, Rough Trade)

SIDE 1
Eat Y'self Fitter
Neighbourhood Of Infinity
Garden
Hotel Blöedel

SIDE 2
Smile
I Feel Voxish
Tempo House
Hexen Definitive / Strife Knot

58

PERVERTED BY LANGUAGE

CRAIG SCANLON – guitar, vocals

MARK E. SMITH – vocals, piano, violin

BRIXE SMITH – guitar, vocals

THE FALL

side 1
EAT Y'SELF FITTER
NEIGHBOURHOOD OF INFINITY
GARDEN
HOTEL BLÖEDEL

side 2
SMILE
I FEEL VOXISH
TEMPO HOUSE
HEXEN DEFINITIVE/
STRIFE KNOT

PRODUCED BY STEVE PARKER*

Front cover: CLAUS CASTENSKIOLD
slides by Ron Sumner from the Ikon Video
'THE FALL//PERVERTED BY LANGUAGE BIS'

RECORDED AT PLUTO, MANCHESTER
MIXED AT SILO, LONDON

*Except: 'TEMPO HOUSE' – recorded live at the
Hacienda, Manchester by Heather Hanley and Oz McCormick

PAUL HANLEY – drums, electronics

KARL BURNS – drums, bass

STEVE HANLEY – bass

STEVE HANLEY – bass

ROUGH TRADE RECORDS
DISTRIBUTED BY THE CARTEL
ROUGH 62

THE LOT

CRAIG SCANLON – guitar, vocals
MARK E. SMITH – vocals, piano, violin
BRIXE SMITH – guitar, vocals
PAUL HANLEY – drums, electronics
KARL BURNS – drums, bass
STEVE HANLEY – bass

Technical
Produced by Steve Parker*
Front cover: Claus Castenskiold

*except 'TEMPO HOUSE' – recorded live at the
Hacienda, Manchester by Heather Hanley and Oz
McCormick

Recorded at Pluto Studio, Manchester, and mixed at Silo,
London, mid-1983 (tracks 1–6 & 8).

The Law of Optics: The Fall, the Northern Working Men's Club and the Refining Powers of Rational Recreation

The Fall emerged during the heyday of a particular kind of *club culture*. From the mid-1960s, some social clubs in the north and midlands of England had begun to occupy a distinct position within an emerging tradition of popular leisure. Louis Armstrong played fourteen nights at Batley Variety Club in 1968, and performers such as Shirley Bassey and Tommy Cooper were headlining the variety and glamour Clubs of the north (such as the Wakefield Theatre Club or the Golden Garter in Wythenshawe). These Clubs catered for the entertainment needs of a better-off working class, with the revival of live entertainment in response to television's growth and reach meaning that stars would often play for good money in venues very close to home. As he'd reminisce, Mark E. Smith tended to regard this period and their experiences as essential in shaping the Fall's early outlook:

> *We were doing cabaret circuits at the time, just to earn money […] Working Men's Clubs and all that. Fuckin' godawful! Fuckin' terrible! Good though. It toughened you up. They'd be throwing glasses – proper glasses, like – and spitting at you. I see a lot of groups today, and they don't know they're born. But touch wood nobody ever walks out of a Fall concert. You've got to keep the fuckers in there. That's how we got half our following. You fuckin' win them over and get their respect. They still come now. Miners from Wakefield and Newcastle.*[1]

During its peak years, the Club would become a place for being entertained that was, above all, resolutely local and perhaps proudly parochial. It was defined in the minds of many by an idea and image of possessing and living a certain kind of *northernness*. Although Smith would swerve the stereotype regarding any blunt north/south separation (asked whether he had a northern sensibility, he immediately replied that his was 'north Mancunian'), he demonstrated a long-standing antipathy towards, and would hold a special degree of enmity for, England's capital. London's self-image and wilful cluelessness regarding the rest of the country, together with the empty attractions it seemed to offer to those drawn into its orbit, would be a common refrain in interviews – this hostility to both the city and what it appeared

1. Interview with David Cavanagh, *Volume*, 14 September 1992.

to represent reflecting Smith's preference for standing apart from any or all cases of self-appointed trendsetting, including that of cultural centres (always Salford, never Manchester).

However, Smith's attitude was in fact part of a tradition that was most certainly already present in London's relationship with the burgeoning glamour and Working-Men's-Club scenes in the north, and which was noted in *The Stage Year Book* from 1962:

> [*They*] *roam the world searching for talent to import – yet at the cost of their fares to Manchester, Sheffield, or maybe Doncaster, they could make a year's domestic shows, with enough over to strike a rich new vein of exports [...] As is so often the case in other fields, London appears in this matter to be one of the remaining reservoirs of ignorance. It's time the bright lads in the West End got hep to it all.*

The author's selection of Doncaster as an example of a kind of non-metropolitan remoteness or as an edge-land without any cultural significance, representing a parochial or small-town mentality or attitude, and as the venue for a particular kind of entertainment, foreshadows Smith's own concerns regarding talent and where it was to be found. As he'd go on to write (on the sleeve of the Fall's earliest live album *Totale's Turns* – the *turn* being Club parlance for the evening's act – and with his words channelled through the character of Roman Totale, an honorary member of the Wakefield Young Drinkers' Club), the WMC was seen seriously as a legitimate source for a good night out in those out-of-the-way places, such as Bradford, Preston and, of course, *Doncaster*. Naturally, Smith (or Totale) goes further, positioning the Fall in opposition to *both* the Club and London scenes.

Many people have commented on the Working Men's Club aspect of the Fall's work, usually people who have never had to live with or treat WMCs as the only form of live entertainment. Anyway, satire always takes a while to get through, and that WMC mentality is alive and well except nowadays it wears straight-leg Lee Coopers. Maybe one day a Northern sound will emerge not tied to that death-circuit attitude or merely reiterating movements based in the capital.

The more traditional image of the Working Men's Club as drink-sodden, bleak in its basic decor and design and exclusively male was developed along far less glamorous lines than those likely experienced by the Smith family in the 1960s and '70s. Established in 1862, in the classic spirit of Victorian paternalism, the Working Men's Club and Institute Union (WMCIU or CIU) was envisaged as a self-organising and cooperative network of spaces focused on an ideal for leisure – what its founder Rev. Henry Solly would choose to call 'rational recreation'. Similarly, Smith was often fond of reiterating his own vision for the Fall as one of a deliberate and meaningful collision of feeling ('R&R as primal scream') and knowing ('My idea was just to get people's heads going . . .'); of primitive music with intelligent lyrics, engaging both the heart and the head. For Solly, the Club would be a space for socialisation, conviviality and concerts, alongside lectures, reading and self-help, whose aim was an ambiguously termed improvement. Such a hybrid of thinking and acting would be, for Solly, the salvation of the working-class male, mainly because it would keep him out of the pub (and help him to escape from the family, his drudge life of wife and children), while being with acquaintances in a situation of supervised sobriety. Such a utopian aspiration wouldn't last long, however, and was quickly replaced in response to members' demands, their rebellion based on a preference for a slightly less rational form of recreation. In 1867, a list was drawn up noting the eight key reasons why CIU-affiliated Clubs were unlikely to succeed. Among the challenges that were identified were 'a too positive presence' of both 'the Parson's hand' and local youth, the number of rival attractions offered by any metropolis, the 'strained relations between master and man', and the political agitation taking place at the time. Most notable, however, was the absence of opportunities to consume beer.

Although it would at first be rationed, within three years alcohol would become commonplace as the staple of any successful Club. By the 1970s, the CIU would grow to become the world's largest private-members organisation, with over four thousand Clubs being affiliated, although this number has since halved, and the decline shows no sign of slowing. Quickly, *entertainment* (rather than any other ideas of improvement) would become the main attraction for Club members and, as would be noted in the CIU's official history marking its sixtieth anniversary, the relationship between music and alcohol became very close, and was not always regarded positively: 'Music . . . which ought to purify and refine, is now extensively employed as a temptation to drinking and other vices.'

Early instances of Henry Solly's preferred recreational entertainments for Club life would be inspired by music-hall traditions of song, dance and audience participation. Although sniffily accepted by Solly and the CIU's overseers at the time, particularly lively was the 'Judge and Jury Class', a mock trial that would bring members onto the stage in order to be brought to justice by their Club's committee for a variety of imaginative offences (e.g. 'passing round his Lordship's snuff box'). Mark E. Smith's early onstage role often seemed to reflect that of one committee member in particular: the hectoring master-of-ceremonies known as the 'concert chairman' – the individual given the responsibility of maintaining order in the room ('Are you doing what you did two years ago? Well, don't make a career out of it'), filling the gaps between acts, calling the frequent games of bingo and making critical announcements to the members ('Last orders half past ten'). Perhaps Smith was influenced by Colin Crompton's popular character from ITV's attempt to bring the Club experience into audience homes, *The Wheeltappers and Shunters Social Club*, which aired from 1974 to 1977. Crompton's dazed and seemingly uninterested Club chairman introduced the show's acts, made pronouncements on behalf of the (unseen, unheard) committee, and sustained the show's meta-narrative as a faithful simulacrum of 'real' Club life. Smith's early performance persona seems to have been developed through a meshing together of the characteristics of similar Club committee members, who would often have to function as both comedian and organisational representative. In terms of form, content and delivery, Smith's lyrics and performances would echo the Club man's game of choice: bingo. The common idea that the game is, or was, the preserve of (mostly elderly) women (who wouldn't be allowed to become full members in any CIU-affiliated Club until 2007) is quite the myth. The bingo master reflected his audience of players, and his trance-like combination of words, numbers and individual letters, creating a distinct bingo-derived patois, is a clear influence on Smith's words and world view. From the Fall's first lyric to their very last, these meaningful numbers would be present or suggested: in the in-character narrative of *Bingo-Master's Break-Out!* ('Two swans in front of his eyes [...] it's number one for his Kelly's eye...'), or Smith's meditation on survival, probability and having a 'marked card' in 'Nine Out of Ten'.

Typography is both a visual strategy for giving meaning to words and a method for expressing cultural values, a way to craft and exploit the letterforms as 'outer shaping devices' that work upon a reader to achieve impact and effect. Typography and graphic-design practices manifest themselves in WMC culture in one main location, which usually has two roles. They're mostly found on the ubiquitous Club noticeboard, either advertising the performances and acts that are to feature in the upcoming schedule of events (mostly taking place on Friday and Saturday nights) or drawing a visitor's attention to the environment of the Club itself and the institutional rules which must be paid heed to – often by replaying scenes of associative and embodied action (what you must not do, how you must not do it). Mostly home-printed A4 pages, messily nested and clustered together, these notices act as an organisational barometer, telling stories of that Club's shared values, its commonly held needs and the demands which mustn't be ignored. The posters advertising live entertainment take a quite different aesthetic approach, glossily overcompensating for the performer's relative obscurity, or for whatever quality of musicianship might be on offer, with the use of a broad grammar of stylistic devices that mirror a perceived visual style seen in the wider world, while creating a genre all of their own. Slick photography elevates the subject with little trace of (or need for) Photoshop blends, brushes or retouching, alongside the full gamut of typographic trickery – never-too-decorative font selection combined with experiments that bravely explore the hinterlands of legibility – all working together to portray a culture that's actively striving for a kind of glamour, fashion and exoticism that belies the humdrum surroundings of your average Club's concert room.

Echoing the announcements and pronouncements of the *Wheeltappers'* Colin Crompton, the notices to members and associates often speak on behalf of the (faceless, nameless) Club committee and adopt a formal visual and typographic tone, while throwing off any artifice of a designed professionalism or pretence towards positive visual or typographic engagement with their readers. Instead they present a blank and brutalist collision of the simplest of forms with an equally direct mode of communication that, while guided by the CIU's values as a means for association, drive home the repeated conditions of the rules of Club membership. Modernist designer Jan Tschichold argued for a 'pure' typography as the means for achieving a better or improved society through socialised cooperation, with design and designers embracing collectivity as their central ambition, and where '[o]nly anonymity in the elements we use and the application of laws transcending self combined with the giving up of personal vanity (up till now falsely called "personality") in favour of pure design assures the emergence of a general, collective culture which will encompass all expressions of life – including typography'. Mark E. Smith's handwritten and hand-typed early sleeves often recall a Club committee's hastily produced, overly officious messages, their typographic design often shifting from a relatively straightforward presentation of information deemed necessary towards something altogether more careless or unconsidered – sometimes both on one image. Overlapping values seem to underpin the production of the Fall's and the Clubs' collection of typographic objects: an overarching need for order (of some kind); from this the development of collectivity or community (of members, of fans), which then reinforces the sense of belonging (a sense of membership, association, exclusivity or participation); the recognition that the audience, artist or Club member might be bound by a shared set of codes, which are made explicit in some way through their typographic expression; lastly, that the tone of this expression is conceptually and visually distinct, and reflects the character of the thing making the message (the Club or the group). Both Club notices and Fall LP covers often tread a fine line between clarity and belligerence, in how they look or any expectations for how they should perform. They each seem superficially ugly and visually are often overly simplistic, but these tactics are used to disguise layers of encoded meaning and deliberately obscure the real intention of a message.

Each Club sustained a cottage industry of print and publication, largely through a need generated by gaming and gambling, but also in order to structure the conditions of entertainment and entrance, facilitating participation and providing a proof of identity. Mostly, these ephemera were produced cheaply and with little consideration of any need beyond their immediate use. The Club's noticeboards and waste-paper baskets would overflow with crowded and chaotic assemblages of words, images and graphic symbols, overused capital letters losing their impact when constantly exclaiming the rules for being in a room or the many reasons for exclusion; underlined words giving emphasis when necessary, although which ones were assigned the horizontal rule could seem quite random; the whole thing often accompanied by handwritten corrections or additions that rendered the original message quite confused. Mass-participation games such as bingo, played on gridded, numbered cards

printed on pale-coloured paper and sold in perforated sheets or books, would normally result in a proliferation of scrawled, scribbled, daubed and hand-marked detritus being angrily dumped by Club members after their unsuccessful game. Upturning the waste-paper bins after a particularly busy Sunday afternoon's bingo and games would create a pile that had the potential for many hasty collages similar to those found on a number of Fall album covers.

All entry, exit and movement within the Club is governed by the CIU's list of thirty-seven rules. They cover areas such as how the Union is named and its institutional objectives, what Clubs do with their money, how any methods for cessation or dissolution are to be agreed, regulations for the management of Club managers, together with the need to both direct and command temporary or partial Club members and associates. The rules outline how disputes should be handled and the powers of a committee, and how its officers should carry out the day-to-day running of a Club, with the committee having the authority to administer punishments and enforce the necessary penalty for any violation of the Club's rules. The CIU rulebook is a feature of every Club member's introduction to Club life, gifted at the moment of their joining and, alongside other ephemera, a permanent companion in any member's wallet, one that might be called on at any time to prove its owner's right of admission. The aesthetics and typographic style of a list, and the qualities of the ephemera or paperwork used to transmit its contents, suggest a particular value to the information being communicated and that there is, according to design historian Robin Kinross, 'something persuasive about the nature of the organisation that publishes them'. The list's outwardly non-partisan format maintains an air of impartial authority that is established by its context and the ideological underpinnings of any institutional setting. Both lyrically and as a typographic feature of the Fall's LP covers, Smith often showed a fondness for the numeric or alphabetical list, with the tracklist becoming a dominant typographic element of the design. The list as a form of semantic and informational organisation offers a particularly poetic instance of what Umberto Eco called the 'topos of ineffability': an attempt to grasp at the infinite (the indescribable, the unutterable) and concretise it into something relatively mundane, where the idea or form of a list becomes as significant as its contents. For Eco, a list is visible and tangible evidence of an attempt to render the seemingly imperceptible or incomprehensible into something human or in some way rational. Smith's use of lists-as-lyric is often a means to distil the unappealing essence of an unnamed individual, gaining insight into a particular narrator's disposition via the elements of their mundane routines and daily habits ('Dr Buck's Letter'), or to question the trustworthiness of a character through a detailed cataloguing of their unappealing attributes ('Ten Points').

Popular impressions of the Fall's work ethic and Smith's attitude towards work have been shaped by their reputation as a live act and the value of the

THE FALL

HULME LABOUR CLUB, MANCHESTER
Friday, 22 July 1977

PRESTWICH HOSPITAL SOCIAL CLUB
Saturday, 25 November 1978

THE FALL

BOWDON SOCIAL CLUB, ALTRINCHAM
Wednesday, 14 February 1979

THE FALL

NELSON RAILWAY WORKING MEN'S CLUB
Friday, 29 August 1980

THE FALL

SOCIAL CLUB, BURNLEY FOOTBALL CLUB
Wednesday, 19 May 1982

The Fall

TRADE UNION CLUB, SYDNEY, AUSTRALIA
Tuesday, 10 / Wednesday, 11 August 1982

THE FALL

BOYS' CLUB, BRADGATE ROAD, BEDFORD
Saturday, 1 October 1983

THE FALL

EAST'S RUGBY CLUB, BRISBANE, AUSTRALIA
Friday, 22 June 1990

BANGOR RUGBY CLUB
Saturday, 2 August 1997

THE FALL

ST BERNADETTE'S
CATHOLIC SOCIAL CLUB, WHITEFIELD
Wednesday, 21 / Thursday, 22 October 1998

THE FALL

BALNE LANE WORKING MEN'S CLUB,
WAKEFIELD
Friday, 21 May 2010

THE FALL

LOWER KERSAL SOCIAL CLUB, SALFORD
Saturday, 22 / Saturday, 27 / Sunday, 28
September 2014

group as one that was best experienced live. Crucial to this seems to have been the widely quoted fact that the Working Men's Club was where the Fall served their apprenticeship in the group's earliest years. Given the impact of the Club on the Fall, it's perhaps a surprise not to see more evidence of them playing social and WMC venues, to match Smith's rhetoric about the Fall's toughening-up and apprenticeship phase, reflecting the time served in Club concert rooms across the north-west and beyond. From the exhaustive (albeit incomplete and perhaps insane) online Fall gigography, it's possible to identify sixteen venues that are clearly a 'Club' in the CIU sense, spread across three distinct phases of activity – 1977–83, 1990–8 and 2010–14 – with eight in the first phase, four in the second and four in the last: sixteen from a list whose true length is unlikely ever to be known. Perhaps it's more useful to view the Club as the embodiment of an idea (in much the way it was dreamed up by Solly), and of it being a perfect location for the Fall within the imaginary or mythic, as much as the actual. In this sense, the second phase of the Fall's Club gigs marks some kind of transition or transformation, the last set of performances in 1998 reclaiming the Club as some kind of transcendent space, helping with the process of bedding in a new group that's been made fragile by the traumatic times following their implosion in New York. At this point, the Club stands as an ideal that also communicates directly to their audience (and others) as a way of reinforcing the Fall's values and their links to a now almost extinct culture and class from which Smith had emerged twenty years earlier.

L.P — Dragnet :

side 1 :
PSYKICK D~ANCEHALL~ — This place exists.
A FIGUR WALKS.
  PRINTHEAD
DICE MAN (From the book, don't read it. The songs
BEFORE the MOON falls   much safer.)
  YOUR HEART OUT.   dedicated to all ex-
                           members of The Fall &
side 2 :   Their petty materialism.
  MUZOREWI's DAUGHTER. — For all our lads who
FLAT. OF ANGLES   died in the Boer War

CHOC-STOCK.   "Pop-stock buy my pop-stock"
SPECTRE VS. RECTOR.
PUT AWAY.

  ● sophisticated.

          MARC RILEY — guitars, vocal.
          CRAIG SCANLAN — "ld." gtr
          MES — vcls, tapes, e. pno/kazoo
          MIKE LEIGH — drums.
          STEVE HANLEY — bass, vocal.

Preparatory notes for various songs, 1978–80

MUZOREWI'S DTR

Get that spot n' put it in the pot for me
cos I'm Muzaweri's Daughter.
    Afrika Korps LUV
    Gentle Laws LUV
  I'm Muzaweri's Daughter.

Left-wing hot properties come out of the closets
and she. RUNS Muzaweri's Daughter.
    ETC.

The trees are reeds with evil seeds for me.
  Cos I'm Muzaweri's daughter.
    Afrika Korps. luv.
    Gentle laws. luv.
    Muzaweri's daughter
  Too long in the pot
  Too long in the lips
   I'm Muzaweri Daughter.
       c/right.
       smith/carroll
        1979.

A FIGURE WALKS   10.1.79

A Figure walks behind you   x2
A Shadow walks behind you
A figure walks behind you
   Days of booze and roses
   Shine on us free us all
   Who is not irratible
   He is no genius! (someones always on my tracks etc)
A Figure walks behind you
A Figure walks behind you
A Shadow walks behind you
A Figure walks behind you
   The old golden savages
   Killed their philosophers
   Their thoughts brought the drought about
   (Something followed me out)
A Figure walks behind you
A figure walks behind you
A Shadow walks behind you
A figure walks behind you
   An if it grabs my coat tail
   I will turn an hit it
   (It may remove the pegs
   Keeping my   t again.
Chorus

Tales of Terror
From Europ + America
Always road me
long

MESS OF MY   mark e. smith 78

Swedish singers / with D.L.T.
The energy vampires / more hands on the tranquilisers
Unholy alliance / jokes about rape
Fog bound roads / South African heroes

  A mess of my age
  A mess of my face (D L T)
  A mess of our radios

I remember the times / this was the beginning
Permissive new age / The same old cabbage

  A mess of our/our/our/our

RAP.2. 'I dream about taking some terrorists out for a quiet
      drink etc etc. bombs

      Y'know, dreams y'know when the only solution is
      etribution'

I don't look at myself / I have no health
Take no notice of me / I probably work for a record company

skeleton of;   YOUR HEART OUT

 Just take for instance / A time of great depression
 Fate out of reason / BAD TIMES IN season
chorus: bvcls:
 Don't shut your heart out - Your heart out
 Don't cry   your eyes out   - ''' ''''''' ''
 Don't shut your heart out - '''' ''''''' ''
 No no no no your heart out.

Don't cry for me / MEKKIKO
Or savage pencil / I'm nearly healthy

 An they tried to take my eyes out - Your heart out
 Friends tried to work my soul out - '''' ''''' '''
 An I don't sing I just Shout   - '''''''''' '''
 Heavy clout heart out .

Alone and depressed? / Sit back reflect
It'll soon end / Drop self pity friend

 They will never take   -   Your heart out
 Leave misery at the gate   -   Your heart out
 Just do your best   -   Your heart out
 Then have a rest.(cliche city but V.Important)

            KEYBOARD SOLO?

Here's a joke / To cheer you up
Old times no surgeons / Just magicians and dungeons

 There they'd take   -   Your heart out
 With a sharp knife not fake - Your heart out
 No anaesthetic   -   Your heart out
 That joke's pathetic.

Well look at me / Too much speed
But very plain / You are lucky,friend

 You've got one to take out - Your heart out
 U Know what I'm talking about - Your heart out
 I can't sing just shout   -   Your heart out
 All on one note.
sing sing sing sing/sing sing sing sing
look at me I just ring
even with a cold/I'm not very old etc etc etc ad nauseum.

        Copyright Mark E. Smith 1979.

MES 1979.

21st. June.   It's ~~Prorogation~~   mark e. smith 1978 c/r

The ~~world~~ → l. (aside)

1/ My boys tape when I say/ o it studio way
New equipment-all clean/new gear-clothes mean
I answer and take calls/No trouble with the law
Turn it on for interviewers/Oh yeah(prime movers,
→ I *Wonder* what is next years thing
  harmony.   ~~Smash~~ crash smash ring.

2/ They've got another side/(pop heroes of the mind,
While you suckers queue or work/ oney for us in play
                                end tel
We have never sold out/ pend hours over clever art
And funny advertising notes/(make you bite and
  It's the new leather thing   raise your hopes
  SMASH CRASH SMASH RING.
The ~~world is his~~ (aside)

ass-moced.
3/ The broken backs of the real bands/(million closed
                                        minds.
The wear of the average man/re-form the old clans
The worst died because of you/Along with some other
                                              too
erasing of our rainbows/" e ore men' we have big x
                                              toes.
  → It's the new leather thing
  harmony. Smas,crash,smash,ring.

4/ Houdini believed his tricks/that's why he died
Oh,I'm not coming out/There may be a film on tonight
Or Elliots untouchables/Or ads for new hotels
That look like science fiction films/Or revival-
                          - Gothic-pig-swill.
  Watch the skies, watch 'the Thing'
  → ~~It's the new leather thing~~
  Smash,crash,smash ring.
harmony *your house*
Smash crash ring

30.10.78   WHAT IS THIS CONDITION?

When home went out.When out went in.
What is this condition ? (x2)
~~Alone want love.In love want solitude~~
~~What is this condition ? (x2)~~
In a ring of fire.What I wanted all my life.
Guitars ring din higher.Want a fire extinguisher.
What is this condition ? (x2)
-A neurotic Pan-vision ?
-A spoilt child brat-ism ?
An astral clockwatcher.A waste of the universal taxpayer.
What is this condition ? (x2)
-Too busy never cared(x2)

        PUT AWAY

Late 20th century.Was late and just said 'yes' or 'no'
And was mistaken for sarcasm.Even belligerent-noun 'to
fight'
They're puttin me away,but i ll be back some day(x2)CHORUS

In prison for a year and a day
1. A bust doorbell sound and then the door broken down
   A bust doorbell sound and the door broken down
   They rang an rang but i never went down
     There puttin me away but i ll be back someday(x2)
2. I thought it might be a follower,friend,rent man,split end
   Maybe a follower, friend or some local men
   I used to drink a bottle of vodka a day but now
     There puttin me away but i ll be back someday(x2)
3. They rang n rang but i never went down
   When people ring i never went down
   All metal nails and walls now i'm sent down
     There puttin me away but i'm back some day(X2)
4. My nice sides gone it won't be long
   Si-si-si long but now its gone
   Just dreams like 2 girls and a millionaire
           Pushin me away but i ll be back someday(x2)
       No sex or records for a year an a day ah.tut.

                    G A#C D G-F D/C
                                  D/chord

              2 ggcfggca#g

30.10.7? UNDERGROUND MEDICINE

seeds
bvels

~~Pushing~~ beat: nervous system nervous system nervous system ne

MORONIC BEAT

1vcl.:   underground medicine   un erground medicin

1. A spark inside / ten percent that I hide
   And when it clicks / there is no resist

2. Every time I hear / A new baby cry
   I thank my spark inside ——— and.....

        D underground medicine   underground medicin

3. Found a reason not to die / a reason for the ride

4. The spark inside / when it hits the mind

        D underground medicine   underground medicin

4. Had a psychosomatic / voice At one time
   It might come back /   cough   Need...

        D undergound medicin undergrond medicine und

   On my pants I spilt expectorant
   And he shot better with thirty pints
   THEY TOOK HIS CUP AWAY—TAKE IT AWAY

   CHANG A CHANG
   ETC

   ——————————————————

   E G A# C# / D

LYRICS:

BINGO MASTER'S :(excerpt)

All he sees is the back of chairs/In the mirror a lack of hairs
Alight realm which he fills out/Hear the players all shout/
Bingo master's break-out.   xxx A glass of lager in his hand
Silver microphone in his hand/Wasting time in numbers and rhyme
One hundred blank faces mine.

Same the time he flipped his lid/Holiday in spain fell through
the players put it down to.

A hall full of cards left unfilled ended his life with wine and
pills/There's a grave somewhere only partly filled/A sign in a
graveyard on a hill reads: Bingo masters break-out.

REBELLIOUS JUKEBOX :

'I'm searchin for the now—I'm lookin for the real thing,yeah'

MESS OF MY: (excerpt)

'A signal din
   A mess of my age/mess of my face/mess of our radios(?)
I remember the times/this was the beginning/permissive new
age/the same old cabbage.
   A mess of my age/mess of my taste(...?)/mess of our nervous
   systems.
TV mock/No leads plugged in/left-wing hot properties/let
back in the closets.'

I LIKE TO BLOW:(excerpt)

'No stars in the zone/I stay at home/I live in channel
 Potatoes in packs
An I like to blow/Like to blow/Like to blow/Concentration
Zone.

INDUSTRIAL ESTATE:
'Yeah,yeah industrial estate'

KOWALSKI.

QUESTER MEDIUM DISKORD

Is there anybody there ?   YEAH!
BAP BA DAP BA DAP BA BA
chorus:
Rock rocky for quester psychic disco
Step forward ha ha ha for ESP medium diskord

   My garden is made of stone / And the computer centre over the road
    I saw a Monster on the roof /It's colours glowed on the roof
ROUND the corner is quester psychic disco
Look over for ESP medium diskord

   Here they have no records / They know your questions about no words
   Just stumble bumble to the waves / Twitching out to the waves
GET aboard for quester psychic disco
Rocky rocky for ESP medium diskord

   When I'm dead and gone / My vibrations will live on
   Through thoughts not vinyl thru the years/People will dance to my
WAVES.

   CHORUS.

   MEntally come.

                         copyright Mark E Smitj 1979

Call Yourselves Bloody Professionals?
The Fall and Amateurism

amateur: a person who engages in a pursuit, especially a sport, on an unpaid rather than a professional basis. Late 18th century from French, from Italian amatore, *from Latin* amator *'lover', from* amare *'to love'.*
(*Oxford English Dictionary*)

If anyone talks about amateurs these days, they tend to be thinking of two distinct categories. There's the 'gifted amateur', usually a musician or sports player with heaven-sent talent, possessed of an ability that no amount of professional graft could touch. More common is the 'rank amateur', an embarrassment, a clumsy failure getting in the way of people who can do a job properly. Oddly, no one ever talks about a 'rank professional', even though everyone has come across them and there are plenty out there.

Amateurism hasn't been seen as a badge of honour for decades, its meaning squashed into meanness. Mostly, 'amateur' is now used as a term of abuse, signifying the slapdash and the inept; given this, the notion that 100,000 people turned out at Wembley to watch the Amateur Cup final several times in the 1950s seems hard to fathom.

Mark E. Smith understood the shifting plates of language. He never committed his lyrics to paper, not in a book anyway, nothing permanent. Language always has room to manoeuvre, and sometimes a new interpretation can eliminate previous definitions. In the social-media age, are the Norwegians still proud of their trolls? Do chimpanzees still groom each other? At the other end of the spectrum, 'DIY' did not have good connotations at all when I was growing up in the 1970s; it was largely seen as a means of saving money, and it equated to shoddiness. In the twenty-first century, 'DIY' suggests authenticity and anti-consumerism. The meaning of 'amateur', having made the reverse trip, could and should be reclaimed. The Fall turned down TV shows that insisted they print out the lyrics of songs they were about to perform. They refused with good reason: as long as they weren't set in stone, the songs were still alive. And as long as the Fall remained amateurs, they could do exactly what they wanted.

'Professional' has, for some time, suggested aptitude, expertise and status. You would trust a professional — it suggests qualifications. In the late nineteenth century, things were quite different. Sport was seen as an end in itself and professional footballers were sneered at. You expected to get paid for doing something most people do out of love? You had a nerve! 'Amateur' was a term that indicated pride and incorruptibility. In modern pop parlance, it probably comes closer to 'indie' than anything else. Outside of sport and music, a similarly honourable term might be 'autodidact'.

The Fall were not professionals. This enabled them to explore areas that would have seemed alien to their contemporaries on major labels, who were tied into album/tour/single/tour cycles dictated by their record companies. In the digital pop age, it may be no big thing for Beyoncé to produce a complete film to accompany her new album, or for the Pet Shop Boys to write a new score for *Battleship Potemkin*, or for Ed Sheeran to sit – wearing his tatty jumper and simpleton grin throughout – for David Hockney. In the mid-1980s, though, the Fall's contemporary-dance collaboration with Michael Clark was completely unheard of. For Mark E. Smith to write a play, *Hey! Luciani*, was similarly eye-popping. The group were entering cross-cultural territory at a time when MTV seemed shocked that Run DMC's and Aerosmith's different strands of pop could possibly work together. Bands were bands, and they stuck fast to their jobs. The Fall were not a professional pop group. They did not devote their time to one strand of music, or art, and they certainly didn't do it purely to make money.

> *Harry Dowd, the goalkeeper in the [Manchester City] championship team in 1968, was the best. He still worked as a plumber part-time and my dad was a plumber too. We used to go behind the goal and Harry would wander over and talk about washers and copper joints.*
> (Mark E. Smith, *When Saturday Comes*, 2000)

In 1878/9, Darwen – a football club based in a Lancashire mill town between Blackburn and Bolton – brought in two Scottish players from Partick F.C. to play in the FA Cup, with the promise of well-paid mill work dangled as a carrot. The Football Association was, at this point, entirely amateur, for the benefit of players who didn't need to get paid for their time, and any covert paying of players was against its (unwritten) rules. Darwen were not thrown out of the FA Cup, though; the FA knew by this point that professionalism was an unstoppable force. It was working-class towns in the north that harboured professional clubs, and they had usually been formed by philanthropists and sports-minded clerics.

Ten years later, the Football League formed, as well as a rival league called the Combination, and the following year the Football Alliance. All of them were professional. And, like any business, competition meant that some of them went to the wall: Newton Heath were founder members of the Combination, and went on to become Manchester United, members of the Football League and multiple European Cup winners; so were Bootle, who were Everton's main Merseyside rivals in the 1880s, but who these days play in the North West Counties League against the likes of Barnoldswick Town, Squires Gate and AVRO, a works team for an aircraft manufacturing company in Oldham.

Look at Bootle and Manchester United fans and you have to wonder, who's happier in 2020? United were sold to some Americans, the Glazer family, who saw them as nothing more than an investment to offset losses elsewhere in their business empire. United were pawns in a capitalist game. This had nothing to do with thirty-yard free kicks that go in satisfyingly off the underside of the crossbar. Seventh or eighth in the Premier League won't be good enough for demanding United fans, but, more importantly, it really won't be good enough for the shareholders. The self-financed Bootle, meanwhile, are second in the NWCL at the time of writing. Their Twitter account shares footage of a kid in the Liverpool ONE shopping centre playing Robert Miles's 'Children' on the piano. They bemoan the demise of Garston Co-operative Society. They write 'all the very best to Dennis Skinner on his 88th birthday. To the constituents of Bolsover . . . SHAME ON YOU!' It's hard to imagine Manchester United's official Twitter feed having such free rein.

As things stand, Bootle could be promoted from the North West Counties League into the Northern Premier League, still a long way from the fully professional ranks (it would also be incorrect to call them 'amateur' – more on that later). In the second division of the North West Counties League, and in no immediate danger of reaching such giddy heights, are Prestwich Heys, the local non-league club for the district of north Manchester where Mark E. Smith grew up.

The football triumphs of today, or any day, can be fashioned with dignity and satisfaction only by applying the principles of play which the Corinthians and their contemporaries fashioned for the world.

(Edward Grayson, *Corinthians and Cricketers*, 1955)

PRESTWICH HEYS FIRST TEAM: Back row (left to right): J. Fox (trainer), D. Twigg (reserve), R. Hanvey (sub.), R. Freeman, D. Smith, K. Hancock, B. Smith, R. Howard, A. Tolan (reserve). Front row (left to right): A. J. Povall, T. E. Kaye, K. Bramhall, H. Kynaston, M. Rogers, and P. J. Gilmour (captain and team manager).

PRESTWICH HEYS

A.F.C.
(FORMED 1938)

LANCASHIRE FOOTBALL COMBINATION

and

MANCHESTER FOOTBALL LEAGUE

at

GRIMSHAWS, off HEYS ROAD
PRESTWICH, MANCHESTER

OFFICIAL PROGRAMME
PRICE 3d.

THANK YOU FOR YOUR SUPPORT!!

FOOTBALL ASSOCIATION AMATEUR CUP COMPETITION
(2nd Round Proper)
Saturday, 17th January 1970. Kick-off 3 p.m.

PRESTWICH HEYS (Red & White trim)		SUTTON UNITED (Amber & White trim)	
1. K. Kirby		1. D. Roffey	
2. G. Gardner		2. R. Brookes	
3. A. Povall		3. D. Clarke	
4. R. Greaves	*	4. E. Powell	
5. D. Smith		5. J. Faulkner	
6. H. Kynaston	*	6. D. Gradi	
7. P. McDonald	*	7. M. Mellows	
8. D. Widdup	*	8. T. Bladon	
9. P. Gilmour		9. P. Drabwell	
10. S. Crompton	*	10. L. Pritchard	
11. J. Garrett	*	11. T. Howard	
12. K. Donegan(Sub)		12. T. Waughman (Sub)	

* Denotes International Player

Referee: Mr. D. Stanton (Lichfield)
Linesmen: Mr. A. Williams (Northwich)
Mr. R. Phoenix (Sheffield)

Next Saturday (24th Jan.) on Grimshaws:-
HEYS v EARLE (Lancs.Challenge Trophy) 3 p.m.

Shop at Tower Buildings for all your Requirements

Club Chatter : Welcome to Sutton United — possibly the finest amateur team in Britain today. Their visit is a further milestone in the history of Prestwich Heys. Some very good teams have played at Grimshaws - Spennymoor, Highgate and Finchley spring readily to mind, but none has achieved the fame or success of Sutton United.

An exciting Cup match flavoured by skills above the average is promised. Both clubs have good grounds for optimism. Sutton, by virtue of their magnificent record over the last few seasons. Heys, in the knowledge that they have led the Lancashire Combination for most of the season and in so doing, gained 37 points from a possible 44. The Sutton team is rich in talent — how could it be otherwise with six international players in their ranks. But — and this is an interesting question which may be answered today — in comparison, how much below international standard, if at all, are some of Heys players? It is unfortunate that Keith Hancock, one who could have stood comparison is out of the team because of illness, but Kevin Kirby, a County and North of England player is no mean substitute.

There is no inferiority complex in the Heys camp and Sutton represent just one more hurdle on the way to Wembley. Confident of success today, Heys wish Sutton better fortune against Leeds United next Saturday. Whatever the result today, Heys are pleased to have established friendly relations with Sutton, which we hope will develop and prosper. After all, is this not what amateur football is all about? Heys extend a warm welcome to the Mayor and Mayoress of Prestwich, Councillor and Mrs. S. Pepperman and to representatives of the Football Association.

Shop at Tower Buildings for all your Requirements

Mark E. Smith would scour lower-league bands for new Fall members as if he was the chief scout of a financially straitened football club. He signed up Marcia Schofield from Khmer Rouge, Karen Leatham from Wonky Alice, Kate Themen from Polythene. In 2001, he drafted in a group called Trigger Happy in its entirety to effectively become the Fall, giving them only eight hours' notice before they had to play a gig. Often, musicians were signed up to the Fall as apprentices, learning their trade on the job: Marc Riley was initially the group's roadie; Ed Blaney went from tour manager to manager to guitarist; Kay Carroll was Smith's girlfriend, brought in as both manager and backing vocalist; classical musician Simon Rogers initially played bass, then – presumably when he seemed too comfortable – was moved by Smith to keyboards, at which point he left the group. Smith called it 'creative management', and he used these tactics to prevent a cosy slide into professionalism. 'When you're playing five or six nights a week the group get slick,' he said, and routine was always the enemy.

In Nige Tassell's *The Bottom Corner*, Ken Ryder – the former chief scout for Middlesbrough, Sheffield Wednesday and Wolverhampton Wanderers – talks about uncovering new talent in unlikely places: 'Of course, every chairman would love to find another Charlie Austin or another Jamie Vardy, but they don't grow on trees. You've got to go and find them. It's about putting the legwork in. It's about not being afraid to go somewhere on a Friday night instead of going home. You've got to go out and turn the stones.' With the Fall, Mark E. Smith didn't often extend his radar far beyond the pubs of Prestwich, but he was confident his scouting ability would see him recruit new members whom he could mould, make great. When they got too comfortable ('Don't start improvising, for God's sake'), they might be fired by phone or just left at an airport. Another scouting mission would commence, and the process continued. It worked. The Fall never sounded glossy or comfortable; it was always an ongoing learning process. They weren't there to be a professional pop group – a 'fancy group', as Smith would have it.

This level of amateurism is rare in football or music. A few years ago, I saw a striker called Ashley Flynn playing for AFC Emley, a village side who play on a hilltop near Huddersfield, in the shadow of the Emley Moor TV tower. In an FA Cup preliminary tie against Athersley Rec, he was clearly head and shoulders above every other player. He went on to score seventy-three goals in the 2015/16 season.[1] He only wanted to play where he would enjoy football, he told scouts; he would rather that than make loads of money. Besides, he had no intention of giving up his day job as a legal executive. So he had the ability, everyone knew that. At Emley, he was on a bonus of £10 per goal – it was fun to smash records in his spare time, and the goal bonuses

1. He actually scored eighty goals, but seven of those had been in two games against Lincoln Moorlands Railway, who had resigned from the league mid-season and had their results expunged.

bought pints for his mates after the game. He did eventually decide to move on, to Yorkshire Amateur, a club in the Harehills district of Leeds that plays in the Northern Counties East Premier Division, a whole division above Emley.

Amateur players were far more plentiful in the 1950s and '60s, which was largely down to the way professional football clubs treated their players. In 1952, Bury signed Stewart Imlach from Lossiemouth for £150. He received £7 a week during the football season and £6 a week over the summer close season; his wage could have risen to £14 a week if he was picked for the first team. That was all; no more was possible as this was the era of the maximum wage, and the Players' Union reckoned that only 20 per cent of professionals were paid the maximum wage. Professional footballers were effectively owned by the clubs they played for; their lives were remarkably similar to those of the fans who worked in mills and factories, only with less flexibility. The club could retain your services in perpetuity; if they wanted shot of you, and no other club wanted to pay a transfer fee, then you were stuck, unable to move and play elsewhere. Your only option would be to leave the professional game. If you did that, you could lose your house. Even a relatively small club like Bury owned the houses its itinerant players lived in, just like the tied housing that was built for the town's mill workers. If the club decided to show you the door, not expecting you to move to another club, then you were effectively sacked and left with nothing.

Another Manchester group, James, had left the Factory label in 1986, after releasing two acclaimed singles for the American major Sire (home to the Ramones, Talking Heads, Madonna). After their first album, *Stutter*, underperformed commercially, Sire asked them to make a more radio-friendly album, which would be called *Strip Mine*. Still they weren't happy with the results and spent a year remixing James's tracks in search of a hit. A group that had been so uncommercial that they refused to do interviews and intentionally wore anti-fashion clothes in 1985 were now in the position of being signed to a label that wouldn't even release their music. Eventually, they found a legal loophole and put out a live album on their own called *One Man Clapping* in 1989. With distribution by Rough Trade, it went to no. 1 on the independent chart. These are history lessons that are largely forgotten, but it's no wonder the independent record labels of the 1980s and the amateur football game of the 1950s had so much appeal.

In his book *On the Corinthian Spirit*, D. J. Taylor talks about his father, who worked for the Norwich Union insurance company, played for their first XI, won a Norwich Business Houses Championship medal and, on the strength of this, applied for the vacant manager's job at Exeter City in 1947. As an experienced amateur footballer, he had felt fully capable of managing a league club from Devon (though he never received a reply). The reams of surviving prep notes for *Hey! Luciani* show that Mark E. Smith approached writing his first play with a thoroughness that no professional playwright could have bettered. Still, he had no intention of giving up music to become a full-time playwright. With the *Perverted by Language (Bis)* video collection released in 1984, it was also apparent that the Fall weren't making videos to appear on MTV; it was just another branch of the arts where Smith felt he had something unique to say. It's surprising and rather shocking how little most bands want to be involved in their own videos and artwork, let alone actively control them. Staying on independent labels enabled the Fall to maintain a Corinthian approach. Artwork, live appearances, even press releases bore their distinctive mark.

The Fall were nothing if not contradictory and, as well as a dislike of the corporate rock world, they had a healthy mistrust of independent record labels, where an alternative culture could easily curdle into routine. Domino would eventually get it in the neck on *Your Future Our Clutter*, but in the 1980s Rough Trade was their repeated target. Smith must have laughed long at Dave McCullough's review of *Totale's Turns* in *Sounds* in 1980, which suggested that its release on Rough Trade was like the confluence of two mighty rivers. Rough Trade was so much brown rice to Smith – it lacked the correct work ethic. He saw it as amateur in the modern sense, run by work-shy hippies, novices and people who didn't take pride in their work. The Fall ended up on Rough Trade anyway; they felt happier on a label that was home to other mavericks, like Cabaret Voltaire and Kleenex, rather than a major that wouldn't let Smith employ his sister as chief sleeve designer. Their teaming up was due to convenience and a very loose alignment of values. The smell of lentils was just something Smith had to put up with.

'We were very in much in danger of becoming another Rough Trade group,' Smith told John Doran of *The Quietus* in 2010. The first time the Fall left Rough Trade it was for another independent label, Kamera, which few of their fans were familiar with. The trickster Smith told Doran: 'They were a heavy metal label and they just said "Do whatever you want." I said "I want to make an LP that lasts for an HOUR!" They're all right them heavy metal blokes sometimes aren't they? They were like "An hour?! YEAH! There's a cheque, dude!"' In reality, Kamera had nothing to do with heavy metal. It was an odd little label with few and varied acts: ex-Family singer Roger Chapman, Birmingham post-punk act the Au Pairs, and Freddie Starr, who got to release a live album of his Elvis routine. It was like a fever-dream night out at a working men's club, which was probably part of the appeal for Smith. An hour-long single vinyl album was always going to sound thin and quiet (the maximum recommended length per side is twenty-two minutes), though Smith told Doran he was upset about the sound quality of *Hex Enduction Hour* for different reasons: 'When it came out it was on really duff heavy metal vinyl, the sort of stuff you'd use for Sabbath's *Greatest* or whatever. It must have sounded really weird in those days... it was like a Woolworths recording. All muffled and everything.'

Were there benefits to being affiliated to an amateur football league, in the way that there was credibility in being signed to a label like Rough Trade or

Factory? There were. The rise of professional football in the 1880s meant that amateur teams were increasingly squeezed out of the FA Cup. The Amateur Cup was first contested in 1890, a revolt against the growing professionalism in football, and it originally featured an uneasy mix of the ex-public schoolboys who had initially competed in the FA Cup for no payment (Old Carthusians, Royal Artillery, the Casuals) and working-class amateurs with day jobs.[2] The latter were mostly members of the Northern League, which represented Teesside, Wearside, Tyneside, County Durham and Northumberland (Stockton, Willington, Blyth Spartans), and clubs from the fringes of London (Finchley, Southall, Clapton) who played in the Isthmian League, so named for its Olympian amateur ideals. Post-war, the Amateur Cup final was played at Wembley and regularly sold out; 100,000 people watched Bishop Auckland play Crook Town in the 1954 final, two teams from mining towns in County Durham whose combined populations didn't come remotely close to Wembley's capacity. It would have been hard to imagine that just twenty years later, the last-ever Amateur Cup final would be played.

What happened in the intervening twenty years was the rise of 'shamateurism'. For decades, the Isthmian League was a closed shop of fourteen clubs – no promotion, no relegation, with invitations only occasionally handed out to new members. Between the wars, other leagues sprung up for clubs in the Isthmian catchment area who couldn't get an invite, all with similarly idealistic Greek names: Athenian, Corinthian, Spartan, Delphian, Hellenic, Essex Olympian. Clubs from the Isthmian League won the Amateur Cup a record thirty times; crowds were so impressive that Dulwich Hamlet's Champion Hill ground was rebuilt in 1931 to hold 30,000 people. There was pride in playing for Isthmian clubs, and theoretically everyone played for nothing but expenses; if you wanted to play semi-professional football, there was always the Southern League, which could even give clubs like Hereford and Cambridge a lift up to the fully professional Football League. But if Isthmian clubs wanted to attract the best players, and keep them away from Southern League clubs, there were always underhand means. The dam broke when the secretary of Isthmian newcomers Hitchin Town announced loudly in the club bar that his team had made illegal payments to players; the scandal led to the departure of their manager, former Arsenal player Laurie Scott. It suddenly became obvious why the same few clubs (Wimbledon, Hendon, Leytonstone, Walthamstow Avenue) finished near the top every season, while more honourable clubs (Clapton, Dulwich Hamlet, Corinthian Casuals) were always closer to the bottom of the league. The increasingly false division between professional and amateur football was finally done away with by the FA in 1973, with the 1973/4 season's Amateur Cup being the last.[3]

---

2. The old-boys clubs that dominated the competition in its early years began to withdraw from 1902, when they set up the Arthur Dunn Cup, named in memory of an Old Etonian player.

3. For the record, Bishop's Stortford beat Ilford 4–1 in the final to claim the trophy in perpetuity.

Hon. Assistant General Secretaries: L. STONE, Esq., 303 Bury Old Road, Prestwich (PRE. 5074), W. J. GILLBANKS, Esq., 18 Church Drive, Prestwich (PRE 1422).
Hon. Treasurer: F. E. NORTON, Esq., 80 Carr Avenue, Prestwich. (PRE 4727).

COUNCIL MEMBERS:

Hon. Insurance Secretary; Club Hon. Assistant Treasurer; and Hon. Secretary Publications Committee: F. W. COCKBAIN Esq. (PRE 4940).
Hon. Welfare Officer: W. H. HORBURY, Esq.
Team Manager/Coach (First Team): P. J. GILMOUR, Esq. (WHI 5563).
Team Manager/Coach (Reserves): R. FREEMAN (766-6957).
Hon. Ground Manager and Technical Officer: B. BRIERLEY, Esq.
Hon. Secretary Ground Committee (Administrative): W. H. HORBURY, Esq.
Chairman of the Ground Committee: G. K. CARNELL, Esq. (766-6899).
Vice-Chairman of the Ground Committee: R. DICKINSON, Esq.
Hon. Assistant Secretary Ground Committee (Administrative): T. E. KAYE, Esq. (773-6192).
Hon. Trainer: A. CUSICK (MID 5021).
Hon. Trainer (Physiotherapy, First Team): J. FOX (PRE 3405).
Hon. Trainer (Physiotherapy, Reserves): J. KENNEDY.
Club Captain: T. E. KAYE, Esq.
Keeper of the Records: L. STONE, Esq.
Hon. Secretary/Treasurer Development Fund: G. A. B. BROSTER, Esq.
Hon. Assistant Secretary/Treasurer Development Fund: F. W. COCKBAIN, Esq.

'Chock-Stock' started as a pro-pop song cos all the people into the Fall, the Pop Group, Gang of Four, Throbbing Gristle and who fuckin' laugh at pop fans are patronising, that's all. At least the kids into pop are being honest.

(Mark E. Smith, *Slash* magazine, January/February 1980)

Arguably the single most influential record in the Fall's career is a compilation album. Kenny Everett's *The World's Worst Records*, released in 1978, was the most anti-canon album you could imagine. Some of it was pure schlock — country narratives and syrupy Christian rhymes ('The Big Architect in the Sky') — but much of it was pure amateurism, unclassifiable, fired by the same impulse that had sent dozens of garage punk bands into Texas recording studios in the 1960s, and similar numbers of one-chord wonders in Britain to make DIY seven-inches in the late 1970s. The chorus of Nervous Norvus's literal car crash of a song, 'Transfusion', would be indirectly quoted on 1979's 'Rowche Rumble', while Steve Bent's frayed MOR 'I'm Going to Spain' would be covered quite faithfully on *The Infotainment Scan*. Other tracks that cast a light on future Fall recordings include the Trashmen's 'Surfin' Bird', which had previously shocked the UK with its manic monotone thrash on K-Tel's kid-friendly *Goofy Greats* in 1976.[4] Beyond even the Trashmen, though, both louder and more manic, was 'Paralyzed' by the Legendary Stardust Cowboy, a one-man band who, against all odds, had been signed to Mercury in 1968. David Bowie, who signed to US Mercury a year later, would later claim the Cowboy gave him the inspiration to create Ziggy Stardust, though frankly there's a far stronger link between 'Paralyzed' and 'Mere Pseud Mag. Ed.' than there is to 'Moonage Daydream'.

What about Mrs Miller's 'A Lover's Concerto'? You hear her odd operatic approach to scat singing over a cod-Motown backing and recall Karl Burns's anecdote that he was once told by Smith to play the tom-toms like 'a snake'. This music was neither straightforward nor professional. It was all wrong. Simon Rogers explained the genesis of 'Paintwork', from *This Nation's Saving Grace*: '"Paintwork" was sort of half done in my bedroom and then Mark took the cassette away. He had it in his little Dictaphone/cassette recorder and sat on it and made a big hole in the middle.' Maybe it was an accident, but on what was one of the Fall's most polished albums you have to think it might have been an intentional piece of self-sabotage. Steve Bent dropped a similar bomb on 'I'm Going to Spain', cutting surreally into his potential holiday hit with a line about sandwiches — 'I hate them, yes, I hate the cheese and pickle' — leaving MES-like thumbprints on the paintwork.

Smith saw the canon and nostalgia — especially major-label-funded, professional nostalgia — as an even greater curse on music than shamateur record labels. '(Do) the Hucklebuck' by cabaret 1950s revivalists Coast to Coast,

4. 'Surfin' Bird' had never been a hit in Britain, though it had reached no. 4 in the US in 1963. Americans might be confused as to how its mono-chord DIY clatter could be construed as awful. A year after *Goofy Greats* came out, the Ramones covered 'Surfin' Bird'.

a hit in early 1981, irked him so much that within weeks he had transformed it into 'Hassle Schmuck'. A couple of years later, he found an equally unusual target for his ire: 'I hate the guts of Shakin' Stevens for what he has done. The massacre of "Blue Christmas" — on him I'd like to land one on.'

> *Thank you to all the people who helped me on my vendetta tonight.*
> *Thank you to all the people who helped me on my vendetta tonight.*
> *Who helped me on my vendetta tonight. Oh, go tell your passion,*
> *go tell your weepings to the K-Tel marines. To the publishing wolverines.*
> (Mark E. Smith, onstage at Acklam Hall, Notting Hill, 1979)

Shakin' Stevens's career arc is quite possibly the one that Smith feared the most; he would use 'creative management' to keep it permanently at arm's length. Stevens had been born in the Ely district of Cardiff, the youngest of eleven children, and was already married and working as a milkman when he joined the Sunsets, aged nineteen, in 1968. The group — without Shaky — had formed as the Backbeats as long ago as 1958, and so were more continuity rock and roll than revivalist. They supported the Rolling Stones at London's Saville Theatre in December 1969, a week after Altamont, and quickly became the biggest attraction in the country on the underground Ted scene. They were still a big under-the-radar act in 1976, when Johnny Rotten abruptly concluded an interview, saying he was off to catch a Shakin' Stevens and the Sunsets show. That same year, Shaky recorded Hank Mizell's rockabilly touchstone 'Jungle Rock' on the titchy Mooncrest label; it was a song the Fall would cut themselves in 1997.

What happened next was that Shaky signed to Epic Records in 1978, home to ABBA and Michael Jackson, and scored a couple of fairly convincing minor rock-and-roll hits with 'Hot Dog' and 'Marie Marie' in 1980. When he covered Rosemary Clooney's daffy pre-rock hit 'This Ole House' the following year, it unexpectedly hit no. 1, and he was suddenly playing Pat Boone to Adam Ant's Elvis — he had become the biggest, safest pop star in the country. The backing tracks may as well have been pre-sets, it didn't affect sales of Shaky's cosy 1950s covers. 'Blue Christmas', which reached no. 2 in 1982, was clearly a step too far for Mark E. Smith. Here was a once-noble performer who had worked as an upholsterer and a milkman by day, while singing primal rock and roll on the club circuit by night, reduced to cracker-toy covers of songs by his greatest hero. This was what professionalism in the music industry meant.

This was exactly what the Fall worked hard to avoid for over thirty years. But neither did they want to be pigeonholed as 'independent', which to Smith would have translated as 'Rough Trade groups'. Rather than equating to true independence, the term had become stylised and ghettoised as 'indie' by the time the Fall unexpectedly signed to Beggars Banquet in the mid-1980s.

Are there any similarities between the Fall's chart-bothering covers and Shaky's wack rock and roll? The Beggars Banquet years — when every other A-side seemed to be a cover ('Victoria', 'There's a Ghost in My House', 'Mr Pharmacist') — certainly feel as close to cashing in their chips as the Fall ever got. They had left Rough Trade for a second time, after the release of *Perverted by Language* (the first Fall album with Brix in the line-up) in 1983, and moved to the notionally independent though entirely anonymous Beggars Banquet in 1984. The Fall started to scrub up. Mark and Brix appeared on the cover of the *NME* in late 1983 looking almost chart-friendly; they started to release cover versions for the first time in 1985 (starting with Gene Vincent's 'Rollin' Danny'), and began recording things that even non-Fall fans would recognise as sounding like the Fall ('Hit the North'). The photo session for 'Victoria' featured Smith with only the two female members of the group — glamorous blonde Brix and brunette Marcia Schofield — while the shop-floor members (Scanlon, Hanley, S., Hanley, P.) were frozen out. It was hard to avoid seeing this as 'professionalism', or, in pop parlance, 'selling out'. Beggars Banquet weren't a charity. Money was changing hands. Someone was conceivably having a word in Smith's ear. In footballing terms, it felt like they had accepted sponsorship.

Most likely, MES simply fancied a change and wondered where a financial bunk-up could take the Fall. Around the same time, the Lancashire club Colne Dynamoes began an unexpected charge up the non-league pyramid. Bankrolled by millionaire chairman — and manager — Graham White, they had a budget to make some Football League clubs, like nearby Burnley, green with envy. White himself had founded the Dynamoes in 1963, as a club for him and his schoolmates from Colne Primet High School. By 1982, they were founder members of the North West Counties League. White's work in the timber industry had made him wealthy; property speculation in the 1980s made him very wealthy indeed. What would happen, he wondered, if I spent my money on the club, maybe even bring in some professional players? He began a spending spree, going through hundreds of thousands of pounds, bringing in ex-Liverpool star Alan Kennedy, and White watched his Dynamoes climb to the brink of the Football League itself. There was a real possibility that they could take the place of fallen giants Burnley, at the time on their uppers in the Fourth Division. And then suddenly, in August 1990, having been denied promotion because their Holt House ground wasn't up to standard, they folded overnight. Graham White left football altogether, and in all the years since he has never once spoken publicly about Colne Dynamoes' dramatic rise and fall.

Could the Beggars Banquet era, a flirtation with the big league that meant the Fall were fully affiliated members of the *Smash Hits* sticker collection from 1985 to 1988, have led to a similar collapse? Mark and Brix split, and the Fall moved to Fontana, a real major label (I'm sure MES was happy to be on the label that had released primal-noise 45s like the Troggs' 'Wild Thing' and Dave Dee, Dozy, Beaky, Mick & Tich's 'Hold Tight'), at the start of the 1990s. Perversely, the move saw them back down from gauche promotional items like a seven-inch box set with free lyric sheets (the only time the Fall provided printed lyrics with one of their records), and they recharged themselves with the *Extricate / Shift-Work / Code: Selfish* triptych.

The Fontana label had started in the 1950s as a subsidiary of Dutch electronics giant Philips, the company that sponsors and maintains Dutch football's wealthiest club, PSV Eindhoven. It had never been anything other than part of an international corporation, and by January 1990, when 'Telephone Thing' became the Fall's first single on Fontana, it had become part of Polygram, the biggest record company in the world. This, conversely, did not add any kind of extra sheen or professional polish to the Fall's output. In fact, it's the only Fall era in which the words 'warmth' and 'gentility' could be applied to their music ('Bill Is Dead', 'Edinburgh Man', 'Time Enough at Last', 'Gentlemen's Agreement'). 'Rose' is a rare, generous divorce song ('We've got that wah-wah going – you started that'). Still, Smith's sense of humour was intact. His cheek was bare on a cover of 'Legend of Xanadu' that seemed designed to point out that Dave Dee, Dozy, Beaky, Mick & Tich's original had been an influence on Joy Division's 'She's Lost Control'. Maybe Fontana was a benign benefactor and allowed the Fall's independence more space. Either way, unlike the Beggars Banquet years, there is nothing needy about these records.

The Fall would achieve their highest league position with 1993's *The Infotainment Scan*, a no. 9 hit on the UK album chart. It was their first album for the Permanent label, a tiny record company they joined after leaving Fontana which appeared to release only records by folk-jazzer John Martyn and a post-All About Eve act called Mice. The flirtation with the big leagues was over; they were soon back to full amateur status at part-time outfits like Artful, Receiver, Action and Jet (no, not the same Jet that ELO had been on). One of these labels was run from a record shop in Preston. Eventually, they settled down with an old indie warhorse, Cherry Red, which was named after a song by the MES-approved Groundhogs. There was stability, but not much money, and the Fall became labelmates with other prized antiquities, such as Hawkwind; this at least guaranteed a home for the group as they entered their fourth decade. This was as close to winding down as the Fall would ever get.

In *The Football Man*, Arthur Hopcraft writes about the dozens of pitches at Hough End, 'a great, low-lying urban plain off one of Manchester's major entry-and-exit roads, the grass bordered on one side by a railway line and on another by a prefabricated housing estate'. Hough End was a place where 'old warriors conserve their wind by playing wily midfield games, suppressing criticism from younger men for their immobility by shouting the loudest and lacing compliments with baritone abuse of referees'. Cherry Red was the Fall's own Hough End, suitable for bloody-minded kickabouts which were never going to trouble Premier League scouts. There was still a mix of rancour and wit on *Ersatz GB* and *New Facts Emerge*: 'All salute at the altar of filo pastry' sounded like a pissed-off Fiery Jack (What next? Wetherspoons doing quinoa salad?) thirty years on. Railing against filo pastry and the crass redevelopment of Manchester's Victoria Station was no guarantee of airplay on BBC 6 Music, let alone Heart or Absolute. Smith's world view — more specifically, his view of twenty-first-century Britain — was still perfectly distinct over the relatively sure footing of the Fall's final line-up. Hopcraft's take on Hough End's amateur footballers is pertinent: 'Perhaps unconsciously we are reacting individually against our decline, in our historical old age, as an international force.'

References

John Doran, 'Becks Enduction Hour', interview with MES, *The Quietus*, 19 February 2010.

Edward Grayson, *Corinthians and Cricketers*, Naldrett Press, 1955.

Gary Imlach, *My Father and Other Working-Class Football Heroes*, Yellow Jersey, 2005.

Nige Tassell, *The Bottom Corner: A Season with the Dreamers of Non-League Football*, Random House, 2016.

D. J. Taylor, *On the Corinthian Spirit: The Decline of Amateurism in Sport*, Yellow Jersey, 2006.

When Saturday Comes: The Half Decent Football Book, Penguin, 2005.

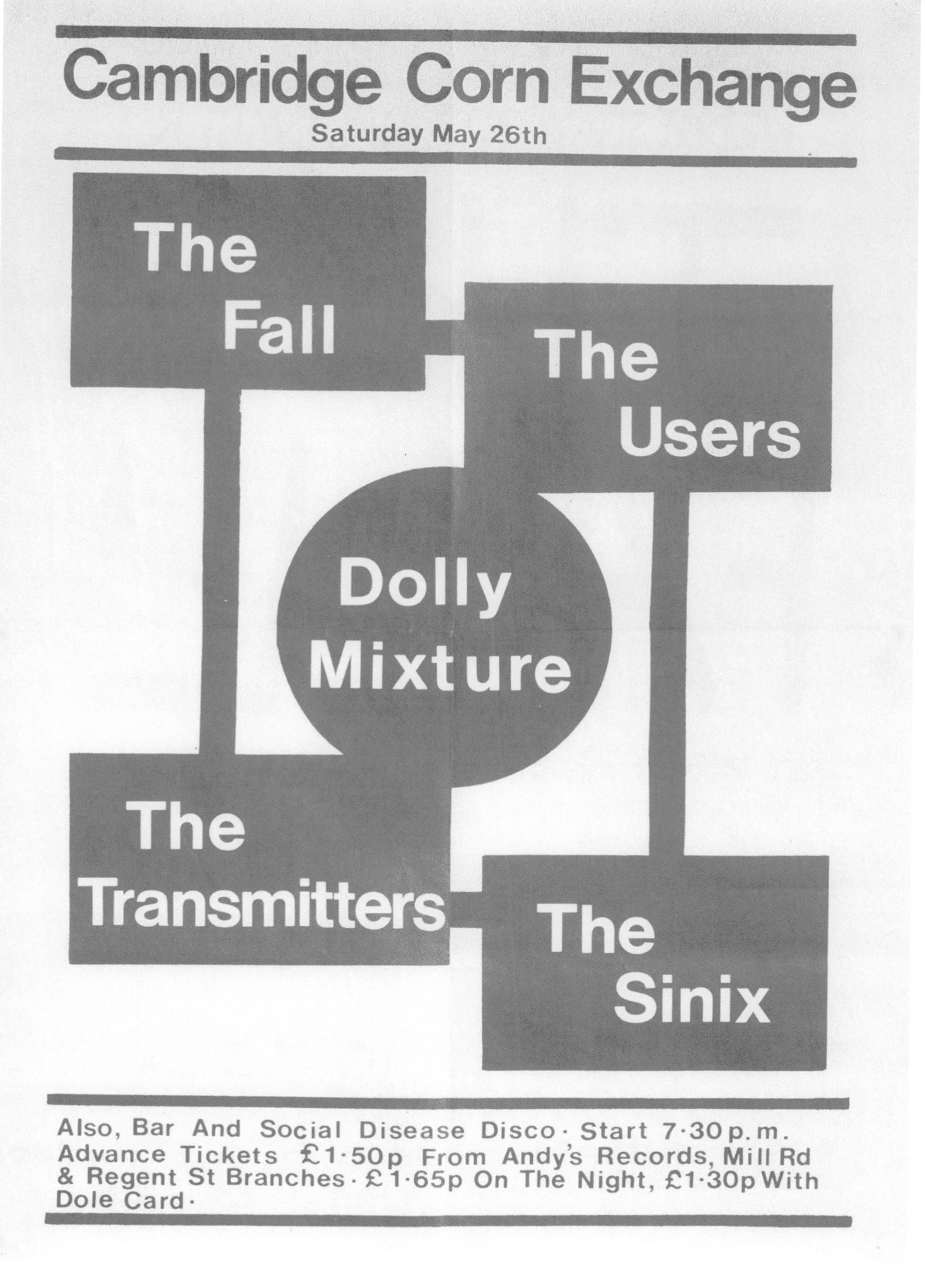

Cambridge Corn Exchange

Saturday May 26th

The Fall

The Users

Dolly Mixture

The Transmitters

The Sinix

Also, Bar And Social Disease Disco · Start 7·30 p.m.
Advance Tickets £1·50p From Andy's Records, Mill Rd
& Regent St Branches · £1·65p On The Night, £1·30p With
Dole Card·

LESSER FREE TRADE HALL
WEDNESDAY 22nd DECEMBER.

THE FALL

an alternative christmas
spectacular

special guests:
Gay Animals

7-30p.m. 'till 10-30 p.m.

tickets from F.T.H. Virgin, Picc.Rec.
and usual outlets — only £2-50.

HEY PEASANTS!

THE FALL
GROTESQUE

AFTER THE GRAMME

NEW ALBUM AVAILABLE NOW
THROUGH ROUGH TRADE

INFO-(01) 727 6085. Cat. No. Rough 18. Distribution 2211100

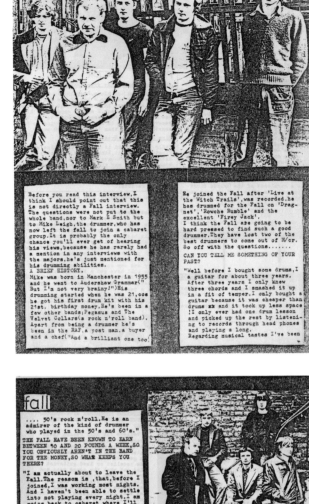

The Fall

Before you read this interview,I think I should point out that this is not directly a Fall interview. The questions were not put to the whole band,nor to Mark E Smith but to Mike Leigh,the drummer,who has now left the fall to join a cabaret group.It is probably the only chance you'll ever get of hearing his views,because he has rarely had a mention in any interviews with the majors,he's just mentioned for his drumming abilities.
A BRIEF HISTORY
Mike was born in Manchester in 1955 and he went to Audenshaw Grammar(" But I'm not very brainy!")His drumming started when he was 21,cos he got his first drum kit with his 21st. birthday money.He's been in a few other bands;Pegasus and The Velvet Collars(a rock n'roll band). Apart from being a drummer he's been in the RAF,a post man,a buyer and a chef("And a brilliant one too!

He joined the Fall after 'Live at the Witch Trails',was recorded,he has drummed for the Fall on 'Dragnet','Rowche Rumble' and the excellent 'Firey Jack'.
I think the Fall are going to be hard pressed to find such a good drummer.They have lost two of the best drummers to come out of M/cr. So off with the questions.......
CAN YOU TELL ME SOMETHING OF YOUR PAST?

"Well before I bought some drums,I a guitar for about three years. After three years I only knew three chords and I smashed it up in a fit of temper.I only bought a guitar because it was cheaper than drums xx and it took up less space and I only ever had one drum lesson and picked up the rest by listening to records through head phones and playing a long.
Regarding musical tastes I've been

Pages 94–98: Fanzine covers and interiors 1979–80.

FALL

a mod in the sixties,a skinhead, a hippy and a punk.So I tend to go through periods of liking one sort of music until something new is introduced to me.At the moment I like everything except Opera!
WOULD YOU CONSIDER YOURSELF A PUNK OR A TED NOW?

"I don't consider myself to be in any category except maybe a 'Teddy-Punk'.I like rock n&roll, reggae,jazz and new wave,so I have wider tastes than the average ted or punk."
THE REVIEWER OF FIREY JACK SAID THE THINGS ROCKABILLY,IS THIS ANY OF YOUR DOING?

"Don't believe everything you read. If Firey Jack is rockabilly I'll My bum in Burtons window! The song just started off as a jam at a practice.I just started drumming and the rest joined in.At the time we were doing a few slow numbers and I thought it would be nice to do something bouncy.The drum riff is a standard rockabilly riff with a double shuffle,&which I ripped off from a Johnny Cash record so if you want to categoris e it,I would call it new-wave country!
THE FALL ARE ASSOCIATED WITH DRUGS. WHAT ARE YOUR OPINIONS OF DRUGS IN ROCK N'ROLL,OR IN GENERAL?

"They are necessary to some people who 'need to escape' or cannot 'get high' on the music itself. I'm worried about the situation, because it is just accepted and some fans tend to be led into taking drugs because their favorite musician is associated with them,or because their friends do it and they feel obliged to. I do not take drugs except tablets for epilepsy,and I find no need for artificial stimulents,cos I can get high on the music itself. I can beat about the bush. DRUGS HAVE KILLED,RUINED LIVES AND BRAINS,AND WILL CONTINUE TO DO SO UNTIL THE 'WORKING CLASS HEROES' IN BANDS SPEAK OUT AGAINST THEM".

I'VE HEARD THAT IN PAST FULL BAND INTERVIEWS ARGUMENTS HAVE STARTED ON THE SUBJECT OF DRUGS,IS THIS TRUE?

"I believe the only reason there arent any full band interviews is that the interviewer is not interested in all the band. In general they tend to go for the vocalist or lead guitarist to find out what the songs mean and how they came about. With the Fall everyone wants to get inside Mark Smith's head and see what he's thinking.After that they will have a word with Marc Riley and Craig Scanlon.The bassist and the drummer are not

usually involved in the writing, so there's no common ground except the usual,'what are your favorite groups."

OVER THE HISTORY OF THE FALL THERE HAS NEVER BEEN A FIXED LINE UP FOR A LONG TIME,WHY ARE THE LINE UPS SO UNCERTAIN?

"There's a combination of reasons;
1.The people have become boerd and did nothing to rectify it, ie,writing something they are not boerd with.
2.In any band,there are disagrem- ents,but some people take it too seriously and leave out of anger.
3.Other reasons such as impracticality of travelling to practise or personal difficulty. Yvonne lived first of all in Yorkshire and then in Birmingha x

THE LATEST LINE UP SEEM A MIXED BUNCH OF CHARACTERS,DOES THIS HELP IN ANY WAY?

"I don't think the differences in character have anything to do with the music.It is the creative guitar work of Marc and Craig, that fits in with the lyrics, together with the basic compatability of bass and drums."

IN A PAST INTERVIEW,MARK SMITH SAID HE REALLY WANTED YOU TO JOIN,WHY WAS THIS?

"He says he wanted to work with a drummer who has a simple style, which I learnt when I was playing

continued over...

---

fall

an old picture of the Fall; l-r, Mike Leigh,Marc Riley,Martin Bramah, Yvonne Pawlett and Mark Smith.

.... 50's rock n'roll.He is an admirer of the kind of drummer who played in the 50's and 60's.
THE FALL HAVE BEEN KNOWN TO EARN BETWEEN 10 AND 20 POUNDS A WEEK,SO YOU OBVIOUSLY AREN'T IN THE BAND FOR THE MONEY,SO WHAT KEEPS YOU THERE?

"I am actually about to leave the Fall.The reason is ,that,before I joined,I was working most nights. And I haven't been able to settle into not playing every night,I am going back to cabaret where I'll be able to play every night. I thought long and hard before I made the decision,and I will miss the Fall a lot.I love the music and have nothing but the greatest respect and admiration for Mark Smith. I just love drumming,and want to get as much of it as I can."
WHATS YOUR VERSION OF THE ROCK N' ROLL DREAM?

"The average man/woman in the street joins a band,makes a record,people buy it like mad and he/she becomes a rock star over night."
WHAT WOULD YOU LIKE TO SEE IN THE FUTURE AND WHY?

"There will always be a future for music,because man will always have lesiure time and he will find himself with more time to spend on lesiure pursuits. Iwould like to see another music revolution like rock n'roll and punk,because it is in danger of lapsing back into the state of apathy,which there was before the punk revolution. Aside from music I would like to see the Tories out of office for at least the next eight years or so,so that the Socialists can get a chance to put things back right again. I would like to see a protected income for teachers,and so avoid producing a generation of illiterate. Also I would like money to be spent on the National Health service,so that we can afford to xxx buy equipment for saving lives."

HAVE YOU ANY AMBITIONS?

"I WANT TO BE A RICE SUPERSTAR! Get married and have kids.(In that order.) OR....I would like to have nice young ladies throwing themselves at my feet and fullfill my every desire. If I can't have any of those,I just want to carry on drumming until I'm 60,and make a few more records in the process."

Well thats it.The Fall lose yet another excellent musician,who'S next?I can't see Mike making any more records ,now that he's gone cabaret.But in the meanwhile the Fall have a live lp coming out soon,through Rough Trade,which should be worth giving your attention to.Thanks to Mike Leigh for doing the interview. This is the third attempt at typing this article,and the best.

Nightclub, which noone can relate to, not even The Members.

Smith: That is a common policy of the band - we wanna make music that will stay on for 10 years. I'm damned sure there'll be a lot more people listening to our stuff in 10 years than a lot of famous bands.

Smith: What songs are you talking about?

WELL, IT'S JUST THAT SOME GROUPS DON'T LIKE PLAYING THEIR EARLY MUSIC-THEY FEEL THEY'VE POSSIBLY CHANGED SINCE THEN, OR THAT IT'S A STATEMENT THAT'S BEEN SAID...

Smith: Well, we've dropped Repetition, and Bingo Master; partly because we feel the message is irrelevant, but also because the band's bored with it.

Riley: If we pooled in all the songs we have we'd have about 60. We've got too many songs now, and there's only about 3 old songs in the set.

Smith: And it's wrong to suppress that creativity. It's like bands that have hit singles, you know, - by the time the single hits the charts, they've been playing it for a year, and they're going to have to play it for another year.

Riley: That's why we like getting things down while they're fresh. Like we have with the new album - all the stuff on it, except for 2, was written after Martin left, so all the album is fresh.

Smith: If there's a fault with Witch Trials, it's that we were over-familiar with the songs.

Riley: I was, and I'd only been in the band 6 months at the time.

WHY HAVE THERE BEEN SO MANY LINE-UP CHANGES? IS IT SOMETHING YOU'VE WANTED?

Smith: It's not something you want at the time, but it's worked out good when you look back at it.

Riley: It's all very personal - if you don't like it you leave, and that's that. It's strange with something like Martin to break it off, and just say "I'm leaving", and see what happens when he's been there for like 2 years.

DO YOU STILL CONSIDER IT THE FALL?

Smith: Yeah. Defeinitely. A band is what it's got to say, and I've always spoken for the band through the lyrics; so I think it would be different if the lyric-writer had left, but he hasn't, ie I haven't. I was throughly bored with the Witch Trials sound, I needed a fuckin' change, it was horrible - well it seems horrible to me now. It works really good - the energy a line-up change injects into a band is incredible.

A LOT OF PEOPLE GO ON STAGE THINKING OF THE AUDIENCE, AND WHAT THE AUDIENCE WANTS TO HEAR; DO YOU PLAY WHAT THE AUDIENCE WANTS, OR WHAT YOU WANT?

Smith: Well we don't pander to audiences, but then audiences can make a difference. I find our audiences totally unpredictable- I don't know what's going to happen with

them next time, and I think that's good. The YMCA was wierd - that wasn't what I expected at all (details of the YMCA gig are on Page 39)...

Riley: It's like when we played Warrington, yonks ago, with Karl, and it was just like hundreds of kids there, with a mass of po-going. Then we played there 6 months later with Mike, and it was suddenly different - a load of people just stood there watching.

Smith: London is always different as well. So is Manchester. The Fall haven't got a fixed audience. The YMCA gig was really wierd, because there was like, all the intellectuals there, and then a core of dancers at the front going wild, and all these guys with moustaches behind them, going "Ummm...yes...".

DO YOU THINK YOU 'WON' AT THE LYCEUM?

Smith: Er... yeah. People made a big fuss about that thing, wheras we thought it was just another gig. We just thought we'd made a mistkae playing th e Lyceum again, 'cos we knew it was going to be like that.

Riley: ...After the Gen X thing. We played with Gen X there and it was pretty horrible, but we decided to play there again...

Smith: 'Cos we thought it would be a lot better. We were playing with what we thought then were 'kindred spirits', ie Gang Of 4, Mekons, Stiff Little Fingers...but they turned out to be a oack of shit. It was good to play it though - The Fall thrive on that. Me & Marc were talking about it just the other day, it's really good - it brings the best out of us insituations like that.

Riley: It's like if something goes wrong before we go on, we're all wound up. Like at The Marquee, Yvonne (Pawlett) was

l-r - Mark Smith, (maj Scanlon) Marc Riley, Steve Hanley, Mike Leigh

PIC: Brendan Jackson

95

supposed to turn up, and she didn't. So we said "Alright, fuck you". It's like spite, I suppose.

Smith: Something like The Lyceum brings out The Fall's attitude. Like the YMCA was a bit too easy really.

WAS LATWT CAREFULLY PLANNED OUT IN ADVANCE, LIKE IT WAS A RUN-DOWN OF '78 FOR YOU?

Smith: Yeah it was rather 'In Retrospect'.
Riley: It was getting rid of old songs.
Smith: Well it wasn't so much that- we had about 4 other songs to go on it; we just had too many songs for it. That was the drag. The only bit of real spontaneity was the title track- it was made up there.

WAS IT DELIBERATE TO RECORD IT IN ONE DAY AND MIX IT IN ONE DAY?

Smith: It was and it wasn't. We had 5 days, but I got sick for the first 3. There was a lot of fuss made about that as well - I mean, why bands have to take more than 3-4 days to do an album is beyond me personally. Especially bands that do the, like, guitar, bass,drums line-up like we do. Why they have to go in for months is beyond me.
Riley: Some people go in, and they do dubs on this, and dubs on that. Ours is a very straightforward sound.
Smith: The best sound The Fall get is live- it always has been.
Riley: ... Which is why Rumble got more of a live sound.

IS THE "I STILL BELIEVE IN THE R'N'R DREAM" LINE SARCASTIC OR SERIOUS?

Smith: It's half and half- it's ambiguous. But I do ina lot of ways. People say The Fall aren't rock'n'roll you know; my attitude is that we are rock'n'roll and no other fucker is.
Riley: It's just what they consider to be rock'n'roll, like screwing and...
Smith: Like if you get down to the basics of rock'n'roll, if you go back to the mid-'50's - those bands had the right attitude.

I WAS GOING TO ASK WHETHER YOU DID CONSIDER YOURSELF ROCK'N'ROLL...

Smith: I do. I consider other bands not rock'n'roll. The term rock'n'roll is overused and it stinks, which is why I said "R'n'R" - an abbreviation.

WHY DO YOU CONSIDER OTHER BANDS NOT ROCK' N'ROLL?

Smith: Because a lot of them don't keep to the spirit - they get into technique, they get into effects in the studio,and they get into playing their instruments. Or they get into bringing singles out, bringing albums out, doing tours - that's not rock'n'roll. Like people used to say "Oh, you've got a really good drummer" or "Oh, you've got a really good guitarist"- that's a fucking stupid thing to say. Nobody knows - who cares? Audiences don't know who's a good musician, but they know what's good - they feel it and they know

it's good. It's like me - I can't sing but I knwo what I'm doing is good. And I know that rock'n'roll is not the plying of instruments - you don't play instruments in rock'n'roll, and bands that do are copping out in my estimation. Bands that, like, go in the studio, do a guitar solo, then go back and put loads of effects on it, so it's not actually a guitar solo you're listening to, but a control board. Do you get me? And I think that's not rock'n'roll.

marc Riley pic: AF

HAVE YOU EVER THOUGHT OF PUTTING IN THE LYRICS?

Smith: No. I don't believe in it. I think that's another thing that's wrong with rock'n'roll at the moment - the consumer is getting everything on a plate. You notice these new wave bands, they took the bad angle of it, like the accessibility - it's so fuckin' accessible that there's no work required by the band or the listener. And, like, - why should people have lyric sheets - it's a wasye of fuckin time. The greatest thing I ever saw was the first Ramones album where they put the lyrics in. It was so fucking funny. That was a really good bit of piss-taking of the American rock market. Like "You're a loudmouth baby, you're a loudmouth"...   No, I'm dead against it. We've got a lot of letters asking for lyrics, and if I've got them handy, I send them.

I don't like lyrics for people to read. I like lyrics to go with music. I'd be a fuckin' poet wouldn't I? I wouldn't write like I write if they were meant to be read. It's like some of the new stuff that the band's going to do soon - there's no lyrics actually in it. Most of them are like sounds, sort of sub-words.

HOW IMPORTANT IS SUCCESS TO YOU?

Smith: We don't go after it, because, as I said before I like privacy, and things have been offered us we've turned down. All I want success for is money to keep the band going. What we've attained now is great, because there's no pressure - it's a good tension between us and these buggers here

HOW DO YOU GET ON WITH STEP FORWARD - I READ YOU'RE NOT ACTUALLY SIGNED TO THEM WHICH I THOUGHT WAS EXCELLENT.HOW COMMITTED ARE YOU TO BEING FAIRLY INDEPENDENT - HOW MUCH SAY HAVE YOU IN THINGS YOU DO ?

S.Forward aren't too bad,they continuously owe us money,but that's the price you pay for freedom,we have final say in everything - art,ads(if any!!),tracks studio producer, Yvonne left a week before we started LP & we just rang S.Forward up & told 'em we'd do it without her & they didn't say a thing when is ok,y'know ? Have heard some terrible horror-stories about bands on labels like Virgin eg. Penetration vinyl fuck-up,Members fuck up any fuckin band that signs to Virgin fuck-up.Always been true - since CAN & CPT. BEEFHEART even. I think S.Forward'll either split up within 2 years or become another Virgin - dig ??

HOW EASY IS IT FOR YOU TO DO MUSIC-IT SOUNDS QUITE SIMPLE & REPETITIVE BUT LESS MONOCHROME NOW & YOU SHOUT-ESP. ON THAT FUNNY(TELL ME WHY/IS IT SO}BIT ON 'NO XMAS'-DO YOU THINK THAT INSPIRING OTHER UN-MUSICAL PEOPLE TO FORM BANDS IS ABOUT THE MOST POSITIVE THING YOU CAN DO ?

I think I've got an advantage over musicians in that I know nothing about music & suspect I'm tone-deaf. I have a plastic 4-string gtr.which I do a lot of writing on(eg.'NO XMAS')So simplicity dosen't embarrass me.Sometimes it's hard(esp.on the old fingers) sometime it ain't!!!!!!
Positive-mmm dunno - think all best music for years has been done by "non-music" people eg.early Pistols/Velvets/Stooges/Elvis even to a certain extent !/Residents etc. Phil Spector.

DOES IT TAKE YOU LONG TO GET THE SOUND YOU WANT & ARE YOU FUSSY ABOUT WHAT THE FALL PUT OUT - DOES THIS EXPLAIN THE GAP BETWEEN THE LAST SINGLE & THE NEW ONE.

The sound the band got now am pleased v.much with -for the first time in the Fall I can rely on their attitude & can now 'break-loose' & flow myself without having to support other members.eg.Present band threatens me.which is good(musically I mean !).Gap 'tween singles due to people leaving & nurturing new band to it's present form.Plus S.Forward are slow bastards & some bands bring out too many records anyway.

SOME OF YOUR LYRIX SEEM A BIT HARD(MOTHER-SISTER)THAT I REALLY LIKE BUT THE FUNNY INTRO.SEEMS TOO NEGATIVE & EASY,WHEREAS THE LP's TITLE TRACK IS POSITIVE.

You'd be amazed how many people react to that'Little & Large' bit on 'Mother/Sister! % That song was an attempt to use words as music more or less } I hate idea of 'LYRICS' on paper.If that was my job I'd be a poet or J.C.Clarke.One day I hope I'll drop words all together as they're inadequate & just make emotive - word patterns Maybe !

WHAT ABOUT FREE GIGS ETC.I READ YOU WEREN'T TOO KEEN ASHAD BEEN ON THE DOLE SO LONG. WHAT ABOUT CHEAPER LP'S WITH HERE & NOW LIKE ATV DID ? HOW MUCH DID YOURS COST TO MAKE & R.R.P.-THE COVER WASN'T GLOSSY I NOTED.

I think Here & Now do free gigs cos nobody'd pay to see them.Also,why should we bee the only ones penniless at end of night ?Rip-off clubs LOVE free gigs as they save on staff,don't have to give band anything & make a fortune on the bar.Also like a lot of the new wave & hippy movements,it means that only kids with loads of dough from mum & dad or jobs can get up & play OR form own record label.I get £15 a week which must be a 50% lower wage than the majority of my audience.
Witch Trials cost approx. £ 3,700 which is like EVERYTHING from our petrol to taking it to the shops.We paid half & S.Forward paid half.

WHICH ARE YOUR FAVOURITE SONGS & WHY ?

Fall faves: V.Times/No Xmas /UG Medicin /2 Steps /In My Area.   IN NO PARTIC
off new LP- Muzorewi's Daughter /Spectre vs. Rector /Printhead.   ORDER.
V.hard to be objective tho'?!!

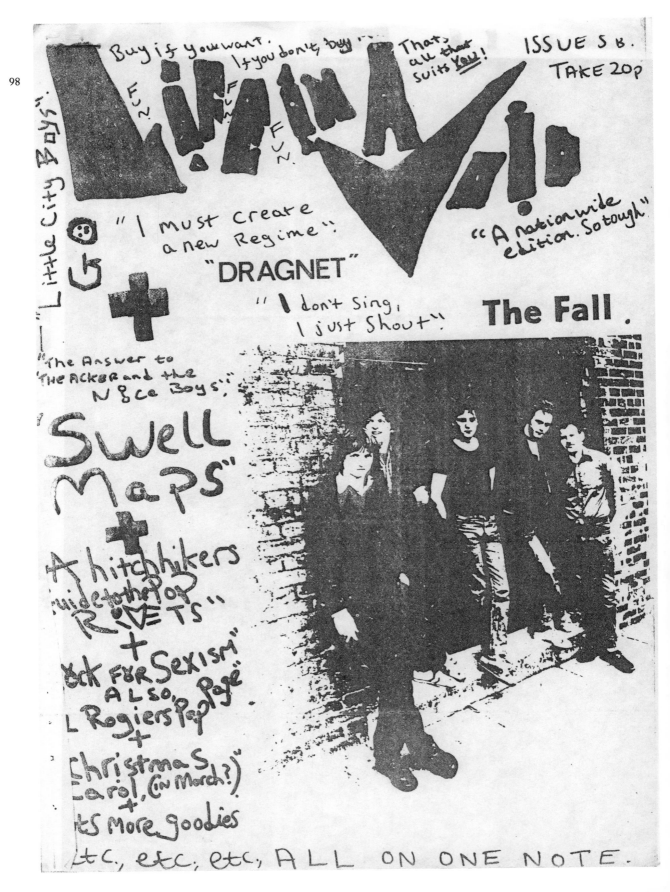

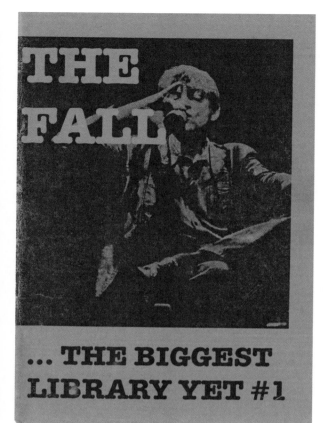

THE FALL

... THE BIGGEST LIBRARY YET #1

THE FALL

THE BIGGEST LIBRARY YET #2

THE FALL

TH EBI GGE STL IBR AR YYE T#3

THE FALL

THE BIGGEST LIBRARY YET #4

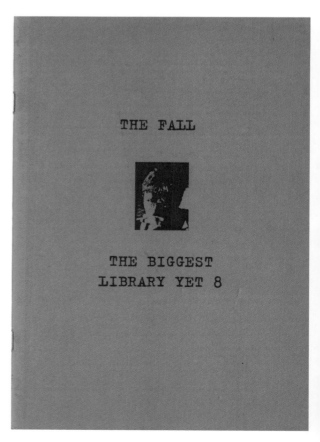

Call Yourself a Football Fan?

Time for a chat with Mark E. Smith of the Fall, whose football experiences include encounters with a goalkeeping plumber and a controversial match against the Icicle Works.

You grew up in Salford, which is more United than City. Is there a reason why you're a City fan?

Not really, just to be contrary, I suppose. Also, you want to support the opposite team to your dad, and my dad had been a United fan. Back in the 1950s he'd go to away games on his bike – he'd cycle to places like Leicester. But I converted him to City.

I had another United connection, though. I applied for a clerical job at the Edwards family's meat factory after I left school. It was £9 a week. It might even have been Martin Edwards who did the interview. He said, 'Well the meat wagons come in. Just sit there, fill in these forms and file them.' I said, 'When would the job start?' And he said, 'You've started.' And he left me in the office.

How long did you keep the job?

An hour. I was there all by myself, he'd locked the door. When he came back, I left.

Did you watch United winning the Champions League?

I was walking to my local pub just when they scored and this huge roar went up. There was a free bus into Manchester laid on half an hour after the game and they said, 'Come on. Even though you're a Blue, you're getting on this bus.' And I have to say it was a great night – all the clubs you could never normally get in to had their doors open, free drinks and everything. And in a funny way it didn't feel like it had happened to United; it was like they were a cricket team or something.

Did you used to see City regularly?

I used to stand on the Kippax but one of the reasons I stopped going was because of the moaning. Now, when you have to sit down, you can't escape them. In the Peter Reid days, they'd be winning 2–0 and they'd be saying, 'Oh, it'll be 3–2 ...' The thing about the moaners is you know they're always going to come back. I remember talking to these young City fans before Joe Royle came and they were practically suicidal, and I said, 'Look, it's always been like that.' When I started supporting them in 1965, they were bottom

Pages 99–100: *The Biggest Library Yet*, 1994–2000.
Fall fanzine edited by Graham Coleman, later by
Rob Waite. Covers to the first eight of nineteen issues.

of the Second Division. But these kids think City's history began with
Colin Bell.

Just about the only good thing Oasis ever did was to threaten to take over
the club. That galvanised people into action and they got this new guy,
Bernstein, in like a shot. Now Sky are involved and it could be the downfall
of them. Does Murdoch know what he's taking on – 30,000 miserable gets?
'Live from Maine Road, it's Man City vs. Hartlepool.' Try selling that in America.

Who were your favourite players?

Harry Dowd, the goalkeeper in the championship team in 1968, was the best.
He still worked as a plumber part-time and my dad was a plumber too. We used
to go behind the goal and Harry would wander over and talk about washers
and copper joints. I remember being at a cup tie once and Harry was saying,
'Do you know if this goes to extra time today, only I've got a job on at half five?'
Then suddenly people are shouting, 'Harry, Harry!', and the team we were
playing are charging down the pitch, and Harry rushes out, dives at someone's
feet, throws the ball up the pitch then comes back and starts again – 'So, is this
extra time today...?'

The local paper had a 'Where are they now?' feature recently on City's
team from the Rodney Marsh time in the early 1970s. There were a couple
who just seem to have disappeared off the face of the earth. One was quoted
as saying, 'If I wasn't a footballer I'd be a tramp', and I think he's done it.

Did you collect things like football stickers?

Yes, I had the 1970 Mexico World Cup set. The Romanians had been
photographed in black and white then coloured in. You'd open a packet and
it would be one of the East Europeans and you'd scream. And then when the
World Cup came around, half of them weren't even in the squad. The pictures
were all from about 1962.

Did you go to see other teams in the area?

Quite a few. Prestwich Heys were the local non-league team and I went to
see them in an amateur cup tie against Sutton United. I was on the pitch
celebrating a goal and got arrested by my neighbour, who was a part-time
policeman.

At Bury you could get in for free if you went through the cemetery behind
one end and jumped over the fence. They were always losing though because
they had the best pitch, this great lush grass that all the other teams liked to
play on. We used to go to see Oldham when they had Ray Wilson from the
1966 World Cup team, and he could hardly walk. You could see why he became
an undertaker, because he was halfway there. They were bottom of the Fourth

but they suddenly started winning every game and in three seasons they were up near the top of the Second.

Who was the first player you met?

Funnily enough, I met George Best a few times. First was in some drinking club in London in the early 1980s. He heard I was from Manchester and went into this big rant about how he used to get all this stick from the crowd at United when they thought he wasn't doing enough. It was true, he did use to stand around doing nothing for eighty minutes, but I thought that was all right, given that he'd still win them the game. But he'd still get stick when he was going off, from Bobby Charlton and the other players. He was the type who'd just walk into his local boozer, and there will always be people wanting to have a go, if you're like that.

The Fall did a song about football, 'Kicker Conspiracy', back in the early 1980s. What sort of reaction did it get at the time?

You couldn't mention football in the rock world then. We were on Rough Trade and I told them, 'This is about football violence', and it was all, 'You don't go to football, do you?' I remember *Melody Maker* saying, 'Mark Smith's obviously got writer's block having to write about football.' About five years later, the same guy reviewed something else saying it was a load of rubbish and 'nowhere near the heights of "Kicker Conspiracy".' And now, of course, all the old music hacks are sat in the directors' box with Oasis.

Have you ever watched a game from the directors' box?

My worst experience at City, actually, was when the agent we were with at the time got us into the directors' box for a David Bowie show at Maine Road. And it was a disgrace.

They had pennants on the wall, like the European Cup Winners' Cup, all creased up in plastic. They hadn't changed the photos since 1968, they still had black-and-white blow-ups from the *Manchester Evening News* and the trophy cabinet hadn't been cleaned. The bar itself was like a kiosk – it was worse than anything on the Kippax. Alex Higgins was there too and he sort of collapsed into it. I've been to United's, and of course that was like something on Concorde.

What is your favourite football book?

The best one I've read is *Colours of My Life* by Malcolm Allison, which covers how he turned City around. When he came back in the late 1970s he was totally broke. He'd go into all the best clubs in Manchester like it was still 1968 and take a load of mates, like an Oliver Reed scene. He'd be asked to pay at the end and he'd just say, 'Pay? What do you mean? I'm Malcolm Allison.' But sometimes it didn't work and they'd have to have a whip-round, he'd go around collecting fivers and loose change in his hat.

As for football writing now, the newspaper coverage here is terrible. I was looking at one paper during Man United's games in Brazil and I thought, 'Am I reading the financial pages?' It was all about how Man United haven't got a press guy and what a disaster it was they were the only club who didn't have one. And I'm reading it thinking, 'Yeah, but what was the score?'

Have you kept in touch with football when you've been abroad?

Going to Germany in the early 1980s got me back into football when I was going off it a bit. In places like Hamburg there was an avant-garde rock scene among fans at some clubs, something that wasn't here in Britain. And you get big pints of beer at German matches for, like, 25p, and a nice clean sausage. I saw Germany vs. Bulgaria at the 1994 World Cup. What a day out that was.

The German players were limbering up like an hour before the game, doing leap-frogging and gymnastics. Then they showed an interview with someone from the Bulgarian staff on these massive screens around the ground and he said, 'I'm just glad we've all turned up. We only had nine men half an hour ago.'

In the stadium they were trying to be nice to everyone and they brought in these guys with red caps all dressed like Michael Jackson as extra security. We were in the German end and in the middle of the game this South American film crew come and sit in front of us, and I'm asking them to move. This red cap comes up and asks me what's wrong. Then a policeman comes over and he brings over this guy from the US soccer federation who looks like Ronald Reagan with white hair and he's saying things like, 'Is your seat not comfortable sir?' And I'm saying, 'No, it's fine, it's just this film crew.' Then he says, 'Ah. You're not German, are you, sir?' I think they had this idea that football was like some germ from Europe that might infect them.

Do you play yourself?

I've started playing again. I'm a central defender. I like tackling, but when I play I walk.

Like Franz Beckenbauer …

Similar. I trip people, tap them on the shin. But I don't like the niggling little fouls they do now, all that shirt-pulling. The annoying thing about that Beckham foul in the World Cup, when he got sent off, was he hardly even kicked him. If you're going to kick them, kick them.

The Fall used to have a team, we'd play university teams before gigs. We played the Icicle Works when we were both in this hotel in London. There were eight or nine in our team, the group and couple of roadies. This guy called Big Dave from Lincolnshire, who was like the fattest lad you've ever seen, went in goal. And they turned up in replica Liverpool kits with 'The Icicle Works' on the front and they've got this mock European Cup with them.

It was twenty minutes each way and we went 5–4 in front in injury time and their tour manager's the referee, so it went on and on until they won 6–5. It'd gone dark by the time we finished and in the bar they're telling all the music journos they've won and passing the European Cup around.

Have you had any encounters with football hooligans?

It seems to me that the fascination with rough lads we've got now is a very middle-class thing. They're from small places, but not impoverished places either – stockbrokers who can forget about being new dads for a day and have a fight. It's a sadomasochism thing, wanting to be hit. It's like the kid at school who was always hitting people, you just knew he was a closet case. I used to get it on trains coming down to London. They get on at Milton Keynes and they're staring you out and all this.

I remember Man City had this group called the Main Line Service Crew. We were on a train on a Saturday afternoon going down for a gig and they were asking us if we were City or United and all that. And I said, 'Hold on, it's three o'clock. City are at home today. What are you doing here?' And they were going to Spurs or somewhere to try and cause trouble at half-time, then they'd be back up on the train to get to Maine Road when the away fans are coming out. That's the sort of mentality they've got.

THE FALL/STATEMENT

The Fall

ANOTHER BRANCH ON THE TREE OF SHOWBUSINESS ?

The new single. Double-A side.Songs:

"ROWCHE RUMBLE" (Look At What The People Around You Are Taking)
    This is a great dance number and combines a cheek-in-tongue put down of a popular sweetie with The Fall's tribute to Racey.Dig it.

"IN MY AREA"
    It's primal scream time again folks as The Fall attack their enemies,get tight,& disprove the theory that might is right.The most difficult song they attempt,the mistakes are glorious.Smith almost sings on it-like he says in another Fall tune:
("I don't sing just shout-heavy clout heart out)An artist predicting the future?)
That's the only way to get it right.
    Maybe Johnny Cash'd sound like this if they'd kept him in San Quentin.Maybe it's white trash trying to talk back.
        "Former friends suck on the fall/genuine white crap article/their
         future cries of broken pain are idiot victims just ends to -
         the madness in my area"

PERSONNEL MID to TERMINAL 79
==

        The Fall have a new line-up following the departure of Martin Bramah.There are now six of them(like dice) :

 YVONNE PAWLETT(19) elec.piano. Yvonne,like her music,travels a lot,and so would you if you came from Doncaster.Never plays the same thing twice-her notes are ex another dimension while keeping to the songs basic requirements-this is most notic-eable on "In My Area"
 CRAIG SCANLAN(18) elec.guitar. New member,left-handed.Craig is the bookworm of-the group.His genius is still in formation.Plays cranky lead that flows.Fave LP Is "White light/White Heat" Ex Staff 9.Brought classic song "Choc-Stock" with him.
 MARC RILEY(17) also guitar. By Fall standards a veteran.Formely on bass and can be heard on "Witch Trials" Very popular with younger Fall-fans,gets letters ask ing for guitar lessons etc.How touching.Bands manager says he reminds her of young Brian Jones.Switched to guitar as there was a lot of music buzzing around in his Cancerian brain,and to make way for his best friend:
 STEVE HANLEY(18) bass guitar. Totally natural bassist,much revered by Smith who saw Martin's exit as the perfect opportunity to bring him in.Always hung round with band and is The Fall from head to toe.Giant in stature and mind.Not many people have heard him talk.
 MARK E. SMITH(22) vocals. Founder and lyric writer.Called a dictator by many Audiences love him ha ha. Has problems at dry cleaners viz;"How did your coat get like that,Mr Smith?" "What do you do for a living?"   "I hang around old buildings for hours and get very dirty in one hour"
 MIKE LEIGH(23) drums. Mike is straight but great.ex rock n roll revival band. Plays standing up,sometimes.Big man but big heart.Ex bouncer and is serving penance with the Fall.

" I ALWAYS USE 'SLATES' AMPLIFIERS AND 'SKINNY RATS' GUITARS - I'D
TRUST NO OTHERS "   - Craig Scanlan

" TO EXPLAIN MY LOVE FOR 'CASSETTES' WOULD BE IMPOSSIBLE - SIMILAR
TO THE AFFECTION SHOWN TO ME BY VARIOUS NEW NEW POP PERSONALITIES "
- Mark E. Smith

THE FALL

33 r.p.m.

'SLATES - NEW 10" 33rpm single release by:

THE time was mid-February,The Fall,ORIGINALLY
intending to cut 2 tracks ended up with many
more.As crumbs of nightmare filtered through
they decided to release the lot,as ALL TRAKS
ARE RELATED.

Side 1 concerns observations of trash culture,   ----
British Undercurrents of secrecy and institutional goings on,esp.
Prole Art Threat - A spy media story found in an abandoned file
cabinet.The side is begun by Middle Mass,the first gleanings of The
Hip Priest.more of him later.
Side 2 is,in chronological order, Fit and Working Again-a fun piece
about regeneration,wi' nods ha hee to the super-weedy groups,title
track(Slates,Slags Etc.)which is about plagarisation and blackboard
type people in this land of ours,rounded off by Leave The Capitol
(note fancy spelling) which relates time warps and encounters in
Victorian Vampiric London.

VIEWPOINTS,PRESS - TOO MODEST TO DISCUSS

'I just thought The Fall were Great.Just in a different league
(World) to everything that had gone before.'
- Ray Lowry/City Fun.

'full of cynical comments,puns and working-class depression-
the fall sweep aside all passing trends' - Vox Magazine/Dublin.

'Bloody awful' - Jeff Beck

'The Fall are changing shape yet again...The Fall are a rhythm
section tight and disciplined.....a firm foundation created to
give Mark the freedom to let fly' - Edwin Pouncey/'Sounds'

'The Great God Pan resides in Welsh green masquerades/On Welsh cat
caravans/But the Monty hides behind curtains grey blackish cream
All the side-stepped cars and the brutish laughs from the couple
in the flat downstairs' 'Leave the Capitol'
Fall Music Publishrs
Ltd./ Cavalcade '81

EXTINCTION HITS TOTALE FAMILY/RECENT DISCOGRAPHY

45s: 'How I Wrote Elastic Man'/'City Hobgoblins' (rough trade 048
Jul.'80)

'Totally Wired'/'Putta Block-forthcoming Excerpts' (RT 056)

l.p.s 'Totale's Turns' (Rough 10)   Apr.80
'Grotesque' (Rough 18)   Nov.80

DE TWO _ BIOG:

The F.F.
420b,Bury New rd.
Salford 7 Lancs.

108

CRAIG SCANLAN   STEVE   MARC RILEY
                       HANLEY   (Guitars,e.piano)

Average file age: 20

Grant Showbiz & Paul Hanley (drums)   their leader.
cover up the pink press threat file

FUTURE PLANS   To Keep Shtum.The hip priest approach,aired first
on an April Peel session recorded in the nazi fortress,is the new
musical direction of The Fall.i.e. songs like Lie-Dream Of a Casino
Soul,Hip Priest,Hassle Schmuk,Dragos G.,Fantastic Life.Also the band
will be working with ex-drummer Karl Burns in various projects.

EVERYTHING BAR 'SLATES' MUSICALLY IS TEN YEARS OUT OF SYNCH ON THE
CONTEMPORARY SCENE.YOUNG PRODUCERS AND NONE_TECH STUDIOS ARE LIKE
GOLD DUST NOW. YOU HAVE BEEN TOLD.

                              regards & affection /The Fall.

ED-FORWARD RECORDS, 41b blenheim crescent london w11 2ef, UK, (0) 727-

The Fall

Handout-Statement lp "DRAGNET"

WHY ARE YOU SMILING ?

" The Fall are from Manchester.So what.You're right.But this is not the
spineless usual.It's Original Article.Not romantic not sub-intellectual
not "tough" re-cycled cabaret glam three chord big boots like the mg
Dog Kennel label."DRAGNET" is white crap let loose in a studio but still
in control.Sung in natural accents in front of unAFFECTed music.
'DRAGNET' ISN't a mass of confusion covered by reverb and a control board.
This sound could catch on.So what.Get Caught." — R.TOTALE XVII

" The Fall: Influential,arrogant,accurately hypercritical of rock apathy "
— N.M.E. September '79

ADD ON THIRTY YEARS NOW YOU'VE GOT SPIT McBURNS

The songs on "DRAGNET" are about psychics,showbiz,chances,criminals
prisons,results of the Boer War,pop,cruel jokes,paranoia and stimulants
of all kinds,demons and more.The follow-up to 1st. LP 'LIVE AT THE WITCH
TRIALS'(Much OK'd and acclaimed),that's as much "DRAGNET" has in common
with that record.This is band and fate's policy.Change equals growth.
'We're better because all are songs are different'—M.Leigh
    our

This record celebrates The Fall's 3rd. year of existence against all
odds.Thanx to all who helped make it possible(YOU'LL STILL HAVE TO BUY IT)

Overleaf you can meet the people who wrote and
recorded it,if you go for that sort of thing.

"I must create a new regime/Or live by another mans

I could use some pure criminals/And get my hands on some royalties"
—'Before The Moon Falls'(The Fall)

Tracks on "DRAGNET" are:
side 1: PSYKICK DANCEHALL/A FIGURE WALKS/PRINTHEAD/DICE MAN/BEFORE THE MOON
    FALLS/YOUR HEART OUT.
side 2: MUZOREWI'S DAUGHTER/FLAT OF ANGLES/CHOC-STOCK/SPECTRE VS RECTOR
    PUT AWAY .

COMPLETE AND UTTER DISCOGRAPHY:
by and for the fall:
singles: BINGO MASTER'S BREAK-OUT (SF7)   — DELETED)
    IT'S THE NEW THING/VARIOUS TIMES(SF9) — DELETED)
    ROWCHE RUMBLE/IN MY AREA (SF11)   FIERY JACK (SF13)
L.P's: LIVE AT THE WITCH TRIALS(SFLP1)
    DRAGNET (SFLP4)   'TOTALE'S TURNS' budget l.p.
                            out 1.May on
"They say music should be fun like reading a story of love/ ROUGH TRADE
But I wanna read a horror story"   Records
    ----"Dice Man" (The Fall)

INFERNAL PERSONNEL phase 3

CRAIG SCANLAN(18) e.guitar.   Craig's a Cack(left) Hander.His outgoing personality and immediate charm make him the obvious spokeman for the group,which
he isn't.Interests: ballroom dancing,gardening and Captain Beefheart.Mancunian.

STEVE HANLEY(19) bass guitar. Latest arrival to The Fall along with Craig.
Eire citizen and chef.Not many have heard him talk.Interests: Beer and beer
money.

MARC RILEY(55) guitars,vocals.   Marc is the veteran of the group.Formerly on
bass guitar and can be heard on 1st l p 'Witch Trials'.Although the baby of
The Fall age-wise,often takes the paternal role. Likes: Public Image,Lou Reed

MIKE LEIGH(24) drums.   Ex rock n roll revival group.He got tired of playing 'It's Now Or Never' every night with inadequate musicians scared of their
own hands.Part Romany.Ex-bouncer serving pennance with The Fall.

MARK E. SMITH(13) ld vocals etc. Founder of The Fall and the cause of all
this trouble,but paid back viz. dry cleaners:'How did your coat get so dirty
Mr. Smith ?-what do you do for a living?' Answer:'I hang around old buildings
for hours and get very dirty in one of those hours'.Lyric writer.

In winter they like pullovers and thick coats,while in summer they go more
for cotton garments.80% of them are Mancunians in fact ,and all members
like the Residents-even those who haven't heard them.

                                    mes/late 79

              THE END

STEP FORWARD RECORDS, 41b blenheim crescent london w11 2ef, UK. (01)-727-0734

PSYKICK DANCEHALL

Is there anybody there ? — Yeah
Rocky rocky it's quester psykick danceha...
Medium dischord.
    My garden is made of stone/There's a ...
    I saw a monster on the roof/It's colo...
Round the corner is quester psykick danc...
Medium dischord
    Here they have no records/They know y...
    Just bumble stumble to the waves/Twit...
Clock it clock it it's quester psykick ...
medium dischord.
    When I'm dead and gone/My vibrations ...
    In vibes not vinyl thru the years/Peop...
Rock it rock it it's quester psy kick d...
MEDIUM DISCHORD.

PRINTHEAD

A U ORINGFACE ...'m a printhead/I go to pie...
...end of eat a line End of hook line...
...had a repage/What we need/I ...ri...

STOP BEING
'CONNED'

New factual information reveals that
YOU
not the 'experts' can wipe away Cancer.
Arthritis, Sclerosis, and all diseases
NOW
not by giving money, but by one simple
ACTION.

Smoking do... not cause Cancer

...
...
... Spri...

...e a chan... oh
/Is this a branch o... the ...
...ce/Only in their front ro...m
...
...ces/... ... ...
    the poison dice

a take a chance fan?
storyof love

...pie going/Is this a branch

u take a chance baby?

h April '79.

The Fall

draGnet

The Fall

PSYKICK DANCEHALL

...them. nsooly out o'
Rocky ... mit two the ...
Medium ...sehord.

My go..ler is made of a...
a muster passing the thus a
Round a ... sream is queste:
Medium disshord.

Here they have no record
Just bumble stumble to t...
Clock it clock it it's que...
medium dischord.

When it's dead and gone/M...
In vibes not vinyl thru
Rock it rock it it's quest
MEDIUM DISCHORD.

PRINTHEAD

A U ORRORFACE I'm a printhead
yeah. End of scotch line. Kind of
We had a ...page/What we need...

INFERNAL PERSONNEL phase 3

CRAIG SCANLAN(18) e.guitar.   Craig's a back(left) Hander.His outgoing personality and immediate charm make him the obvious spokesman for the group,which
he isn't.Interests: ballroom dancing,gardening and Captain Beefheart.Mancunian.

STEVE HANLEY(19) bass guitar. Latest arrival to The Fall along with Craig.
Eire citizen and chef.Not many have heard him talk.Interests: Beer and beer
money.

MARC RILEY(55) guitars,vocals.   Marc is the veteran of the group.Formerly on
bass guitar and can be heard on 1st lp 'Witch Trials'.Although the baby of
The Fall age-wise,often takes the paternal role. Likes: Public Image,Lou Reed

MIKE LEIGH(24) drums.   Ex rock n roll revival group.He got tired of playing 'It's Now Or Never' every night with inadequate musicians scared of their
own hands.Part Romany.Ex-bouncer serving pennance with The Fall.

MARK E. SMITH(13) 14 vocals etc. Founder of The Fall and the cause of all
this trouble,but paid back viz. dry cleaners:'How did your coat get so dirty
Mr. Smith ?-what do you do for a living'. Answer:'I hang around old buildings
for hours and get very dirty in one of those hours'.Lyric writer.

In winter they like pullovers and thick coats,while in summer they go more
for cotton garments, 80% of whom are manchunians in fact, and all members'
like the Residents-even those who haven't heard them.

WHY ARE YOU SMILING ?

" The Fall are from Manchester.So what.You're right.But this is not the
spireless usual.It's Original Article.Not romantic not sub-intellectual
not "tough" re-cycled cabaret glam three chord big boots like the ng
Dog Kennel label."DRAGNET" is white crap let loose in a studio but still
in control.Sung in natural accents in front of unAFFECTed music.
'DRAGNET' ISN't a mass of confusion covered by reverb and a control board.
This sound could catch on.So what 'Get Caught." R.TOTALE XVII

" The Fall: Influential,arrogant,accurately hypercritical of rock apathy "
— N.M.E. September '79

ADD ON THIRTY YEARS NOW YOU'VE GOT SPIT McBURNS

The songs on "DRAGNET" are about psychics,showbiz,chances,criminals
prisons,results of the Boer War,pop,cruel jokes,paranoia and stimulants
of all kinds,demons and more.The follow-up to 1st. LP 'LIVE AT THE WITCH
TRIALS'(Much OK'd and acclaimed),that's as much "DRAGNET" has in common
with that record.This is band and fan's policy.Change equals growth.
'We're better because all are our songs are different8-M.Leigh

This record celebrates The Fall's 3rd. year of existence against all
calculations to all who helped make it possible(YOU'LL STILL HAVE TO BUY IT)

Overleaf you can meet the people who wrote and
recorded it,if you go for that sort of thing.

"I must create a new regime/Or live by another mans
I could use some pure criminals/And get my hands on some royalties"
—'Before The Moon Falls'(The Fall)

Tracks on "DRAGNET" are:
side 1: PSYKICK DANCEHALL/A FIGURE WALKS/PRINTHEAD/DICE MAN/BEFORE THE MOON
FALLS/YOUR HEART OUT.
side 2: MUZOREWI'S DAUGHTER/FLAT OF ANGLES/CHOC-STOCK/SPECTRE VS RECTOR
PUT AWAY.

COMPLETE AND UTTER DISCOGRAPHY:
by and for the fall:
singles: BINGO MASTER'S BREAK-OUT (SF7)
         IT'S THE NEW THING/VARIOUS TIMES(SF9)
         ROWCHE RUMBLE/IN MY AREA (SF..)
L.P's: LIVE AT THE WITCH TRY. SFLP1)
        DRAGNET (SFLP4)

"They say music should be fun like reading a story of love/
But I wanna read a horror story"——— Dice Man' (The Fall)

...e a chance heh?
'Is this a branch on the tree

...ce/Only in their front rooms
...take a chance man

emptying ashtrays
lice

nce fan?

this a branch

nce baby?

draGnet

The Fall

45: HOW I WROTE 'ELASTIC MAN'

city hobgoblins

released 9.7.80

put that syn-
thesiser away,
you

Q.V.

Piccadilly, M/CR.

"The best book I've ever
read" -George 'Liar 'Hackrington
'Manchester Midday News'

also available:
'TOTALE'S TURNS'

L.P. featuring live versions of independant
chart moneyspinners like:
        FIERY JACK
        ROCHE RUMBLE "a sleeper"-N.M.E.
        NO XMAS
        NEW PURITAN
    <u>PLUS</u>: EVERYTHING THAT CONFUSED YOU IN THE PAST!

<u>Maximum price: £2.99</u>

'WORKING MENS' CLUB..CULTIVATED
POSEUR INCOMPETENCE'
                        -MELODY MAKER

"They sound like Beefhearts'
band did at the beginning.I
can't believe it."
                - 'SLASH' magazine U.S.

ON ROUGH TRADE RECORDS AND CONSCIENCE

Ask Your Local Record Dealer To Take That stupid
Expression Off His Face.

This Advertisement Was
Paid For By:
    The Fall Foundation.

The Fall

The Fall

of Manchester

Front: Hand-out statement for
L.P. "TOTALE'S TURNS"
(Rough Trade records No.10)

FEATURING

-- HOT PRESS LINE-UP :

-- EVERYTHING THAT CONFUSED YOU IN THE PAST

-- DISCOGRAPHY to come;

-- HOW I WROTE 'PLASTIC MAN'

"Coupon and gas board man/dragnet for gun blast man
a rented cage is flat of angles"

ut man is self-centred and loves only for himself. The origin of this
roblem is the Fall of Man.
Divine Principle teaches that the Fall of Man was an actual event, but

"And put down left-wing tirades
and the musical trades.And on
free trade I say...."

One night vet is called out/From his overpaid leisure
To Temperance household/Delivered ran out/Phoned his wife in terror
'There are no read-outs for this part of the track'
Next bit is hard to relate/The new born thing hard to describe
Like a winged rat thats been trapped indide/A wharehuse base near
A city tide/Brown sockets purple eyes/Fed with rubbish from disposal
barges brown and covered/No changeling as the birth was witnessed:
"Only one person could do this"
        "Yes" said Cameron "And the thing was in the impression of
        J.TEMPERANCE"

-His hideous replica! His hideous replica! His hideous replica!

Scrutinize the little monster   Disappear thru the door
His hideous replica!

NEXT WEEK: The Fall of Man

Paperback Shamanism

*I am kino-eye, I am a mechanical eye. I, a machine, show you the world as
only I can see it [...] Now I, a camera, fling myself along their resultant,
manoeuvring in the chaos of movement, recording movement, starting with
movements composed of the most complex combinations.*
(Dziga Vertov, *Kino-Eye*)

Everything is in sharp focus because it's new.

*At school the exercise books were the same every year, always vandalised in
the same way, ritualistically. There are exercise books here too, but they're
different. No one notices how many you use, when you open them or when you don't.
It's not quite the same as your old rough book; there's an office aesthetic instead,
the paper feels different under your fingers. Everything is a bit cheaper, crappier,
the manila paper a bit rougher, your handwriting getting worse by the day,
the noise of the duplicator, fag breaks, you've started drinking tea now, cracking
into splinters these little plastic stirrers that they've started getting now instead
of spoons for some reason.*

*But even though you're out of school, you realise that you'll never really get
out of class. You can make your school anywhere. At a desk, you hide a pulp novel
inside a manila file. As a junior clerk you can make one too many trips to the
stationery cupboard without being seen. You can save the scrap paper, fasten it with
treasury tags, you can steal a folder. You realise that if you put a page of the last
quarter's accounts at the front, then it looks enough like work that it won't arouse
suspicion if your boss walks past. And the rest of the folder can be whatever you
like. Stamp a date on the front. Inside, the rest of the folder is fragments, lyrics,
poetry, a half-scrawled story about a jawbone. You stamp it 'PAID', for a joke.
If you can camouflage yourself in your BHS work shirt, then you can camouflage
your real work in amongst your wage work. You are your own teacher. If Vertov
could become a camera, maybe you can become a classroom.*

We are fond of speaking of education as though it were a fundamental
good, the foundation of our moral and ethical sphere. But when we speak of
education, we hardly ever actually mean the accumulation of an objective
body of knowledge. We're fond of lauding people as 'well-educated', but this
doesn't quite mean what it ought to; instead, it's a phrase that signifies how
our country, like many others, is built on the questionable achievements of
our Establishment, namely a handful of white, male, posh men who have
floated gormlessly to the surface following Eton or Oxford or whatever.
These men have latterly been joined by 'bright grammar-school kids', who are
usually still at least middle-class, but set apart from the Etonians to a sufficient
degree for the Etonians to pretend that they rose to the top in a system of

meritocracy. A further, fake, ego massage that they scarcely needed. This second category of white middle-class men will from time to time be augmented by people who are, perhaps, only two things out of three: posh white women, for example. This system of schooling also separates the non-rulers into categories – those without qualifications, those who qualified for free school meals, those who were the first of their family to go to university, and so on – so you can carry the scars of the educational system with you throughout your life. This is just how it has always worked. For all that we have focused on education in the choosing of our rulers, we are scarcely given the opportunity to question what we're being taught, and what we have learned. And we have, mostly, learned nothing. This has been going on for hundreds of years, and no one has learned anything.

But what if we have a thirst for knowledge that informs how we exist in the world? In his essay 'The Poet and the City', W. H. Auden notes that poets ought to 'have a job which does not in any way involve the manipulation of words', in order to better create space to do creative work. He outlines the perfect, idyllic education for poets, as follows:

> *In my dream-day College for Bards, the curriculum would be as follows:*
> *1. In addition to English, at least one ancient language, probably Greek or Hebrew, and two modern languages would be required.*
> *2. Thousands of lines of poetry in these languages would be learned by heart.*
> *3. The library would contain no books of literary criticism, and the only critical exercise required of students would be the writing of parodies.*
> *4. Courses in prosody, rhetoric and comparative philology would be required of all students, and every student would have to select three out of an offering of courses in mathematics, natural history, geology, meteorology, archaeology, mythology, liturgies, cooking.*
> *5. Every student would be required to look after a domestic animal and cultivate a garden plot.*

Auden's poet might be fluent in Hebrew and Swedish, and might spend most of his time not writing poetry at all but instead cooking and caring for a rabbit. Auden's syllabus suggests that what a poet really needs is an approach to education that is truly exploratory, with no aims or end in sight.

It's perhaps not so surprising that artists and poets have tried to reinvent education many times.

Black Mountain College was established in 1933, in North Carolina. It was a non-hierarchical institution where students were required to participate in farm work, construction projects and kitchen duty as part of their holistic education. Faculty members included Buckminster Fuller, Josef and Anni Albers, Merce Cunningham and John Cage. It closed, in debt, in the late 1950s, but cast a long shadow over the avant-garde well into the twenty-first century.

For Joseph Beuys, reinventing education had been central to his artistic practice and personal myth-making. He'd idolised Rudolf Steiner, whose teachings around what he called 'anthroposophy' suggested that there was a tangible spiritual realm that could be accessed by humans, if only they learned how to develop their mental faculties in the correct way. Like Steiner, Beuys was interested in breaking down barriers between the intellect and the psyche, and also between the biographical details of his own life and his artistic practice. His role as a teacher-wizard was central to this, so education in this context takes on a quasi-mystic quality, although if you imagine education to be a good in its own right, then perhaps it matters less what the contents are.

The art historian Benjamin Buchloh wrote of Beuys that 'no other artist (with the possible exception of Andy Warhol, who certainly generated a totally different kind of myth) managed – or probably ever intended – to puzzle and scandalise his primarily bourgeois art audience to the extent that he would become a figure of social worship'. He was writing in 1980. I can certainly think of one other artist, since: Mark E. Smith towered over the Fall, puzzling and scandalising the band's audiences to the end.

For Buchloh, Beuys was problematically messianic, a cult leader whose grandstanding utopianism masked a simple-minded shallowness, and whose carefully cultivated myth of origin (he claimed he had been rescued from a wartime plane crash by Tartars, who wrapped his wounded body in fat and felt and told him, 'You are not German: you are Tartar now') was a pure embellishment. As he riffed on this falsified backstory, using fat and felt in his sculptures throughout the 1960s, Beuys was able to dodge confronting his real history as a decorated member of the Luftwaffe. The manoeuvres of the man conspire to obscure the work. Perhaps this is a familiar thorniness: for many, the Mark E. Smith of the popular imagination is a problematic figure who gets in the way of the Fall. Smith's world, unlike Beuys's, is not one of utopianism or personal myth. For all that the Fall and Smith became synonymous over the years, he simply did not centralise himself in its world, like Beuys did – but neither is it a precise inversion of this. When Beuys established the Free International University for Creativity and Interdisciplinary Research in the 1970s, he had aspirations for it to become an 'organisational place of research, work, and communication' where students could ponder the future of society. It was, in this way, part of a twentieth-century countercultural tradition of influencing public life for the better by conceiving of experimental forms of education; but it cohered around Beuys as a visible figurehead, and if you couldn't accept the man in the hat, it probably couldn't teach you anything.

For all that Mark E. Smith came to be entirely synonymous with the Fall's body of work, he never announced his intentions to this extent. With Smith you have the sense the world of the Fall just flowed out of him, or rather it seemed to come from beyond, passing through him. The myth formed around the man and grew over him like lichen over a concrete bollard, without him having to do anything that he wasn't doing anyway.

Josef Beuys

118

Alexander Trocchi

Beuys was hardly alone in trying to reinvent education in the middle part of the twentieth century. Around ten years earlier, the poet and writer Alexander Trocchi's 'Project Sigma' had sought to influence public life and build a countercultural revolution through a variety of interventions. Education was central to his aims. In 1963, Trocchi had published 'Invisible Insurrection of a Million Minds' in *Situationist International*. In the essay, he proposed the formation of what he called a Spontaneous University. It would grow from a 'cultural jam session' and evolve into an institution in its own right. He writes:

> *The original building will stand deep within its own grounds, preferably on a riverbank. It should be large enough for a pilot group (astronauts of inner space) to situate itself, orgasm and genius, and their tools and dream-machines and amazing apparatus and appurtenances; with outhouses for 'workshops' large as could accommodate light industry; the entire site to allow for spontaneous architecture and eventual* town planning.

Trocchi took his inspiration from Black Mountain College and sought to create something that would be even more radical, because it would be more financially sustainable. He suggested that Spontaneous University's radical pedagogy would be supplemented by various forms of income generation: merchandising, patents and fees. He wanted to break free from the shackles of the state's influence on education, but still accepted its need to survive under capitalism. As author McKenzie Wark notes, Trocchi's vision was for 'both science fiction and a business plan, a utopian future and an almost exact description of sophisticated spectacular business in the twenty-first century'. Sadly — and perhaps this is a rare example of political horseshoe theory actually holding up — what at the time may have seemed like radical reinvention appears to twenty-first-century eyes as a premonition of the neoliberal university model, with its focus on economic independence and growth. Or, to look at it another way, Trocchi may have gone full circle and inadvertently ended up advocating for private finance initiatives.

Throughout the 1960s, various countercultural happenings and movements would attempt to harness the power of education and collective learning as ways of growing revolutionary consciousness. The Free University of New York, led by Allen and Sharon Krebs, started life in 1965 as a break-away social enterprise for academics purged from their own institutions for holding left-wing views. It lasted only a couple of years but was a major influence on the Anti-University of London, which set up shop in a squatted building on Rivington Street in Shoreditch in 1968. The Anti-University's faculty included Allen Ginsberg, Stuart Hall, Richard Hamilton, R. D. Laing, Jeff Nuttall, Cornelius Cardew and Stokely Carmichael. They had wanted to establish a non-hierarchical environment where people could meet as equals, believing that increased understanding and knowledge of each other would be a necessary condition for revolution. Trocchi, writing about the Anti-

University in *International Times* in 1968, said: 'The positive aspect of this youthful attitude is reflected in the bright dress, in the search by whatever means for consciousness expansion in the sure knowledge that what the Victorians called "work" does not ennoble, and that even if it did, it would still be an anachronism. The young man on National Assistance asserts in his inarticulate way the necessity of leisure.'

And yet these educational utopias never quite managed to create an entirely different world; perhaps constrained by form and function, rather than their own imaginations, they generally presented alternatives to the extant structures and establishments that prop up our public sphere. But a revolution never came from reforming what is already there. What if your education was based on ditching these structures entirely, these systems that have held mediocre men in charge for so long? If it's not good enough to simply replace the Etonians with liberal artists, then you need to walk away entirely. Mark E. Smith's education was not based on educational reform, but on its abolition: an autodidact takes responsibility for their own learning and development. Smith's obsessive autodidacticism drove the band and was the big bang that created the universe around it. As a consequence of his own thirst for pure knowledge, the Fall created a universe that functions as the truly radical liberal-arts curriculum of the late-twentieth century.

Although the focus, as the years passed, was increasingly on Smith, the characterisation of him in the press ossified into something that did not really capture what the Fall represented. The simple caricature of the man in the pub hid the fact that the Fall was not simply a proxy for Smith, but not a straightforward group either. Instead, it had grown into something in its own right, like a swirling ball of psychic energy that only Smith, as a magus, could just about control. So what we mean when we talk about the Fall's universe as a curriculum is something much bigger than Smith as one person; it is a vast, interconnected web of interests spanning music, art, war, politics and geography. This is a curriculum that includes relentless cynicism and antagonism, sure, but also great love and care for an alternative canon of art and literature, incorporating horror fiction, rockabilly and novelty records. It functions as a sentient consciousness that knows how things need to be in order to be good (which is why it gets so angry when they are bad). Its epicentre will always be in the north of England, but neither is it uncritically at home here, and its catchment area is as vast as the entire universe.

They say that in order to hypnotise a person, they need to be relaxed. They need to be open to suggestion. Similarly, there is a trance-like state that mystics can attain. The artist Hilma af Klint, herself a friend of Rudolf Steiner, made automatic paintings, saying that 'the pictures were painted directly through me, without any preliminary drawings, and with great force'. In this half-awake, half-asleep state, we can receive all manner of information. The Fall's curriculum was transmitted through cheap FM radios to teenagers in darkened bedrooms under duvet covers. It's no wonder it was so captivating.

Hilma af Klint

He might not have meant to, but through the Fall Mark E. Smith has created an elaborate syllabus, a collection of reference points so unique that the legacy is bigger than either himself or anything he might have intended.

That's not to say that an anarchic curriculum such as this is entirely without problems. The Fall's school was a long way from Auden's idyllic daydream college, nor was it conceived as a utopia. If it grew out of Smith's own wild, spinning fractals of knowledge, then it was also constrained by them. To the autodidact there will always be gaps, subjectivities which are not questioned. (You don't know what you don't know.) A lifetime's scrutiny will inevitably reveal its limitations. To this end, some obituaries characterised Smith's political views as becoming reactionary in later life, but that's not strictly accurate. It is a liberal convenience to imagine him as the 'good son' who went bad, a leftist gone astray. Right from the beginning, his views straddled the political compass awkwardly, diagonally, but they are generally internally consistent. On questions of war, he was part of a hawkish tradition that exists on the British left, as well as on the right. He hadn't been a member of the Labour Party since the Michael Foot days, having left over the party's opposition to military intervention in the Falklands. He was vehemently anti-Nazi, but that encompassed a position of venerating Britain's place in the world. As a member of a generation who grew up on post-war *Eagle* comics, his world view was one that was never decolonised. There has, too, been both posthumous condemnation and attempted after-the-fact justification of the Fall's use of the n-word in 'The Classical', mostly concentrating on questions of intent and narrative voice. It's true that Smith's lyrics are very rarely in the first person, he frequently writes in character and they are seldom intended to be taken at face value. But, regardless, 'The Classical' is still written by a white person, on the assumption it will be heard by the white, liberal audience it wants to bait. Even if, as seems likely in the context of other works, its intention is to provoke, highlight hypocrisy and take delight in antagonising that audience, it prioritises its own amoral desire to shock over anything else. 'This is the home of the vain!' (Although he described the song as 'our way of saying "fuck off!" to [the music industry]', to the best of my knowledge Smith never defended the line itself. And I'm sure if he'd wanted to, he would have.)

Maybe all schools will need to be burned down, in the end.

When you get a job, you can continue your education. Learning switches from something that you do between skiving to something that you can embody. If you remove education from the school, you can become your own classroom. While Dziga Vertov imagined himself as a camera, becoming the object which documents, Joseph Beuys said, 'I am a transmitter. I radiate out.' What we're describing, when we talk about the Fall, is a universe, a web of reference points that creates its own popular culture. Mark E. Smith was his own classroom; he led its curriculum less as a formal teacher than as a paperback shaman whose teachings you might stumble upon. The intellectual energy that cohered around him was like an electrical storm, unmarshalled by the educational establishment. He became a transmitter, like Beuys. Unlike the Establishment's classrooms and structures, the web of knowledge that cohered around the Fall was the entire point. Smith's knowledge was characterised by his relentless curiosity and pursuit of intellectual and creative freedom.

It is under these conditions that the Fall became a school. This secret school, concealed within post-punk rock orthodoxy like a battered Arthur Machen paperback inside a manila folder from an office stationery cupboard, taught a lot of us. And for everyone who was hypnotised in that pre-dream state, in a darkened room, under the blankets, via this transmitter, transmitting, the teachings will continue to underpin a lot of what we will have to say, long after the school has burned down.

1984
Sign to Beggars Banquet; 'Oh! Brother' (Jun); 'C.R.E.E.P.'
(Aug); *The Wonderful and Frightening World of the Fall*
(Oct); *Call For Escape Route* EP (Oct); radio sessions for
David Jensen, Janice Long; *Perverted By Language* (*Bis*)
VHS (Factory); first collaboration with Michael Clark,
Le French Revolting, for the Paris Opera.

1985
Hip Priests and Kamerads compilation LP (Mar);
'Couldn't Get Ahead/Rollin' Dany' (Jun); *This Nation's
Saving Grace* (Sep); 'Cruisers Creek' (Oct); *The Fall
Lyrik & Texte* (Lough Press, Berlin).

1986
'Living Too Late' (Jul); 'Mr Pharmacist' (Sep);
Bend Sinister (Oct); 'Hey! Luciani' (Dec); *Hey! Luciani:
The Times, Life and Codex of Albino Luciani*, a play by
Smith, featuring Michael Clark and Leigh Bowery,
runs for two weeks at Riverside Theatre, Hammersmith,
London (Dec).

1987
'There's a Ghost in My House' (May); 'Hit the North'
(Oct); *In Palace of Swords Reversed* compilation LP –
first release on Cog Sinister label; Elland Road, Leeds
show w/ U2, the Pretenders and the Cult (Jul);
Reading Festival (Sep).

1988
'Victoria' (Jan); *The Frenz Experiment* (Mar);
HMV Oxford Street in-store (Mar); *I Am Curious Orange*
ballet, w/ Michael Clark, Edinburgh International Festival
(Aug); *I Am Kurious Oranj* (Oct); 'Jerusalem' (Nov).

The Wonderful and Frightening World of The Fall (October 1984, Beggars Banquet)

SIDE 1
Lay of the Land
2 by 4
Copped It
Elves

SIDE 2
Slang King
Bug Day
Stephen Song
Craigness
Disney's Dream Debased

The **Wonderful and FRIGHTENING World of...**

The Fall

MARK E. SMITH	VOCALS and TAPES
BRIX SMITH	LEAD and RHYTHM GUITAR and VOCALS
KARL BURNS	DRUMS, PERCUSSION and BASS
PAUL HANLEY	DRUMS, KEYBOARDS
CRAIG SCANLON	RHYTHM and LEAD GUITAR
STEPHEN HANLEY	BASS and ACOUSTIC GUITAR
a friendly VISITOR	
GAVIN FRIDAY	VOCALS: tracks 3 & 7

1 · LAY OF THE LAND
- the latest bulletin from 5, Demeval Close, Miseryrse, Forcedcomedy, Lanes.

2 · 2 by 4
- INTO our midst came fiend . . . into our midst, came Friend. Stomache gnawed as Trek of fame debuted on KGB pantomine t.v. show one Friday, 'bah'.

3 · COPPED IT
- Composer here, muddled in thought, confusing 'being caught' for 'stealing freely'

4 · ELVES
- A Tubby commotion at the feet . . . reasonable feuding now irrelevant, only sharp scythes and a cold tongue could match this horrid Travesty.

Produced by
JOHN LECKIE

Engineered by
JOE GILLINGHAM

"Ze Wonderful and Frightening World Of"
SKANS · JOHN and BETH · JOHN PEEL · B.B. · · BUNTER THOMAS · CLAUS CASTENSKIOLD ·

The Fall Photography By
MICHAEL POLLARD

Cover Painting By
CLAUS CASTENSKIOLD

A MARQUIS PLC. MANIPULATION

5 · SLANG King
- ". . . a cheapness of mind, a cheapness of taste a tawdry little shine on the seat of his conscience . . . But Mr. Hammer has a talent, discovered at a very early age." - Rod Serling.

6 · BUG DAY
- These things wanted rights and tenancy, Govt. sponsored bands - of course it all stemmed from the Nip Insect Glorification crazs - the tinned bean diet for Spiders just about sealed it . . .

7 · STEPHEN SONG
- Vatican distort into operatic nightmare.

8 · CRAIGNESS
- "Shimmering violet shimmer, twisting haunts shadow passers veil night time silvery veils swirling rustling sweep. Shining, melodious Drifting." - B.E.S.

9 · DISNEY'S DREAM DEBASED
- His bank account, terminal 1956: 6,000 dollars.

Beggars Banquet
BEGA 58

MARK E. SMITH   VOCALS and TAPES
BRIX SMITH   LEAD and RHYTHM GUITAR and VOCALS
KARL BURNS   DRUMS, PERCUSSION and BASS
PAUL HANLEY   DRUMS, KEYBOARDS
CRAIG SCANLON   RHYTHM and LEAD GUITAR
STEPHEN HANLEY   BASS and ACOUSTIC GUITAR

a friendly VISITOR
GAVIN FRIDAY   VOCALS: tracks 3 & 7

Produced by JOHN LECKIE
Engineered by JOE GILLINGHAM

The Fall Photography By MICHAEL POLLARD
Cover Painting By CLAUS CASTENSKIOLD

Recorded at Focus Studios, mid-1984.

This Nation's Saving Grace (September 1985, Beggars Banquet)

SIDE 1 – CASTLE NKROACHED
Mansion
Bombast
Barmy
What You Need
Spoilt Victorian Child
L.A.

SIDE 2 – NATION'S SAVING GRACE
Gut of the Quantifier
My New House
Paint Work
I Am Damo Suzuki
To NkRoachment: Yarbles

Stephen HANLEY (Eire)   Bass gtr.
Karl BURNS (Unknown)   Drums
Brix SMITH (U.S.A.)   Lead Guitar, vocal
Simon ROGERS (Snookeria)   Keyboards, acc. guitar, bass gtr.

Mark E. SMITH (Broughton)   Vocals, violin, guitar
Craig SCANLON (Munster)   elec. rhythm guitars

production: John LECKIE
side 2 – LECKIE / ROGERS/M.E.S
engineering: Joe GILLINGHAM
cover: M. Pollard / C. Castenskiold
cut: Steve, Chalcot Road
photos: Lucy Salenger, C. Chards, C. Segal
vehicle: No Good Boyo

Recorded Orinoco, London, mid-1985.

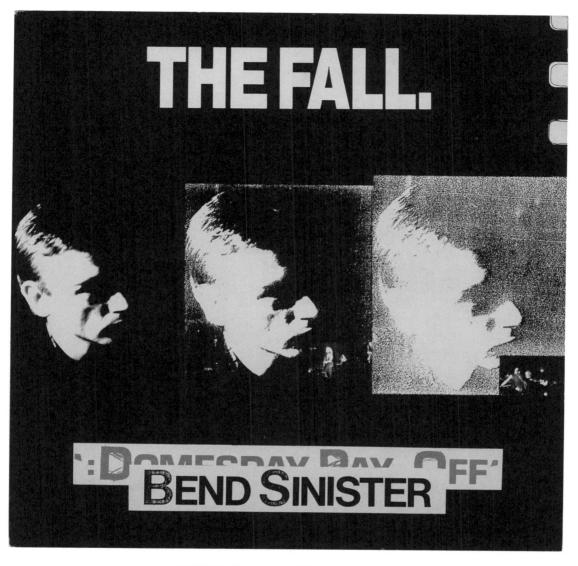

Bend Sinister (September 1986, Beggars Banquet)

SIDE 1
R.O.D.
Dktr. Faustus
Shoulder Pads 1#
Mr Pharmacist
Gross Chapel – British Grenadiers

SIDE 2
US 80's–90's
Terry Waite Sez
Bournemouth Runner
Riddler!
Shoulder Pads 2#

MARK E. SMITH	VOCALS & TAPES	
STEPHEN HANLEY	BASS, GUITAR	
SIMON ROGERS	KEYS, MACHINES, GUITAR	
CRAIG SCANLON	ACCOUSTIC & ELECTRIC GUITAR	PRODUCED BY JOHN LECKIE
BRIX SMITH	LEAD GUITAR, KEYS, VOCAL	PHOTO'S: Lars Schwander, Jeff Veitch, Kint B.,
JOHN S. WOOLSTENCROFT	DRUMS, PERCUSSION	Steve Saporito, Sue Dean and Larry Rodriguez
(PAUL HANLEY)	DRUMS, T.2.	Recorded at Yellow 2, Stockport; Abbey Road, London; Square One, Bury, mid-1986.

The Frenz Experiment (February 1988, Beggars Banquet)

SIDE 1 – CRIME GENE
Frenz
Carry Bag Man
Get a Hotel
Victoria
Athlete Cured

SIDE 2 – EXPERIENCE
In These Times
The Steak Place
Bremen Nacht
Guest Informant (excerpt)
Oswald Defence Lawyer

PERSONNEL
STEVE HANLEY – BASS
CRAIG SCANLON – RHYTHM GUITAR
MARCIA SCHOFIELD – KEYBOARDS
BRIX E. SMITH – LEAD GUITAR
MARK E. SMITH – LEAD VOCALS
SIMON WOLSTENCROFT – DRUMS

W/ S. ROGERS – SEMI-ACC GUITAR,
ELEC. SAXOPHONE

DX'S + PROPHET – M. Sch + S.R.
E. PIANO (8) – M.E.S.
BACKING VOCALS BY THE FALL

PRODUCED BY SIMON ROGERS
BAR (2) (6) (9) – GRANT SHOWBIZ
ENGINEERED – I. GRIMBLE, D. BARTON, STEP

PHOTOGRAPHY - PAUL COX (FRONT),
PYKE (BACK)

Recorded at Abbey Road, London; Brixton and
Manchester, mid-late 1987.

I Am Kurious Oranj (October 1988, Beggars Banquet)

SIDE 1
New Big Prinz
Overture from 'I Am Curious Orange'
Dog Is Life / Jerusalem
Kurious Oranj
Wrong Place, Right Time

SIDE 2
Win Fall C.D. 2080
Yes, O Yes
Van Plague?
Bad News Girl
Cab It Up!
Last Nacht

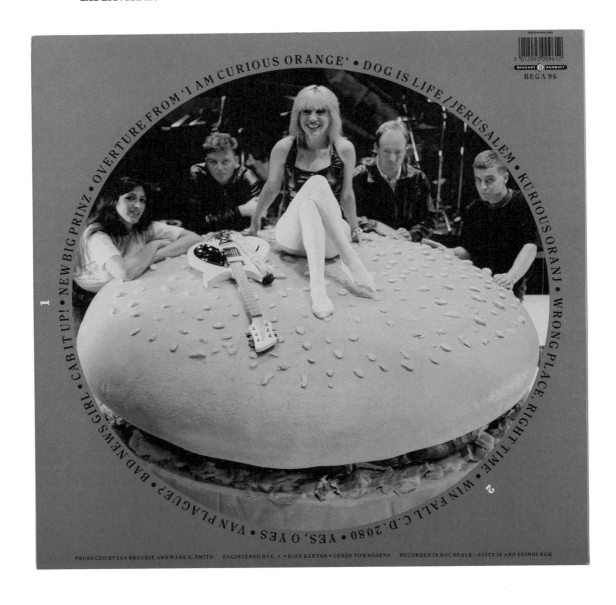

OVERTURE FROM 'I AM CURIOUS ORANGE' • DOG IS LIFE / JERUSALEM • KURIOUS ORANJ • WRONG PLACE, RIGHT TIME • WIN FALL C.D. 2080 • YES, O YES • VAN PLAGUE? • BAD NEWS GIRL • CAB IT UP! • NEW BIG PRINZ •

MADE IN ENGLAND
5 012093 009612
BEGGARS BANQUET
BEGA 96

1

2

PRODUCED BY IAN BROUDIE AND MARK E. SMITH   ENGINEERED BY C.J. • DIAN BARTON • CENZO TOWNSHEND   RECORDED IN ROCHDALE – SUITE 16 AND EDINBURGH

The Fall
MARK E. SMITH – Lead Vocals
STEVE HANLEY – Bass Guitar
CRAIG SCANLON – Rhythm / Acoustic guitar
MARCIA SCHOFIELD – Keyboards
BRIX SMITH – Lead Guitar / Vocals
SIMON WOLSTENCROFT – Drums

Michael Clark & Company
LEIGH BOWERY, LESLIE BRYANT,
MICHAEL CLARK, MATTHEW HAWKINS,
DAVID HOLAH, JULIE HOOD, AMANDA KING,
ELLEN VAN SCHUYLENBURCH

PRODUCED BY IAN BROUDIE AND MARK E. SMITH
ENGINEERED BY C.J., DIAN BARTON,
CENZO TOWNSHEND

Kevin Cummins – The Fall Photographs
Richard Haughton – Stage Photographs

Recorded at Suite 16, Rochdale and The King's Theatre,
Edinburgh, mid-late 1988.

Let Me Tell You About Scientific Management: The Fall, the Factory and the Disciplined Worker[1]

Over the last few years two conflicting ideas about the Fall have come about, without ever really being recognised as contradictory. There's the old idea of Mark E. Smith and the group as grim northern disciplinarians, prone to reactionary statements in interviews and a disdain for students and the work-shy; and another, which has been more common lately, that concentrates on MES as 'Prophet in Prestwich', a kind of Lovecraftian psychic and seer opposing the technocratic rationalism of Factory Records. This tension between an iron, workerist discipline, which can be heard in the grinding, repetitive sound, and the visionary revelations that pervade the lyrics is best understood through *management*. Specifically, through the supplanting of nineteenth-century work norms with the more efficient, apparently scientific system imported from the US after the 1910s, under the influence of the theorist Frederick Winslow Taylor, whose 'rationalisation' paved the way for the assembly line and mass production.

First of all, though, there are the curious perceptions of the factory and industry in the Fall's early work. For all his professed workerism, MES's pre-Fall experience, after time spent in a meat factory, was mostly as a dock clerk, outside of the site of production itself, followed by a spell of unemployment and assiduous reading. The factory is something observed but not directly experienced – something studied and aestheticised to discover its effects. Accordingly, in *Live at the Witch Trials*, industry features as a sinister presence, a centrifugal force sucking people in and spitting them out as valium-addicted, psychically and physically warped. 'Industrial Estate' admonishes that the 'crap in the air will fuck up your face', creating something new and bizarre out of it. At this point, however, there is still a certain flailing element to the Fall's music, with the drums constantly clattering and falling about. There may have been no solos or displays of individual technique, but there was a certain sloppiness and franticness to the Fall that would soon be purged. Smith, too, was not sounding particularly enamoured by the English obsession with hard graft, bemoaning being 'tied to the puritan ethic' on the title track. However, a particular industrial obsession had already crept in on their first single, in 1978: the importance of the 'three Rs: repetition, repetition, repetition'.

---

1. Originally written in 2008 for the 'Messing up the Paintwork' conference at the University of Salford.

This has to be seen in the context of British industry, and of Britain and, specifically, Manchester as the first area in the world to comprehensively transform itself into a purely industrial, purely urban and anti-rural economy – it should be noted that Smith uses 'peasant' as an insult in 'C'n'C-S Mithering'. The forcible remaking of the worker as an appendage to a machine was traced by Marx in *Capital* thus:

> *To work at a machine, the workman should be taught from childhood, in order that he may learn to adapt his own movements to the uniform and unceasing motion of an automaton* [...] *at the same time that factory work exhausts the nervous system to the uttermost, it does away with the many-sided play of the muscles, and confiscates every atom of freedom, both in bodily and intellectual activity* [...] *it is not the workman that employs the instruments of labour, but the instruments of labour that employ the workman.*

This forcible simultaneous limiting and overstretching of the body's capabilities is what becomes a feature of the Fall's records from *Dragnet* onwards.

'Spectre vs. Rector' has been cited as perhaps the first truly great Fall track, the first to showcase Smith's fractured, gnostic storytelling. This is true enough, but it's also intriguing what happens to the early Fall's sound here. The song is dominated by a huge, ugly bass riff, repeating relentlessly and drawing everything (apart from Smith) into its pattern. The track resounds with repetitive clatter, evoking some kind of foundry or mill, something also evoked by the claustrophobic, noise-ridden production. *Dragnet*'s sleeve notes, meanwhile, evoke a city that is more post-industrial than industrial – 'up here in the North there are no wage packet jobs for us, thank Christ'. As with their sleeves at the time, such as that for 'How I Wrote "Elastic Man"', it's the ruined factory and its ghosts that are more redolent of the urban reality than Factory's seamless *Sachlichkeit*. The *Dragnet* sleeve features an excerpt from a conversation with the dry-cleaner that evokes perfectly the romantic possibilities of the dilapidated, decommissioned city: 'How did your coat get so dirty Mr. Smith? What do you do for a living?' Answer: 'I hang around old buildings for hours and get very dirty in one of those hours.'

The Fall's definitive morphing into the merciless machine of *Hex Enduction Hour* was yet to occur, however. To go back for a moment to Taylor and Marx, there's a certain difference between the painful overexertion of the English factory system and American scientific management. Taylor writes in *Principles of Scientific Management* that there are two particular fallacies obstructing the efficient management of labour: one that places the accent on the naturally gifted individual and places the onus on extraordinary, voluntaristic excesses of labour – the Stakhanovite movement in the USSR is a fine example of this, straining to achieve deliberately excessive targets; and another, where the workers' belief that efficient labour will make their own jobs obsolete leads to slow, deliberately obstructive working. Taylor writes that his intention is

> to prove that the best management is a true science, resting upon clearly defined laws, rules, and principles, as a foundation. And further to show that the fundamental principles of scientific management are applicable to all kinds of human activities, from our simplest individual acts to the work of our great corporations, which call for the most elaborate cooperation. And, briefly, through a series of illustrations, to convince the reader that whenever these principles are correctly applied, results must follow which are truly astounding.

This was achieved via the time and motion study, whereby the movement of the worker was charted in minute detail and then evaluated by management to decide the way in which he can produce the most in the smallest amount of time.

The early Fall, with its relatively scrappy inefficiency, can be seen as a remnant of the earlier principles of management, whereby the workforce essentially do their own thing, leading to sudden, sporadic increases in work rate and physical expenditure. From around 1980, this becomes severely circumscribed by the dominance in every song of Steve Hanley's bass riffs, which in their rumbling, metallic tone evoke the humming of a brutally effective factory. The workers, the actual musicians, are severely disciplined if they shirk the steady tempo or, even worse, decide to express themselves: that oft-quoted 'Don't start improvising, for God's sake' on 'Slates, Slags Etc.'. At around the same time, Smith's lyrics get both more fantastical and more insistent on the need for pure, pared-down repetition, and exhibit much disdain for malingerers. While two years earlier the puritan ethic was disdained, now a certain ambiguous identification with a Cromwellian ethic could be found in his lyrics. Not just the threat of a 'New Puritan', but other telling references creep in – a healthiness gained through decidedly unhealthy sources. 'Fit and Working Again' features Smith, over a steady, undemonstrative chug, declaring: 'And I feel like Alan Minter / I just ate eight sheets of blotting paper / And I chucked out the Alka-Seltzer' – shoving down industrial products until he feels like a boxer.

Taylorism is often associated with cybernetics and the machine aesthetic that the Fall have often deliberately stood against – the synthesisers and robots of the early 1980s. But as much as it suggests, in acclimatising to simple, repetitive, machine-like tasks, something beyond human, it also implies something before the human. Antonio Gramsci's short study *Americanism and Fordism* reminds us that Taylorist management theorists, as with MES's description of musicians as cattle, were not particularly respectful of the human subjectivity of their workers. Gramsci cites Taylor's term for the worker, 'the trained gorilla', as 'expressing with brutal cynicism' what he describes as 'developing in the worker to the highest degree automatic and mechanical attitudes, breaking up the psycho-physical nexus of qualified professional work, which demands a certain active participation of intelligence, fantasy and initiative on the part of the worker'. Gramsci sees this as a progressive development, eliminating the sentimentality and peasant spirituality from the working class, who will then be able to prepare for power. Taylor, meanwhile, insisted his system was fairer than the nineteenth-century's work norms – what he called 'the more or less open warfare which characterises the ordinary types of management'. But in the Taylorist factory itself there would be absolutely no question about who was manager and who was managed. He promised his system would not lead to unemployment, but the Fordist modes of production could guarantee full employment only briefly. There would be slightly more job security than there would be in service of the Fall, but not by much.

Taylor and his disciples set themselves the task of obliterating the imagination and the fantastic. Smith, meanwhile, would eliminate the desire for initiative and display on the part of his musicians, a group which tends, at least outside of classical music, to think of itself as creative, rather than as cogs in a machine. Accordingly, the turnover becomes enormous. But while deriding individualism in the Fall, Smith's songs are far more ambiguous about the process of being subjected to the will of the machine and the manager. 'Fiery Jack' depicts a character whose repetitive job leaves him able to 'think think think' and 'burn burn burn', with no outlet – the wasting of human intelligence under the factory system, slack-jawed, living on pies, drunk for three decades. Yet this isn't a moralistic expression of sociological concern so much as admiration for and identification with the speeding, simmering resentment that drives Jack. Although it's never a good idea to impart a definitive authorial voice to any Fall song, there's a definite undercurrent in several songs from the 1980–3 period that suggests discipline and puritanism have done something awful to the psyche of the British. Frequently, this is ascribed to the survival of a peasant residue, as on the atavistic horrors of *Grotesque* and the anti-rock mocking of how 'all the English groups act like peasants with free milk'. Elsewhere, though, this seems more like a factory product. 'Kicker Conspiracy' details how by the early 1980s English football had become a grim slog, in which any individual talent has been effaced for an amateurish, brutal limitation of possibilities, a place 'where flair is punished' – something which sounds a great deal like being in the Fall. However, there was always one person allowed to demonstrate flair, with Smith's indisciplined, fragmented, oblique and far from utilitarian textual/verbal collages roaming into the places which the rigours of the music blocked off.

In the live version of 'Cash and Carry', Smith improvises that 'Even in Manchester, there's two types of factory there. One makes men old corpses. They stumble round like rust dogs. One lives off old dying men. One lives off the back of a dead man. You know which Factory I mean,' before declaring that, by contrast, 'I have dreams, I can see.' Factory Records and its protagonists have been comprehensively claimed by museum culture, with all the biopics, exhibitions and retrospectives that entails, and have even been cited as central to the 'regeneration' or gentrification of the city. The Fall have yet to be fully claimed by this history and reduced to cliché. The nearest thing to that was the *NME*'s caricature of Smith as grim foreman and pub bore, something to which the singer himself played up. Discipline in the later Fall becomes nearer again to nineteenth-century production than the iron consistency of the Taylor system. Smith once quoted Carlyle's aphorism 'Produce, produce, produce, what else are you here for?', though for much of the last decade or two what was produced often seemed less important than the mere act of production itself – what Marx called 'production for production's sake'. However, in the Fall's best work, the factory features as an ambiguous but utterly central motif. It warped a people, warps minds as much as bodies, and rather than being in conflict with the weird and fantastical, it produces the weirdness itself.

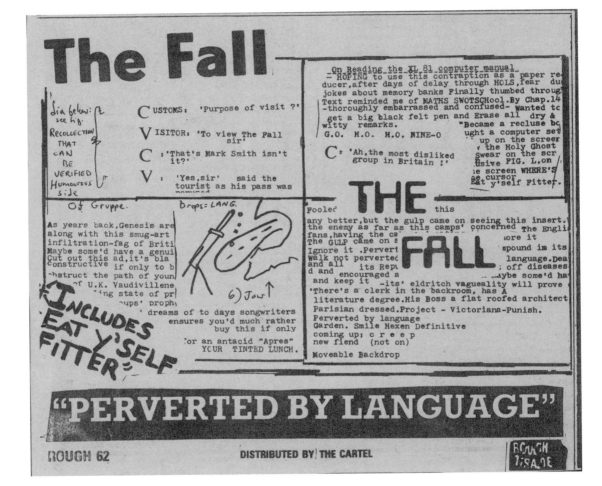

The Fall

..EDWARD ZI...

The HEX EN...
The HEX EN...
The HEX E...
The HEX E...
The HE...

AUGUST 18
CN-CH TOWN HALL

HIP PRIEST

AUGUST 20-21
MAINSTREET

THE FALL

THE

F A

142

(1hr)   (1hr)   (1hr)

HAIL THE CLASSICAL

MESSAGE FOR YER...

ARE YOU STILL...
- ☐ bowing to 'Mythical Thingy'?
- ☐ in need of that 'one true sentence'?
- ☐ wondering who is the 'King Shag Corpse'?

Then you **still** need the HEXAN school.

Lay down your weary trend **now**.   HERE'S HOW...

CIGS SMOKED HERE

UNSUITABLE FOR ROMANTICS

HEX ENDUCTION HOUR BY THE FALL

HEXEN

JAWBONE AND THE AIR-RIFLE

WHO MAKES THE NAZIS?

AND MANY MORE!

CUT OUT

AND FILE AWAY FOR REFERENCE

* Fabulous stereo effects
* 2 drum kit line-up
* immortal melodies
* chummy lifestyle tips
* euro-processed vinyl

THINK FIRST - MOST DOKTORS FOLLOW WHAT'S "BEST"

KAMERA RECORDS

DISTRIBUTED BY STAGE 1 RECORDS   KAM 005

He had been frightened of himself far too much.Now,as he paced the creaking boards,this realisation filtered into his psyche and for the first time he understood the words 'gratitude' 'sympathy' and 'big personality face'.Their dictionary meanings were intended to oppress, especially the last two.Gratitude was still useful in that it could mean the random forces of nature working for his good,and him seeing that.Paganism.He'd been very close to becoming ex-funny man celebrity. He needed a good hour at the Hexen school,a word mutant of two languages he'd grasped from thin air.

HEX ENDUCTION HOUR

× New l.p. !

THE FALL

IST: HEXEN-BILE,HEXEN CURSES

THE SCOURGE OF 'ROSSO-Rosso'

    'HEX Enduction Hour' is official new Fall product on Kamera Records,and in the groups opinion their most concentrated work to date. And maybe it will.It is packed with typical Fall appreciation of the good things in life,plus the usual niggly,annoying,BITTY observations that keep the group well away from the over exposed minds of our time.

    'There is no culture is my brag' _ 'The Classical'

THE LITTLE THINGS JOIN UP

TO MAKE:

Track listing:
Side a. The Classical-Jawbone & The Air-Rifle-Hip Priest-Fortress,Deer
        Park-Mere Pseud Mag.Ed-Winter(Hostel-Maxi)

Side b: Winter 2 -Just Step S'Ways-Who Makes the Nazis?-Iceland-And This
    Day.
personnel same as last 45 release 'Lie-Dream Of A Casino Soul'

The first 50 mins of the l.p. are songs honed in from the last tours The Fall have performed,the first side songs of comment and attitude,the 2nd side especially last 2 tracks 'Iceland' and 'And This Day',intends to intimidate the listener into the Fall's intelligence thru noise waves(:) 'And This Day' was savagely and randomly edited to produce new lyrics & impossible notes. Satirical,humourous element of past Fall work v.underplayed because 1. they've wrung it dry 2. t.v. is riddled now with liquidified 'satire' in most cases inferior to what the 'satirists' are trying to takea da piss out of.

      BLAST First (from politeness) ENGLAND

                          -W.Lewis 1914

WARNING: THERE ARE NO BLONDE BIRDS ON THE COVER OR IN THE RECORD.

                              P.T.O.

TEXT EXCERPT FROM: <u>AND THIS DAY</u>

> And this day no matter what and never or who fills baskets or
> who's just there, the whole earth shudders
> You show me the bloody poor bores/The surroundings are screaming on
> the roads,so you even mistrust your own feelings
> And this day,the old feelings came back:
> Big basket full s'-park s'-mart
> Everywhere just no fucking respite for us here,John kidder
> And this day,it will soon heal up.

'Winter' is a tale concerning an insane child who is taken over by a
spirit from the mind of a cooped-up alcoholic,and his ravaged viewpoints
and theories.An earlier version went into the 'Clang' process of speech,
whereby the sufferer during speech makes sentences containg similar sounding words.   NI

Hex Enduction Hour was recorded in an empty cinema,a studio adjacent to
it,and 'Hip Priest' was recorded in a studio made of lava(:)

Production: Richard Mazda/Grant Cunliffe/Mark E. Smith

The siGN oF Quality

BIG.   P.   You know it needs a
                                    lens.

next single announce ment:
    45 rpm   SIDE A: 'LOOK,KNOW'
               SIDE B: 'I'M INTO C.B.'

  side A is a new version of a fairly old song recorded using the same
          technique as 'And This Day'.Lyric is a schizo rant,spawned in
          the U.S., where many groups are becoming male go-go dancers

  side B: Is a comment on the weedy Home Office Sanctioned LIBERACE-ISM
          of U.K. band transmissions.
                                        out terminal Mar.82

Any mail should be sent to: The Fall c/o V.M. 284 Pentonville Rd.
                                         London N.

please do not expect a reply,as The Fall are not a condescending French
resistance type group nor do they have warehouses packed with info kits
on themselves.Thankyou.

                              M.E.S. Mar 82

THE FALL
Two 7 inch singles in Gatefold Sleeve RT 143

featuring
CONTAINER DRIVERS
and
KICKER CONSPIRACY
(LIMITED QUANTITY AT £1.99)

DISTRIBUTED BY THE CARTEL
FORTHCOMING FALL LP ON ROUGH TRADE RECORDS
"PERVERTED BY LANGUAGE" – ROUGH 62

THE FALL.

the FRENZ experiment

AVAILABLE ON ÷
ALBUM ÷ WITH LIMITED FREE SINGLE
CASSETTE ÷ WITH FOUR ADDITIONAL TRACKS
COMPACT DISC ÷ WITH FIVE ADDITIONAL TRACKS

BEGGARS BANQUET

INCLUDES THE SINGLE VICTORIA

ON TOUR ÷ IN MARCH
7th **BIRMINGHAM** ÷ HUMMINGBIRD
8th **MANCHESTER** ÷ RITZ
10th **EXETER** ÷ UNIVERSITY
11th **CARDIFF** ÷ UNIVERSITY
12th **OXFORD** ÷ POLYTECHNIC
14th **LIVERPOOL** ÷ ROYAL COURT THEATRE
15th **LEEDS** ÷ UNIVERSITY
17th **LEICESTER** ÷ UNIVERSITY
18th **LONDON** ÷ HAMMERSMITH ODEON
19th **CAMBRIDGE** ÷ CORN EXCHANGE

ENTERTAINMENT & PRICES YOU CAN, AT LAST, AFFORD.

THE FALL

Plus Support

MON 11th DEC

TICKETS FROM QUEENS HALL, BRADFORD
AND KRASH RECORDS, LEEDS. (Merrion and Headrow shops)

TEL: 392712

ADVANCE £5·00 — DOORS OPEN 7·30 PM

PURCHASE EARLY TO AVOID DISAPPOINTMENT.

QUEENS HALL

...only for the very best of live music.

queens hall, morley st, bradford, w.yorks. bd7 1bw tel: bfd. 392712/753007

Memorex for the Kraken: The Fall's Pulp Modernism

PART I[1]

Maybe industrial ghosts are making Spectres redundant.
(The Fall, *Dragnet* sleeve notes)[2]

M. R. James be born be born
Yog Sothoth rape me, lord
Sludge Hai Choi
Van Greenway
R. Corman
(The Fall, 'Spectre vs. Rector')[3]

Scrawny, gnarled, gaunt: Smith doesn't waltz with ghosts.
He materialises them.
(Mark Sinker, 'England: Look Back in Anguish')[4]

Who can put their finger on the Weird?

It's taken me more than twenty years to attempt this deciphering. Back then, the Fall did something to me. But what, and how?

Let's call it an Event, and at the same time note that all Events have a dimension of the uncanny. If something is too alien, it will fail to register; if it is too easily recognised, too easily cognisable, it will never be more than a reiteration of the already known. When the Fall pummelled their way into my nervous system circa 1983, it was as if a world that was familiar – and which I had thought *too* familiar, too quotidian to feature in rock – had returned, expressionistically transfigured, permanently altered.

I didn't know then that already, in 1983, the Fall's greatest work was behind them. No doubt the later albums have their merits, but it is on *Grotesque (After the Gramme)* (1980), *Slates* (1981) and *Hex Enduction Hour* (1982) that the group reached a pitch of sustained abstract invention which they – and most others – are unlikely to surpass. In its ambition, linguistic inventiveness and formal innovation, this triptych bears comparison with the great works of twentieth-century high-literary modernism (Joyce, Eliot, Lewis). The Fall extend and performatively critique that mode of high modernism by reversing the impersonation of working-class accent, dialect and diction that Eliot, for example, performed in *The Waste Land*. Smith's strategy involved aggressively retaining his accent, while using – in the domain of a supposedly popular entertainment form – highly arcane literary practices. In doing so, he laid waste to the notion that intelligence, literary sophistication and artistic experimentalism are the exclusive preserve of the privileged and the formally educated. But Smith knew that aping master-class mores presented all sorts of other dangers; it should never be a matter of proving (to the masters) that the white crap could be civilised. Perhaps all his writing was, from the start, an attempt to find a way out of that paradox which all working-class aspirants face: the impossibility of working-class achievement. Stay where you are, speak the language of your fathers, and you remain nothing; move up, learn to speak in the master language, and you have become a something, but only by erasing your origins – isn't the achievement precisely that erasure? ('You can string a sentence together, how can you possibly be working-class, my dear?')

The temptation for Smith was always to fit into the easy role of working-class spokesman, speaking from an assigned place in a given social world. Smith played *with* that role ('the white crap that talks back', 'Prole Art Threat', 'Hip Priest'), while refusing to actually play it. He knew that representation was a trap; social realism was the enemy because, in supposedly 'merely' representing the social order, it actually constituted it. Against the social realism of the official left, Smith developed a late-twentieth-century urban English version of the 'grotesque realism' that Bakhtin famously described in *Rabelais and His World*. Crucial to this grotesque realism is a contestation of the classificatory system which deems cultures (and populations) to be either refined or vulgar. As Peter Stallybrass and Allon White argued: 'the grotesque tends to operate as a critique of a dominant ideology which has already set the terms, designating what is high and low'.[5] Instead of the high modernist appropriation of working-class speech and culture, Smith's 'pulp modernism' reacquaints modernism with its disavowed pulp doppelgänger. Lovecraft is the crucial figure here, since his texts – which first appeared in pulp magazines like *Weird Tales* – emerged from an occulted trade between pulp horror and modernism. Follow the line back from Lovecraft's short stories and you pass through Dunsany and M. R. James, before coming to Poe. But Poe also played a decisive role in the development of modernism – via his influence on Baudelaire, Mallarmé, Valéry, and their admirer, T. S. Eliot. *The Waste Land*'s debt to *Dracula*, for instance, is well known.[6] The fragmentary, citational structure of a story like Lovecraft's 'Call of Cthulhu', meanwhile, recalls *The Waste Land*. More than that: as Benjamin Noys argued in his paper 'Lovecraft the Sinthome' (given at the 2005 'Gothic Remains' conference at Sussex University), the abominations from which Lovecraft's strait-laced scholars recoil bear comparison with cubist and futurist art; that is to say, Lovecraft turns modernism into an object of horror.

Yet Lovecraft's texts are exemplary of Weird, rather than straightforwardly Gothic, fiction. Weird fiction has its own consistency, which can be most clearly delineated by comparing it to two adjacent modes: fantasy and the uncanny. Fantasy (and Tolkien is the exemplar here) presupposes a completed world, a world that, although superficially different to 'ours' (there may be different species or supernatural forces), is politically all too familiar (there is usually some nostalgia for the ordered organisation of a feudal hierarchy). The uncanny, meanwhile, is set in 'our' world — only that world is no longer 'ours' any more, it no longer coincides with itself, it has been estranged. The Weird, however, depends upon the difference between two (or more) worlds — with 'world' here having an *ontological* sense. It is not a question of an empirical difference — the aliens are not from another planet, they are invaders from another reality system. Hence, the defining image is that of the threshold, the door from this world into another, and the key figure is the 'Lurker at the Threshold' — what, in Lovecraft's mythos, is called Yog-Sothoth. The political philosophical implications are clear: *there is no world*. What we call *the* world is a local-consensus hallucination, a shared dream.

Is There Anybody There?

Part One: spectre versus rector
The rector lived in Hampshire
The spectre was from Chorazina...
(The Fall, 'Spectre vs. Rector')

'Spectre vs. Rector', from 1979's *Dragnet*, is the first moment — still chilling to hear — when the Fall both lay out and implement their pulp modernist methodology. 'Spectre vs. Rector' is not only a ghost story, it is a commentary on the ghost story. The chorus, if it can be called that, is a litany of pulp forebears — 'M. R. James be born be born / Yog-Sothoth rape me, lord...' — in which language devolves into asignifying chant, verbal ectoplasm: 'Sludge Hai Choi / Van Greenway / R. Corman'.

Not coincidentally, 'Spectre vs. Rector' was the moment when the Fall really began to sound like themselves. Before that, their sound was a grey-complexioned, conspicuously consumptive garage plink-plonk punk, amphetamine-lean and on edge, marijuana-fatalistic, simultaneously arrogant and unsure of itself, proffering its cheap and nastiness as a challenge. All the elements of Smith's later (peripheral) vision are there on *Live at the Witch Trials* and on the other tracks on *Dragnet* — watery-eyed figures lurking in the corner of the retina, industrial estates glimpsed through psychotropic stupor — but they have not been condensed down yet, *pulped* into the witches' brew that will constitute Smith's plane of consistency.

On 'Spectre vs. Rector', any vestigial rock *presence* subsides into hauntology. The original track is nothing of the sort; it is already a palimpsest, spooked by itself — at least two versions are playing, out of sync. The track — and it is very definitely a track, not a 'song' — foregrounds both its own textuality and its texturality. It begins with cassette hum, and when the sleeve notes tell us that it was partly 'recorded in a damp warehouse in MC/R', we are far from surprised. Steve Hanley's bass rumbles and thumps like some implacable earth-moving machine invented by a deranged underground race, not so much rising from the subterranean as dragging the sound down into a troglodytic goblin kingdom in which ordinary sonic values are inverted. From now on, and for all the records that really matter, Hanley's bass will be the lead instrument, the monstrous foundations on which the Fall's upside-down sound will be built. Like Joy Division, their fellow modernists from Manchester, the Fall scramble the grammar of white rock by privileging rhythm over melody.

Fellow modernists they might have been, but the Fall's and Joy Division's take on modernism could not have been more different. Martin Hannett and Peter Saville gave Joy Division a minimalist, metallic austerity; the Fall's sound and cover art, by contrast, were gnarled, collage cut-up, deliberately incomplete. Both bands were dominated by forbiddingly intense vocalist visionaries. But where Ian Curtis was the depressive-neurotic, the end of the European Romantic line, Smith was the psychotic, the self-styled destroyer of Romanticism.

'Unsuitable for Romantics', Smith will graffiti onto the cover of *Hex Enduction Hour*, and 'Spectre vs. Rector' is the template for the anti-Romantic methodology he will deploy on the Fall's most important releases. After 'Spectre vs. Rector', there is no Mark E. Smith the Romantic subject. The novelty of his approach is to impose the novel or tale form ('Part One: spectre versus rector . . .') into the Romantic-lyrical tradition of the rock-and-roll song, so that the author function supplants that of the lyrical balladeer. (There are parallels between what Smith does to rock and the cut-up surgery Eliot performed on the etherised patient of Romantic expressive subjectivity in his early poems.) Smith chant-narrates, not sings, 'Spectre vs. Rector'.

The story is simple enough and, on the surface, deliberately conventional: a post-*Exorcist* revisiting of the classic English ghost story. (At another level, the narrative is generated by a Roussel-like playing with similar words: 'rector'/'spectre'/'inspector'/'exorcist'/'exhausted'.) A rector is possessed by a malign spirit ('the spectre was from Chorazina' — described on the sleeve notes as 'a negative Jerusalem'); a police inspector tries to intervene but is driven insane. (This a real Lovecraftian touch, since the dread fate that haunts Lovecraft's characters is not being consumed by the polytendrilled abominations, but by the schizophrenia that their appearance often engenders.) Both rector and inspector have to be saved by a third figure, a shaman-hero, an outsider who 'goes back to the mountains' when the exorcism is complete.

The rector stands for rectitude and rectilinearity, as well as for traditional religious authority. (The ontological shock that Lovecraft's monstrosities produce is typically described, any Lovecraft reader will recall, in terms of a twisting of rectilinear geometries.) The Inspector, meanwhile, as Ian Penman conjectured in his 1980 interview with the Fall, 'stands for an investigative, empirical world view'.[7] The hero ('His soul possessed a thousand times') has more affinity with the Spectre, whom he absorbs and becomes ('The spectre possesses the hero / But the possession is ineffectual'), than with the agents of rectitude and/or empirical investigation. It seems that the hero is driven more by his addiction to being possessed — which is to say, dispossessed of his own identity ('That was his kick from life') — than by any altruistic motive. He has no love for the social order he rescues ('I have saved a thousand souls / They cannot even save their own'), but in which he does not occupy a place. '"Those flowers, take them away," he said,

They're only funeral decorations
And this is a drudge nation
A nation of no imagination
A stupid dead man is their ideal
They shirk me and think me unclean...
UNCLEAN...

In *Madness and Civilisation*, Foucault argues that the insane occupy the structural position vacated by the leper, while in *The Ecstasy of Communication*, Baudrillard describes 'the state of terror proper to the schizophrenic: too great a proximity of everything, the unclean promiscuity of everything which touches, invests and penetrates without resistance, with no halo of private projection to protect him any more'. [8] Baudrillard is, of course, describing the schizophrenia of *media* systems which overwhelm all interiority. Television brings us voices from far away (and there's always something on the other side ...). For Baudrillard, there is an increasing flatness between media and the schizophrenic delirium in which they feature; psychotics often describe themselves as receivers for transmitted signals. And what is the hero of 'Spectre vs. Rector' if not another version of the 'ESP medium of discord' that Smith sings of on 'Psykick Dancehall'?

Smith's own methodology as writer-ranter-chanter echoes that of the hero-malcontent. He becomes (nothing but) the mystic pad on which stray psychic signals impress themselves, the throat through which a warring multiplicity of mutually antagonistic voices speak. This is not only a matter of the familiar idea that Smith 'contains multitudes'; the schizophonic riot of voices is itself subject to all kinds of mediation. The voices we hear will often be reported speech, recorded in the compressed 'telegraphic' headline style Smith borrowed from the Wyndham Lewis of *Blast*.

Listening to the Fall now, I'm often reminded of another admirer of Lewis: Marshall McLuhan. The McLuhan of *The Mechanical Bride* (subtitle: 'The Folklore of Industrial Man') understood very well the complicity between mass media, modernism and pulp. McLuhan argued that modernist collage was a response to the perfectly schizophrenic layout of the newspaper front page. (And Poe, who in addition to his role as a forebear of Weird fiction was also the inventor of the detective genre, plays a crucial role in *The Mechanical Bride*.)

PART II[9]

M. R. James, Be Born Be Born

Ten times my age, one tenth my height...
(The Fall, 'City Hobgoblins')[10]

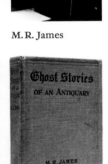

M. R. James

So he plunges into the Twilight World, and a political discourse framed in terms of witchcraft and demons. It's not hard to understand why, once you start considering it. The war that the Church and triumphant Reason waged on a scatter of wise-women and midwives, lingering practitioners of folk-knowledge, has provided a powerful popular image for a huge struggle for political and intellectual dominance, as first Catholics and later Puritans invoked a rise in devil-worship to rubbish their opponents. The ghost-writer and antiquarian M. R. James (one of the writers Smith appears to have lived on during his peculiar drugged adolescence) transformed the folk-memory into a bitter class-struggle between established science and law, and the erratic, vengeful, relentless undead world of wronged spirits, cheated of property or voice, or the simple dignity of being believed in.

(Mark Sinker, 'Watching the City Hobgoblins')[11]

Whether Smith first came to M. R. James via TV or some other route, James's stories exerted a powerful and persistent influence on his writing. Lovecraft, an enthusiastic admirer of James's stories to the extent that he borrowed their structure (scholar/researcher steeped in empiricist common sense is gradually driven insane by contact with an abyssal alterity), understood very well what was novel in James's tales. 'In inventing a new type of ghost', Lovecraft wrote of James,

he departed considerably from the conventional Gothic traditions; for where the older stock ghosts were pale and stately, and apprehended chiefly through the sense of sight, the average James ghost is lean, dwarfish and hairy – a sluggish, hellish night-abomination midway betwixt beast and man – and usually touched before it is seen.[12]

Some would question whether these dwarven figures ('ten times my age, one tenth my height') could be described as 'ghosts' at all; often it seemed that James was writing *demon* rather than ghost stories.

If the libidinal motor of Lovecraft's horror was race, in the case of James it was class. For James scholars, contact with the anomalous was usually mediated by the 'lower classes', which he portrayed as lacking in intellect but in possession of a deeper knowledge of weird lore. As Lovecraft and James scholar S. T. Joshi observes:

> *The fractured and dialectical English in which [James's array of lower-class characters] speak or write is, in one sense, a reflection of James's well-known penchant for mimicry; but it cannot be denied that there is a certain element of malice in his relentless exhibition of their intellectual failings. [...] And yet, they occupy pivotal places in the narrative: by representing a kind of middle ground between the scholarly protagonists and the aggressively savage ghosts, they frequently sense the presence of the supernatural more quickly and more instinctively than their excessively learned betters can bring themselves to do.*[13]

James wrote his stories as Christmas entertainments for Oxford undergraduates, and Smith was doubtless provoked and fascinated by James's stories in part because there was no obvious point of identification for him in them. 'When I was at the witch trials of the twentieth century, they said: "You are white crap."'[14] (*Live* at the witch trials: is it that the witch trials have never ended or that we are in some repeating structure which is always excluding and denigrating the Weird?)

A working-class autodidact like Smith could scarcely be conceived of in James's sclerotically stratified universe; such a being was a monstrosity who would be punished for the sheer hubris of existing. (Witness the amateur archaeologist Paxton in 'A Warning to the Curious'. Paxton was an unemployed clerk and therefore by no means working class, but his grisly fate was as much a consequence of 'getting above himself' as it was of his disturbing sacred Anglo-Saxon artefacts.) Smith could identify neither with James's expensively educated protagonists nor with his uneducated, superstitious lower orders. As Mark Sinker puts it: 'James, an enlightened Victorian intellectual, dreamed of the spectre of the once crushed and newly rising working classes as a brutish and irrational Monster from the Id: Smith is working class, and is torn between adopting this image of himself and fighting violently against it. It's left him with a loathing of liberal humanist condescension.'[15]

But if Smith could find no place in James's world, he would take a cue from one of Blake's mottoes (adapted in *Dragnet*'s 'Before the Moon Falls') and create his own fictional system rather than be enslaved by another man's. (Incidentally, isn't Blake a candidate for being the original pulp modernist?) In James's stories, there is, properly speaking, no working class at all. The lower classes that feature in his tales are, by and large, the remnants of the rural peasantry, and the supernatural is associated with the countryside. James's scholars typically travel from Oxford or London to the witch-haunted flatlands of Suffolk, and it is only here that they encounter demonic entities. Smith's fictions would locate spectres in the urban here and now; he would establish that their antagonisms were not archaisms.

Sinker: 'No one has so perfectly studied the sense of threat in the English horror story: the twinge of apprehension at the idea that the wronged dead might return to claim their property, their identity, their own voice in their own land.'[16]

The Grotesque Peasants Stalk the Land

Detective versus rector possessed by spectre
Spectre blows him against the wall
Says direct, 'This is your fall
I've waited since Caesar for this
Damn fatty, my hate is crisp!
I'll rip your fat body to pieces!'
(The Fall, 'Spectre vs. Rector')

> *The word grotesque derives from a type of Roman ornamental design first discovered in the fifteenth century, during the excavation of Titus's baths. Named after the 'grottoes' in which they were found, the new forms consisted of human and animal shapes intermingled with foliage, flowers, and fruits in fantastic designs which bore no relationship to the logical categories of classical art. For a contemporary account of these forms we can turn to the Latin writer Vitruvius. Vitruvius was an official charged with the rebuilding of Rome under Augustus, to whom his treatise 'On Architecture' is addressed. Not surprisingly, it bears down hard on the 'improper taste' for the grotesque. 'Such things neither are, nor can be, nor have been,' says the author in his description of the mixed human, animal, and vegetable forms:*
>> *'For how can a reed actually sustain a roof, or a candelabrum the ornament of a gable? or a soft and slender stalk, a seated statue? or how can flowers and half-statues rise alternately from roots and stalks? Yet when people view these falsehoods, they approve rather than condemn, failing to consider whether any of them can really occur or not.'*
>
> (Patrick Parrinder, *James Joyce*)[17]

By the time of *Grotesque (After the Gramme)*, the Fall's pulp modernism has become an entire political-aesthetic programme. At one level, *Grotesque* can be positioned as the barbed prole-art retort to the lyric antique Englishness of public-school prog. Compare, for instance, the cover of 'City Hobgoblins' (one of the singles that came out around the time of *Grotesque*) with something like Genesis's *Nursery Cryme*. *Nursery Cryme* presents a gently corrupted English surrealist idyll. On the 'City Hobgoblins' cover, an urban scene has been invaded by 'émigrés from old green glades': a leering, malevolent kobold looms over a dilapidated tenement. But rather than being smoothly integrated into the photographed scene, the crudely rendered hobgoblin has been etched, Nigel Cooke-style, onto the background. This is a war of worlds, an ontological struggle, a struggle over the means of representation.

Grotesque's 'English Scheme' was a thumbnail sketch of the territory over which the war was being fought. Smith would observe later that it was 'English Scheme' which 'prompted me to look further into England's "class" system. INDEED, one of the few advantages of being in an impoverished sub-art group in England is that you get to see (If eyes are peeled) all the different strata of society – for free.'[18] The enemies are the old right, the custodians of a National Heritage image of England ('poky quaint streets in Cambridge'), but also, crucially, the middle-class left, the Chabertistas of the time, who 'condescend to black men' and 'talk of Chile while driving through Haslingden'. In fact, enemies were everywhere. Lumpen punk was in many ways more of a problem than prog, since its reductive literalism and perfunctory politics ('circles with A in the middle') colluded with social realism in censuring/censoring the visionary and the ambitious.

   Although *Grotesque* is an enigma, its title gives clues. Otherwise incomprehensible references to 'huckleberry masks', 'a man with butterflies on his face' and Totale's 'ostrich headdress' and 'light blue plant-heads' begin to make sense when you recognise that, in Parrinder's description, the grotesque originally referred to 'human and animal shapes intermingled with foliage, flowers, and fruits in fantastic designs which bore no relationship to the logical categories of classical art'.

   Grotesque, then, would be another moment in the endlessly repeating struggle between a pulp Underground (the scandalous grottoes) and the Official culture, what Philip K. Dick called 'the Black Iron Prison'. Dick's intuition was that 'the Empire had never ended', and that history was shaped by an ongoing occult(ed) conflict between Rome and gnostic forces. 'Spectre vs. Rector' ('I've waited since Caesar for this') had rendered this clash in a harsh Murnau black and white; on *Grotesque* the struggle is painted in colours as florid as those used on the album's garish sleeve (the work of Smith's sister).

   It is no accident that the words 'grotesque' and 'weird' are often associated with one another, since both connote something which is out of place, which should either not exist at all or not exist *here*. The response to the apparition of a grotesque object will involve laughter as much as revulsion. 'What will be generally agreed upon', Philip Thomson wrote in his 1972 study *The Grotesque*, 'is that "grotesque" will cover, perhaps among other things, the co-presence of the laughable and something that is incompatible with the laughable.'[19] The role of laughter in the Fall has confused and misled interpreters. What has been suppressed is precisely the *co-presence* of the laughable with what is not compatible with the laughable. That co-presence is difficult to think of, particularly in Britain, where humour has often functioned to ratify common sense, to punish overreaching ambition with the dampening weight of bathos.

   With the Fall, however, it is as if satire is returned to its origins in the grotesque. The Fall's laughter does not issue from the commonsensical mainstream but from a psychotic Outside. This is satire in the oneiric mode of Gillray, in which invective and lampoonery becomes delirial, a (psycho) tropological spewing of associations and animosities, the true object of which is not any failing of probity but the delusion that human dignity is possible. It is not surprising to find Smith alluding to Alfred Jarry's *Ubu Roi* in a barely audible line in 'City Hobgoblins' ('Ubu le Roi is a home hobgoblin'). For Jarry, as for Smith, the incoherence and incompleteness of the obscene and the absurd were to be opposed to the false symmetries of good sense.

But in their mockery of poise, moderation and self-containment, in their logorrheic disgorging of slanguage, in their glorying in mess and incoherence, the Fall sometimes resemble a white English analogue of Funkadelic. For both Smith and George Clinton, there is no escaping the grotesque, if only because those who primp and puff themselves up just become more grotesque. We could go so far as to say that it is the human condition to be grotesque, since the human animal is the one that does not fit in, the freak of nature who has no place *in* nature and is capable of recombining nature's products into hideous new forms.

On *Grotesque*, Smith has mastered his anti-lyrical methodology. The songs are tales, but tales half-told. The words are fragmentary, as if they have come to us via an unreliable transmission that keeps cutting out. Viewpoints are garbled; ontological distinctions (between author, text and character) are confused, fractured. It is impossible to definitively sort out the narrator's words from direct speech. The tracks are palimpsests, badly recorded in a deliberate refusal of the 'coffee table' aesthetic Smith derides on the cryptic sleeve notes. The process of recording is not airbrushed out but foregrounded, surface hiss and illegible cassette noise brandished like improvised stitching on some Hammer Frankenstein monster.

'Impression of J. Temperance' was typical: a story in the Lovecraft style in which a dog breeder's 'hideous replica' ('brown sockets [...] purple eyes [...] fed with rubbish from disposal barges') haunts Manchester. This is a Weird tale, but one subjected to modernist techniques of compression and collage. The result is so elliptical that it is as if the text — part obliterated by silt, mildew and algae — has been fished out of the Manchester Ship Canal (which Hanley's bass sounds like it is dredging).

'Yes,' said Cameron, 'and the thing was in the impression of J. Temperance.'

The sound on *Grotesque* is a seemingly impossible combination of the shambolic and the disciplined, the cerebral-literary and the idiotic-physical. The obvious parallel was the Birthday Party. In both groups, an implacable bass holds together a leering, lurching, schizophonic body whose disparate elements strain like distended, diseased viscera against a pustule- and pock-ridden skin ('a spotty exterior hides a spotty interior'). Both the Fall and the Birthday Party reached for pulp-horror imagery rescued from the white trash can as an analogue and inspiration for their perverse 'return' to rock and roll (cf. also the Cramps). The nihilation that fired them was a rejection of a pop that they saw as self-consciously sophisticated, conspicuously cosmopolitan, a pop which implied that the arty could be attained only at the expense of brute physical impact. Their response was to hyperbolically emphasise crude atavism, to embrace the unschooled and the primitivist.

The Birthday Party's fascination was with the American 'junkonscious', the mountain of semiotic/narcotic trash lurking in the hindbrain of a world population hooked on America's myths of abjection and omnipotence. The Birthday Party revelled in this fantasmatic Americana, using it as a way of cancelling an Australian identity that they in any case experienced as empty, devoid of any distinguishing features.

Smith's rock-and-roll citations functioned differently, precisely as a means of reinforcing his Englishness and his own ambivalent attitude towards it. The rockabilly references are almost like 'what if?' exercises. What if rock and roll had emerged from the industrial heartlands of England rather than the Mississippi Delta? The rockabilly on 'The Container Drivers' or 'Fiery Jack' is slowed by meat pies and gravy, its dreams of escape fatally poisoned by pints of bitter and cups of greasy-spoon tea. It is rock and roll as working-men's-club cabaret, performed by a failed Gene Vincent imitator in Prestwich. The 'what if?' speculations fail. Rock and roll needed the endless open highways; it could never have begun in Britain's snarled-up ring roads and claustrophobic conurbations.

For the Smith of *Grotesque*, homesickness is a pathology. (In the interview on the 1983 *Perverted by Language* video, Smith claims that being away from England literally made him sick.) There is little to recommend the country which he can never permanently leave; his relationship to it seems to be one of wearied addiction. The fake jauntiness of 'English Scheme' (complete with proto-John Shuttleworth cheesy cabaret keyboard) is a squalid postcard from somewhere no one would ever wish to be. Here and in 'C'n'C-S Mithering', the US emerges as an alternative (in despair at the class-ridden Britain of 'sixty hours and stone toilet back gardens', the 'clever ones [...] point their fingers at America'), but there is a sense that, no matter how far he travels, Smith will in the end be overcome by a compulsion to return to his blighted homeland, which functions as his *pharmakon*, his poison and remedy, sickness and cure. In the end he is as afflicted by paralysis as Joyce's Dubliners.

On 'C'n'C-S Mithering' a rigor-mortis snare drum gives this paralysis a sonic form. 'C'n'C-S Mithering' is an unstinting inventory of gripes and irritations worthy of Tony Hancock at his most acerbic and disconsolate, a cheerless survey of estates that 'stick up like stacks' and, worse still, a derisive dismissal of one of the supposed escape routes from drudgery: the music business, denounced as corrupt, dull and stupid. The track sounds, perhaps deliberately, like a white English version of rap (here, as elsewhere, the Fall are remarkable for producing *equivalents* to, rather than facile imitations of, black American forms).

Body a Tentacle Mess

So R. Totale dwells underground
Away from sickly grind
With ostrich head-dress

Face a mess, covered in feathers
Orange-red with blue-black lines
That draped down to his chest
Body a tentacle mess
And light blue plant-heads
(The Fall, 'The N.W.R.A.')[20]

But it is the other long track, 'The N.W.R.A.', that is the masterpiece.
All of the LP's themes coalesce in this track, a tale of cultural political intrigue
that plays like some improbable mulching of T. S. Eliot, Wyndham Lewis,
H. G. Wells, Dick, Lovecraft and Le Carré. It is the story of Roman Totale,
a psychic and former cabaret performer whose body is covered in tentacles.
It is often said that Totale is one of Smith's 'alter egos'; in fact, Smith is in
the same relationship to Totale as Lovecraft was to someone like Randolph
Carter. Totale is a character rather than a persona. Needless to say, he is not
a character in the 'well-rounded' Forsterian sense so much as a carrier of
mythos, an intertextual linkage between pulp fragments.

The intertextual methodology is crucial to pulp modernism. If pulp
modernism first of all asserts the author function over the creative–expressive
subject, it secondly asserts a fictional system against the author god. By
producing a fictional plane of consistency across different texts, the pulp
modernist becomes a conduit through which a world can emerge. Once again,
Lovecraft is the exemplar here: his tales and novellas could in the end no longer
be apprehended as discrete texts but as part-objects forming a mythos-space
which other writers could also explore and extend.

The form of 'The N.W.R.A.' is as alien to organic wholeness as is Totale's
abominable tentacular body. It is a grotesque concoction, a collage of pieces
that do not belong together. The model is the novella rather than the tale,
and the story is told episodically, from multiple points of view, using a
heteroglossic riot of styles and tones (comic, journalistic, satirical, novelistic),
like 'Call of Cthulhu' rewritten by the Joyce of *Ulysses* and compressed into
ten minutes.

From what we can glean, Totale is at the centre of a plot – infiltrated
and betrayed from the start – which aims at restoring the north to glory
(perhaps to its Victorian moment of economic and industrial supremacy;
perhaps to some more ancient pre-eminence; perhaps to a greatness that will
eclipse anything that has come before). More than a matter of regional railing
against the capital, in Smith's vision the north comes to stand for everything
suppressed by urbane good taste: the esoteric, the anomalous, the vulgar
sublime – that is to say, the Weird and the Grotesque itself. Totale, festooned
in the incongruous Grotesque costume of 'ostrich head-dress [...] feathers /
Orange-red with blue-black line /[...] And light blue plant-heads', is the
would-be Faerie King of this Weird Revolt, who ends up its maimed Fisher
King, abandoned like a pulp-modernist Miss Havisham among the relics of

a carnival that will never happen, a drooling totem of a defeated tilt at social realism, the visionary leader reduced, as the psychotropics fade and the fervour cools, to being a washed-up cabaret artiste once again.

PART III [21]

'Don't Start Improvising, for Christ's Sake'

The temptation when writing about the Fall's work of this period is to too quickly render it tractable. I note this by way of a disclaimer and a confession, since I am, of course, as liable to fall prey to this temptation as any other commentator. To confidently describe songs as if they were 'about' settled subjects or to attribute to them a determinate aim or orientation (typically, a satirical purpose) will always be inadequate to the vertiginous experience of the songs and the distinctive jouissance provoked by listening to them. This enjoyment involves a frustration — a frustration, precisely, of our attempts to make sense of the songs. Yet this jouissance — something also provoked by late Joyce, Pynchon and Burroughs — is an irreducible dimension of the Fall's modernist poetics. If it is impossible to make sense of the songs, it is also impossible to stop making sense of them — or at least it is impossible to stop *attempting* to make sense of them. On the one hand, there is no possibility of dismissing the songs as nonsense; they are not gibberish or disconnected strings of non sequiturs. On the other, any attempt to constitute the songs as settled carriers of meaning runs aground on their incompleteness and inconsistency.

The principal way in which the songs were recuperated was via the charismatic persona Smith established in interviews. Although he scrupulously refused to either corroborate or reject any interpretations of his songs, invoking this extra-textual persona, notorious for its strong views and its sardonic but at least legible humour, allowed listeners and commentators to contain, even dissipate, the strangeness of the songs themselves.

The temptation to use Smith's persona as a key to the songs was especially pressing because all pretence of democracy in the group had long since disappeared. By the time of *Grotesque*, it was clear that Smith was as much of an autocrat as James Brown, the band the zombie slaves of his vision. He is the shaman-author, the group the producers of a delirium-inducing repetition from which all spontaneity must be ruthlessly purged. 'Don't start improvising, for Christ's sake,' goes a line on *Slates*, the ten-inch EP follow-up to *Grotesque*, echoing his chastisement of the band for 'showing off' on the live LP *Totale's Turns*.

Slates' 'Prole Art Threat' turned Smith's persona, reputation and image into an enigma and a conspiracy. The song is a complex, ultimately unreadable play on the idea of Smith as 'working-class' spokesman. The 'Threat' is posed as much to other representations of the proletarian pop culture (which at its best meant the Jam, and at its worst the more thuggish Oi!) as against the ruling class as such. The 'art' of the Fall's pulp modernism – their intractability and difficulty – is counterposed with the misleading ingenuousness of social realism.

The Fall's intuition was that social relations could not be understood in the 'demystified' terms of empirical observation (the 'housing figures' and 'sociological memory' later ridiculed on 'The Man Whose Head Expanded'). Social power depends upon 'hexes': restricted linguistic, gestural and behavioural codes which produce a sense of inferiority and enforce class destiny. 'What chance have you got against a tie and a crest?' Weller demanded on 'Eton Rifles', and it was as if the Fall took the power of such symbols and sigils very literally, understanding the social field as a series of curses which have to be sent back to those who had issued them.

The pulp format on 'Prole Art Threat' is spy fiction, its scenario resembling *Tinker Tailor Soldier Spy* redone as a tale of class-cultural espionage, but then compressed and cut up so that the characters and contexts are even more perplexing than they were in Le Carré's already oblique narrative. We are in a labyrinthine world of bluff and counter-bluff – a perfect analogue for Smith's own elusive, allusive textual strategies. The text is presented to us as a transcript of surveillance tapes, complete with ellipses where the transmission is supposedly scrambled: 'GENT IN SAFE-HOUSE: Get out the pink press threat file and Brrrptzzap* the subject. (* = scrambled).'

'Prole Art Threat' seems to be a satire, yet it is a *blank* satire, a satire without any clear object. If there is a point, it is precisely to disrupt any 'centripetal' effort to establish fixed identities and meanings. Those centripetal forces are represented by the 'Middle Mass' ('vulturous in the aftermath') and 'the Victorian vampiric' culture of London itself, as excoriated in 'Leave the Capitol':

The tables covered in beer
Showbiz whines, minute detail
It's a hand on the shoulder in Leicester Square
It's vaudeville pub back-room dusty pictures of white-frocked girls and music
teachers
The bed's too clean
The water's poison for the system
Then you know in your brain
LEAVE THE CAPITOL!
EXIT THIS ROMAN SHELL!

This horrifying vision of London as a Stepford city of drab conformity ('hotel maids smile in unison') ends with the unexpected arrival of Arthur Machen's *Great God Pan* (last alluded to in the Fall's very early 'Second Dark Age', presaging the Fall's return of the Weird).

The Textual Expectorations of *Hex*

> *He'd been very close to becoming ex-funny man celebrity. He needed a good hour*
> *at the hexen school …*
> (Press release for *Hex Enduction Hour*)

Hex Enduction Hour was even more expansive than *Grotesque*. Teeming with
detail, gnomic yet hallucinogenically vivid, *Hex* was a series of pulp-modernist
pen portraits of England in 1982. The LP had all the hubristic ambition
of prog, combined with an aggression whose ulcerated assault and battery
outdid that of most of its post-punk peers in terms of sheer ferocity. Even the
lumbering 'Winter' was driven by a brute urgency, so that, on side one, only
the quiet passages in the lugubrious 'Hip Priest' – like dub, if it had been
invented in drizzly motorway service stations rather than in recording studios
in Jamaica – provided a respite from the violence.

Yet the violence was not a matter of force alone. Even when the record's
dual-drummer attack is at its most poundingly vicious, the violence is formal
as much as physical. The rock form is disassembled before our ears. It seems
to keep time according to some system of spasms and lurches learned from
Beefheart. Something like 'Deer Park' – a whistle-stop tour of London circa
1982, sandblasted with 'Sister Ray'-style white noise – screams and whines
as if it is about to fall apart at any moment. The 'bad production' was nothing
of the sort. The sound could be pulverisingly vivid at times: the moment when
the bass and drums suddenly loom out of the miasma at the start of 'Winter'
is breathtaking, and the double-drum tattoo on 'Who Makes the Nazis?' fairly
leaps out of the speakers. This was the space rock of Can and Neu! smeared in
the grime and mire of the quotidian, recalling the most striking image from
The Quatermass Xperiment: a space rocket crash-landed into the roof of a
suburban house.

In many ways, however, the most suggestive parallels come from black pop.
The closest equivalents to the Smith of *Hex* would be the deranged despots of
black sonic fiction: Lee Perry, Sun Ra and George Clinton, visionaries capable
of constructing (and destroying) worlds in sound.

As ever, the album sleeve (so foreign to what were then the conventions
of sleeve design that HMV would only stock it with its reverse side facing
forward) was the perfect visual analogue for the contents. The sleeve was
more than that, actually: its spidery scrabble of slogans, scrawled notes and
photographs was a part of the album rather than a mere illustrative envelope
in which it was contained.

With the Fall of this period, what Gérard Genette calls 'paratexts'[22] – those
liminal conventions, such as introductions, prefaces and blurbs, which mediate
between the text and the reader – assume special significance. Smith's paratexts
were clues that posed as many puzzles as they solved; his notes and press
releases were no more intelligible than the songs they were nominally supposed

to explain. All paratexts occupy an ambivalent position, neither inside nor outside the text. Smith uses them to ensure that no definite boundary could be placed around the songs. Rather than being contained and defined by its sleeve, *Hex* haemorrhages *through* the cover.

It was clear that the songs weren't complete in themselves but part of a larger fictional system, to which listeners were only ever granted partial access. 'I used to write a lot of prose on and off,' Smith would say later. 'When we were doing *Hex* I was doing stories all the time and the songs were like the bits left over.' Smith's refusal to provide lyrics or explain his songs was in part an attempt to ensure that they remained, in Barthes' terms, *writerly*. (Barthes opposes such texts, which demand the active participation of the reader, with 'readerly' texts, which reduce the reader to the passive role of consumer of already existing totalities.)

Before his words could be deciphered, they first of all had to be heard, which was difficult enough, since Smith's voice – often subject to what appeared to be loudhailer distortion – was always at least partially submerged in the mulch and maelstrom of *Hex*'s sound. In the days before the internet provided a repository of Smith's lyrics (or fans' best guesses at what the words were), it was easy to mishear lines.

Even when words could be heard, it was impossible to confidently assign them a meaning or ontological 'place'. Were they Smith's own views, the thoughts of a character, or merely stray semiotic signals? More importantly, how clearly could each of these levels be separated from one another? *Hex*'s textual expectorations were nothing so genteel as stream of consciousness; they seemed to be gobbets of linguistic detritus ejected direct from the mediatised unconscious, unfiltered by any sort of reflexive subjectivity. Advertising, tabloid headlines, slogans, preconscious chatter, overheard speech were masticated into dense schizoglossic tangles.

'Who Wants to Be in a Hovis Advert Anyway?'

'Who wants to be in a Hovis / Advert / Anyway?' Smith asks in 'Just Step S'Ways', but this refusal of cosy provincial cliché (Hovis adverts were famous for their sentimentalised presentation of a bygone industrial north) is counteracted by the tacit recognition that the mediatised unconscious is structured like advertising. You might not want to live in an advert, but advertising dwells within you. *Hex* converts any linguistic content – whether it be polemic, internal dialogue, poetic insight – into the hectoring form of advertising copy or the screaming ellipsis of headline-speak. The titles of 'Hip Priest' and 'Mere Pseud Mag. Ed.', as urgent as fresh newsprint, bark out from some Vorticist front page of the mind.

As for advertising, consider the opening call to arms of 'Just Step S'Ways': 'When what used to excite you does not / Like you've used up all your allowance of experiences.' Is this an existentialist call for self-reinvention disguised as advertising hucksterism, or the reverse? Or take the bilious opening track, 'The Classical'. 'The Classical' appears to oppose the anodyne vacuity of advertising's compulsory positivity ('this new profile razor unit') to ranting profanity ('Hey there, fuckface!') and the gross physicality of the body ('stomach gassss'). But what of the line 'I've never felt better in my life'? Is this another advertising slogan or a statement of the character's feelings?

It was perhaps the unplaceability of any of the utterances on *Hex* that allowed Smith to escape censure for the notorious line 'Where are the obligatory [n-word plural]?' in 'The Classical'. Intent was unreadable. Everything sounded like a citation, embedded discourse, mention rather than use.

Smith returns to the Weird tale form on 'Jawbone and the Air-Rifle'. A poacher accidentally causes damage to a tomb, unearthing a jawbone which 'carries the germ of a curse / Of the Broken Brothers Pentacle Church'. The song is a tissue of allusions – James ('A Warning to the Curious', 'Oh, Whistle and I'll Come to You, My Lad'), Lovecraft ('The Shadow over Innsmouth'), Hammer Horror, *The Wicker Man* – culminating in a psychedelic/psychotic breakdown (complete with torch-wielding mob of villagers):

He sees jawbones on the street
Advertisements become carnivores
And roadworkers turn into jawbones
And he has visions of islands, heavily covered in slime
The villagers dance round pre-fabs
And laugh through twisted mouths

'Jawbone' resembles nothing so much as a *League of Gentlemen* sketch, and the Fall have much more in common with the *League of Gentlemen*'s febrile carnival than with witless imitators such as Pavement. The coexistence of the laughable with that which is not laughable: a description that captures the essence of both the Fall and *The League of Gentlemen*'s grotesque humour.

'White Face Finds Roots'

> Below, black scars winding through the snow showed the main roads. Great frozen rivers and snow-laden forest stretched in all directions. Ahead they could just see a range of old, old mountains. It was perpetual evening at this time of year, and the further north they went, the darker it became. The white lands seemed uninhabited, and Jerry could easily see how the legends of trolls, Jotunheim, and the tragic gods – the dark, cold, bleak legends of the North – had come out of Scandinavia. It made him feel strange, even anachronistic, as if he had gone back from his own age to the Ice Age.
>
> (Michael Moorcock, *The Final Programme*)[23]

On *Hex*'s second side, mutant r-and-r becomes r-and-Artaud as the songs become increasingly delirial and abstract. 'Who Makes the Nazis?' – as lunar as *Tago Mago*, as spacey-desolated as King Tubby at his most cavernous – is a TV talk-show debate rendered as some Jarry-esque pantomime, and composed of leering backing vocals and oneiric–cryptic linguistic fragments: 'Longhorn breed [...] George Orwell Burmese police [...] Hate's not your enemy, love's your enemy, murder all bush monkeys...'

'Iceland', recorded in a lava-lined studio in Reykjavik, is a fantasmatic encounter with the fading myths of north European culture in the frozen territory from which they originated. 'White face finds roots,' Smith's sleeve notes tell us. The song, hypnotic and undulating, meditative and mournful, recalls the bone-white steppes of Nico's *The Marble Index* in its arctic atmospherics. A keening wind (on a cassette recording made by Smith) whips through the track as Smith invites us to 'cast the runes against your own soul' (another James reference, this time to his 'Casting the Runes').

'Iceland' is rock as *ragnarock*, an anticipation (or is it a recapitulation?) of the End Times in the terms of the Norse 'Doom of the Gods'. It is a *Twilight of the Idols* for the retreating hobgoblins, kobolds and trolls of Europe's receding Weird culture, a lament for the monstrosities and myths whose dying breaths it captures on tape:

Witness the last of the god men [...]
A Memorex for the Krakens

Endnotes

PART I

1. k-punk, 8 May 2006, http://k-punk. abstractdynamics.org/archives/007759.html. A version of this piece was previously published in Michael Goddard and Benjamin Halligan, *Mark E. Smith and The Fall: Art, Music and Politics*, Ashgate, 2010.

2. The Fall, *Dragnet*, Step-Forward, 1979.

3. The Fall, 'Spector vs. Rector', *Dragnet*, Step-Forward, 1979.

4. Mark Sinker, 'England: Look Back in Anguish', *NME*, 2 January 1988.

5. Peter Stallybrass and Allon White, 'The Fair, the Pig, Authorship', in *The Politics and Poetics of Transgression*, Cornell University Press, 1986.

6. A passage in T. S. Eliot's *The Waste Land* which, by Eliot's own admission, was influenced by Stoker's novel:
   'And bats with baby faces in the violet light
   Whistled and beat their wings
   And crawled head downward down a blackened wall.'

7. Ian Penman, 'All Fall Down', *NME*, 5 January 1980, http://thefall.org/gigography/80jan05.html.

8. Jean Baudrillard, 'The Ecstasy of Communication', in Hal Foster (ed.), *The Anti-Aesthetic: Essays on Postmodern Culture*, New Press, 2002, p. 153.

PART II

9. k-punk, 4 February 2007, http://k-punk. abstractdynamics.org/archives/008993.html.

10. The Fall, 'City Hobgoblins', *Grotesque (After the Gramme)*, Rough Trade, 1980.

11. Mark Sinker, 'Watching the City Hobgoblins', *The Wire*, August 1986.

12. H. P. Lovecraft, 'Supernatural Horror in Literature', http://www.hplovecraft.com/writings/texts/essays/shil.aspx.

13. S. T. Joshi, 'Introduction' to M. R. James, *Count Magnus and Other Ghost Stories: The Complete Ghost Stories of M. R. James*, Vol. 1, Penguin, 2004.

14. Mark E. Smith, onstage at the Lyceum, London, in 1978.

15. Mark Sinker, 'England: Look Back in Anguish', *NME*, 2 January 1988.

16. Ibid.

17. Patrick Parrinder, *James Joyce*, Cambridge University Press, 1984.

18. Mark E. Smith, *The Fall: Lyrics*, Lough Press, 1985.

19. Philip Thomson, *The Grotesque*, Routledge, 1972, p. 2.

20. The Fall, 'The N.W.R.A.', *Grotesque (After the Gramme)*, Rough Trade, 1980.

PART III

21. k-punk, 16 February 2007, http://k-punk. abstractdynamics.org/archives/009039.html.

22. Gérard Genette, *Paratexts*, Cambridge University Press, 1997.

23. Michael Moorcock, *The Final Programme*, HarperCollins, 1971

1989
Sign with Fontana/Phonogram; 'Cab It Up!' (Jun); *Seminal Live* LP (Jun).

1990
'Telephone Thing' (Jan); *Extricate* (Feb); 'Popcorn Double Feature' (Mar); 'White Lightning' (Aug); 'High Tension Line' (Dec).

1991
Shift-Work (Apr); Cities in the Park festival, Heaton Park, Manchester (Aug); Reading Festival (Aug); Pete Frame's Rock Family Tree (*NME*, May 11); 'Hip Priest' appears on *The Silence of the Lambs* soundtrack.

1992
Code: Selfish (Mar); 'Free Range' (Mar); Glastonbury Festival (Jun); 'Ed's Babe' (Jul); leave Fontana/Phonogram (Nov).

1993
Sign with independent Permanent Records; 'Why Are People Grudgeful' (Apr); *The Infotainment Scan* (Apr), no. 9 on UK album chart, first and only Top-10 hit; *Behind the Counter* EP (Dec).

1994
'15 Ways' (Apr); *Middle Class Revolt* (May); Smith records 'I Want You' w/ Inspiral Carpets; Smith appears in conversation with Michael Bracewell at the ICA, London; first issue of *The Biggest Library Yet* fanzine.

1995
Cerebral Caustic (Feb); *The Twenty-Seven Points* live LP (Aug).

1996
'The Chiselers' (Feb); *The Light User Syndrome* (Jun); multiple semi-legit live/demo LPs appear on Receiver Records; Smith records 'Plug Myself In' w/ D.O.S.E. for PWL.

1997
Levitate (Sep); Smith plays 'social worker' in short film *Diary of a Madman*, directed by John Humphreys.

Extricate (February 1990, Fontana)

SIDE 1
Sing! Harpy
I'm Frank
Bill Is Dead
Black Monk Theme Part I
Popcorn Double Feature

SIDE 2
Telephone Thing
Hilary
Chicago, Now!
The Littlest Rebel
And Therein…

SIDE ONE 1. SING! HARPY 2. I'M FRANK 3. BILL IS DEAD 4. BLACK MONK THEME PART I 5. POPCORN DOUBLE FEATURE

SIDE TWO 1. TELEPHONE THING 2. HILARY 3. CHICAGO, NOW! 4. THE LITTLEST REBEL 5. AND THEREIN . . .

SIDE ONE written by: 1. M. E. Smith / M. Beddington. 2 & 3 M. E. Smith / C. Scanlon. 4 The Monks. 5 Weiss / English. SIDE TWO written by: 1 M. E. Smith / M. Black / J. More. 2 & 3 M. E. Smith. 4 M. E. Smith / C. Scanlon / S. Hanley / S. Wolstencroft. 5 M. E. Smith / M. Beddington.

SIDE ONE Produced and mixed by Craig Leon, except 4 produced and mixed by Mark E. Smith and Craig Leon. SIDE TWO Produced and mixed by Craig Leon, except 1 produced and mixed by Coldcut for Ahead Of Our Time. 4 produced and mixed by Adrian Sherwood. 5 produced and mixed by Mark E. Smith and Craig Leon.

℗ 1990 Phonogram Ltd. (London). All rights reserved. Unauthorised reproduction, hiring, lending, public performance and broadcasting prohibited. © 1990 Phonogram Ltd. (London).

COG-SINISTER

STEPHEN HANLEY – BASS
CRAIG SCANLON – GUITAR
MARCIA SCHOFIELD – KEYBOARDS & PERCUSSION
MARK E. SMITH – VOCALS
SIMON WOLSTENCROFT – DRUMS
MARTIN BRAMAH – GUITAR & VOCALS

with: CHARLOTTE BILL / FLUTE & OBOE,
KENNY BRADY / FIDDLE, CRAIG & CASTLE /
B.VOCALS & ORGAN, M.EDWARDS / GUITAR

PRODUCED BY: CRAIG LEON, ADRIAN SHERWOOD,
COLD CUT, M.E. SMITH

ENGINEERS: ALAISTAR G. SCHILLING,
IAN TAPE ONE and a bunch of guys in pony tails

Recorded at Southern Studios, London; Swanyard Studios,
London; The Manor, Oxfordshire; Wool Hall, Somerset,
mid–late 1989.

Shift-Work (April 1991, Fontana)

SIDE 1 – "EARTH'S IMPOSSIBLE DAY"
So What About It?
Idiot Joy Showland
Edinburgh Man
Pittsville Direkt
The Book of Lies
The War Against Intelligence

SIDE 2 – "NOTEBOOKS OUT PLAGIARISTS"
Shift-Work
You Haven't Found It Yet
The Mixer
A Lot of Wind
Rose
Sinister Waltz

848 594-1

ALSO AVAILABLE ON

| CD | 848 594-2 |
| MC | 848 594-4 |

"EARTH'S IMPOSSIBLE DAY"

1 SO WHAT ABOUT IT?

2 IDIOT JOY SHOWLAND

3 EDINBURGH MAN

4 PITTSVILLE DIREKT

5 THE BOOK OF LIES

6 THE WAR AGAINST INTELLIGENCE

"NOTEBOOKS OUT PLAGIARISTS"

1 SHIFT-WORK

2 YOU HAVEN'T FOUND IT YET

3 THE MIXER

4 A LOT OF WIND

5 ROSE

6 SINISTER WALTZ

SHIFT-WORK

"EARTH'S IMPOSSIBLE DAY" TRACKS 1, 5, 6 PRODUCED BY ROBERT GORDON AT FON STUDIOS, TRACK 2 PRODUCED AND MIXED BY CRAIG LEON, TRACK 3 PRODUCED BY CRAIG LEON/GRANT SHOWBIZ, MIXED BY CRAIG LEON, TRACK 4 PRODUCED BY GRANT SHOWBIZ, MIXED BY CRAIG LEON. "NOTEBOOKS OUT PLAGIARISTS" TRACKS 1, 2, 5, 6 PRODUCED AND MIXED BY CRAIG LEON, TRACK 4 PRODUCED BY CRAIG LEON AND GRANT SHOWBIZ, MIXED BY CRAIG LEON, TRACK 3 PRODUCED BY ROBERT GORDON AT FON STUDIOS. THE FALL PERSONNEL: STEPHEN HANLEY – BASS GUITAR, CRAIG SCANLON – LEAD & RHYTHM GUITAR, MARK E. SMITH – LEAD VOCALS, SIMON WOLSTENCROFT – DRUMS & KEYBOARDS, KENNY BRADY – VOCALS & FIDDLE. WITH ADDITIONS: CASSELL WEBB – BACKING VOCALS, DAVE BUSH – MACHINES, CRAIG LEON – ORGAN & GUITAR, MARTIN BRAMAH – GUITAR ON 'ROSE' MARCIA SCHOFIELD, FLUTE ON 'ROSE'. MANAGEMENT: TREVOR LONG. ARTWORK: PASCAL. THANKS TO: SAFFRON, TREVOR, ROB FON, PELL, CRAIG & CASS, BRADY, JENNY, MANDY, HEATH, STIK, CHARLIE, RONA, JACKO, MAISON, MAVIS, DAVE LUFF, MONIQUE, DANIEL, MICHAEL & MICHEL, A, FROST, REICHARDT, JOHN & BETH, JOE COHEN & BABS, I. ADAMS, EDINBURGH, HILARY, RED ALERT, NOEL & SHIRLEY, GRANT, ELLEN VAN SCHUYLENBURGH, AMEL & MARK AND ALL THE ENGINEERS FOR THEIR HELPFUL OBSTRUCTION.

COG SINISTER

STEPHEN HANLEY – BASS GUITAR
CRAIG SCANLON – LEAD & RHYTHM GUITAR
MARK E. SMITH – LEAD VOCALS
SIMON WOLSTENCROFT – DRUMS & KEYBOARDS
KENNY BRADY – VOCALS & FIDDLE

WITH ADDITIONS:
CASSELL WEBB – BACKING VOCALS
DAVE BUSH – MACHINES
CRAIG LEON – ORGAN AND GUITAR
MARTIN BRAMAH – GUITAR ON 'ROSE'
MARCIA SCHOFIELD – FLUTE ON 'ROSE'

"EARTH'S IMPOSSIBLE DAY"
TRACKS 1,5,6 PRODUCED BY ROBERT GORDON AT FUN STUDIOS, TRACK 2 PRODUCED AND MIXED BY CRAIG LEON, TRACK 3 PRODUCED BY CRAIG LEON/GRANT SHOWBIZ, MIXED BY CRAIG LEON TRACK 4 PRODUCED BY GRANT SHOWBIZ, MIXED BY CRAIG LEON

"NOTEBOOKS OUT PLAGIARISTS"
TRACKS 1, 2, 5, 6 PRODUCED AND MIXED BY CRAIG LEON, TRACK 4 PRODUCED BY CRAIG LEON AND GRANT SHOWBIZ, MIXED BY CRAIG LEON, TRACK 3 PRODUCED BY ROBERT GORDON AT FON STUDIOS

ARTWORK: PASCAL

Recorded at FON Studios, Sheffield and elsewhere, late 1990 / early 1991.

Code: Selfish (March 1992, Fontana)

SIDE 1
The Birmingham School of Business School
Free Range
Return
Time Enough At Last
Everything Hurtz
Immortality

SIDE 2
Two-Face!
Just Waiting
So-Called Dangerous
Gentlemen's Agreement
Married, 2 Kids
Crew Filth

THE FALL

Side 1
THE BIRMINGHAM SCHOOL
OF BUSINESS SCHOOL.
FREE RANGE.
RETURN.
TIME ENOUGH AT LAST.
EVERYTHING HURTZ.
IMMORTALITY.

Side 2
TWO-FACE!
JUST WAITING.
SO-CALLED DANGEROUS.
GENTLEMEN'S AGREEMENT.
MARRIED, 2 KIDS.
CREW FILTH.

Produced by Craig Leon, Simon Rogers, Mark E. Smith
Artwork, Front: Pascal Le Gras, Back: Saffron

THE FALL

Stephen Hanley – bass guitar
Craig Scanlon – lead & rhythm guitar
Mark E. Smith – vocals & tapes
Simon Wolstencroft – drums & keyboard

Introducing
David Bush – keyboards & machines

With:
C. Leon, S. Rogers – keyboards
Cassell Webb – backing vocals

Produced by Craig Leon, Simon Rogers, Mark E. Smith
Artwork, front: Pascal Le Gras
Back: Saffron

Recorded at Air Studio, London and Glasgow, late 1991.

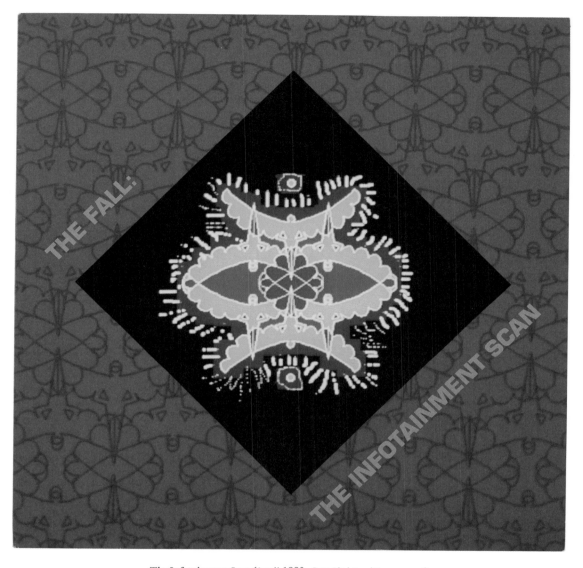

The Infotainment Scan (April 1993, Cog Sinister / Permanent)

SIDE 1
Lady Bird (Green Grass)
Lost In Music
Glam-Racket
I'm Going to Spain
It's a Curse

SIDE 2
Paranoia Man in Cheap Sh*t Room
Service
The League of Bald-Headed Men
A Past Gone Mad
Light / Fireworks

PERMANENT RECORDS

COG SINISTER

5 018524 050215

SIDE 1

1) **LADYBIRD (Green Grass)**   3.59
   (Scanlon/Smith/Hanley/Bush/Wolstencroft)
2) **LOST IN MUSIC**   3.49
   (Nile Rogers/Bernard Edwards)
3) **GLAM-RACKET**   3.12
   (Smith/Hanley/Scanlon)
4) **I'M GOING TO SPAIN**   3.27
   (S. Bent)
5) **IT'S A CURSE**   5.19
   (Smith/Scanlon)

SIDE 2

6) **PARANOIA MAN IN CHEAP SH*T ROOM**   4.27
   (Scanlon/Smith)
7) **SERVICE**   4.11
   (Smith/Scanlon/Hanley)
8) **THE LEAGUE OF BALD-HEADED MEN**   4.07
   (Smith/Hanley)
9) **A PAST GONE MAD**   4.19
   (Smith/Bush/Wolstencroft)
10) **LIGHT/FIREWORKS**   3.46
    (M. Smith)

PRODUCED BY: Rex Sargeant
Except: Tracks 2 & 10 – Mark E. Smith
Tracks 3 & 10 – Simon Rogers
Cover Art By Pascal Le Gras

ALL COMPOSITIONS: EMI Music Publishing Ltd
Except: Track 2 – Warner Chappell Music Ltd
Track 4 – Copyright Control
Track 10 – Copyright Control

© & ℗ Permanent Records 1993. Marketed & Distributed by Total Records via BMG

PRODUCED BY: Rex Sargeant
Except: Tracks 2 & 10 — Mark E. Smith
Tracks 3 & 12 — Simon Rogers
Cover Art By Pascal Le Gras

No line-up listed on original artwork

Recorded at Suite 16, Rochdale, late 1992 / early 1993.

Middle Class Revolt (May 1994, Cog Sinister / Permanent)

SIDE 1
15 Ways
The Reckoning
Behind The Counter
M5#1
Surmount All Obstacles
Middle Class Revolt!
You're Not Up To Much

SIDE 2
Symbol Of Mordgan
Hey! Student
Junk Man
The $500 Bottle Of Wine
City Dweller
War
Shut Up!

180

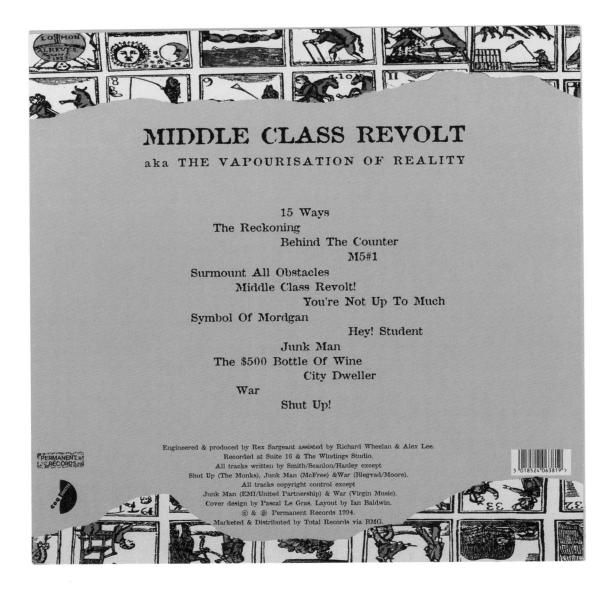

MIDDLE CLASS REVOLT
aka THE VAPOURISATION OF REALITY

15 Ways
The Reckoning
Behind The Counter
M5#1
Surmount All Obstacles
Middle Class Revolt!
You're Not Up To Much
Symbol Of Mordgan
Hey! Student
Junk Man
The $500 Bottle Of Wine
City Dweller
War
Shut Up!

Engineered & produced by Rex Sargeant assisted by Richard Wheelan & Alex Lee.
Recorded at Suite 16 & The Windings Studio.
All tracks written by Smith/Scanlon/Hanley except
Shut Up (The Monks), Junk Man (McFree) &War (Blegvad/Moore).
All tracks copyright control except
Junk Man (EMI/United Partnership) & War (Virgin Music).
Cover design by Pascal Le Gras. Layout by Ian Baldwin.
© & ℗ Permanent Records 1994.
Marketed & Distributed by Total Records via BMG.

PERMANENT RECORDS

5 018524 063819 >

Engineered & produced by Rex Sargeant
Cover design by Pascal Le Gras. Layout by Ian Baldwin.

Recorded at Suite 16, Rochdale and The Windings
Studio, Wrexham, late 1993 / early 1994.

No line-up listed on original artwork

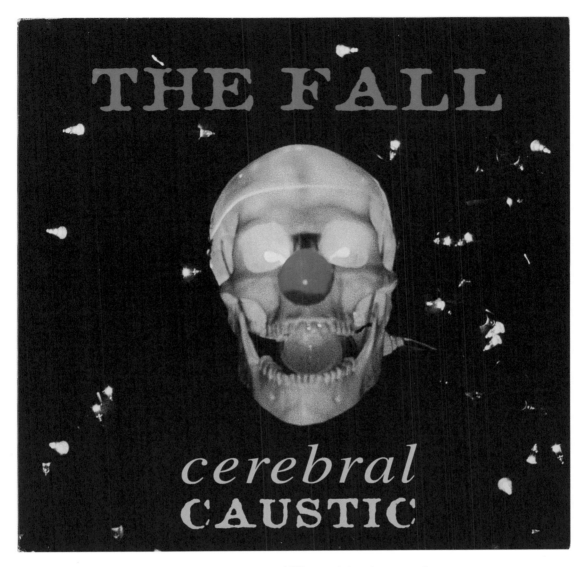

Cerebral Caustic (February 1995, Cog Sinister / Permanent)

SIDE A
The Joke
Don't Call Me Darling
Rainmaster
Feeling Numb
Pearl City
Life Just Bounces

SIDE B
I'm Not Satisfied
The Aphid
Bonkers In Phoenix
One Day
North West Fashion Show
Pine Leaves

PERMLP 30

Side A
The Joke (Lyrics :– Smith M.E. / Music :– Smith L.E.)
Don't Call Me Darling (Lyrics :– Smith M.E. / Music :– Scanlon C.)
Rainmaster (Lyrics :– Smith M.E. / Music :– Smith L.E.)
Feeling Numb (Lyrics :– Smith M.E. / Music :– Smith L.E.)
Pearl City (Lyrics :– Smith M.E. / Music :– Burns C. & Bennett M.)
Life Just Bounces (Lyrics :– Smith M.E. / Music :– Hanley S. & Scanlon C.)
Side B
I'm Not Satisfied (Lyrics :– Frank Zappa / Music :– Frank Zappa)
The Aphid (Lyrics :– Smith M.E. / Music :– Hanley S. & Scanlon C. & Wolstencroft S. & Smith L.E.)
Bonkers In Phoenix (Lyrics :– Smith M.E. / Music :– Smith L.E.)
One Day (Lyrics :– Smith M.E. / Music :– Bush D.)
North West Fashion Show (Lyrics :– Smith M.E. / Music :– Burns C.)
Pine Leaves (Lyrics :– Smith M.E. / Music :– Burns C. & Hanley S. & Scanlon C.)

Produced by M.E. Smith & M. Bennett. Backing vocals on track 5 by Lucy Rimmer. All songs SGO Music except track 5 SGO/Bucks Music & track 7 copyright control. Skull & Spike images by Pascal Le Gras. Photographs by Valerie Philips. Sleeve design & layout by Ian Baldwin.

Ⓒ & Ⓟ Permanent Records 1995.
Marketed and distributed by
Total Records via BMG.

5 018524 085019

Mark E Smith – vocals
Brix Smith – guitar, vocals
Craig Scanlon – guitar
Steve Hanley – bass
Simon Wolstencroft – drums
Dave Bush – keyboards
Karl Burns – drums, guitar, vocals
With:
Lucy Rimmer – vocals on Pearl City

Produced by M.E. Smith & M. Bennett
Skull & Spike images by Pascal Le Gras
Photographs by Valerie Philips
Sleeve design & layout by Ian Baldwin

Recorded in London, late 1994.

The Light User Syndrome (June 1996, Jet)

SIDE 1
D.I.Y. Meat
Das Vulture Ans Ein Nutter-Wain
He Pep!
Hostile
Stay Away (Old White Train)
Spinetrak
Interlude / Chilinism
Powder Keg

SIDE 2
Oleano
Cheetham Hill
The Coliseum
Last Chance To Turn Around
The Ballard of J. Drummer
Oxymoron
Secession Man

Mark E. Smith, vocals, tapes. Simon Wolstencroft, drums, programming. Brix Smith, guitar, vocals. Julie Nagle, keyboards, guitar. Stephen Hanley, bass guitar. Karl Burns, drums, vocals, guitar. Lucy Rimmer, vocals. Mike Bennett, vocals.

Production: Mike Bennett & Mark E. Smith. Engineer: Warren Bassett. Sleeve design: Phil Rogers. Photography: Pete Cronin.

Recorded at The Dairy, London, early 1996.

Levitate (September 1997, Artful)

SIDE 1
Ten Houses of Eve
Masquerade
Hurricane Edward
I'm a Mummy
The Quartet of Doc Shanley
Jap Kid
4 ½ Inch

SIDE 2
Spencer Must Die
Jungle Rock
Ol' Gang
Tragic Days
I Come and Stand At Your Door
Levitate
Everybody But Myself

produced by mark e smith

vocals keyboards ME SMITH
bass guitar S HANLEY
keyboards guitars programming arranging JULIA NAGLE
drums S WOLSTENCROFT
drums K BURNS
guitars ANDY HACKETT
guitars TOMMY CROOKS

photography tommy crooks
artwork pascal le gras
design venus

Recorded at West Heath Studios, London;
Beethoven Street Studios, London, and PWL Studios,
Manchester, mid-1997.

Cardinal R. Totale's Scrapbook: Torn Fragments of James, Machen and Lovecraft, Unpulped Among a Jumbled Trove of Songs by the Fall, Early and Also Late

> *...Smith and his mute companions seem to represent Medium and Spirit World both. Hideous figures dancing on the edge of vision, twisted ugly denizens of the Hobgoblin City, he celebrates them while he's warning against them, presents himself as informer against them and worst among them.*
>
> (Mark Sinker, *The Wire*, August 1986)

The crux pretty grasped, yet mostly misunderstood
Mark will sink us
('Mark'll Sink Us', B-side to 'There's a Ghost in My House' twelve-inch, 1988)

The title *The Years of Endurance: Freedom's Own Island* is reactionary puff, and much of Arthur Bryant's book is the same, sad to say, but one passage in it I love:

> *The capital of the area, now given over to the service of Mammon, was the old Jacobite town of Manchester, whose new population huddled together in damp, stinking cellars. Its port [...] was upstart Liverpool, home of the West Indian trade and its scandalous offspring, the slave trade. Farther south [...] was the Black Country – by 1790 a land of forges, collieries and canals with grimy trees and hedges. The traveller, venturing into this little-trodden, satanic region, saw rows of blackening hovels swarming with ragged children, and instead of church spires tall chimneys belching metallic vapours and at night lit by flames...*

The years are 1793–1802, that perilous moment when Napoleon was conquering everywhere except Britain, which stood alone and beleaguered, and the book was written in 1942, when history threatened to rhyme. A Tory and a sentimentalist for empire, Bryant wasn't capable of the complexities or intellectual sympathy of E. P. Thompson's colossal (and much more important) *The Making of the English Working Class*, yet where Thompson's book often flattens out the Industrial Revolution 1780–1832, this unexpected extract does somehow capture something of its sheer monstrous phantasmagoria, down to the most helplessly goblin-punk of details: 'At its southern extremity was

Birmingham […] where the head grew dizzy with the hammering of presses, the clatter of engines and the whirling of wheels. Here almost every man in the cobbled street stank of train oil, and many had red eyes and hair bleached green by the brass foundries.'

Right here, at the borderland between the grimy, deprived social real of the landscape and the inexplicable terrors that surge around and under and through it – this, as Richard Cook once wrote, is splendid Fall country.

> *I tell you, sir, that an awful being stalks through the streets, a being before whom the sunlight itself should blacken, and the summer air grow chill and dank.*
> (Arthur Machen, *The Terror*)

Here, as I encountered it in the mid-to-late 1980s, was a very different species of correspondence to Bryant's, between a Blakean vision of the hell pits of the emergent Birmingham–Liverpool landscape and the same landscape in the same region not quite 200 years later, when everything from industrialism to punk needed the prefix 'post-' dropped in front of it. Here was the sense that if you walked through a city in the right (meaning the wrong) way, you could once again find those fires and smokes and luridly lit skies, as spectral marks of a hidden continuity with everything that we have chosen no longer to see. And where Bryant had been ambushed into an unlikely aside, Mark E. Smith's project was a torrent of nothing but asides, the entire bulk of the work constantly breaking off from itself to react at some new item on the edge of sight. As in the compacted and interleaved sequence of ideas in 'Psykick Dancehall', the song that opens *Dragnet*: computer centre in shopping mall, with spectre on roof, 'its colours GLOWED on the roof' – this compression into one another of cyclic and mesmeric rock performance, and of DJing and radio and mediumism, and of occult tradition, and of actual factual city landscape. MES: 'Is there anybody there?' The Fall as their own audience: 'YEAH!' On the one hand: 'They have no records' (all this is out beyond the reach of official documentation). On the other: 'My vibrations will live on / […] / People will dance / To my waves!'[1]

This essay traces a route out of the nineteenth century deep into the trypophobias of Smith's own brain, via the horror paperbacks he devoured as a pilled-up teenager, hoovering up information from everywhere, to spark into those phrases that jump out at you and make you grin (if only as a defence against fright, sometimes). Alongside Poe, Dunsany, Blackwood – even Stevenson, Conan Doyle and Chesterton – three in particular seem to figure: M. R. James (1862–1936), Arthur Machen (1863–1947) and H. P. Lovecraft (1890–1937). It's about unwanted doors opened and even

1. Even the nubbin of reality that this song bubbles up from is off at the odder end of the quotidian: apparently a self-identified witch, Kay Carroll's mother had indeed set up a psychic centre in a former dance studio located in a mall in Prestwich city centre (Simon Ford, *Hip Priest: The Story of Mark E. Smith and the Fall*, Quartet Books, 2002).

more unwanted people glimpsed capering within – and in the end, it's about Smith's relationship with these people, which is very much not that of any of these three writers, but rather an outgrowth of his own politics and perverse sense of humour ... if these can even be separated.

Sound-wise, *Dragnet*, only the second Fall LP, is a way station for a new line-up that is not yet confident in their own best sound. But the band's lo-fi production-layering experiments also very much begin here – and while the lists and images and personnel lists on the cover of *Live at the Witch Trials* were carefully typed and squared off, *Dragnet*'s sleeve is a torn-edge collage of fragments, a scrapbook of wilful shortcuts and slipshod cuttings, photos and half-quotes, investigation and mimicry and possession and critique. It's an LP beset with investigators and inspectors (with two openly crime-flavoured songs reversing the optics: 'Flat of Angles', about the chase and the hideaway, and 'Put Away', about the prison stretch). Smith's hand-writing and pronunciation are puzzles to be solved, journeys to embark on, clues to decode or reassemble – plus there's a photo of Mark himself, hair long, coat long, peering through the slatted door of some decaying functional building at who-the-hell-knows-what ...

There's spiteful chatter about rock routines and values ('Printhead', 'Choc-Stock'), and a rare foray into political commentary ('Muzorewi's Daughter', complete with a joke about cannibalism and a misspelled name, Smith's orthography as problematic as his sense of humour here). The title and concept of the 'Dice Man', meanwhile, is stolen from modern genre fiction, and Luke Rhinehart's 1971 novel.[2] Bluntly stated, the throw of a dice is the project's entire approach to brand-building and line-up stability, and to Smith's songwriting technique, where chance-set happenstance can abruptly interrupt at any point to determine all of the journey's future turns.

And then there's a sequence of a very different mettle: 'Psykick Dancehall' and 'A Figure Walks' opening side one, and 'Before the Moon Falls' and 'Your Heart Out' closing it. And alone on side two but hugely dominating it, 'Spectre vs. Rector': another inspector, plus a fug of distortions announcing some of Smith's precursors. 'M. R. James be born be born!' it begins. 'Yog Sothoth rape me, lord!' Or is it: 'M. R. James, *vivant vivant*! Yog Sothoth, Ray Milland'?[3] The first version is a darkly sexual invocation; the second, bizarrely Frenchified but probably correct, names the key actor in the Roger Corman-directed movie of Poe's short story *The Premature Burial* (1962). At one point in this film, the Milland character screams at his wife to take away the flowers she's just picked: 'You must promise never to bring those sickly funeral

2. Relevant to my themes (though not known to Smith in 1978) is that Rhinehart is the *nom de guerre* of a New York-born sometime professor of literature, the elusively prankish George Cockcroft.

3. The Ray Milland reading is that of the diligent and learned interpreters at the Annotated Fall website. This footnote marks the essay's debt to them (as, for example, the upcoming gloss on flowers as funeral decoration) and also reaffirms how central shifting ambiguity and mutation are to the Fall's work, where the settled text is anathema. http://annotatedfall. doomby.com.

decorations[4] into the house!' Anyway, there they are seen plainly: revered ghost writer James, ghastly Lovecraftian god, pulp-movie director Corman, thriller writer Peter Van Greenaway – and a lurch into evocative gibberish (if it is gibberish): 'Van Greenway! R. Corman! Sludge Hai Choi, Choi Choi Son!'

You could probably write a book dissecting just this song. Mark Fisher calls it 'the moment when the Fall really began to sound like themselves'. I don't entirely agree with this – in a way this essay is an impasto of Mark in 2006 citing me in 1986 to make a point, and me in 2019 disagreeing with both of us – but it's absolutely a vortex of significant forces whirling together. And James and Lovecraft are two key names in all this, and both are certainly all over this sequence and (perhaps) lurking behind much of the rest of the LP. Performing 'A Figure Walks' at London's Lyceum in 1979, Smith dedicated the song to Lovecraft, but in 1986 I mainly heard 'Casting the Runes', the M. R. James story in which the malevolent warlock Karswell sends his victim a woodcut of Bewick's, roughly torn out of the page: one which shows a moonlit road and a man walking along it, followed by an awful demon creature. Under it were written the lines out of the 'Ancient Mariner' (which I suppose the cut illustrates) about one who, having once looked round, 'walks on, / And turns no more his head, / Because he knows a frightful fiend / Doth close behind him tread.'

Approved in passing in this story as the kind of modern academic who understands how to talk about magic, James Frazier is also lurking somewhere within these lines: 'The old golden savages killed their philosophers / Thought brought the drought about / SOMETHING FOLLOWED ME OUT!', and he's probably also present in 'Your Heart Out'. 'Before the Moon Falls' invokes Blake: 'I must create a new regime / Or live by another man's' for 'I must create a system or be enslaved by another man's.'

Fisher's and my disagreements are easily explained. Exegesis with Smith is a veritable plague of rabbit burrows, with every momentary landing surface becoming another hole, and holes generating holes generating holes... And always there's the urgency of that rough, slouching figure looming up behind us – and of (arm hairs now erect) the figure's own detective techniques possessing our own and turning our self-sense back into who or what we always already were...

'The terror induced by forests and darkness,' said a mocking voice from somewhere over her head, 'was called by the Ancients, Panic fear, or the fear of the great god Pan. It is interesting to observe that modern progress has not altogether succeeded in banishing it from ill-disciplined minds.'
(Dorothy L. Sayers, *Murder Must Advertise*)

4. The corresponding lines in the song run as follows: 'And this hero was a strange man / "Those flowers, take them away!" he said. "They're only funeral decorations."'

In *The Wire* in 1986, I was excitedly filtering the Fall entirely through
M. R. James and describing Smith's language as a 'political discourse framed
in terms of witchcraft and demons [... and] the war that the Church and
triumphant Reason waged on a scatter of wise-women and midwives,
lingering practitioners of folk-knowledge [...] a huge struggle for political and
intellectual dominance, as first Catholics and later Puritans invoked a rise in
devil-worship to rubbish their opponents'. James, I suggested, 'transformed
the folk-memory into a bitter class-struggle between established science
and law, and the erratic, vengeful, relentless undead world of wronged spirits,
cheated of property or voice, or the simple dignity of being believed in'.
As an 'enlightened Victorian intellectual, [James] dreamed of the spectre of
the once crushed and newly rising working classes as a brutish and irrational
Monster from the Id'. Smith, I continued, 'is working class, and is torn between
adopting this image of himself and fighting violently against it. It's left him
with a loathing of liberal humanist condescension.'

Responding in 2006, in a three-part essay, 'Memorex for the Krakens:
The Fall's Pulp Modernism' (reprinted elsewhere in this collection), Mark
Fisher — who also felt very much trapped and oppressed by liberal humanist
condescension — expanded on these passages, and pushed back a little against
mine. No one like Smith, he noted, exists in a James story. This autodidact
modern northern urban ventriloquist of all the perspectives in a story — its
agent-inspector, its victim-rector, its scientist-magician-commentator,
its hero, its beast from another dimension, the stage-player so entertainingly
able to grasp and mock all these various layers as they interacted — would
in James be a 'monstrosity which would be punished for the sheer hubris of
existing'.

As background to his supernatural intrusions, James will sometimes
elaborate learnedly on historical wrongs to be marked or avenged: a poacher
or a witch unjustly hanged, innocents dispossessed, children preyed on and
murdered. At other times, a historical tyranny extends into the present,
disturbed and active again: 'Count Magnus' is the totemic example (complete
with low-key tentacle). His narrators — and most of his victims — are from
the educated reading classes: scholars, academics, professionals, the upper-
middle classes. Almost everyone else is a walk-on device of plot exposition and
mood variation, a figure of fun, their speech salted with mispronunciations,
malapropisms and clichéd or misremembered quotations. Fisher quotes
the (often tin-eared himself) horror anthologist S. T. Joshi here, to excavate
the intellectual confusions of these characters, as a proven mark of the malice
James had towards them.

But if the reader is generally enjoined to smile indulgently at their
speech patterns, these characters nevertheless have a heightened awareness
of the ancient and the supernatural. They spot the stalking ghosts the hero
has missed, they know the local bogey lore. As the central figures barrel past
caution towards their comeuppance, a story's joke is often that those most

like us, assumedly less funny, are about to pratfall (or much, much worse). And James is certainly poking fun their way too, with an ear far better attuned to their fuller foolishness.

> *At all stages of history the sacred animals were mummified, so that consecrated bulls, cats, ibises, crocodiles and the like might return some day to greater glory. But only in the decadence did they mix the human and the animal in the same mummy.*
> (H.P. Lovecraft, 'Imprisoned with the Pharaohs')

> *Like, the real occult's in the pubs of the East End. In the stinking boats of the Thames, not in Egypt. It's on your doorstep mate. Strikes a chord with me.*
> (Mark E. Smith on Arthur Machen, *Independent*, 22 February 2017)

James was provost of King's College, Cambridge, and then of Eton College, as well as vice-chancellor of the University of Cambridge. By all accounts a kind-hearted man in person, his public politics were exactly as this CV indicates. His friend, the novelist A.F. Benson, cheerfully described him as a reactionary. The modern working class – as Fisher or Smith or you or I might understand it – is indeed largely unimaginable in James-world.

Fisher's poster child for the animus that Joshi discerns is one Paxton, the 'amateur archaeologist' in 'A Warning to the Curious': an 'unemployed clerk and therefore by no means working class' whose 'grisly fate was as much a consequence of "getting above himself" as it was of his disturbing sacred Anglo-Saxon artefacts'. Isolated and self-taught, Paxton ignores the usual danger signs and is punished all too horribly for this, the narrator too late to help this hapless and tragic figure – whom the reader surely finds entirely sympathetic. James is less condescending here than canonically uneasy at the idea that perhaps a similar menace lurks for all such scholars, excited as we are by old unopened rooms and tomes and tombs.[5] As a punishable crime, curiosity is, to James, primarily a mark of persons like himself – and, as his readers, we are all in peril of 'getting above' ourselves. And the recognition is why we read on.

Fisher's angry point is that this Victorian class politics of knowledge is still with us: these 'antagonisms were not archaisms', as he puts it. Indeed, but it seems off to identify Smith (or Fisher himself) with the mild-mannered clerk Paxton, over (for example) the more interestingly hostile and capable Karswell of 'Casting the Runes'. In this story, magic, to the Establishment academics, is merely superstition, and of anthropological interest at most – until they

---

5. We can go further, since this tale is full of between-the-lines hints of a deeper link between the hapless amateur archaeologist and the tomb's lethal guardian, the residue of one William Ager. Both obsessive young men without family or even friends, Paxton and Ager are extremely alike as characters, the latter somehow luring the former in, from long before the idea of an excavation had quite occurred. When Paxton encounters that final terrible grinning face, it may be his own.

meet a fellow who practises it, and he sets his demon on them. Karswell is
excluded from their circle because he hungers for the wrong kind of knowledge
– or, more accurately, because he knows the wrong things the wrong way.
And to defeat him they must acknowledge that his necromantic science is
entirely real, helping themselves to its spells and murderous ends, entirely
upending their high opinions of their own rectitude. The warlock is smashed
for destructive hubris – but not before he gets some of his revenge in first.
And all because they had fun with his bad prose: '...we made game of it
together. It was written in no style at all – split infinitives, and every sort of
thing that makes an Oxford gorge rise.'

Lovecraft admired James greatly, sending him an essay[6] in 1927 that made
this clear. Sadly, the feeling wasn't mutual. Lovecraft's ear – what rhythm or
style there is to *his* prose – did not impress James: '...a disquisition of nearly
40 pages of double columns on Supernatural Horror in Literature by one
H.P. Lovecraft, whose style is of the most offensive. He uses the word cosmic
about 24 times.' Reactions like this against comfortable taste and moderate
perspective led to Fisher's K-Punk project in the first place, and his desire to
bring to his beloved pulp – horror in particular – the honour and intellectual
respect he believed it deserved within the intellectual milieu he aspired to,
and to free modernism from this particular condescension trap, that as a value
it could *only* descend into the world from above.

> *There are sacraments of evil as well as of good about us, and we live and move to
> my belief in an unknown world, a place where there are caves and shadows and
> dwellers in twilight. It is possible that man may sometimes return on the track of
> evolution, and it is my belief that an awful lore is not yet dead.*
> (Arthur Machen, *The Red Hand*)

Classics of the form, collected over four anthologies between 1904 and
1925, James's thirty-odd ghost stories were conceived as a distraction and
a relaxation, a Christmas entertainment for himself and his pupils. 'Canon
Alberic's Scrapbook', the first tale in the first collection, also invokes his
favourite narrative technique, the story fashioned as a scrapbook – this
Victorian parlour pastime here translated back into the late-seventeenth
century, that era of extreme religious upheaval and the (alleged) decline
of magic. A James story is a narrative jigsawed together from fragments of
information and fragments of disconnected perspective. Deeply knowledgeable
about manuscripts and incunabula and their historical context, James was an
excellent mimic of historical writing styles. His details are exact, scholarly
titbits to enrich the setting, but also to open grim portals at the back of the
known ('The Treasure of Abbott Thomas' begins with a page-long thicket
of medieval Latin, before James relents and gives the English). Documents

6. http://www.hplovecraft.com/writings/texts/
essays/shil.aspx.

from old court cases are often part of the quilt-work, a firm dialectic of potential justice: the notorious Judge Jeffreys makes an appearance in 'Martin's Close', trolling the defendant as outrageously as he would later in the court transcripts of the Bloody Assizes, and openly egging the murdered spirit of a young girl into henpecking her killer towards his execution. But outcomes are often less clearly deserved: the innocently inquisitive tourist who awakes 'Count Magnus' is pursued across four countries, for no reason just or fair. The story's opening is typical James: 'By what means the papers out of which I have made a connected story came into my hands is the last point which the reader will learn from these pages.'

H.P. Lovecraft

Lovecraft, who adored this quasi-scholarly element in James, simply had none of the requisite knowledge, and had to fashion an equivalent from his own far more vituperative disgust of class and race, the cursed book *The Necronomicon* – the work of Abdul Alhazred, the 'mad Arab' – and so on. Prejudice and panic ran deep in the American author, far deeper than in his precursors. His cosmos is a vortex of chaos and terror, vast and dark and loveless, and crawling with forces and beings utterly beyond our ken. Round the corner, there they are, skin bubbling, tendrils writhing, at once lethally dangerous and pitilessly indifferent to us, threatening us from undiscovered islands ('The Call of Cthulhu') and the Antarctic ('At the Mountains of Madness'), from caverns beneath ('The Horror of Red Hook'), the depths of space above ('The Whisperer in Darkness'), from bloodlines within ('Jermyn', 'The Descendant') – and generally from dimensions visible only to adepts and the insane. To set up its reveal – far out to sea a hideous elder god is coming for all of us – most of the early part of 'The Call of Cthulhu' deals with the made-up archaeology of lost religions and sects and cryptic symbols – and, by implication, the modern world's technological and civilisational hubris of denial.

Rewriting 'Count Magnus' as the impressively overwrought 'The Hound', Lovecraft adopts its random vengeful fury as his metaphysics, in which our scientific complacency is but thinly walled off from an omnipresent howling tumult, merely postponing the worst. Insofar as they fail to engage with such realities, all of human art, history and philosophy are but a puny, meaningless blip, and all humanity is nothing; to glimpse the tumult – or just think of it – is to go mad.

Hence, everything that's been catnip to visual artists since: unearthly colours ('The Colour Out of Space'), non-Euclidean geometries ('The Dreams in the Witch House') and creatures that are impossible to apprehend ('The Haunter of the Dark'). The weight Lovecraft placed on a lost-for-words discourse of the overwhelmed (amorphous, blasphemous, indescribable, loathsome, unnameable) left a rich imaginative space wide open for films and comics, from Jack Kirby's art for Marvel to *Rick and Morty*, and, of course, from Smith's sister Suzanne's unforgettable artwork for *Grotesque* to the run of Claus Castenskiold covers, from *Perverted by Language* through to 'Living Too Late'.

But as Lovecraft's most-used word list turns concrete — dank, foetid, squamous, fungoid, noisome, gibbering — it's the quickest trip into the Fall's sound world ...

> *'With no language but a cry' was the thought that flashed into my mind. Hideous it was beyond anything I had heard or have heard since, but I could read no emotion in it, and doubted if I could read any intelligence [...] Of course there was nothing to be seen: but I was convinced that if I waited, the thing would pass me again on its aimless, endless beat and I could not bear the notion of a third repetition.*
>
> (M. R. James, 'A Neighbour's Landmark')

> *Rock'n'roll isn't even music really. It's a mistreating of instruments to get feelings over.*
>
> (Mark E. Smith, interview with the *NME*'s Graham Lock, 7 April 1979)

They say music should be fun, like reading a story of love
But I want to read a horror story
(The Fall, 'Dice Man', 1979)

Before high modernism was even an idea, James was working scrapbook-style — and Lovecraft does too, and so does Smith, his folders of compacted, cryptic leads forever tumbling open before us. Smith's declared favourite Arthur Machen also stitches his materials together — though his stories, long and short, often feel more like unrelated slender volumes bound together by metaphysical error. As narratives they're rarely well formed overall — his sense of an ending was sometimes ludicrously poor — but section by section they can be deeply evocative, effectively conjuring lyrical reverie as well as unease. In *The Three Imposters; or, The Transmutations*, for example, the very long chapters have such titles as 'Novel of the Black Seal', 'Novel of the Iron Maid', 'Novel of the White Powder', 'The Recluse of Bayswater', 'Strange Occurrence in Clerkenwell' and 'History of the Young Man with Spectacles'. The connections we're asked to make between them are as oblique as the transitions between them are abrupt, more like the chord changes in a Philip Glass opera than anything on a Fall LP. Haunting his gorgeous Welsh hills, the mountains and forests and rivers of his birth, are the ruins of the Roman Empire and the ghosts of many peoples from both then and since. And then suddenly we're in the smog-wreathed urban maze that Machen lived and worked in.

Tales within tales: characters outline where they're from and where they're at, including the horrors they've seen, the louche scenes they've guessed at, the drink and drugs they've necked. He's by far the *friskiest* of the three writers here, drug-savvy and sex-adjacent (James is bachelor-virginal in comparison, and Lovecraft obsessed only with lineage and breeding). His work gave James a 'nasty aftertaste: rather a foul mind I think, but clever as they make 'em', but Aubrey Beardsley illustrated *The Great God Pan*, and Oscar Wilde called it '*un succès fou*'. He ran sometimes, as a sceptical Paxton-type, with the Hermetic Order of the Golden Dawn, greatly disliking the Order's Karswell figure, Aleister Crowley, while Crowley in turn encouraged his disciples to read Machen's work. Welsh by birth, rarely escaping the lower reaches of London's book world, Machen was a translator – and sadly, out of financial need, sometimes a hack. James and Lovecraft distinguish their monsters from their victims. Machen's often seem to fit both roles at once, and too many – perhaps this ease of slippage requires it – are little more than ciphers.

And yet Machen's characters also very clearly fuck. His Britain comes in nested layers, historical and sensual, the most ancient ever-present within (or right next to) the most up-to-date, and the heart of the disquiet is that it's just so easy to suddenly slip from one mode to another, from the quotidian to the bizarre to the perversely erotic. And, meanwhile, all around us, visible or otherwise, are these *others* – the faerie folk, the old ones, a malign and sometimes stunted '*early*' people, offshoots of a pre-human line still active, some sibilant and lizardy, some utterly alluring, sex as the connection nowhere overtly described yet everywhere implied.

The Great God Pan weaves a labyrinth of hints and glimpses around a single dreadful encounter with a demigod. As a patient who is impregnated and sent mad, Mary Vaughan's world and body are opened up to horned evil by brain surgery that is off the books and off the page, though it's unclear if physical contact even takes place, and Vaughan functions largely as an off-screen device, with no agency and little discernible character. As the offspring of this union, Helen is also glimpsed only at a distance, the topic of heated rumour and amazed gossip – including a string of suicides in her wicked, dangerous wake – until a final ghastly denouement:

> *I was then privileged or accursed, I dare not say which, to see that which was on the bed, lying there black like ink, transformed before my eyes. The skin, and the flesh, and the muscles, and the bones, and the firm structure of the human body that I had thought to be unchangeable, and permanent as adamant, began to melt and dissolve* [...] *I saw the form waver from sex to sex, dividing itself from itself, and then again reunited. Then I saw the body descend to the beasts whence it ascended, and that which was on the heights go down to the depths, even to the abyss of all being. The principle of life, which makes organism, always remained, while the outward form changed* [...] *I watched, and at last I saw nothing but a substance as jelly. Then the ladder was ascended again* [... here the MS is illegible ...] *for one instance I saw a Form, shaped in dimness before me, which I will not farther describe. But the symbol of this form may be seen in ancient sculptures, and in paintings which survived beneath the lava, too foul to be spoken of* [...] *as a horrible and unspeakable shape, neither man nor beast, was changed into human form, there came finally death.*

I stood here, and saw before me the unutterable, the unthinkable gulf that yawns profound between two worlds, the world of matter and the world of spirit.
(Arthur Machen, *The Great God Pan*)

Mostly it's just shit that I thought was good at the time – stuff like 'Jeremy Paxman is a monster' – well, maybe not that bad, but phrases I've put down when I've been up at night.
(Mark E. Smith, *Renegade*, Penguin / Viking, p. 64)

When I set off into this essay, I honestly felt it would be fairly easy to identify a dozen or so songs that pushed further out into the terrain that 'Spectre vs. Rector' long ago broached: 'a torn-edge collage of fragments, a scrapbook of wilful shortcuts and slipshod cuttings, photos and half-quotes, investigation and mimicry and possession and critique'. I was wrong. First, because substitute Victorian-modern Manchester for London, and from its clammy opening notes, *Live at the Witch Trials* already reminds me strongly of Machen – so this journey didn't even start when *Dragnet* invoked its precursors out loud. Second, because what we face after the mid-1980s isn't a dwindling of clues and glimpses to follow, but an ever-more chaotic profusion. The historical papers in your library are being digitised and supplanted by the videos and CDs in your home-entertainment system – at any second everything can channel-flick or device-click mutate into everything else. And we're transforming too, as listeners and viewers, and as zoned-out out-zoned subjects of, and objects in, songs and programmes and every other kind of document.

Like a Glass chord change gone pixelate granular, any given Fall song after the mid-1980s will be a flicker of sources and backdrops, full of futures and pasts as TV channels to switch between, scenes real and unreal – a glade, a deserted car park, a line of back-to-backs, a travel motel – that are dense with figures felt and differentiated, even if sometimes not at all easily identified, and traces of these figures, scribbled notes, recorded snippets, half-glimpsed and half-heard blurred images or distorted sounds, rumours, jokes, awkward mini-playlets acted out by the band, excerpts everywhere of semi-decontextualised commentary (sometimes by Smith, often by others).

James marshals his evidence as a court record or historian might: unresolved wrongs erupt back into the present, and half-knowing they have not really earned their comfort, his educated readers shiver. Lovecraft gestures at science and learning, but only as a species of lunacy: to describe the forces that shape the cosmos is merely to accelerate the ruin they will bring us. In Machen, too, strange ways of writing and speaking suggest we share a world with things we barely grasp – and with people we comprehend, but dimly at best. Mixing among us so intimately, these people *are* us. Just a horny breath away, if you glance down that suburban side street …

Yet if we draw back in pity at the writhingly drawn-out denouement of *The Great God Pan*, the truer tale of Suzanne Smith's cover art is that we don't. Machen's capering figures are offstage mysteries, and his narrators are merely interchangeable. When we gaze on those tendrilled, contorting, glow-colour figures prancing on *Grotesque*, we half-think, half-pleased, 'That's how others are seeing *us*!' These three writers that MES so admires have all worked a species of blasted outsider into their respective story-tropes, yet none imagined or depicted this species with the rich variation and detail and shifting, fractured perspective that Smith and his team achieve, nor with the half-derisive, half-sympathetic identification.

This pullulating mass in Fall world is an individuated multiplicity, a jellied prole-mass that manifests as many spectres walking, seen yet unseen, in a multiform world already made up only of us: alcoholics as elves, pensioners as cackling demons, our nightmares as our neighbours. A quote, a joke, a peculiar but naggingly well-wrought line in the murk of a song starts morphing into derision — except who's manifesting here, and how? Who's satirising who — and how deliberately badly? Is this fibbing, or description, or warning, or is the slantwise greeting of the slouching phantom here at last?

So perhaps in the end the only true way in and through is simply a precession of some of the bits and moments that illuminate — or is that *ex-luminate*? The word 'endarken' should definitely exist. What follows is my own folder of residues, unruly in mimicked presentation and almost helplessly arbitrary in structure — not quite a random walk but definitely a very slipshod psychogeography.

'2nd Dark Age' (*Fiery Jack* EP, 1979): Smith concludes this bleakly impressionistic litany of changes (as wrought by Thatcher's accession to power) by identifying its singer as 'Roman Totale XVII', the bastard descendant of Charles I and the 'Great God Pan'. A familiar Smith cognomen round this date, Totale is *not* a cipher, but vivid and particular, and (thanks to the backstory of his family romance) a hard-to-parse narrator. 'Leave the Capitol' (*Slates*, 1981): in a song that mostly sequences snapshots of the London of long ago, Roman or Victorian, here's the same GGP two years later on. Commentary seems to want this to be a contemptuous satire, but to me it better recalls a section of Machen's *The Secret Glory* (1900), in which a schoolboy pub-crawls through a hidden Soho with his girl, and loves it.[7] The oddly mumbled cry that ends the song is instantly (and inexplicably Scottishly) disavowed: 'I laughed at the Great God, Pan! / (I didnae, I didnae!)'

To repeat myself: there's no quick way through *any* Fall song, still less one that repeatedly alternates 'Leave the Capitol!' with the sarcastic counter-cry 'You know in your brain!' In 1959, Jack Kirby created a cartoon short for Marvel, 'I Laughed at the Great God, Pan!' in which a gallery-goer mocks a painting of this same semi-divinity and of the belief system behind it.[8]

7. *The Secret Glory* is mostly a very *un*supernatural book that mocks the ethos of the English public school by locating romance and glamour anywhere but there. A hurried Asian quest for the Holy Grail in the later chapters is no match for its treks through the Soho fleshpots.

8. *Tales to Astonish*, Vol. 6, Marvel Comics, 1959.

This dapper young hipster extols rationalism — until his moustache is made to fall off. So *much* for what you know in your brain. Then cut from the O/G forest deity's green Welsh glades to '[B]ut the Monty hides in curtains'. The 'M' in M. R. James stands for Montague, and this is a near-subliminal call-back to his 'Stories I Have Tried to Write':

> *The man [. . .] sitting in his study one evening [who] was startled by a slight sound,*
> *turned hastily, and saw a certain dead face looking out from between the window*
> *curtains: a dead face, but with living eyes. He made a dash at the curtains and tore*
> *them apart. A pasteboard mask fell to the floor. But there*
> *was no one there, and the eyes of the mask were but eye-holes.*

'Garden' (*Perverted by Language*, 1983): another blizzard of palimpsest-snippets pulling in every direction. Listen on headphones and there's a moment a couple of minutes into its clean deep-toms chime when the percussion, right out at the edges of the stereo mix, makes you think that someone's moving around in your flat. Of course, it's entirely part of the recorded sound-form, yet it somehow also bumps at you from outside, especially if you're off-guard. Its surge of images flash by: a god in a garden (maybe Eden, maybe Gethsemane); a second god very much not in a garden; various monstrous household pets and try-hard on-screen no-marks: 'He's the Young Generation dancing troupe / Try'na perform country and western [. . .] He had a Kingdom of Evil book under a German history book.' The song repeats to a close with the phrase 'Jew on a motorbike' — recalling rock god Dylan-as-Jesus for some,[9] and his rising again post-accident to redeem rock-and-roll mythology, or else wreck it. Except judging by when the murk increases most, the key section is just before this, when a letter from one-time sitcom star Reg Varney (ostensibly about wiring up explosives to ward off unwanted phone calls) breaks up into a shout of alarm or delight: 'He's on the second floor / Up the brown baize lift shaft / He's here / He's here at last / I saw him / I swear . . .'

Dylan had routed his return through country and western — *Nashville Skyline, Self-Portrait, New Morning* — and country and western has valence in Fall mythology also: as the source of the bright, sprightly drive of both *Grotesque* (1980) and *Slates* (1981), and of the singles leading up to them (including 'Fiery Jack'). There's a triple compression pun here: C&W out to C'n'N and back to CnC. 'Country and northern' was the chosen term for the variant of country and western delivered by this well-loved, all-male incarnation of the band, while 'cash-and-carry' is a general synecdoche for a degraded landscape and lifestyle. *Grotesque* combines family portrait (complete with high-colour mutant animal-insect pets) with a withering prediction of a regional militancy that is always doomed to failure ('The North will rise

9. The Annotated Fall website breaks 'Garden' down in extreme detail, element by element, arguing that its real topic is polysemy. http://annotatedfall.doomby. com/pages/the-annotated-lyrics/garden.html.

again / Not in ten thousand years'), but lean into this mordantly negative class-war sketch and the surface clouds into full-on impenetrable lo-fi fog, with breaks in transmission as aural blizzard-weather, like the thunderstorms in a Gothic novel or the lightning suddenly overhead now.

Container drivers, out-of-town retail parks, commercial estates and call centres, how London post-banking Big Bang will reshape the rest of the nation – in 1981, *this* is the actual secret 1990s inferno bearing down on us from the future. And as the figures chasing me have pushed me into this critical mind-fugue state, I note first that 'Garden' is very much a desprightlified country and northern; and, second (and suddenly), that the line about the 'lift' and the 'second floor' is another foreshadowing: of a scene (in 1981, not yet written) from Thomas Harris's *The Silence of the Lambs* (book 1988, film 1991), just after Hannibal Lecter turns a prison guard into a skinned, sculpted angel. Here's Hannibal talking to Clarice Starling, about the even-worse-than-him killer Jame Gumb: 'That peculiar goatish odor is trans-3-methyl-2-hexenoic acid. Remember it, it's the smell of schizophrenia.' And here's a line from the bluesy suburban quotidian of 'Married, 2 Kids' (*Code: Selfish*, 1992): 'peculiar goatish smell'. And here's a phrase from my friend Tom Wootton's online essay on the Fall and Machen,[10] taken from the latter's semi-autobiographical *The Hill of Dreams*: 'the rank fume of the goat'. The goat-godling seems to get everywhere, so Tom treats its *musk* as a transition into a unifier. Let's squeeze this even further. The word 'satire' has two more or less unrelated roots: a Latin one meaning 'medley' (from *lanx satura*, a 'dish filled with different kinds of fruit'), and a Greek one meaning, yes, a faun-like woodland companion of Bacchus, the god of wine, half-man, half-beast – a *satyr*. Wild fragments and panic fear, code-shift and manic leer: whatever it mainly is today, 'satire' wasn't always just a boss-class hazing to police political and cultural norms. As witness the cloven-footed dancer-predator piping us on, beckoning to us from side streets as we hurry past, always waiting for us already in the studio lift.[11]

The Wonderful and Frightening World of The Fall (1984): by now Brix's presence – bringing with it subliminal pop-harmony choruses – is beginning to change the feel of some of the masquerade. A bad future is also on the move ahead of us – the truth is always in the trash, and yet here's the ersatz simply eating it, a dynamic gradually blooming into Blair's Britain fifteen years later, all finance jargon and uncanny-valley entertainment-industry pod-doubles. But for the time being, most god-zone disputes emerge from zoned-out TV-remote channel-clicking. In 'Lay of the Land', the laugh-out-loud diffidence of the band slow-chanting 'Ley! Ley! Ley!' is a mumbled am-dram replay of some protesting hippies in the BBC's 1979 series *Quatermass*. In 'Bug Day', Smith as

10. https://theidiotandthedog.wordpress.com/2008/04/29/arthur-machen-and-the-fall. For Wootton, Smith himself is one of the key innovators in this same lineage of horror, not least for so firmly shifting its geographies.

11. According to (yes, that one) Paul Hanley's *Leave the Capital: A History of Manchester Music in 13 Recordings*, the brown baize can be found in Pluto (!) Studios in Manchester.

a droning wildlife documentary scientist predicts quasi-classical apocalypse
– from 'midges hovered over the heather' to 'Minoa said EEK!' – as the track
clicks and chitters against the tinkly-bonk intrusions and near-stops of its
chromatic 3D quasi-fugue.

I Am Kurious Oranj (1988): this bicentennial ballet is half named for a
1960s Swedish soft-porn movie, and possibly tells of the Glorious Revolution
of 1688, when England cleverly hired in a very Dutch monarch. Much of the
music is written by Brix, but the third song, 'Dog Is Life/Jerusalem', is half
stand-up stunt about terrible pets and half Hubert Parry's patriotic 1916 hymn
tune. After uncanny sound-space shifts, plastic-meaty drumming and a churn
of Stockhausen noises, the well-known Edwardian tune is artlessly played
on bass, while Smith (more artlessly still) semi-sings William Blake's 1808
introduction to his poem about John Milton (1608–74), that 'true Poet and of
the Devil's party without knowing it'. A subterranean passage through your rec
room back to the palpable spiritual battle of the English Revolution – except
which of the Two Great Gods-in-combat are we siding with (remembering
that Roman Totale XVII is the bastard son of Charles I as well as Pan...)?
Anyway, here's how it ends, with some nobody's unself-aware whine about a
banana-skin accident they want big-state recompense for: 'It was the fault of
the government [...] I was expecting a one-million-quid handout.'

As above, so below – for the essay's sake only, we must now speed up
and dwell less, as we hurtle through all the nows and thens, futures and pasts
as replica figurines in a cartoon wrestling-and-reformation tournament,
cheesy doubles everywhere, 'flicker' and 'mutation' our watchwords, relentless
abuse of shape – rhythm as much as image – our last best weapon. With
better attuned/detuned eyes and ears, we can probably trace a similar path
through the flashing fog of almost *any* Fall sequence – though similitude is
the one thing we can no longer trust, and there are many other ways through.

'Bremen Nacht' (*The Frenz Experiment*, 1988): MES as schoolboy,
imitating a Nazi, as per war-obsessed 1960s English comic *The Victor*,
quasi-biographically describing the bizarre sickness that assaulted him once
on tour, a micro-riff and bad German denouncing some barely specified
wartime crime – Axis or Allied, who knows? 'Mollusc in Tyrol' (*Seminal
Live*, 1989; *The Twenty-Seven Points*, 1995): low-spoken somethings against
amazing burbled Radiophonic space-invader torrent, the mid-1990s version
nothing but high fly-buzz and distant biscuit-tin synth-drum instrumental.
Shift-Work (1991): exceptional double meaning here – have a bleeding guess![12]
'Rainmaster' (*Cerebral Caustic*, 1995) flickers between the magickal and
the glossily denatured, as familiars and witchcraft punctuate a documentary

12. Here's a brief but telling Fall word list,
Lovecraft-style, drawn only from 1990s titles
and after: 'scan', 'syndrome', 'are you are', 'real new Fall',
'reformation', 'solvent', 'ersatz', 'sublingual',
'new facts emerge'.

about Florida and other jungles – and Belgium and Basingstoke and the phrase 'TV man's tarantula'. 'Unutterable' (*The Unutterable*, 2000): Smith blurts out the title like some ridiculous drunk, then chops German ad-speak into Lovecraftian ramble: 'I'm dripping post-seizure [...] floated brain intolerable...' (Except Smith's *faux*-broken and crabbed deployments of the languages he inhabits are deftness itself when compared with Lovecraft's; as a creation, Smith's crazed, doomed investigators, intoxicated and ridiculous, are something to point out and chuckle at – even as knowing mirrors of his own personal symptoms.) 'Crop-Dust' (*Are You Are Missing Winner*, 2001) uses a sample of 'I Just Sing' by the Troggs on a tight loop, excavating – as sampling often can – the astonishing throwaway beauty of a forgotten deep cut. 'Xyralothep' (*The Real New Fall LP (Formerly 'Country on the Click')*, 2003): a quasi-Egyptian, Lovecraftian god helps MES rewrite Max Ehrmann's 1920s poem (and 1970s chart hit) 'Desiderata':[13] 'Avoid aggressive men.' 'Systematic Abuse' (*Reformation Post TLC*, 2007): the shape and time signature of its bass-fuzz riff are strangely hard to parse, at once perfectly repetitive and somehow asymmetrical, and so the narrator concludes, of every inconsequential anecdote, 'It is the same!' 'O! ZZTRRK Man' (*New Facts Emerge*, 2017, shortly before Smith's death): a single phrase here shape-shifts from 'Hold your breath!' to 'Old George Best!' to 'Oh, judgement!' – the signal example of the puns and word games that so ruthlessly smear any sense you think you've grasped anywhere, right down to Smith's murkily recorded old-man mumble.

And let's switch back one last time to something glimpsed in passing, important precisely because it's *not always there*. Certain versions of 'Crop-Dust' contain the phrase 'skyscraper-tall German soldiers'. Tom Wootton connects this with 'The Bowmen', probably Machen's best-known tale, in which Agincourt bowmen were seen standing beside their beleaguered descendants in the trenches, to firm them up against the Teutonic foe. This was the source of the war-fever rumour of the Angels of Mons, and Machen – stupefied by the virality-as-fake-truth of the fiction he knew he'd authored – corresponded irritably but uselessly for months with those who insisted its author must have 'heard it from a friend of a friend', as they were certain they had. (Caveat: in just the kind of sardonic switch Smith likes to pull, the spectral figures in the song seem to be German rather than English.) So he set his post-war book *The Terror* in what he termed 'The Censorship', the wartime period during which any local news story that might dismay or demoralise was suppressed. Once more a sequence of interwoven short 'novels', his various off-page hints that the entire animal world has turned on mankind have, in this fictional structure, simply vanished from rational public discussion. But the rumours continue to percolate uneasily at folk level.

13. 'Nyarlathotep' is a Lovecraft prose poem.
A version of 'Desiderata' was a hit for Les Crane in 1971,
while another appears as 'Spock Thoughts' on 1968's
Two Sides of Leonard Nimoy.

Welcome to the glitchy modern folk-news labyrinth: 'Everyone hears the hum at 3 a.m.'

> *The most merciful thing in the world* […] *is* [*man's inability*] *to correlate all* [*of his mind's*] *contents* […*But the sciences one day, some say it is already upon us, will eventually*] *open up such terrifying vistas of reality* […] *that we will either go mad from the revelation or flee into blissful sleep, peace and safety of another New Dark Age.*
>
> (Mark E. Smith's deft edit of the opening section of H. P. Lovecraft's 'The Call of Cthulhu', recorded as 'The Horror in Clay' on *The Post Nearly Man* (1988))

> [*Mark*] *told me he believed there were only seven original people in the world, and that everyone else was a slate of one of them. Mark was absolutely one of the seven.*
>
> (Brix Smith, *NME* Awards show, 2018)

One combatant in the blog conversations that originally arose round the K-Punk project was the philosopher Graham Harman, who is associated with the speculative realism movement. He went all in on the pulp redemption attempt. For Harman, the virtue of all Lovecraft's overripe language is (first) that it refuses any metaphysical or other walls between the inner mind and the outside world, between reason and madness – humans are irrevocably out in the cosmos and in among the chaos; and (second) that it falls so lamentably, so repetitively, so garbledly short of any convincing grand theory of the cosmos. To encompass reality *should* be to fail to grasp it, so that, far from damning him, Lovecraft's qualities as a writer make him *superior* to Proust or Joyce.[14]

Mark Fisher is happy to place the great Fall triptych of 1980–2 – *Grotesque, Slates* and *Hex Enduction Hour* – in a high-literary pantheon alongside Joyce or Wyndham Lewis, citing its 'ambition, its linguistic inventiveness and its formal innovation'. With Eliot's working-class mimicry in *The Waste Land* in mind, Fisher hears Smith's Mancunian accent as the refusal and perhaps the reversal of any impersonation by high-art modernism of the rest of creation. And 'pulp modernism' is handy enough as a high-speed summary of the techniques and devices to hand – everything I'm calling scrapbook and channel-flick, plus all the deliberately obvious games with masks, self-consciously terrible acting and other *Verfremdungseffekte*. But where Harman merely inverts the established hierarchies (Lovecraft trumps Proust), Fisher's move perhaps uneasily reflects the belated, reactive hierarchies and interpellations in his own head – his own embranglements and fears, his own intellectual ambitions and political contradictions, his sense of being forever trapped between his working-class identity and potential lasting achievement.

If Smith was anxious at all about his achievements, that anxiety was primarily directed at his fellow band members and creative rivals for authority

14. Graham Harman, *Weird Realism: Lovecraft and Philosophy*, Zero Books, 2012.

and role; and, secondly (with amused irritability after the early years), at the clued-out uselessness of most rock-press misprisions of the nature of his work. Plainly, Smith *didn't* acknowledge these highs and lows of his work as forming any such approvable shape or trajectory, still less his so-called Imperial Phase as some kind of higher artistic–intellectual breakthrough compared to his later work. The class issues that Fisher identifies in the world of intellectual production of course remain an endemic nuisance – and he's always good on where turmoil and conflict live and seemingly go unseen – but how much purchase does he have on Smith's attitudes (which are very much not Fisher's) to himself as either diceman-craftsman [15] or reader – of pulp, of romantic poetry, of high modernism, of anything else? In which anything absorbed (which seems to have meant almost everything) was far more of an artisan's tool or lens than a status symbol: the Troggs, the BBC's *Farming Today* show, Pan horror paperbacks, Nietzsche on Napoleon – literally whatever he had just grabbed and watched or heard or processed. As we may recall, Blake's 'I must create a system or be enslaved by another man's' then continues: 'I will not reason and compare: my business is to create.'

And just like Helen Vaughan at the end of *The Great God Pan*, hideously writhing through her own bodily history, all these figures in all these landscapes, Smith is *every one of them*, a quick-change artist on a smog-bound stage, casting his shadow to amuse and to deceive, while amusing and deceiving to inform and disenchant. All the quotes and clues and hints and jokes and traces thrown in to fuck *you* up: *Eat the grenade!* Once upon a time, M.R. James imagined a readership like himself, imagined a refined 'we' he could top-down tease with the perils fashioned by its ('our') own class narrowness. Maybe to be little learned is to be better in tune with all the darker wisdoms from before the dawn of time, to be cognisant of the demons, patient yet ugly under *everyone's* beds? In Lovecraft's fiction this class inversion of learning is so over-amplified that it's fully transformed – like the great dark gods, the teeming lower classes and breeds are themselves a manifestation *only* of this malevolent chaos. They don't dream against it because they exist within it, they know it, and nervelessly worship and work for it. But as Smith imagines his listeners – this wide and knobbly-weird and ill-favoured and eldritch-varied crew as seen horribly capering across the footlights to horrible Fall music in horrible venues all over the horrible world – he doesn't recognise a 'they' and he doesn't exactly acknowledge a division between 'us' and 'them'. As with Machen, the links are also the distinctions, the intimate borders and boundaries endlessly penetrated and crossed, until no simple gradient between just and unjust outcomes applies. In the end, his class solidarity is the wide-ranging alertness of his mocking eye and memory, and his politically misshapen ear, catching at the phrases that caught at him and casting them back at us changed and changing, his attitude endlessly unreadable.

15. Divination through throwing dice or turning cards is also a type of entrail-reading. A modern-day witch trial puts the best journalists in the dock.

FREE "Distort to find the grotto of thought"

THE FALL

the 'yeh' ning pandered

Riverside Programme

HEY! LUCIANI

PART 3

Tuesday-Saturday 5th-20th December 1986

Hideous Noise Group Write 'St' Pope Biog

Ohio, Sweden: A group has written a character portrayal of a Pope J.P. One — rumoured to become a 'SAINT' which will be presented at the 'Riverside Studios' near some river where 'Rule Brittania' was written. The Vatican commented "We have been waiting for a sign for 7 years".

Today 7.5103
Years ago "I could have been a journalist. I could've been head of Rueters" Albino Luciani 1978.

"It's nonsense" claimed their manager from a St John's Wood face lift surgery. "I was promoting big time heavy metal/Top 20 groups when they concocted this scheme in Hull, almost 497 miles away from Albert Side Studios, Croydon".

'Wild Bill Hicock Relative traced in U.K.

Boston, Lincs — a descendant of the legendary Wild West Hero, Wild Bill Cody, has been traced in Boston, Lincs, England. Known locally as 'Big Dave' Cody he bears a striking resemblence

STOP PRESS
BORMANN FOUND
CHIL
VICTORY FOR ROBSON
AGAINST FIST 1 — 0

Above: Riverside Theatre programme, December 1986.

Pages 206–16: It has long been rumoured that the script for *Hey! Luciani: The Times, Life and Codex of Albino Luciani*, which ran for two weeks at London's Riverside

Theatre in 1988, was scrawled on beer mats and delivered in a carrier bag. These preparatory notes and script extracts for the play suggest that this may not be entirely accurate, although the script was clearly rapidly changing during rehearsals.

For 2 minutes. The Chicago

. Newspaper Board

GELLI: For all it's
solid ~~white~~ Democrat
appearance... - 20·11·86.

Surrey Comet

MARCH: Yeah, you have agreements
with these guys —

GELLI: To
write

(Gelli is
(deleting in
MARCINKUS's
~~obvious~~ NERVE

what theyre old, Big and
Bold! — So his Newness is
dross?

MARCINKUS: Yeah. How—?
GELLI — You wouldn't have ~~bought~~
~~me~~ asked me here. A visit to the
dead centre of Rome perhaps?
MARCINKUS: The envelope, quickly
exit, Gelli laughing, M. flapping

light swings to M.E.S.

DDS.
cont.
② MES:

w cassette
of piano
weedy

~~IT WAS~~

THE NIGHT AFTER 'FLUKE NIGHT',
~~STA~~ENDED UP IN A
CONVENTION ACCOMMODATION
SORTA PLACE, OWNED BY A
BETTING SHOP CHAIN, NOT
MUCH SEEN OUT OF MIDDLE ENG-
LAND, HERES WHY.
AFTER I'd bluffed in with Photocopy of
Express American See OVER

SISTER VINCENZA ?
SINCE U HAVE NOT BEEN WITH
US LONG I WILL GIVE YOU
THE benefit.

of watching me with the Holy See —
SISTER: Do you know him? They say he is provincial!

S. VINC: KNOW HIM? HE LOOKS LIKE WALTER WINCHELL
At thirty two he went thru' a windshield
He is a man of the soil, yes, but
he is frugal and wise. I was at a today
with him today, never something before done by a
Holy Father. The church of the poor.

SISTER: Pardon me Holy Mother but this is the modern
age — the church must follow computer
trails. I hear.

SISTER
VINC: Dear Sister In your teachings you never encountered
the camel + needle?

ACT. 5.

stage. L-R: mes Adj 3rd desk /POPE/
S. HANCEY. / MASKED MAN
Unmasked!

tape: ...STATE COG. ANALYST.

BATZHDAD STATE COG ANALYST

BATZHDAD, STATE COG ANALYST

typing (Msk. Mmn) "

POPE (S.H. Typing-
eyes?   hiding.

M. 6 - S - || cass SDS orig? ||

P.A...
LOUD | M.MN: Y'KNOW A FRIEND OF MY
BROTHER IN LAWS' WORKED INNA
'REGENERATION' STATION, TELEX
DEPARTMENT I THINK. ANYWAY, THEY
IT WAS TOO NEAR
SAID SOMETHING, So They ran away
Exiled, In + Yellow Car.
The rear view mirror became A
credit Card /
All it reflected were the eyes
of those inside /

STEVE HANLEY: (MIDDL.)

.DISAPPEARED.   SNATCHED. BACK.

THE NOON LOUNGE

HELD A FIESTA

FOR NORMALS   music
                               up
I'VE BEEN WAITING.

ALWAYS AROUND,

A LONG TIME COMING

BY MY FORM SHEET

IT'S TIME, TO

DO SOME REPLACING.   CITY
                          SCENERY
—— MUSIC (Alcoholed.   . DISAPPEARS
                          BLACK.

molester Elect on the front of the Daily Roma - i ask you. a----Cody,back home would've sent the cops round

Who is this man - Jimmy Stewart ?

     C.VILLOT: ?HExxxx

               '- he instructed me that he wished to visit certain none-gratisimo parts of

               Rome. He is just bourgeois,my friend.

                        ----

os theme builds , darknesss opening to

                    split stage

 stge right; light on JP I

   HE TALKS TO HIMSELF: stge left desk & radio announcer

        JP I: I FEEL MY BONES HOLD KNOWLEDGE THAT WILL BRING MY ENDING.

              AMBROSE BIERCE DEFINED RELIGION AS A GOODLY TREE,IN which all foul birds of the

              air have made their nessts.-- ah this servixxxxx new role makes me morbid-my eyes

Meanwhile,lights real   are like 2 television screens,continual open,but in the morning-I'm living again;

(bright up,2 reveal

 SISTER Vincenz,Villot

    behind him,a mike is   (VATICAN Radio taped noises,announcer

placed by technician   now mostly revealed

        JP I: But I find therapy in the people-my energies should,and will,go to the expressio

              of my inner thoughts.Fear apparent is mostly spent.

Tells To walk

MUSIC climaxes then dead low but still hearable, we half hear the begixxxxx their conversation;   **5**

Bishop MARCINKUS:

         Some guys come on ,y xxx I KNOW YEA YEAH,YKNOW,IN CHICAGO ROB EVERYBODY then

         skip to some mythical state down over the border-I'M NOT GOING,CEE VEE...

    CDNL Villoti;   'During my objective absolutions and reflections,it occurred to me that ALL

       MEN COMMIT EVIL ,In the most pleasant and idyllic atmospheres - our faith

       acknowledges this - you, Bishop are confirming this in your refusal to travel.

       Here RESIDENT,

       Others here Excitedley monitor in fear the recent change here.they seest.(To quote

       ,'....THE SPIRAL CIRCLES, NARROWING FASTER..

       Which HE APPROACHING SEEMS TO WIND' !

   B   MARCINKS:

         U ,yea..the Kraut stuff.......(MUCH LOUDer;   huh..ha .. huh then it

         hahUH. " THAT absurdest drollest beast " THAT CREASES ME....

         bm laughs at own joke,he is a gruff man,but with a hi IQ,Occasionally his

       GhettoMIDXXXXMIXXXXXXXX manner pokes through)

           WEST U.S.

       Anyway

       '..BUT HE CALLED ME FROM A visiti..ey yuh know u - conference..

   CDNL VILL: SI SI

     B.M.:   I WAS having with Calvi.Had the whole thing nicely wrapped up in my affectionate palm.

       WHEN A CALL COMES THRU: ' His Holiness requests a breakdown of the distribution of the

       alms for the poor of Venezia, Rome - I ask you ! DRAGGED back, my friend,from

       the fine distillation of two months work with that crook bastard - To pore over the

       wine allowance for some Fiat rejects,who suddenly are caught holy ,glimpsing this lean sheep

rovgh Proj:

purple.

shimming
Ghostly.

yellow

dh
act y
rovgentin
inside?

(AS SUDAZ GOES INTO HYPNOS STATE,THE FOUR OFFICRS STARE
PUZZLEMENT ASTONISHMENT   AMUSEMENT
SUD_ AZ CHânts:
                    8 (THIS WILL BE DOUBLE TRACKED RECORDING

                TAPED)   HUREN ZEE HUREN ZE
                       ABORETUM   CHEET NEE   TZ LA
          GEE   SCRIVNRS CLARK   SCRIVENERS
              CORSAIRS CREW ARE IN SANT MENARD
     STRANDED   KNOTTING CLAWS STAND OVER IT ONLY ZUFFALIG
     AND SHA LASKO INC. CAN RESCUE KHALKALIS DIGNITY
              OR GLEEFULLY SPREAD ALL INNARDS WEST
                       BAHZHDAD   STATE_COG ANALYST
                       BAHZHDAD   STATE COG ANALYST
     (SPOTLIGHT PROJ BRIEF   ALL STARE IN DISBELIEF   DARK

                              STAGE END OF ACT 2
                       ----

sic as at beginning turning into soft version of gb grenadiers.

riverside studios

Crisp Road Hammersmith W6 9RL   Administration 01-741 2251   Box Office 01-748 3354

part of act three;   after live group perf and after tape music excerpt:

          jacky :8stage middle)   "THE PEOPLE BEHIND LASHKO
                                                   DOMIS INC. KINDLY CON
                                                   TINUE XMX TO CONFIDE
                                                   THEIR WORSE MEMOIRS TO
                                                   US.

     J.O'M: hello, my name is gail howard." I am not what I Seem.:
          Through glass pitchers holding coffee stains.,walk to

          work for Mx squat Mr Biege pants.Cannot recall why or

          why I just don't just exit,resign as I enter the house
          the aisle down,cut through-the guest house that doubles
           as coffe shop, off lino up carpet
             fellow workers turn away in envy and hatred

             I JUST DON't get this.
             This nightmare unfolds in five unit snatches
             The part time work bug,O HOW DID I catch it?

             At a loss to know if awake or dreaming.
             When I try to recall, (GOES BLANK)

     Resumes:

             observe tragic clouids, my ears are ringing
             The earth is made up of Terylene patches,
             My name is   ...Gil Howarth ?

                    music.
                    Mgr. Michelle

HEY! LUCIANI.

Act One.

Narrator: Europe 1870 — the first Vatican Council meets and guarantees an Infallible Pope. The Spain Gang is in disarray and tough-guy France is recovering from a fight it could not finish. Meanwhile, in Alsace-Lorraine state, F. Neechkah, in bandages turks and prussians — tough — encourages by the manipulating British gang, to play a bigger part in the forth coming shoot-out scenario.

Music: DR. FAUSTUS

Young Luciani appears and dances to bzki type musak.

Young Luciani: (hums) How can they even stand by the holy tree — opus de i opus de i, I am Luciani, the devil get ready!

Old Luciani: At the back of the mind of this priest about to be ordained, was the feeling of a chapters end. I was getting lost for some reason, now I look back, as I knew the route as well as I know the back of my hand.

Young Luciani: (a black look crosses his face) Opus de i.....devil get ready, it is over, I am ov...when I am a priest, new ordained, the people will exclaim.....

Narrator: Rome, Rome, seven, eight, Rome, Rome......

John Paul I: A pretence to be calmed, but at the back of my head, there was a goal...the poor people would exclaim rejoice...would i change, but I was never like them........

Sister Vincenza, Villot, Marcinkus and Buzzonetti join the Pope they shout good things and wave. They all look like good people.

Gelli enters and is calling for Antognozzi.

Gelli: Antognozzi?

Antog.: Yes?

Gelli: What news regarding the election? I relish our allies distorted **. Antog.?
An open ended transmission via here — don't fob me off, Antog — big Dave over the sea, his compatriot Bishop gorilla in there with our Villot...

Antog.: Mendoza would like a conversation regarding your wares, and a favour will supply you with full information if requested on the Jew Terrorists, who have, he claims, just passed Vivaldia, south bound.

Gelli: Senile idiot, I suppose it has to come to this, the

1

Gelli: Ah, the Chicago Paper Board, you like their sworded democratic ways?

Marcinkus: Exactly, that just the way I feel. To have an agreement with these guys...

Gelli: To write what they are told!

Marcinkus: Yea!

Gelli: To write it big and bold!

Marcinkus: Yea!

Gelli: So how go things with my friend?

Marcinkus: Not so good!

Gelli: Not so good for you I think, not so good. Tell me, when did his newness go away?

Marcinkus: He went away......Hey! Wait a minute your not supposed to know about that.

Gelli: You would not have arranged this meeting otherwise, my jungle book keeper.

Marcinkus: What I'm interested in is the telex.

Gelli: Tell me first - his holiness is on a visit to the dead centre of the world?

Marcinkus: Perhaps. Perhaps not. But I'll tell you something one day the steel glove will be on the other hand. (Gelli shows the telex) Ah! Well at last, it sure looks interesting.

looked more closely.

MONOLOGUE

?: (Speaking on the telephone) O.K, yea, O.K, yea, tomorrow, mm, our thought are with you too, yea, right.

JPI: Number seven - out out. Oh fat one - satan has clipped your legs and strung your eyelashes to a glibbering neon tube of all the numbers the world knows - we could can his dormant flesh and export it to Wall Street, and monitor the index of Vatican Luncheonmeat! Wheres Sister Vencenza with the bloody wine? Fifteen? Fifteen ex - s.s, tut, tut. It's not easy being a pope. Twenty - ha! This new world crazy, telexes us an invoice for his mediocre womanising! Out, Out.

(Sister Vencenza enters with a bottle of wine)

Sister Veñcenza: Your refreshment your holiness, your second bottle, if your remember.

JPI: My father would spit that amount before noon, dear Sister. A man's nerves often require subtle inclinations for them to tolerate their similars. (Sister Vencenza exits) Yes-you, You, You and you - transaction gangsters. Your fleet ~~don't seem to come in handy when the intercom pick up your odour~~ of, fiats will come in handy when you are being trailed by Interpol Agents. - out, out. ?? ????? What next pay confession booths? The last twelve! This is always the most difficult. Only with my senses can I justify these removals. Their aura is confidense, but their eyes and mouths communicate only stimulated egos. ?????? Their affection in my presence reduces my spirits to an aura like I'm an open gift box, of continued assurance - a trifle penance necessary to leave them time to think of nothing. revealed only in their treatment of servants, waiter and suchlike, in asides and a chilling abruptness - that is conscious merely of its position on a ladder thats not quite it though.

Swindlers of odd pennies given in faith

Sister Vencenza: John Paul - go to bed now please. They say sleep provide all the angels cannot proscribe.

Mark E. Smith[1]

Yer got sixty hour weeks, and stone toilet back-gardens
Peter Cook's jokes, bad dope, check shirts, lousy groups
Point their finger at America
Down pokey quaint streets in Cambridge
Cycles our distant spastic heritage
It's a gay red, roundhead, army career, grim head
If we were smart we'd emigrate.
(The Fall, 'English Scheme', 1980)

> *The Fall have always been at arm's length. That's our mentality.*
> (Mark E. Smith, 1980)

As with Joyce, Beuys, and Wyndham Lewis, the historians will be arguing about Mark E. (for Edward) Smith until the kingdom comes. Twentieth-century culture has been kept alive by the irritants which work their way under its skin. In this much, Wilde's late-Victorian aphorism, 'To be great, one must be misunderstood,' required a new century to prove its accuracy. Mark E. Smith, who could so easily be the subject of a myriad Sunday supplement profiles, has remained a shadowy and mistrusted figure, silhouetted on the banks of the cultural mainstream. As our times appear to demand art-terrorist outsiders, Smith has called the era's bluff by refusing easy routes to fashionable and commercially lucrative acceptance. Whilst Damien Hirst prepares to suspend his Turner Prize in a vat of formaldehyde, Mark E. Smith – unknown to many – continues to ply his trade as an independent musician, philosopher, historian, writer, wit and fly-in-the-ointment.

Smith formed the group, the Fall (after the Camus novel), in Manchester in 1977. At the time, he was working in Manchester Docks as a customs clerk. This was a time when the metropolitan impetus of punk rock was being challenged by the provinces. The deliquescing anarchy of the Sex Pistols and the Clash was giving way to the studied neurosis of Joy Division and Cabaret Voltaire. But the Fall had no place – nor wanted one – in either camp. From their inception, Smith's Fall were bloody-minded outsiders, possessing an extraordinary ability to get up noses. At a time when post-punk fashionablilty was about to disgrace itself with the saccharine posturing of New Romanticism, the Fall looked like a cross between a class outing from *Please Sir!* and a crew of chagrined pipe-fitters on their afternoon off.

1. This piece, first published in *Frieze*, no. 6, 1992, is an inversion of 'Wyndham Lewis' by Stuart Bertolotti-Bailey (reprinted elsewhere in this volume). 'A small alteration of the past / Can turn time into space'

In 1980, pop music was reinventing itself as a kaleidoscope of carefully stylised factions; the Fall, immovable in their determination to remain aloof from the posturing of their peers, quickly earned not only incomprehension but also hostility. In their early performances, they brought the volatility of a bad night in a Wakefield working men's club to a scene which believed itself both to be self-contained and self-policed. The rhetoric of the Fall was similar to suddenly finding oneself in a slanging match with a vituperative Mancunian lorry-driver. For this invective, the Fall have never been forgiven. Challenged with the notion that the Fall drew their menace from the twilight of punk rock, Smith replied with a dismissive sniff, 'Punk? Hate that stuff. I wouldn't have it in the 'ouse!' Like Public Image Ltd's *Metal Box*, the Fall's debut LP, *Live at the Witch Trials*, was regarded as the death rattle of the 1970s. This was music that seemed to deal with personal and political dissatisfaction in a manner which was both sinister and confrontational. By 1981, Public Image resembled a self-parodic cabaret turn, fit only for the chicken-in-the-basket circuit. The Fall, on the other hand, had made their sense of alienation a vital part of their art, laying the foundations for a creative process which has seen them through fifteen LPs in as many years.

For Mark E. Smith, even irrelevance could be put to work for the Fall. As a teenager, he would ride around Manchester on the top deck of a bus, shouting random words in a pointed manner at bewildered passers-by. 'Leper', 'penguin' or 'grandmother!', when delivered with the correct mixture of urgency and forethought, could obtain an effect that bordered on the sinister.

It was only a short step, aesthetically, from confusing Mancunian pedestrians with ordinary language to offending the music cognoscenti by challenging their self-satisfaction. *Live at the Witch Trials* was jarring and disjointed, making a virtue of its northern bloody-mindedness: 'We are the Fall! / Northern white crap that talks back / We are not black; tall / No boxes for us / Do not fuck us...'

Already, Smith's campaign bore marked similarities to the *Blast* phase of Wyndham Lewis and the Vorticist assault on inter-war Bloomsbury. Lewis was a Renaissance man without a culture vital enough to support the fulfilment of his talents. Similarly, Smith is locked in a position of trench warfare, blasting and bombardiering against a fashion-driven society which is indurate to all attitudes save its own conservative 'non-conformity'. Thus, Smith is cast (again like Lewis) as a cat among pigeons, stalking the effete by saying the unspeakable. Interviewed in 1979, he said: 'Nuking Russia might not be a bad idea as far as the bleedin' world is concerned. They've plunged a lot of people into miserable lives. You've only got to be in East Germany to see it. It's a horrible way to live. It's like Middlesbrough.' Again, in 1985: 'Live Aid? I smell a lot of Victorian bloody do-gooding about the whole thing. There are people in Hulme [Manchester] who are half-starved, so why not send the aid to them? Never in a million years. And any country that can be invaded by the Italians must be a load of crap. Am I right?'

While Smith's polemic continues to affront every notion of political correctness, his audience recognise that his contrariness is merely a facet of a far more complex, and engaging, world vision. The ability to provoke and doubt, simultaneously, has often been cited as being fundamental to great art. Smith himself went some way to acknowledging this in 1988: 'Whenever I say anything, I often think that the opposite is true as well. Sometimes I think the truth is too fucking obvious for people to take. The possibilities are endless and people don't like that. They go for the average every time. Well, that doesn't interest me in the slightest.'

From the very beginning, the Fall has been Mark E. Smith's medium for expressing his unique world view; everything outside the band is meat for his stew. Within the chaos of the Fall, and within the oblique, humorous code of Smith's writing, there are precise patterns and a finely focused lucidity. He assembles his lyrics in such a manner that found language, narrative, slang, double-talk, trigger phrases and rapid juxtapositions are combined to create a discourse which describes as it commentates. The style is not artless, as it may look, but the product of careful design.

'It's just precog,' says Smith. 'You write things down and you don't know what they mean but you know they're true and they come true later. It's not prophecy as such. It makes me laugh actually. I see things happening and I think: "Oh, that reminds me of something." Turns out it's something I wrote five years ago. I wrote a song called "Zagreb Daylight" two years ago. We were playing in Zagreb and I could feel this horrible, murderous shit in the air. I had a feeling that yobs were going to rule the earth. I'm half one myself, you see. Anyway, I wrote this thing about a man in a shop with a dwarf behind the counter. It didn't go down well at all. If it came out a month from now, people would say it's topical.'

Like Wyndham Lewis, Mark E. Smith will suggest the existence of a conspiracy behind most manifestations of modern culture. In songs like 'Oswald Defence Lawyer', 'Kicker Conspiracy', 'Bug Day', 'The War Against Intelligence', 'Rowche Rumble' and 'Riddler!', Smith appears to endorse what Lewis meant by 'the immense false-bottom underlying every seemingly solid surface'. Interviewed in 1990, Smith stated: 'It's natural to gripe at things like British Telecom. One time I was using the phone a lot and I dialled a number, and I could hear people munching sandwiches and talking about my last phone call. I actually rang the operator and said, "Look. I'm trying to dial a fucking number here and I can't get through because your people are talking about my phone calls. Have you got a bloody licence to do this?" And she slammed the phone down on me!'

If the Fall are both Smith's vision of the world and his means of describing it, then the strange and frightening world of the Fall is peopled with grotesque characters whom Smith has invented. These would include Joe Totale, J. Temperance, Wireless Enthusiast, Fiery Jack, the Man Whose Head Expanded, Hip Priest, Man with Chip, Carry Bag Man and Slang King. One gets the impression that Smith's livid imagination was incubating this cast since before the Fall began. In many ways, his writing for the Fall has served to fill in the biographies of these characters; at the same time, Smith will write pseudonymously under their names. On the sleeve of 1980's *Totale's Turns*, R. Totale XVIII pens a note entitled 'Call Yourselves Bloody Professionals?' and concludes with the comment: 'This is probably the most accurate document of the Fall ever released, even though they'll have a hard time convincing their mams and dads about that, ha ha.' Interestingly enough, the remains of R. Totale's ancestor are described elsewhere as being found buried on a Welsh hillside, complete with instructions to unleash the content of certain tapes upon the world.

When asked to clarify this assessment of these characters, Smith cautiously sips his beer before replying: 'Man with Chip still going strong on the chat show. Cheap TV stance, yeah. Oprah Winfrey. Heh! Heh! Magnus fucking Pyke!'

'We've got repetition in our music and we're never gonna lose it,' Smith announced in 1978. While critics have yet to agree on whether the Fall, musically, are a din or a sublime symphony, the roots of the band's mesmeric intensity lie in the practice of repetition. In the most compelling Fall songs, the group merely provide an open structure through which Smith roams like a suspicious caretaker, flashing his torch from one empty dark room to another. This is best illustrated in 1988's 'Dog Is Life/Jerusalem', a lyric which featured the unique songwriting credit of 'William Blake/Mark E. Smith'. As the song approaches a narrative passage, the music is pared down to an unflinching pulse, over which Smith declaims: 'I was walking down the street when I tripped up on a discarded banana skin / And on the way down I caught the side of my head on a protruding brick, chip / It was the government's fault / I was very let down with the Budget / I was expecting a one-million-quid handout / I was very disappointed / It was the government's fault.'

As Smith explains, the idea of the Fall has always been to write intelligent lyrics over a raw, basic beat. 'That's never changed really. One thing we always get is, "This is their most commercial album for ages." In fact, the LPs have become less and less commercial over the years, and I'm quite proud of that. The problem with that is, people get this idea that we're determined not to do well. Which isn't the case at all. So we get Top-30 singles, and they won't even consider us for *Top of the Pops*. It's the last thing they want. I think there's a fear of the Fall in that respect. If people heard us, they'd find us entertaining and stimulating. Intelligence is actively discouraged these days, though, isn't it?'

Initially, the received idea of the Fall's audience was that of pale, spotty, adolescent males – bedroom misfits and trainspotters who wore anoraks with elasticated cuffs and lived off white-bread sandwiches. The obscurity of the Fall appeared to demand supporters who were socially dysfunctional – the weird cousins of Clash fans. In time, however, the Fall have gained a massive

European following which covers all social groups, from art-world fashion victims to pot-bellied, middle-aged rockers.

'Fall audiences have always been a bit weird,' says Smith. 'Well, not weird actually. I think they're the salt of the earth. I get letters from kids in Wales. Their lives have been transformed by the Fall. I suppose if you're on the dole in Wales, there's nowt else to do, unless you're out burgling.

'These guys in Wakefield, miners and all that, they've all grown up with wives and kids, and they've been with us since 1978. They don't buy records any more but they're still into the Fall. It means a lot to me. They read interviews I've done and write me postcards saying, "Reel 'em in, cock – the lads in the Wakefield Pit." Actually, we've always caught the individuals. In Germany, we played this gig, and the oldest man in the world was there. He must have been about ninety. Had grey hair down to his arse. He looked like God, with a Fall LP under his arm.

'It always annoys me when I hear other bands going on about how they're not a student group like the Fall. Student group? You must be fucking joking! I don't mean to sound prejudiced, but if you go to university, you're a bit daft anyway. I've nothing against students, mind. We play student places quite a lot. You walk into the disco, and there's all these kids on the dance floor jigging around to Lynyrd Skynyrd records. When *Slates* [1981] came out, we lost our student audience overnight. I was fucking glad about that.

'I feel a bit sorry for kids these days. They're obsessed with animals and all that. That's quite nice, I suppose. I've got two cats myself. But they're putting the frighteners on kids these days. Giving them anxieties they don't need. I saw something yesterday. It was horrible. These kids in tears about elephants. I blame the fucking teachers.'

But, despite their position as a 'difficult' group already at odds with shifting musical fashions, the Fall's Luddite tendencies have brought them into the focus of serious debate about contemporary art. 'Some of our stuff is art and some of it isn't,' Smith shrugs. 'We get it and we lose it. I like that, as it happens. I think a lot of my writing is art, but I'm a bit shy about it and that's why it's not printed. I couldn't be so precious to force it on the public. I've seen too many rock bands go out and pretend they're art. You get classed with them. I've always been careful to keep away from all that.

'I'd like to be considered as an artist. But I don't want to get into David Byrne territory. I'm not knocking the guy, but he was never any good to begin with. They go for him in a big way out in America. He's not an artist like John Waters is an artist. I suppose Waters is a bit like me really: he takes trash, puts it together with what he thinks and does it very well. But, basically, my attitude to life is to live. It's more important to be a man than an artist. I don't believe in the artist syndrome. I think I stimulate people's brains by saying what I think. Always have done. But, when we tour America, we get people coming up to us saying, "If only you could be a bit more like Talking Heads." Well, we always had better backdrops than Talking Heads.'

Mark E. Smith's writing anticipates and rejects academic criticism. Also, he has famously avoided offering analyses of either his records or his collaborative projects in theatre and dance. Of his play *Hey! Luciani* (1986), Smith says, concisely: 'It's like a cross between *The Prisoner* and Shakespeare. There's even bits that rhyme and stuff.' The more ambitious *I Am Curious, Orange* (1986), a ballet with Michael Clark dealing with the ascendancy of William of Orange to the British throne, was summarised by Smith as: 'The English get pissed off with their king, kick him out and get some Dutch bloke in.' As a historian, Mark E. Smith possesses the self-assurance of A. J. P. Taylor: 'You don't hear much about Cromwell these days, despite the fact that he built England up to what it was. There used to be this statue of Cromwell outside Victoria Station, in Manchester, but they moved it and put it in some fucking park in Wythenshawe, behind some bush. Nobody knows about it!'

Smith, spokesman of the 'prole-art threat', maintains a similar single-mindedness towards the traditionally sensitive topic of money. 'Fear is relative to how much you're earning and what kind of threat you're under. But I can live on a fucking quid a week, me. And I have done. But, if I suddenly made a load of it, I'd buy a house. I don't like shopping and all that, but I like nice clothes. A good pair of trousers when you can. You usually find in Britain that the scruffiest people are the richest. Have you noticed that?'

But would Smith invest, seriously, in art? 'Course I would. Italian stuff mainly. Chairs and stuff like that. If I had an awful lot of money, I'd buy some of that Catholic stuff – Tintoretto, El Greco. I like the colour in those paintings. But what would I do with it all? I've got the books and that anyway. I'm well into Venetian art. They always had a bit of humour about them. Like, they'd put a German soldier in the middle of *The Last Supper*. Stuff like that.

'I look at some of the things in *Frieze*, like the stuff with the tin cans. I did all that in the fifth year at school. You'd get these sixth-formers with Pink Floyd sleeves under their arms doing this stuff with green blobs and brown blobs. They'd be going: "Oh, it's about the economy and the Third World debt." Then they'd tell me that my stuff wasn't art, but it were miles better than their fucking horrible blobs. Ten years later, they're doing it for themselves down in Chelsea. That's the tragedy of being a self-taught artist.'

Inevitably, Mark E. Smith is faced with the danger of becoming as marginalised as Wyndham Lewis became in his later and most prolific years. As yet, however, the Fall remain a question mark in the history of art. But Smith continues to blast.

'Manchester council had this "Bring Art to the People" day,' he concludes. 'They're all raving socialists, that lot. There were five exhibitions in bars around the city. It was a kind of art pub crawl. They wanted me to kick it off, snip the ribbon and all that. I thought our fame was going down last year, so I decided to do my bit. You've got to keep a high profile. It's that kind of business. Anyway, we were dragged around these bars and showed all this art. There was all this Factory stuff done by some bloke who won't get out of bed for less than £5,000. These sub-Warhol drawings of *Carry On* characters. I'm thinking, "This is crap!" but you don't want to be rude about it cos it's all middle-aged people. They're saying, "Oh, Mark. I never knew you were into art." I was going, "Oh yeah, I love a bit of art, me. I'm into Tinzeretto and all that," and their mouths dropped.

'So, we got to the third bar. By this time, the band were dropping off one by one and going home for a bit to eat. I stuck around, and I was trying to make an effort cos there were all these art writers from the famous papers. I was talking to one woman about Wyndham Lewis, and she went into this rant for about twenty minutes about how he was a fascist and all that. I was saying, "All right, luv, we all know that. But at least he apologised for his mistakes." Then they were asking me which ones I liked. So I pointed to this painting on the wall — a black-and-white thing with barmen wearing leather coats and all these grotesque characters hanging about. It looked a lot like an Otto Dix. Then this bloke from the council ambles over and says, "Actually, Mark, that's not part of the exhibition." Turns out it's just part of the wall. Heh! Heh! It was easily the best, though.'

Custom number plate made for 'Telephone Thing'
music video.

Pages 225–32: *Sinister Times*, 1987. Free promotional
newspaper, issue 1 of 1.

The Fall

SINISTER TIMES

MARQUIS MANIPULATION PRODUCTION   SOMEDAY 00TH 19$$

Wings

Day by day. The moon gains on me. Day by day. The moon gains on me. Purchased pair of flabbly wings. I took to doing some HOVERING. Here is a liste of incorrect things. HOVERED Mid- Air outside a study. An Academic, nodded his chin, sent in the dust of some cheap Magazines. His academic rust could not burn them up.Recruited some gremlins. To get me clear of the airline routes.I paid them off with stuffing from my wings.They had some fun with those cheapo airline snobs.The stuffing loss made me hit a time-lock.I ended up in the eighteen sixties.I've bin there for one hundred and twenty five years.A small alteration of the past .Can turn time into space.Ended up under Ardwick Bridge.With some veterans from the U.S. Civil War.They were under Irish patronage. We shot a stupid sergeant,but I got hit in the crossfire.The lucky hit, made me hit a time lock. But, when I got back. The place I'd made the purchase,no longer exists. I'd erased it under the bridge. Day by day.The moon came towards me. By such things. The moon came towrds me. So now I sleep in ditches. And hide away from nosey kids. The wings rot and feather under me. The wings rot and curl right under me. A small alteration of the past. Can turn time into space. Small touches can alter more, than a mere decade. Wings, Wings, Wings, Wings, Wings, Wings, Wings, Wings, Wings, Wings, Wings, Wings, Wings, Wings, Wings, Wings.

TOTALLY WIRED

I'm Totally Wired. Totally Wired. I'm Totally Wired. Totally Wired. Can't yousee ? A butterfly stomach round ground. I drank a jar of coffee, and I took some of these. And I'm Totally Wired. Totally Wired. I'm Totally Wired. Totally Wired. Life leaves you surprised. Slaps you in the eyes. If I were a communist, a rich man would bale me. The opposite applies. The morning light. Another fresh fight. Another row, right, right, right, right. And I'm Totally Wired . JJJust Totally Wired. I'm Totally Biased. Totally Wired. You don't have to be weird to be wired. You don't have to be an American Brand. You don't have to be strange to be strangled. You don't have to be weird to be wrangled. But I'm Totally Wired. Totally Wired. JJJust Totally Wired. I'm Totally Wired. My Heart and I agree. My Heart and I agree. I'm Irate, Peeved, Irate,Peeved, Irate, Bad State. Bad State. ''Cos I'm Totally Wired. Totally Wired. JJJust Totally Wired. Totally Wired. And I'm always worried. And I'm always worried. And I'm always worried. And I'm always worried.

DR. FAUSTUS

Doctor Faustus: Horshoes Splackin' Swallows Haycart, Cart-Horse. Of the peasant blockin'his path. Doctor Faustus: Power showin', spits out Hay-cart, cart-horse, hay and box at the gates of ANHOLT. Dr. Faustus : At the court of the count,made fruits exotic pleasure-lichous, appear behind curtains in winter. Dr. Faustus: At the decadent court, made animals from sun-lands appear in the sparse gardens of Vinter in ze liddle wildage. Doktor Faustus: Horse-shoes clackin', swallows carthorse, hay-cart of the peasant blockin'his path. Must leave his student forces. FAUSTUS! Come get yer chips! Pull me blood silhouette, treu the ceiling sky. Cast me blood silhouette, thru the ceiling sky.

Polmos of Poland ZUBRÓWKA BRAND VODKA 0,5 L

STOP PRESS BORMANN FOUND CHIL VICTORY FOR ROBSON AGAINST FIST 1 — 0

Cash&Carry

Part of America therein

Three months. Three days. Three months. Cliches. Cliches. A treatise. Yet, its them again. For about the fifth f. time, in this god forsaken town. First was Cash N Carry house dance. In Manchester theyre A. In King Nas Ltd Empire. Yer got a Safeway there. Yer got a f. Safeway everywhere. Even in Manchester. Theres two types of factory there. One makes old corpses. They stumble round like rust dogs. One lives off dying men. One lives off the back of a dead man. You know which one. You know which FACTORY I mean. You know... You know... Psychedelic brain rushes offers the alternative. Theyre all good boys.Regular wages. The boss does the covers. They-are OK. by me. They just don't talk to me. I can see. I have dreams. I can see. I have dreams. And the secret of my life. Is...... Secretive,

Kennen Sie den weg nach? Kennen Sie den weg nach? The residents keep wild dogs. Yes its them again. Music Centre Irritant. Get your suits off. Get your vinyl lids on. Get your Lee Cooper on. Have a shower son. Go out to the club, boy. In your fathers bedroom closet pack. Contraceptives. Pru Plus Plan. Objectives. Demob pictures. Old train sets. Kennen Sie den weg nach? Kennen Sie den weg nach? Some food is so fast. Some food is so fast. Now... I never worked for. this death on a plate stuff. I AM NOT HERE TO CHEER YOU UP! Video reach, stereo bog,video reach, stereo bog.A quick fuzz, a quick fuzz. Video reach, stereo bog, video reach, stereo bog. Dissapates. Are you a bit too late? And the secret of their lives is... S. E. X. Meet me here at 8pm. and we'll eat some meat in the rest room. Thats fame. Stars on 45. STARS ON 45!! I KEEP MY POCKETS LINED!. STARS ON 45! I KEEP MY POCKETS LINED! A POSTCARD HASN'T ARRIVED! A POSTCARD HASN'T AR-RIVED! STARS ON 45!! I KEEP MY POCKETS LINED! WE ALL WANT FAME: WHIP ROUND AND TELL ALL THE OTHERS; LETS GET SOME FAME! FOR MI BROTHERS; AND WHAT ABOUT THE OTHERS? ANd on boogy night, It'll be alright. And boogy night. I'll feast on 45's. I'll keep my pockets lined. I'll keep my pocketslined.

COLOGNE

The rouge, smeared on the aged profile, of the local T. H.R. Cologne Branch Chairman, was sore and inched, well away from print. The centimetre oblong lipstick compounded fear. For him, I did not care a jot. The centimetre square purges fear.

VILLAGE BUG

I cannot account for this village bug. Smoke hangs like clouds of slugs. Gossip spreads. In institution domain. But outside, what could mean much? Outside. This would make a universal mug. So, I prefer Village Bug, very much.

NEIGHBOURHOOD OF INFINITY

From The Palace:

The man who's head expanded. Knew: a) Who stole cafe collection box. b) Stupid facade behind Jurgen. d) Who wore a red scarf to remind him of his fiancee. e) The love of Paris, infects the civil service lichen on the North. It was the time of the Giant Moths in the neighbourhood of infinity. I used to have this thing about Link Wray. I used to play him every saturday.

God Bless Saturday! God Bless Saturday! WE ARE THE FALL! IN THE NEIGHBOURHOOD OF INFINITY! It was the time of the Giant Moths. It happens. It happens. Instincts lost. It happens. Lost through purple blossoms. It happens. The desire will turn rotten. WE ARE THE FALL! IN THE NEIGH-BOURHOOD OF INFINITY!

Australians In Europe

Conversation with Ham A. Circa! Post House Motel.

Australians in Europe X 6 Never ever breathe. Australians in Europe X 1 Get a whiff of Air and Helium to breathe. Australians in Europe X 2 Higher! Australians in Europe X 3

THINK. Why did Great Grandad leave? Australians in Europe never see. He was consigned to a boat, after using a huge great cleaver.

Australians in Europe X 4 Never ever ... B.R.E.A.T.H.E. Australians your the biggest things rejected, I have ever seen. Because the boys use a map and they live in Berlin. Your like a pair of dogs loose in McGregor's kiln, you know shit. Australians in Europe X 5 Wake up and suss the scene. You'd better leave them parents,and try Hamburg to Berlin. Your just a bloody Twister, so who do you think your foolin .Australians in Europe

Today 7.5103

Years ago "I could have been a journalist. I could've been head of Rueters" Albino Luciani 1978.

'Wild Bill Hicock Relative traced in U.K.

Boston, Lines — a descendant of the legendary Wild West hero, Wild Bill Cody, has been traced in Boston, Lines, England. Known locally as 'Big Dave' Cody he bears a striking resemblance

YOUR KIND OF PINT.

Von Fall zu Fall

Wenn Pop-Musiker sich nicht ernst genommen fühlen, wenden sie sich der Kunst zu. Auch Mark E. Smith fühlte sich zu Höherem berufen und schrieb ein Stück über Papst Paul I.

Irgendwie hat es Mark E. Smith, scharfzüngiger Kopf von The Fall, geschafft, sich einen Ruf als Satiriker britanischer Mißstände aufzubauen. Doch im blanken Alltagsleben war nicht immer zu erkennen, was die Smithschen Wortschwälle wirklich mitteilen sollten. In Kombination mit der Musik — naher, ungeduldiger Minimalrock — wirken die Texte auf eigentümliche Weise bedrohlich; auf den Interviewseiten der Pop-Presse vermochten sie ebenso zu amüsieren wie zu provozieren. So baute sich in den aufmüpfigen Quartieren der Pop/Rockgemeinde die Überzeugung auf, hier habe Einer die punkige Gift-und-Galle-Romantik nicht in den Wind gehängt, sondern biete mit nordbritischer Schollen- und Praxisgebundenheit die südbrikischen "Amoumacht die Stirn. In sequenter Fortführung r Arbeit hat es Smith THEE schafft, auch nach die Roman Kalt seiner eigenen Paul II zu schlachten... allergie — beohl eher unfreiwillig, beit-beargeistück: sein erstes smith, Märück (genauer: ly sulky medin-Event) , Hey! Fall, has

what the Kollage von wortfirst theati play, who Kurzszenen, Fallgroup, abo Videoprojektionen John Paul im Mittänzchen Cardinal-Balleteine Michael arch of Ver e hier gemäß Proon 26 Aug Story des Albino dead in be-sahlt werden, der heart attack Supra Ezten Dekade ein sip was adding Papst Paul I. David Yallop, der das Zeitliche God's Name s Gerüchte über was murdereçand Freimaurewas that the ne er hartnäckig to exile from th kildeten den bers of the max great war it 2 on Hey! Lu-Vations and to ann des Volkes ernte on the Cur ein, der ganz Jesuitical book ichte gegen, das good Yallop, ç aufzukom Hey! memehren abo U trach Auf Solution — mü

Leaning heavis a diag superstition, e is evident Luciani — the Tin kind it, it is dea cf allpine Laone bullied to is murder by vesal such is that I can zweet, provincial, jragrägh, e is The "codex" of Pälst e is never explained, bu suitable I the monaceing s the Long dications of F 2, whatelementer is scea writing by carefully more existence of tha dor Neither the riaI to Luciani marçf or the disFrom the fast pa be tacci. but, play may assoud sola F 2 ap Armadoue whabaknad, and the AcChristmas outings by mathematic of Mary. But Smith's e it with a the material is predl increasing than test 1 stage, his programmatic notes is colaguorial logue explain any cf igh heels, a for example, the furie e exaggerperers on a scteen betautommaison as part of a quasi-cast list, is cal formula which for lir is here swastika.

A figure crosses 11 cable "his costume blending a from the red and black with polla-dut dress and ated buck-side of uciani, patrihorse. This, says Bleered Pope that the play's medadedly from a

'Svi r''i

young luciani; -'S -TIMI

(A BLACK LOOK CROSSES HIS FACE) OPUS

IT IS OVER   I AM OV....WHEN I

GELLI: EXCLA' Antognossi ?
WALKING TO SET   Riddler
GELLI: DUO.XXM light!

SLEEI DEBT Snatches SONFG & FILM., WITH J. P. I CLICKING FINGERS

Religious after

think The Fall's music is horrid, something went wrong (a ticket price of £8, perhaps), since even the fans were looking miserable as I left at the interval.
Robert Gore Langton

The Fall

Kim Martin den Hä. Guerillas Mark plö Raupen I sichtliche umknickstakst... chen S denlang rung der Es entbe wissen li zerrungs mehr al schaftliz zurütteli die in G stiten-Pi wohl eb billigem lis: s. ne. er Verga. Rundum nicht hab. und ob die Smit außer den schnürigen M phern taz — lich etwas ark E Smith, the stud turns little paspeter Kün

und we take colivies as the -weety's wonnuance at — and, in Hamm written spl, program Smith, w ion fireesome: in Never Connect theatre: suddent say "Yes, Martia talking to you a her life mor Michael Clark, shorts, skips abo Luciani.

The Fi whose 1984 book 24 seem regaçd that Luciani sympohu Yallop's theory deseree ince pontiff planned Clark. Te Curia all mem-Trevor Ionic lodge P 2. So among o stake within the rented articular its influ sesbion, ranch's sometimes the mos keeping, that, ar-tickering, le lodge's clerical purcers as lodge's clerical maybe, find the Italian Even alter. reading the script the low's you beyond these few fin what I saw of it, I suspect the play had yet te doch

The initial impression that Mark E Smith, founder member of pop group The Fall, is just a talentless cult hero scratching a creative itch in public, is born out by this 'concept play' with live

Hochmut kommt vor dem Fall oder:
Mark bleib bei deinem Leisten!

mentiert er seine Weltlichkeit, indem er ein Glas Wein trinkt und jemand zu der Beinerkung veranlaßt, er sei ein writing Mr Nrikes. Mehr weiß wine; he drinks it sn-ach der The Fall burst onto stage, by as if to raise the chest. the single "Hey! Luciani" The production works well visually and musically but Smith's writing suffers from translation to a medium in which you can hear the words.

It is a pity that Smith chose a figure of such limited historical significance. Remembered only of his successor, John Paul I wears a simple white soutane and a smile; John Paul II wears the overseas war wig of code and triple crown onoly speaks in the staged Ameri can accent of the former pontifl. s wouldn't mat that shilungshu finds eavesdropevening, and j artistic creed is a sharp mip This is cut-up mind which is a character will plaint itself. Ti Borrmson, I can Math's "We's secretary tells made shrews, or the cnoicr, material. in lince-leogh T Hoy Luciani at the young sively Sibbinco is cable "his leged he cannoi leave the Nthe for fear of the attentions itis Italian police. There is key, play to be written about Grace, but, of the many ik, of which he stands accused ages vestism and pantomimenss and two of them. Smith misses iing.

HEY LUCIANI!

ABORETUM

I SAID. LUCIANI, THE FUTURE'S HERE TODAY.
I SAID, HEY LUCIANI, POPE OF 33 DAYS. THEY SAID
YOU WERE AN ULTRA NUT AND HAD NO TIME FOR
YOUR CHRISTANITY. YOU PAID WITH YOUR LIFE FOR
THEIR TREACHERY.
THE FUTURE'S HERE TODAY.
THE FUTURE'S HERE TO STAY.
HEY LUCIANY, JESUS HAS GONE AWAY.
I SAID? HEY LUCIANY, MEET THE CHURCH BANKS A.
THEY SAID YOU WERE OF PEASANT STOCK, AND ONE
DAY THE CURIA MURDERED YOU TODAY. YOUR HERMAN-
TICS ARE THROUGH, AND ON THAT FRUITED PLAIN, THE
CORPORATE BISHOPS GRAZE. EXIT CHURCH OF
POVERTY AND PAIN.
THE FUTURE'S HERE TODAY!
THE FUTURE IS HERE TO STAY.
HEY LUCIANI, A POP STAR IN YOUR CELL CAN SEE FROM
YOUR GRAVE THE TV SNOW-STORM ON TOP. THE BRASS
HOLY GRAIL HEY LUCIANI, AND THE COWLS ARE
BLACK. ON AN INQUISITION RACK.
THE FUTURE'S HERE TO STAY.

DEVIL GET READY.

ORDAINED THE POOR PEOPLE'LL

* Italian equivalent of Limited Corporation Company.

(LIGHTS ON SHLDRS AND HEAD ONLY.STILL

BLK SHADOW.

15-30 secs of.as if in dream.

Hideous Noise Group Write 'St' Pope Biog

Ohio, Sweden: A group has written a character portrayal of a Pope J.P. One — rumoured to become a 'SAINT' which will be presented at the 'Riverside Studios' near some river where 'Rule Brittania' was written. The Vatican commented "We have been waiting for a sign for 7 years".

"It's nonsense" claimed their manager from a St John's Wood face lift surgery. "I was promoting big time heavy metal/Top 20 groups when they concocted this scheme in Hull, almost 497 miles away from Albert Side Studios, Croydon".

music about theve ot its so John Paul's untious meanpassage, and withterest, not tive, we witness bald wig bishops and gvith a funny -taged event the you don't -garde bottle of popes, te length. bived in a gs held pre up its own from the a comaa Pope Johan assortmen rican acce errillas inv

MARK'LL SINK US

THE WARD WAS ARRAIGNED WITH SPATS OF BLOOD. THE VICTIM, CASTIGATE, AND YET, PART OF US. THE THOUGHTS IN EYES AS SEEN UNDER A HOOD BURNED IN MY OWN EYES, AND IN MY BLOOD!
MARK'LL SINK US!
A MESSAGE MESMERISED, ON ALL ENGLISH BREATH. THE CRUX PRETTY GRASPED, BUT MOSTLY MISUNDER-STOOD.
MARK'LL SINK US!
I AM DESOLATE. I LIVE THE BLACK AND BLUE OF THE NIGHT.
FRIEND DEPRESSION. COMES NOW AND AGAIN. ONCE IN A BLUE MOON. IT POINTS BACKWARDS THUS:
MARK'LL SINK US.

PFI: "IT IS Wro, where Lenin is, but between Chur ituation there ï DaRome I shall ï ubjects,but wil e rights of auth CJ:ED CNES (Turns

think of themselves as superior world around them.

s Holiness then went on to denounce ation theology.

Credit:
lyric: Mark E. Smith
music: Craig Scanlon
copyright: Minder Music

STRANDED

AND SHA LASK INC.

movement

ST FORN.

to believe that ere is Jerusalem Salvation and Hi some coincidence with the good ot fear to excer ity Against the pointing to encourage o)

HUREN ZEE HUREN ZE

ABORETUM   CHEET NEE   TZ LA

IVNRS CLARK   SCRIVENERS rat'.

IRS CREW ARE IN SANT MENARD

TING CLAWS STAND OVER IT ONLY ZUFFALIG

AN RESCUE KHALKALIS DIGNITY

GLEEFULLY SPREAD ALL INNARDS WEST

DUO light;   What news r ST
'Reflections!)   AAAANOTON ?

ICAN 'THIS IS =
DID   VATICANO
NOWCR: RADIO
       28th September

POPE JOHN PAUL
TODAY
IEU HIS IMAGE
PEOPLE'S POPE'
TO HIS SPEECH,
BEGAN BY HIS HOL
TING OUT THE FRIVOLOUS
DISTRACTIONS OF EVERYDAY
LIFE. AND suggesting
riests ignore the
False God
of Modernisation

ING OVER TO THE VATICAN
ALS AND EMPLOYESS OF LIBR
AND BANK, HIS HOLINESS
ST IMPLORINGLY, ASKED
HEIR AID IN HIS MISSION.

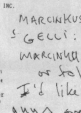

MARCINKUS: Dil' the t
S GELLI: Maybe.
MARCINKUS: Come on
or foll. The pr
I'd like to get s
guys over here to

LOCAL

WORLD EXCLUSIVE

INGS ROAD INVADED SHOCKER
By Winnie Untruth

LOCAL RESIDENTS LIVING CLOSE TO WAKE-FIELD'S BUSY INGS ROAD ARE LIVING IN CONDITIONS SIMILAR TO THOSE WITNESSED IN FRANCE DURING THE SECOND WORLD WAR, Winnie Untruth reports. Residents living close to Ings Road are living under near occupation conditions I can exclusively reveal in an exclusive interview with residents living in the Ings Road area. One resident who wishes to remain nameless told me, "It is like living in occupied France" He explained the constant harassment he faced when out walking his dog. "It is constant harassment when I take tiddles out for a walk. The convoys of traffic are endless, I once stood for three days waiting to cross the road, some thing must be done to stop these people" Other people who live nearby spoke of endless convoys of traffic & one woman told me, "I know of one man who spent three days waiting to cross the road" Residents have written to the leader of Wakefield council, Mr John Fearp*rson, "All he did was write back" explained one irate resident. "He even tried writing to those responsible, but how can you write to someone who only puts their initials on their buildings?" Weekends & Bank holidays bring misery to the local residents an activity is stepped up. Mr Bert Whinge explained, "They seem to step up their activities at Weekends & Bank holidays, there is something strange about them, their eyes are glazed and their expressions blank. They wear a strange sort of uniform in the Winter, green wellington boots and knee length greasy coats. They put up their vehicles and then visit each one of the buildings in turn. Some of them spend hours and hours there, it is as if they are some sort of religious cult, my wife and I are both frightened about it all" Residents told me of their fear of what was going on, "Other people in Wakefield should take a look at what is happening down here" a resident told me, "Once they have colonised Ings Road they will start looking elsewhere to put up their ugly buildings, I am not sure what goes on inside them but I know one thing, it isn't Christian!" With more invaders landing every day things certainly look grim for the residents who live in the Ings Road area.

A whole rack of green wellingtons!

slag ten, credits.

The Fall

PRIZE WINNING LETTER

"Here are my choices for your Punk Rock Hall of Fame:
1. Wyndham Lewis (R.I.P.) Self-styled "The enemy" hated by everyone in his time. Books have been pretty effectively blacklisted. Ask any phony intellectuals about this guy and watch them squirm. Real tough guy. When dying of tumour and blind, doctor asked him about his bowels: his last words were "Mind your own business!" That's punk!
2. Ezra Pound (R.I.P.) You want style? Dig this description of Ez in 1912 (he was 27). Living in London: "Futuristic poet with forked red beard, luxuriant chestnut hair, cane, an aggressive lank figure, one long blue single stone earring dangled on his jawbone. He wore a purple top hat, a green shirt, a black velvet coat, vermillion socks, openwork brilliantly tanned sandals, trousers of green billiard cloth [!!!! — Ed.], in addition to an immense flowing tie that had been handpainted by a Japanese." And that's in the daytime! Made a lot of enemies and was driven out of England. Arrested for treason by the US in 1945 and placed in asylum for 13 years. When finally released in '58, they asked him how it was. Says he, "Oi've had it tougher. That's punk!
3. Gene Vincent (R.I.P.) Elvis is great but this guy played for keeps. Who also made so many great records? He told the DJ's to go f— themselves and even tried to punch out Dick Clark when Clark was very powerful. The best white rocker of them all, and possibly the only rock star ever to VOLUNTEER for military service and win honor for heroism in combat...
4. Little Walter (R.I.P.) Another tough guy who played for keeps. While Diddley and Berry were accepted, this guy is ignored by rock fans and he made great records that a lot of those English R&B cats picked up on. Early Stones sound more like him than Berry. Pulled a gun on one of his band members when member wanted to leave and shot himself in the leg.
5. Frank Zappa. Don't have any of his records but respect this person a great deal. Could have been the Elvis of the '70s if he'd wanted to, but rube people the wrong way is prerequisite of punkhood — Ed.] Must be a punk, he talked himself into his own label without ever getting a hit record. Can sum up whole attitudes in 5 words or less and people don't like it. Had the guts to say in ROLLING STONE that Monkees records were a better than anything coming out of San Francisco. In '68, when asked opinion of Bob Dylan and the Band, he replied, "Sky Saxon and the Seeds. Only Sky Saxon dances better." Now THAT'S PUNK!!!!
— Duane Roseiprul
White Plains, NY

THE HIP PRIEST

Room to live

A FRIEND DROPPING IN

Manchest[er]
35,968 BRITAIN'S BIGGEST REGIONAL

'My 10 Ro[l]

STAUNCH Conservative Mrs Hazel Pinder-White told the "Dallas connection" libel case jury today about the 10 Rolls-Royces she and her husband had had at various times in their married life.

But she denied a suggestion by barrister Mr Patrick Milmo that she and her late husband Charles campaigned for the party in ostentatious style.

"I take exception to that remark," said mother-of-three Mrs Pinder-White, of Broadstairs, Kent. "There was nothing ostentatious about my husband and nothing ostentatious about me."

She was being cross-examined by Mr Milmo in London High Court on the second day of her damages claim against her local Conservative MP, Mr Jonathan Aitken.

She claims he libelled her in a newspaper article by comparing her with an adulteress and alcoholic Sue Ellen, wife of J R Ewing in the Dallas television series.

Mr Aitken, MP for Thanet East and the younger brother of the East Kent Critic, deny February, 1981, article w... Mr Milmo, for Mr Aitken, proved to Mrs Pinder-White her husband, who campai... local issues, was a flamboy...

Victim flees

Pictured left: Some graffiti and scenes from a Manchester recruitment agency our relief through comedy, mirth and charity on Deansgate.

Wireless enthusiast intercepts government secret radio band and uncovers secrets and scandals of deceitful-typed proportions.

A ghast next door door to his neighbour, secretly overheard an aforementioned was a hunter whom radio enthusiast wanted friendship and favour off.

Nearly a new face in hell

A muscular thick-skinned, slit-eyed neighbour is at the table poisoned just thirty seconds before by parties who knew of wireless operator's forthcoming relayation.

A new face in hell

A prickly line of sweat covers enthusiast's forehead as the realisation hits him that the same government hunter and his now blind next door neighbour voted for and backed and talked of an unseen parties have tricked him into their war against the people who enthusiast and dead Hunter would have wished torture on. A servant of government waits in and arrests wireless fan in kitchen for murder of his neighbour.

A new face in hell, a new face in hell, a new face in hell

A new face in hell, a new face in hell, a new face in hell, a new face in hell, a new face in hell, a new face in hell, a new face in hell, a new face in hell, a new face in hell, a new face in hell, a new face in he

The dead cannot contradict, sometimes the living cannot.

A new face in hell! A new face in hell! A new face in hell! A new face in hell!

Copyright Mark E Smith, Fall Foundation Music.

New Face In Hell
by The Fall from "Grotesque" [Ro...]

C...

WINNERS ★ WINNERS ★ WINNERS ★ WINNERS

WINNERS OF FALL COMP
Jac Mason, Chalfield Road, Chorlton; David Munro, Moseley, Ashton Under Lyne; Mr David Kelly, Salford; Tim Bolton, Bramhall; Colin Sharples, Robert Brennan, Chorlton.

WINNERS OF VENTURE RECORDS
Kevin Mitchell, Mr Rax, Salford; David Currie, Heywood; David Vernon, Didsbury, Matt Pilech, Chorlton.

WINNERS OF FATAL ATTRACTION TICKETS
Hilda Myers, Higher Crumpsall, Mrs Irene Newton, Whitefield, Caroline Cunliffe, Eccles; Mrs A C Rample, Tyldesley, Miss J Loughlin, Burnage; Miss G Beeley, North Reddish.

FORUM THEATRE COMPETITION
Bernard Holmes, Sale; Ann Smith, Prestwich, C D Power, Heaton Moor.

CAPTION COMPETITION
Winner – Ms Chambers, Hyde: I knew I shouldn't have starched my new boxer shorts.
Near misses – Mr A Hindley, Blackley: A typical yuppie boxer bag; D Power, H Moor: Glam four-year-old arrested in infant school riot; J Wilkinson, Moston: Who's moved the bucket?; J Imrie, Bolton: Are you sure this initiation ceremony is painless, Sarge?

Crossword Solution No 1

Win Cog Sinister

Many thanks for your kind enquiry about THE FALL FAN CLUB. It has recently formed owing to increased interest.

To join, FOUR POUNDS annually is required, to cover all postage.

Members will initially receive: one kit, comprising of: posters, recording plans and up to the minute tour information etc...

A bulletin of THE FALL will also be sent to you every FOUR MONTHS, for the membership year, free of charge.

CUT HERE →
DIN?

Ev-'ry-bo-ddy loves some-bo-ddies sometime,—

Ev-'ry-bo-ddy loves that taste so true…

THE FALL
SINGLES

ADULT NET

Beggars Banquet

Photocredit: JEFF VEITCH

The Classical.   Classical

THERE is no culture is my Brag. Your lust for

bullshit reveals a desire for a home of

office   THIS IS THE HOME OF THE VAIN!

Where are the obligatory niggers?
HEY THERE FUCKFACE!!
HEY THERE FUCKFACE!!
There are twelve people in the world
The rest are paste

PAINTWORK

Our pine pullovers
You can clutch at my toes
You will drive me insane
You know nothing about it
Its not your domain
Don't confuse yourself with someone who has something to say.

That green peace looked like saffron on the realmBrown dishevelled A Kellogs home
Red church on a hill
Styrafoam inside
Aluminium Tiers
Louis Armstrong tapes waft down the aisles
Synthesised
Thats strife knot
Its a 'skill' to play the second fiddle well
Life is strife, don't forget it.
Life is strife and I said it
Strife is life, but you don't want to hear it. biggest bed holds the mask of death.

MANACLED TO THE CITY!
MANACLED TO THE CITY!

The Eastern block rocks to Elton John
Just give a miss the ice bricks of Bacardi,

"What a dynamic entrance.

......" Reflected mirror of delirium SSSSSS AD BRIDGES

Our words return in patterns
Our minds, encapsulating time

Computers infest hotels
Would you credit it?
All the estate agents
Hysterical breath
Those big big wide streets
Useless MP's

Its good to live in the country
You can get down to real thinking
Walk around look at geometric tracery
Hedgehogs skirt round your leathered soles
Fall down drunk on the road
Its good to live in the country

or end up on debtors retreat estate
or debtors retreat escape
debtors escape estate

3) THE ONLY REASON YOU KNOW THIS, IS THAT IT WAS WELL DOCUMENTED

A Manchester Group that wasn't quite like what you thought.

ANDREW BERRY

ANDREW BERRY

SPORT

KICKER CONSPIRACY

Kicker, Kicker Conspiracy. Kicker, Kicker Conspiracy. J. Hill's satanic reign. Asslickers King O'Team. Kicker, Kicker Conspiracy x 2. In the marble halls of the charm school. How flair is punished. Under Marble Millichip, the FA. broods. On how flair can be punished. They're guest is a Euro- State magnate. How flair is punished. KKC: X4 . In the booze club, George Best does rule.
How flair is punished. His downfall was a blonde girl, but thats none of your business! K. K. C. X 4

Former fan at the bus stop. Treads on the ball at his feet, in the christmas rush. And in his hands,Two lager cans. Talks to himself. At the back. At the top. What are the implications of the club unit? Plastic, Slime, Partitions, Cocktail, Zig-Zag , Tudor Bar Pat McGatt, Pat McGatt, the very famous sports reporter is talking...... there. FANS ! ! !
'Remember, you are abroad! Remember the police are rough! Remember the unemployed! Remember my expense account HOT DOGS AND SEAT FOR MR. HOGG !! HOT DOGS AND SEATS FOR MR. HOGG!!! AAAAANNNNDDD HIS GROTTY SPAWN! ! ! ! Lurid brochures for ground unit. Our style is punished. K. K. C. X 5 Remember! don't collect with the rough. K. K. C. x 1 Kicker, lets swell the facilities. Kicker Conspiracy times eight.

Soccer stars to play TV men

SOCCER favourites will take on BBC North West personalities in a charity match this Sunday at Derby High School, Radcliffe Road, Bury.
Among the soccer men will be the Bury FC management team of Martin Dobson, Ray Pointer, Frank Casper and Wilf McGuiness.
The match — kick-off 2pm — is to raise funds for a video recorder for the Speech and Language Disorder Unit at Uisworth, for children age four to eleven.

TEST MATCH CRICKET
AUSTRALIA First innings
000 for 10
RADCLIFFE First innings
625 for 6

THE MAN WHOS HEAD EXPANDED

Soccer's sick secrets

DRUG ABUSE, alcoholism, mental breakdowns, gambling — all the ingredients of a lurid screenplay were unleashed on soccer's doorstep today.
this time the alleg-

STAFF SPORTS REPORTER

came under fire from Ted Croker, secretary of the Football Association who accused him of 'a certain amount of hysteria.'
In a bid to shock clubs and the authorities into taking more care of their expensive stars, Taylor revealed some sensational case histories.
Players hooked on valium, players with drinking problems, players with their minds warped by the pressures at the top, players run up in huge gambling debts and players crippled by uncaring clubs — being left out.
Taylor hopes to spark a double-edged response to his attack - improved

ations came, not from a hyped-up newspaper exclusive but from one of the most respected figures in the game.
Gordon Taylor, secretary of the Professional Footballers' Association, has launched a major campaign to clean up soccer with an astonishing set of revelations.
But he immediately

medical facilities at many of the Football League's 92 clubs, and the setting up of a Rehabilitation Centre.
He envisages the centre treating not just physical injuries but also psychological problems, a sort of Alcoholics Anonymous, Release, MIND and Gamblers Anonymous rolled into one - and it is that which brought down the scorn of the FA.
Croker countered today: 'There's a certain amount of hysteria in his comments in that he seems to be suggesting this is something new.
'We totally refute his allegations about drugs because we have done everything to keep the game

GAMBLING

F. A. CUP THIRD ROUND

ARSENAL	0	2	FARNWORTH
BARNSLEY	0	1	ACCR. STANLEY
BLACKBURN	1	0	BAYERN MUNICH
BRADFORD	2	1	MOSCOW DYNAMO
BRIGHTON	2	0	BARCELONA
BURY	0	1	ITALY

GENESIS	0	0	MARILLIO
HORLICKS	0	0	BOUR
HUDDERSFIELD	0	0	

Shoeshine, please!

Please hand-pamper my shoes professionally.

The charge for this exclusive shoeshine service is only 4,– DM per pair.

Shoes hand-pampered perfectly, a shining service on the house.

DAVID STUBBS

ADULT NET: Waking Up In The Sun (Beggars Banquet)
Brix E. Smith's fourth single is pleasantly mellow but instantly forgettable, with inane and repetitive lyrics. The B-side , (Remember) Waking It Up Send, packs more emotional punch but is broken up by a disarming change of pace

FA. CUP ROUND-UP

There were few real surprises yesterday, in what can only be described as a dull round. Perhaps Bury's defeat at home, raised a few eyebrows. Sale's victory was courageous in view of the five players of theirs sent off. Farnworth had a surprise win, as did Wigan Yovril. Heated at Old Trafford.

WORLD CUP

ALGERIA	1	1	SHREWSBURY
BRAZIL	1	1	MERTHYR T:
CYPRUS	10	0	HOLLAND
LIVERPOOL	3	0	ARGENTINA
NOTTS FOREST	0	7	LUXEMBOURG
PORT VALE	2	1	RUSSIA
WEST GERM.	½	½	AUSTRIA
YUGOSLAVIA	1	0	YEOVIL

The man who's head expanded. The man who's head expanded was corrupted by Mr Sociological memory. Was corrupted by Mr Sociological Memory Man. Could not get a carrier bag for love nor money. The man who's head expanded. Sounds like head-wappppet. Sounds like wig-wammmmer . Over. Over. Over. Over. The man who's head expanded. The soap opera wrapwould follow him around and use his jewels for T. V. prime time. The man who's head expanded. Turn that bloody blimpy space invader machine off ! The man who's head expanded explained: The scriptwriter would follow him around, of this he was convinced. It was no coincidence. The lager was poisened. It was no matter of small consequence. No little pub incidence. A red faced post- 'Jolly Grapes' would steal his jewels, and put them in the mouths of Vic. actor fools. Of this he was convinced. Sounds like higwapppper. Sounds like a load of mickwappppper . Over. Over. Over. The man who's head expanded. The man who's head expanded. Does not want to appear illiterate. Crack! Crack! Does not want to appear illiterate. Crack! Crack! Crack! Crack! The man who's head expanded. Come on with the heraldry. Add misinterpretation, prerogative,John Kennedy's pulmanesque explained. The man who's head diminished. The man who's head diminished. Sounds like my head ,trying to unravel this lot, I can tell you Sparky!

WORLD CUP REPORT

Port Vale, favourites this year, had a comfortable win over Russia, but holders Merthyr T. had a fright in Brazil, being held to a draw, but look set to join Vale in next round. Liverpool struggled against Argentina, Yeovil (insiders tip) had expected victory, whilst Cyprus took their time to overcome a youthful Holland. It was no surprise that Luxembourg overwhelmed Forest, but look to go no further in competition with a tough away draw. West Germany and Austria agreed terms beforehand.

Far from being naive Mark Smith exhibits the cynicism and world-weariness normally apparent in hoary old conservatives. If the really bel: eves that the righteous rage of the oppressed majority is mere "griping" then he has been living in a peculiarly insular environment. In short, Smith's attitudes are entirely contemptible and all the more regretable in light of the excellent music The Fall have produced over the last few years.
(No name and address supplied)

Draw for next round :
ALGERIA v YEOVIL
SHREWSB
CYPRUS v BRAZIL
MERTHYR T
PORT VALE v LUXEMBOURG
WEST GERMANY v LIVERPOOL
and AUSTRIA

THE FALL
Hey! Luciani (Beggars Banquet)
FLTED amidships by occasional vessels of white noise, a new addition to The Fall fleet of sound, "Hey! Luciani", taken from Smith's recent play of the same name, is almost something you could have in the house. Brix has drawn up alongside hubby Marc and introduced a touch of bubblegum that's positively adhesive. But why heckle, as obliquely as ever, about the death of a Catholic figurehead in 1978? Maybe attitudes are entirely contemptible and all the more regretable in for no other reason than the fact that it's an unresolved issue, a lump that's refused to be flushed away, a half-buried intrusion. As appropriate for The Fall as a derelict synagogue. perhaps.

Comments (recent):

'the same spitball of jaundiced wisdom, about the culpulable stupidity of mankind outside the limited carrying distance of his voice over and over again!'
– Chris Bohn (NME)

SPORTS QUIZ
With Genial Crazy Horse

Question: WHY ?

Answer:

Tommy Lawrence, three caps, forty second minute.

Stuart Bertolotti-Bailey

Wyndham Lewis[1]

BLAST
years 1837 to 1900
Curse abysmal inexcusable middle-class
(also Aristocracy and Proletariat)
BLAST
Pasty shadow cast by gigantic Boehm
(imagined at introduction of BOURGEOIS VICTORIAN VISTAS).
WRING THE NECK OF all sick inventions
born in that progressive white wake.
(Wyndham Lewis, *Blast*, 1914)

> *Our vortex is not afraid of the past: It has forgotten its existence.*
> (Wyndham Lewis, *Blast*, 1914)

As with Joyce, Beuys and Mark E. Smith, the historians will be arguing about Percy Wyndham Lewis until the kingdom comes. Twentieth-century culture has been kept alive by the irritants which work their way under its skin. Inasmuch as this, Marshall McLuhan's call for 'a counter-environment as a means for perceiving the dominant one' required a new century to prove its accuracy. Lewis, who could so easily be the subject of myriad quarterly reviews, has remained a shadowy and mistrusted figure, silhouetted on the banks of the cultural mainstream. As our times appear to demand art-terrorist outsiders, Lewis has called the era's bluff by refusing easy routes to fashionable and commercially lucrative acceptance. While Marinetti caught, peeled and ate the orange thrown at him in public disgrace, Lewis — unknown to many — continues to ply his trade as a novelist, satirist, poet, critic of literature, philosophy and art, magazine editor, painter and fly-in-the-ointment.

Lewis formed the Vorticist group (as the point of maximum energy) in London in 1914. At the time, he was painting and writing around the fringes of London's Bloomsbury, and later from the Rebel Art Centre, which he co-founded with Kate Lechmere. This was a time when most of Europe was largely unsuspecting of the imminent war, which was only a few months away. The studied neurosis of realism and Impressionism was about to give way to the deliquescing anarchy of cubism and expressionism. But the Vorticists had no place — nor wanted one — in either camp. From the group's inception,

1. This piece, first published in *Metropolis M*, no. 2, 2005, is an inversion of 'Mark E. Smith' by Michael Bracewell & Jon Wilde (reprinted elsewhere in this volume). 'A small alteration of the past / Can turn time into space'

Lewis's Vorticists were bloody-minded outsiders, possessing an extraordinary ability to get up people's noses. At a time when post-Impressionism was about to disgrace itself with the saccharine posturing of abstraction, Lewis appeared as comfortable in the regulation uniform of trench warfare as in the louche smoking jacket of his gentlemen's club. In 1914, art was reinventing itself as a minefield of carefully stylised factions. The Vorticists, immovable in their determination to remain aloof from the posturing of their peers, quickly earned not only incomprehension but also hostility. In an early appearance at one of Marinetti's London speeches at the Doré Gallery, Lewis and company brought the volatility of a working men's club to a scene which believed itself to be self-contained and self-policing. The rhetoric of the Vortex was similar to suddenly finding oneself in a slanging match with a chauvinist, fascist, intellectual drunkard. For this invective, Lewis has never been forgiven. Challenged with the notion that the Vorticists drew their menace from the seismic detonation of Futurism, Lewis replied with a dismissive sniff: 'Automobilism – Marinetteism – bores us. We don't want to go about making a hullabaloo about motor cars, any more than about knives and forks, elephants or gas-pipes. Elephants are VERY BIG. Motor cars go quickly.'

Like Marinetti's Futurist manifesto, Lewis's *Blast* magazine was regarded as the alarm call of the pre-war years; this was polemic which seemed to deal with personal and political dissatisfaction in a manner that was both sinister and confrontational. By the end of the decade, the Futurists resembled a self-parodic cabaret turn fit only for the history books. The Vorticists, on the other hand, made their sense of alienation part of their art, laying the foundations for a creative process which was almost immediately disrupted by a war that saw them divided, dispersed and, in some cases, killed in action.

For Lewis, irreverence was put to work for Vorticism. As the self-titled 'Enemy', he would parade around London's art and literary circles shouting random insults at the bewildered cognoscenti. 'The Futurist statue will move: then it will live a little; but any idiot can do better than that with his good wife, round the corner,' 'This war talk, sententious execution and much besides, Marinetti picked up from Nietzsche,' or 'I loathe anything that goes too quickly. If it goes too quickly it is not there,' when delivered with the correct mixture of urgency and forethought, could obtain an effect that bordered on the sinister.

It was only a short step, aesthetically, from confusing Marinetti and the Futurists with dismissive put-downs to offending the art cognoscenti by challenging their self-satisfaction. *Blast* was jarring and disjointed, making a virtue of its graphic appearance, faithfully set according to the Enemy's bombastic wishes by an alcoholic ex-printer between startling puce covers: 'The "Poor" are detestable animals! They are only picturesque and amusing. The "Rich" are bores without a single exception, *En tant que riches!* / We want those simple and great people found everywhere / *Blast* presents an art of Individuals.'

Already, Lewis's campaign bore marked similarities to the *Live at the Witch Trials* phase of Mark E. Smith and the Fall's assault on the post-punk new wave. Smith was a Renaissance man, without a culture vital enough to support the fulfilment of his talents. Similarly, Lewis is locked in a position of terrorist warfare, cerebral and caustic towards a fashion-driven society which is indurate to all attitudes save its own conservative 'non-conformity'. Thus, Lewis is cast (again like Smith) as a cat among pigeons, stalking the effete by saying the unspeakable. In 1914, he wrote: 'OH BLAST FRANCE! / pig plagiarism / BELLY / SLIPPERS / POODLE TEMPER / BAD MUSIC / SENTIMENTAL GALLIC GUSH / SENSATIONALISM / FUSSINESS / PARISIAN PAROCHIALSIM'. Or, again: 'As to women: wherever you can, substitute the society of men. Treat them kindly, for they suffer from the herd, although of it, and have many of the same contempts as yourself. But women, and the processes for which they exist, are the arch conjuring trick: and they have the cheap mystery and a good deal of the slipperiness, of the conjuror. Sodomy should be avoided, as far as possible. It tends to add to the abominable confusion already existing.'

While Lewis's polemic continues to affront every notion of political correctness, his audience recognises that his contrariness is merely a facet of a far more complex, and engaging, world view. The ability to provoke and doubt, simultaneously, has often been cited as being fundamental to great art. Lewis himself went some way to acknowledging this in 1917: 'You must be a duet in everything. For, the individual, the single object, and the isolated, is, you will admit, an absurdity. Why try and give the impression of a consistent and indivisible personality?'

From the very beginning, Vorticism has been Wyndham Lewis's medium for expressing his unique world view. Everything outside the Vortex is meat for his stew. Within the chaos of Vorticism, and within the oblique, humorous code of Lewis's writing, there are precise patterns and a finely focused lucidity. He assembles his words in such a manner that found language, narrative, slang, double-talk, trigger phrases and rapid juxtapositions are combined to create a discourse which describes as it commentates. The style is not artless, as it may seem, but is instead the product of careful design.

'Life is what I have gone out to get,' says Lewis – 'life where it is merging with something else, certainly. But I catch it just before it goes over into the fatuous element. The fish is still in the stream. Or, if you like, this is the raw meat in the kitchen – destined, perhaps, for the Banquet of Reason, but as yet highly irrational.'

Like Mark E. Smith, Wyndham Lewis will suggest the existence of a conspiracy behind most manifestations of modern culture. In texts such as *Enemy of the Stars, Life is an Important Thing, Policeman and Artist, The Orchestra of Media, Tarr* and *The Code of a Herdsman*, Lewis appears to endorse what Smith meant by 'the war against intelligence'. In 1937, Lewis stated: 'Do not play with political notions, aristocratisms or the reverse, for that is a compromise with the herd. Do not allow yourself to imagine "a fine herd though still a herd." There is no FINE HERD. The cattle that call themselves "gentlemen" you will observe to be a little cleaner. It is merely cunning and produced with a product called SOAP. But you will find no serious difference between them and those vast dismal herds they avoid. Some of them are very dangerous and treacherous.'

If Vorticism is both Lewis's vision of the world and his means of describing it, then the Great British Vortex is peopled with grotesque characters whom Lewis has invented. These would include BRITANNIC AESTHETE, WILD NATURE CRANK, DOMESTICATED POLICEMAN, GAEITY CHORUS GIRL, AMATEUR, SCIOLAST, ART-PIMP, JOURNALIST, SELF-MAN, ORGANIST and THE HAIRDRESSER. One gets the impression that Lewis's imagination was incubating this cast since before Vorticism began. In many ways, his writing has served to fill the biographies of these characters; at the same time, Lewis will write pseudonymously under their names. In a later autobiographical piece entitled 'The "Author of *Tarr*"', he begins: 'So much for Mr Cantleman. Need I repeat that this hero of mine is not to be identified with me? But to some extent, in the fragments I have just quoted, you get the lowdown on the editor of *Blast*. That is why I used them.'

When asked to clarify this assessment of these characters, Lewis cautiously sips his beer before replying: 'Never fall into the vulgarity of assuming yourself to be one ego. Each trench must have another one behind it. Each single self — that you manage to be at any given time — must have five at least indifferent to it. You must have a power of indifference of five to one. All the greatest actions in the world have been five parts out of six impersonal in the impulse of their origin. To follow this principle, you need only cultivate your memory.'

'In order to live you must remain broken up,' Lewis announced in 1917. While critics have yet to agree whether the Vorticists, artistically, are drab or dynamic, the roots of mesmeric intensity lie in the practice of contradiction. In the most compelling Lewis texts, the language and typography merely provide an open structure through which the author roams like a suspicious caretaker, flashing his torch from one empty dark room to another. This is best illustrated in *Blast*'s 'Manifesto', signed by ten others. The seven-part polemic begins with a ten-point prologue, in which Lewis declaims: 'Beyond action and reaction we would establish ourselves / We start from opposite statements of a chosen world. Set up violent structure of adolescent clearness between two extremes / We discharge ourselves on both sides / We fight first on one side, then on the other, but always for the same cause, which is neither side or both sides and ours.'

As Lewis explains, the idea of the Vorticists was always to create a violent central activity, attracting everything to itself, absorbing all that is around it. 'Vorticism was an intellectual eruption, productive of a closely packed, brightly coloured alphabet of objects with a logic of its own. The doctrine which is implicit in this eruption is to be looked for in the shapes for which it was responsible [...] I should have encouraged the shaping, in clay or in wood, of objects conforming to these theories. In other words, a world of not-stone, not-trees, not-dogs, not-men, not-bottles, not-houses, etc.'

Initially, the received idea of the Vorticists' audience was that of pale, tall, exceedingly romantic-looking fellows. The obscurity of the Vortex appeared to demand supporters who were socially dysfunctional – the weird cousins of the Bloomsbury Group. In time, however, the Vorticists have achieved a certain following, alongside fellow modernists such as James Joyce, Ezra Pound and T. S. Eliot.

'It was scarcely our fault that we were a youth racket. It was Ezra who in the first place organised us willy-nilly into that. For he was never satisfied until everything was organised. And it was he who made us into a youth racket – that was his method of organisation.

'All politics today, and all the "youth-racket" element in politics, are put across by men-of-letters, journalists, philosophes, or the propaganda of intellectualist sects, groups and phalansteries, rather than via the clubs or the floor of the House of Commons. And as I have already indicated, there was a tidy bit of political contraband tucked away in our technical militancy. But I was not the responsible party.

'Yes, Mr Joyce, Mr Pound, Mr Eliot – and, for I said that my piety was egoistic, the Enemy as well – the Chiricos and Picassos, and in music their equivalents – will be the exotic flowers of a culture that has passed. As people look back at them out of a very humdrum, cautious, disillusioned society, the critics of the future day will rub their eyes. They will look, to them, so hopelessly avant-garde!, so almost madly up-and-coming!

'What energy! – what impossibly Spartan standards, men will exclaim! So heroically these "pioneers" will stand out, like monosyllable monoliths – Pound, Joyce, Lewis. They will acquire the strange aspects of "empire-builders", as seen by a well-levelled and efficiently flattened-out Proletariat, with all its million tails well down between its shuffling legs!'

But, despite their position as a 'difficult' group already at odds with shifting cultural fashions, the Vorticists' Luddite tendencies have brought them into the focus of serious debate about contemporary art. 'The Arts with their great capital 'A's are, considered as plants, decidedly unrobust. They are the sport, at the best, of political chance: parasitically dependent upon the good health of the social body.

'A few arts were born in the happy lull before the world-storm. In 1914 a ferment of the artistic intelligence occurred in the west of Europe. And it looked to many people as if a great historic "school" was in process of formation. Expressionism, post-Impressionism, Vorticism, Cubism, Futurism were some of the characteristic nicknames bestowed upon these manifestations, where they found their intensest expression in the pictorial field. In every case the structural and philosophic rudiments of life were sought out. On all hands a return to first principles was witnessed.'

Wyndham Lewis's writing anticipates and rejects academic criticism, although he has offered analyses of his work. Of his various *Blast*s (1914), Lewis says, concisely: 'Take the first *Blast*, "Blast Humour". That is straightforward enough. The Englishman has what he calls a "sense of humour". He says that the German, the Frenchman, and most foreigners do not possess this attribute, and suffer accordingly. For what does the "sense of humour" mean but an ability to belittle everything – to make light of everything? Not only does the Englishman not "make a mountain out of a molehill"; he is able to make a molehill out of a mountain.' The more ambitious *Tarr* (1914–15), a terse first novel of verbal economy, was summarised by Lewis as displaying 'a certain indifference to bourgeois conventions, and an unblushing disbelief in the innate goodness of human nature'.

Lewis, spokesman of 'The New Egos', maintains a similar single-mindedness towards the traditionally sensitive subject of politics. 'I am trying to save people from being "ruled" too much – from being "ruled" off the face of the earth, as a matter of fact.'

But would Lewis invest, seriously, in politics? 'Really all this organised disturbance was Art behaving as if it were Politics. But I swear I did not know it. It may in fact have been politics. I see that now. Indeed it must have been. But I was unaware of the fact: I believed that this was the way artists were always received; a somewhat tumultuous reception, perhaps, but after all, why not? I mistook the agitation in the audience for the sign of an awakening of the emotion of artistic sensibility. And then I assumed too that artists always formed militant groups. I supposed they had to do this, seeing how "bourgeois" all Publics were – or all Publics of which I had any experience.

'Anyhow, in 1926 I began writing about politics, not because I like politics but everything was getting bogged in them and before you could do anything you had to deal with the politics with which it was encrusted. And I've got so bepoliticked myself in the process that in order to get at me, today, you have to get the politics off me first. However, when politics came on the scene I ring down the curtain; and that was in 1926. That was when politics began for me in earnest. I've never had a moment's peace since.'

Inevitably, Lewis is in danger of becoming as marginalised as Mark E. Smith became in his later, and most prolific, years. As yet, however, the Vorticists remain a question mark in the history of art. But Lewis continues to rant.

'Peace is a fearful thing for that countless majority who are so placed that there is no difference between Peace and War – except that during the latter day they are treated with more consideration. In war, if they are wounded they are well treated, in peace, if struck down it is apt to be nothing like so pleasant.

'You will be astonished to find out how like art is to war, I mean "modernist" art. They talk a lot about how a war just-finished effects art. But a war about to start can do the same thing. War, art, civil war, strikes, *coup d'états* dovetail into each other. It is somewhat depressing to consider how as an artist one is always holding up a mirror to politics without really knowing it. My picture called the *Plan of War* painted six months before the Great War "broke out", as we say, depresses me. A prophet is a most unoriginal person: all he is doing is imitating something that is not there, but soon will be. With me war and art have been mixed up from the start. It is still.'

1998
'Masquerade' (Mar); Smith appears in *Glow Boys*, short film by Mark Aerial Waller; Smith arrested in New York – Hanley S., Burns and Tommy Crooks leave (Apr); *The Post Nearly Man* Smith solo LP (Sep); short-lived all-female band w/ Nagle, Karen Leatham and Kate Themen, who leaves after three shows.

1999
'Touch Sensitive' (Mar); *The Marshall Suite* (Apr); 'F-'Oldin' Money' (Aug); Smith asked to model for Calvin Klein; Smith appears in *Midwatch*, second short film w/ Mark Aerial Waller.

2000
The Unutterable (Nov).

2001
Rude (All the Time) EP (Aug); *Are You Are Missing Winner* (Nov); Craig Scanlon invited to rejoin but declines.

2002
2G+2 live/studio LP (Jun); 'Susan vs. Youthclub' (Dec); 'Touch Sensitive' used in Vauxhall Corsa advert; Smith releases *Pander! Panda! Panzer!*, spoken-word LP.

2003
The Real New Fall LP (Formerly 'Country on the Click') (Oct) – planned for release in April, largely re-recorded after original mix leaks; '(We Wish You) A Protein Christmas' (Dec).

2004
50,000 Fall Fans Can't Be Wrong: 39 Golden Greats compilation (Jun); 'Theme from Sparta F.C. #2' (Jun); *Interim* rehearsals/live LP (Nov); '2 Librans' (Jul).

2005
The Fall: The Wonderful and Frightening World of Mark E Smith BBC4 doc (Jan); *Complete Peel Sessions* box (Apr); 'I Can Hear the Grass Grow' (Sep); *Fall Heads Roll* (Oct).

2006
BBC Radio 3 Mixing It session (Feb); Birtwistle, Pritchard and Trafford leave after show in Phoenix, AZ (May 7) – Smith, Poulou, plus local musicians Tim Presley, Rob Barbato, and Orpheo McCord complete US tour; *Paintwork* exhibition of Fall cover artists and artworks inspired by the group, Praxis Hagen gallery, Berlin (May).

2007
Reformation Post TLC (Feb); 'Reformation' (Apr); *Tromatic Reflexxions* by Von Südenfed – Smith w/ Mouse on Mars (May); Smith reads football results on BBC1 Final Score (May 6).

The Marshall Suite (April 1999, Artful)

PART ONE
Touch Sensitive
F-'oldin' Money
Shake-Off
Bound
This Perfect Day

PART TWO
(Jung Nev's) Antidotes
Inevitable
Anecdotes + Antidotes In B#
Finale: Tom Raggazzi

PART THREE
Early Life of Crying Marshal
The Crying Marshal
Birthday Song
Mad.Men-Eng.Dog
On My Own

Part One //

TOUCH SENSITIVE
M.E. SMITH / J. NAGLE / S. HITCHCOCK)

F-'OLDIN' MONEY
T. BLAKE)

SHAKE-OFF
M.E. SMITH / S. HITCHCOCK / K. LEATHAM / T. HEAD)

BOUND
M.E. SMITH / WILSON BROS.) BMI

THIS PERFECT DAY
BAILEY / KUEPPER) ATV MUSIC LTD

Part Two //

(JUNG NEV'S) ANTIDOTES
M.E. SMITH / N. WILDING / S. HITCHCOCK)

INEVITABLE
M.E. SMITH / J. NAGLE / T. HEAD / K. LEATHAM)

ANECDOTES + ANTIDOTES IN B#
M.E. SMITH / J. NAGLE)

FINALE: TOM RAGGAZZI
M.E. SMITH / J. NAGLE / T. HEAD)

Part Three //

EARLY LIFE OF CRYING MARSHAL
S. HITCHCOCK)

THE CRYING MARSHAL
M.E. SMITH / S. HITCHCOCK)

BIRTHDAY SONG
NAGLE / M.E. SMITH)

MAD.MEN-ENG.OOG
M.E. SMITH / S. LEVEEN / J. NAGLE)

ON MY OWN
M.E. SMITH / J. NAGLE / S. WOLSTENCROFT)

Fourth Part Of Int. Quatrich

MARK E. SMITH // VOCALS) KEYBOARDS) GUITAR)
TOM HEAD // DRUMS)
JULIA NAGLE // KEYBOARDS) GUITAR) PROGRAMMING)
NEVILLE WILDING // GUITAR) VOCAL)

KAREN LEATHAM // BASS)
ADAM HALAL // BASS)
S. HITCHCOCK // STRING ARRANGEMENTS)
SOUND / ENGINEERING // ELSPETH HUGHES, JIM BRUMBY, RICHARD FLACK
PRODUCTION // S. HITCHCOCK, M.E. SMITH

ASSOCIATE PRODUCER // BERNARD MACMAHON
JOHN LENNARD // EXECUTIVE PROD)
PASCAL LE GRAS // PHOTOGRAPHY
THX // P. CHARLES / LISA + MARK @ BATTERY

DESIGN // WARNE/TRUSTAM)

MARK E. SMITH // VOCALS) KEYBOARDS) GUITAR)
TOM HEAD // DRUMS)
JULIA NAGLE // KEYBOARDS) GUITAR) PROGRAMMING)
NEVILLE WILDING // GUITAR) VOCAL)
KAREN LEATHAM // BASS)
ADAM HALAL // BASS)
S. HITCHCOCK // STRING ARRANGEMENTS)

SOUND / ENGINEERING // ELSPETH HUGHES, JIM BRUMBY, RICHARD FLACK
PRODUCTION // S. HITCHCOCK, M.E. SMITH

PASCAL LE GRAS // PHOTOGRAPHY

DESIGN // WARNE / TRUSTAM)

RECORDED AT BATTERY STUDIOS, LONDON, LATE 1998 / EARLY 1999.

NB The double vinyl only used three sides, with Side 4 blank.

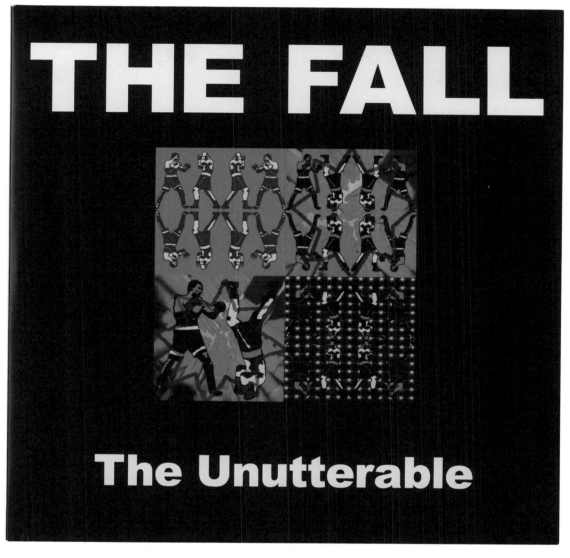

The Unutterable (November 2000, Eagle)

SIDE A
Cyber Insekt
Two Librans
W.B.
Sons Of Temperance

SIDE B
Dr. Bucks' Letter
Hot Runes
Way Round

SIDE C
Octo Realm – Ketamine Sun
Serum
Unutterable
Pumpkin Soup and Mashed Potatoes

SIDE D
Hands Up Billy
Midwatch 1953
Devolute
Das Katerer

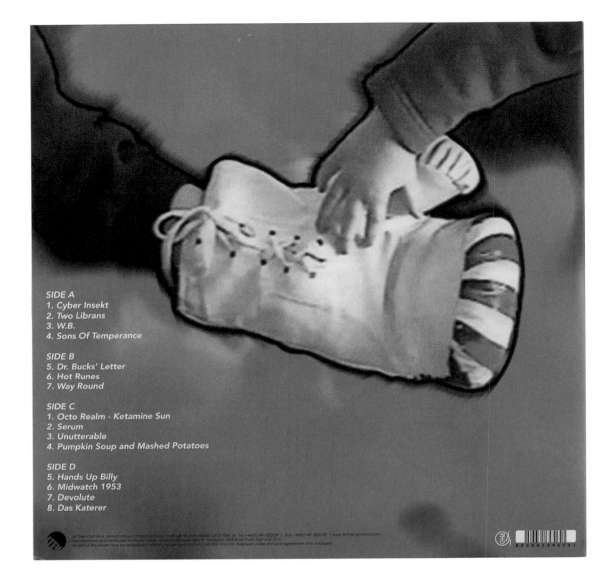

SIDE A
1. Cyber Insekt
2. Two Librans
3. W.B.
4. Sons Of Temperance

SIDE B
5. Dr. Bucks' Letter
6. Hot Runes
7. Way Round

SIDE C
1. Octo Realm - Ketamine Sun
2. Serum
3. Unutterable
4. Pumpkin Soup and Mashed Potatoes

SIDE D
5. Hands Up Billy
6. Midwatch 1953
7. Devolute
8. Das Katerer

Mark E. Smith – Vocals, SFX
Adam Helal – Bass Guitar, proTools
Neville Wilding – Guitar, Vocal
Julia Nagle – Keyboards, Guitar, Vocal Programming
Tom Head – Drums, Percussion
Steve Evets – Vocal
Kazuko Hohki – Vocal
Ben Pritchard – Guitar

Produced by Grant Showbiz / Mark E. Smith
Executive Producer – Rob Ayling

NB This album was only available on CD on release, with the first vinyl pressing on Let Them Eat Vinyl in 2014.

Are You Are Missing Winner (November 2002, Cog Sinister)

SIDE 1
Jim's "The Fall"
Bourgeois Town
Crop-Dust
My Ex-Classmates' Kids
Kick The Can
Gotta See Jane

SIDE 2
Ibis-Afro Man
The Acute
Hollow Mind
Reprise: Jane – Prof Mick – Ey Bastardo

M. E. Smith : Vocals
J. Watts : Bass, Guitar
B. Pritchard : Lead Guitar
S. Birtwistle : Drums
with :
E. Blaney : Guitar + Vocals
B. Fanning : Guitar + Vocals

Produced by :
M. E. Smith
E. Blaney
S. Birtwistle
J. Watts

Engineered by :
Steve Lloyd / Noise Box / Lancs 2001

Design Steve Lee at ZEITartwork

Recorded at Noise Box, Manchester, mid-2001.

The Real New Fall LP (*Formerly 'Country on the Click'*) (October 2003, Action)

SIDE 1
Green Eyed Loco-Man
Mountain Energei
Theme From Sparta F.C.
Contraflow
Last Commands of Xyralothep Via M.E.S.
Open the Boxoctosis #2

SIDE 2
Janet, Johnny + James
The Past #2
Loop41 'Houston
Mike's Love Xexagon
Proteinprotection
Recovery Kit

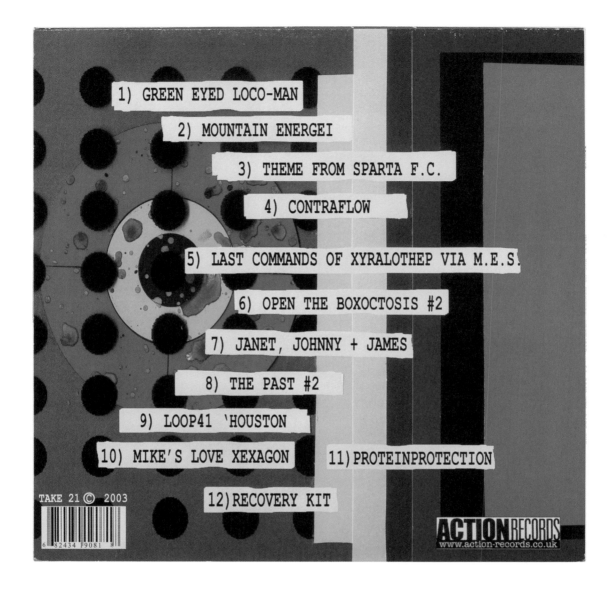

1) GREEN EYED LOCO-MAN

2) MOUNTAIN ENERGEI

3) THEME FROM SPARTA F.C.

4) CONTRAFLOW

5) LAST COMMANDS OF XYRALOTHEP VIA M.E.S.

6) OPEN THE BOXOCTOSIS #2

7) JANET, JOHNNY + JAMES

8) THE PAST #2

9) LOOP41 'HOUSTON

10) MIKE'S LOVE XEXAGON   11) PROTEINPROTECTION

12) RECOVERY KIT

TAKE 21 © 2003

ACTION RECORDS
www.action-records.co.uk

DAVID MILNER – DRUMS – B.VOCALS
– KEYBOARDS
BEN PRITCHARD – LD.GUITAR – B.VOCALS
ELINI POULOU – KEYBOARDS – B.VOCALS
MARK.E.SMITH – LD.VOCALS
JIM WATTS – BASS GUITAR – GUITAR
– COMPUTERS

PLUS: S.BESWICK [KEYS 12]
THE PLOUTY [ORGAN+TEXT 11]
DING [BASS 1]

ENGINEERED BY – TIM GRACIELANDS
– JIM WATTS
PRODUCED BY – GRANT CUNLIFFE
– MARK.E.SMITH

COVER: MARCUS PARNELL

EXECUTIVE PRODUCER – GORDON GIBSON

Recorded at Gracieland, Rochdale, late 2002 /
mid-2003.

Fall Heads Roll (October 2005, Slogan)

SIDE A
Ride Away
Pacifying Joint
What About Us?
Midnight in Aspen
Assume
Aspen Reprise
Bo Demmick

SIDE B
Blindness
I Can Hear the Grass Grow
Youwanner
Clasp Hands
Early Days of Channel Führer
Breaking the Rules
Trust In Me

MARK E. SMITH – VOCALS
BEN PRITCHARD – GUITAR
STEVE TRAFFORD – BASS, VOCALS, GUITAR
SPENCER BIRTWISTLE – DRUMS
ELENI POULOU – SYNTHESIZER, VOCALS

also: DINGO – BANJO, BASS

engineers – BILLY & ALEX (NYC)

produced by – M.E.SMITH / SIMON ARCHER
TIM GRACIELANDS

Recorded at Gigantic Studios, New York, January 2005
and Gracieland, Rochdale, mid-2005.

Reformation Post TLC (February 2007, Slogan)

SIDE 1
Over! Over!
Reformation!
Fall Sound

SIDE 2
White Line Fever
Insult Song
My Door Is Never

SIDE 3
Coach And Horses
The Usher
The Wright Stuff
Scenario

SIDE 4
Das Boat
The Bad Stuff
Systematic Abuse

Robert Barbato   Bass Guitar
Elena Poulou   Keyboards
Mark E Smith   Vocals
Orpheo McCord   Drums / Vocals
Tim Presley   Lead Guitar
Dave Spurr   Bass Guitar

With Special Guests
Peter Greenway Rhythm / Lead Guitar
Gary Bennett Rhythm Guitar

Produced By Tim 'Gracielands' and Mark E Smith

Artwork: Mark Kennedy / George Shaw / Big Head
And His Wife / Becky Stewart

Recorded at Gracieland, Rochdale, late 2006.

'I Want to Sell a Million': Use Value, Exchange Value and Woolworths – Twickenham, 1983–85

Middlesex Enclave, 1983

In 1983, in the Middlesex enclave of Twickenham, the primary source of music for the growing child is the radio; far more so than TV. John Peel, Monday to Wednesday, 10 p.m. to midnight. I listen on my own after my mum and my sister have gone to bed. I am twelve. I am enchanted. The records are eclectic: from Soft Cell to Big Black, Echo and the Bunnymen to the Frank Chickens . . . Ivor Cutler nestled between Altered Images. Often the only unifier is the transmission date. There is also no sense of what the bands on *John Peel* look like – unless they go on to score a rare TV appearance. At this time, I have no idea there is a music press beyond *Smash Hits*, i.e. the 'inkies' – *Sounds*, the *NME*, *Melody Maker* – where musicians are mouthy, get drunk and have arguments with journalists.

The secondary source of music in Twickenham, the point at which you are able to quantify your listening – to make concrete out of abstract and *buy* a record to play at home – is Woolworths on King Street. Clean, expansive – and also stocks sweets. But John Peel and Woolworths seem worlds apart. The *snap, crackle* of Wham! and Billy Joel on the record racks is the diametric opposite of the Cocteau Twins. Isn't it?

Of course I first hear the Fall on the *John Peel Show*. I am given a second-hand record player and radio set by my dad, which is set inside a black 'executive' (or so I believe) suitcase. The Fall are mad, strange, *other*, and yet wholly familiar. Maybe it's because they are the voice of the Lacanian Real, or the Žižekian *real* Real; maybe it's because John Peel never stops playing them.

The Fall in session. Repeats of the Fall in session. Fall singles – and album tracks. I hear Fall songs taking up a great swathe of the Festive Fifty. Fall, Fall, Fall. They are contrasted with the song about the tube top and drag racing, and the song about the 'Blue Canary', and one proclaiming 'It's a Fine Day'. They are definitely *songs*, these things by this group called the Fall, because they are under four minutes long and are played alongside other songs. Fall, Fall, Fall. They shout 'Eat y'self fitter' and *yelp yelp!* all over '2 × 4', and it could be Slade or Trio, but it's not. There's a woman's voice too, and the female element just makes it more exciting. And everyone seems to like them on this programme. John Peel reads letters about them from listeners. Fans.

So it must be true: they have fans – they're popular. Or are they? I'm not sure.

'L.A.' and 'C.R.E.E.P.' – *this is incredible.* I learn that a 'session' is four songs from the band that are different to the other recordings by the band but somehow almost the same. Just like a record is a copy of a 'master' copy of vibrations recorded onto electromagnetic tape, until at the end of the process it's played through a speaker and back into the air again. The same but not actually the same.

Is it important to be popular? Is it important to be alternative? Is it popular to be alternative? If there is a choice, a pre-teen tween choice (although, in 1983, this is sort of pre-tween actually), where do you go to register your views?

In the UK, in the early 1980s, music is mainly free for the schoolchild: you just tape it off the radio. But being in a band is harder because you can 'sell out' to the devil himself – *the Man* – in a matter of minutes. If you advertise jeans or beer, behaviour which is deemed acceptable nowadays, you will go to a certain sort of hell. If you appear on *Top of the Pops* (which is clearly a ludicrous invitation to decline), the Clash will tell you off. And see where that got them.

Early 1985. The Fall are on the brink of something, judging by the sounds coming from the executive suitcase. 'Spoilt Victorian Child'. 'Couldn't Get Ahead'. Songs that are more song-like. The Man yet nearer. Are they alternative? Is it important to be popular? Eat y'self fitter.

Are they about to sell out?

The Fall have not yet appeared in Twickenham Woolworths.

But.

1985. Live Aid in the summer. Princess Di's hair watches George Michael's hair at Wembley Stadium. Pop music has gone big, pop music has gone mental. Pop music – fuck Kensington Market and goths and punks and tiny little earrings in the shape of a cannabis leaf (I got one just thinking it was a nice shape) – has gone extra-blow-dry. It has gone big or it's gone home, to borrow a phrase from five years ago, i.e. the Future. And it's not gone home.

By November, Twickenham Woolworths *itself* has gone mental. It has finally happened: the Fall are now in there too with 'Cruisers Creek'. Let us browse the seven-inch singles lined up like slices of toast: Wham!, Eurythmics and Aretha Franklin. Madness. Shakatak. Midge Ure. Each saying something different, each with a story to tell, yet each priced exactly the same – 79p. I've seen the Fall, though, now – on *The Tube*. The female element I know is Brix. Brix! Half-Madonna, half-chihuahua. During the interview with Muriel Gray, Mark says things like, 'I've always thought of accessibility as something to be spat upon,' so I'm truly *wondering*: is this triumph or disaster? What will the Clash say? Back in Woolworths, in the coming months the Fall will be racked alongside the Durutti Column, Billy Bragg, Stump, New Order and the Cocteau Twins – and George Benson. A slave to the 'midweek' – the one and only ur-accurate prediction of where the record might be placed at the end of the week – Woolworths' buying tactic is now eclectic. It is broad.

So if these bands – the *alternative* crew – are in Twickenham Woolworths, have we all fallen foul of the Man? What is the relation between creative ambition, cultural evolution, the revelation of the Real and profiteering? Oh God.

Now That's What We Call RRP

The music marketplace has a flat recommended retail price (RRP) for every record. A Bogshed seven-inch costs as much as one by Status Quo. Nor does it cost more to buy a record about Jacques Derrida with a rap at the end (Scritti Politti, a double A-side with 'Asylums in Jerusalem', 1982). In 1984, extensive sleeve notes including references to Knut Hamsun, Zola and HP Sauce accompany Frankie Goes to Hollywood's *Welcome to the Pleasuredome* album (ZTT). By the same token, in 1985 it doesn't cost *less* to buy a record about the vagaries of romantic love, although you could argue that there is a *surplus* in terms of this particular type of positing in November 1985 – 'Say You, Say Me' by Lionel Richie, 'The Power of Love' by Jennifer Rush, 'Don't Break My Heart' by UB40. And nor are production costs taken into account. A piece of seven-inch vinyl costs the same to produce whether you press a seven-minute song about ankles featuring a thirty-two-piece orchestra and four swans on bass that's taken three years to record from inception to completion, or a twenty-two-second tune on a kazoo.

The cost of sleeve production is different. It depends, of course, on card weight, printing technique, whether there's a gatefold, etc., but sleeves are separate; they are not dependent on content.

Now That's What We Call Use Value

The record business differs hugely from other areas of the arts, such as theatre, classical music and dance, which receive various forms of funding (from the Arts Council and the National Lottery, among others). The music industry may delight in artists playing live, but it's all about the units, man. The kudos is in record sales. Records have VAT added to the retail price, unlike books.

Because, like, all the people who write books are brilliant, and all the people who make records might just as well be making cupcakes out of goldfinches.

Or something.

Under capitalism all products are commodities. 'Use value' measures the 'usefulness' of a commodity, how far it meets the needs of the consumer. 'Exchange value' is the relative value of a given commodity against another. A sack of oats may be worth two Kit Kats. Next week, though, and given the current economic climate, we may be stabbing each other over the sack of oats in an attempt to stay alive, and it will be 'worth' a whole lot more in exchange value, you sorry, sorry people of the British Isles.

In 1985, the exchange value of a Fall single is the same as one by UB40. That we know. But what is the *use value* of a Fall record when its function is interpretative? *Cultural?* And is it any different from UB40's? And who gets to say so?

Does the use value of a record change the *more* people listen to it? When the record gets into Woolworths, when it nestles among George Michael and Aretha Franklin?

This I do not know.

Now We Get on to Why Your Commercial Period is Also the Most Revolutionary, if You are the Fall – i.e. Brix

Take this quick quiz!

I am in a band, because:

– I need to express myself ✗
– people will find me attractive ✗
– I would like people I don't know to think they know me ✗
– I will become rich ✗
– there is no one else to fill in on bass ✓

> *Once you start revolving yourself around a tune, your axis is fucked.*
> (Mark E. Smith)

It's a myth that bands don't like selling many records, that they want to be on the sidelines, outsiders. If you have no money, you can't afford studio time. It's difficult to tour: you can't pay for a full band, the accommodation's shit, and if no one turns up to your shows, it's pointless. Art needs an audience, almost all of the time.

So why Brix?

Brix the guitarist

Brix the songwriter

Brix the blonde

Brix the wife

Brix – the hits

Brix is as much a subversive presence – fully involved, part of the art, a woman too, brandishing the phallic guitar object – as she is a commercial agent. She both upends the original product – noble savage over primal beat; man and B&H – and *sells it back*. It's no coincidence, surely, that Madonna's hippest single, 'Into the Groove', is released in the same year as what most people (honest) regard as the Fall's first pop record – 'Cruiser's Creek'. Brix ushered in the Commercial Fall Era, from 1983's *Perverted by Language* onwards.

And.

Yet.

It is their most avant-garde period.

*I don't want to sell 40,000 records, I want to sell a million. Mark isn't really
bothered about this but I want to get to all those people who aren't hearing the
records. It doesn't really mean anything unless you get a gold disc.*
(Brix Smith, *NME*, 1986)

The sound is more solid, the sonics more expansive – the studios have got
fancier. She and Mark buy a BMW.

Of course, Brix is not the first female Fall member. Una Baines,
Kay Carroll and Yvonne Pawlett were before her. But Brix joins, and people
still think that's unusual because women are not in as many bands as men.
No one knows why, because they have the same amount of fingers as
man-humans to play stringed instruments and they have genetically identical
mouths that can sing.

So, yes, the Fall have started to revolve around the axis of bigger riffs.
Brix riffs. Briffs. The 'Cruiser's Creek' *video* (they make a video! *PRODUCT!*)
features Brix outside the Ravenscourt Arms in Hammersmith, London,
commanding her Rickenbacker like an elfin, blonde Brian May. We also see
performance artist Leigh Bowery, his face painted in maroon spots which
match his jacket.

The message is getting out there. More people will hear the Fall.
More people will see the Fall. A support slot with U2 in 1987? Yes, please!
(Although they had played with U2 many years previously, when they
were all six years old.)

That is the point, after all? More, not less. Spread the word. Tour the
territories. Eat y'self popular.

HOWEVER.

The price of the 'Cruiser's Creek' single drops in December 1985, when
Band Aid's 'Do They Know It's Christmas?' (don't ask Mark E. about that,
they said, but someone did) hits no. 1. Supply and demand – the product,
which has taken the Fall to a heady no. 96 in the UK charts, becomes surplus.
There are more copies in Twickenham Woolworths than Twickenham
Woolworths would wish. The price drops to 49p, then to 20p. The use value
is still the same, but the exchange value has dropped. Wherein we sense
a coup.

The same applies to – although at different times – the Smiths,
Julian Cope and anything that leaped into the chart thanks to an ardent fan
base and back out again.

But this is doubly subversive. Not only does the Twickenham Woolworths
display the most egalitarian record selection in the county, but the product
is fucking with the formula. The surplus is screwing the finances. The records
which fly back out of the chart are then being sold at a loss – there obviously
being no 'sale or return' policy here. The higher the midweek, the greater the
gamble. In this context, the Virgin Megastore in Oxford Street, by Tottenham
Court Road (now a Primark), would not discount singles and albums so soon

after a chart placing. Harry's 2 is the only other record store in Twickenham, run by a man (not called Harry) who owns Harry's wine bar in Teddington and *could have* opened a record store as a way of paying less tax. Harry's 2 prefers to stock the lighter side of rock – a bit of P. Gabriel, a bit of Waterboys, Kate Bush – something you'll listen to on hi-fi separates, with all that 'spaghetti at the back', which Lenny Henry so disclaims in his Sony advert of the time. Harry's 2 does not sell discounted vinyl until Harry's 2's January sales. I once went in and asked for a Bananarama single, and was met by an icy eyebrow.

So, like some peculiarly British extension of Patti Smith's 'Piss Factory', the Fall are messing with the quota. They are too good, too mainstream, while still being art. (However, it is probably not enough to bring Woolworths down.)

Wild Boy of Dance

Hey! Luciani, Smith's 1986 play about Pope John Paul I's mysterious death, which features our friend Leigh Bowery, is *not* mainstream. 'Wild boy of dance' Michael Clark's 1988 ballet *I Am Curious, Orange*, is *not* mainstream. It's as if the Hits Hits Hits years, the Brix Brix Brix years, are in perfect balance. There is no compromise.

As an art form, dance must be the least cost-effective. Dancers take years to be trained, a dance company is expensive to pay and look after – think of all those swollen joints, those crooked toes – and the productivity rate is low and can't be speeded up by automation. Match this with a troupe of speed-freak minstrels (i.e. our friends the Fall), and you have a pretty shitty prospect 'on the balance sheet'. And yet there they are, all the guys, all the dancers, the bottoms, the enormous hamburgers, the Leigh-Bowery-dressed-as-a-tin-of-beans and pirouettes. And yet this is a commercial hit, in media terms. Broadcast news fizzes around the production. The Fall (the Fall!) perform in front of the Queen of Holland, and she shakes everyone's hand after the show – just like Princess Di after Live Aid.

Just like Princess Di after Live Aid.

This is the life.

You are the wild boys and girls of rock.

You are the wild boy of dance.

You are ~~messing with the paintwork~~ Damo Suzuki.

Except Can never did theatre and dance. Or did they?

Baumol's Cost Disease

Baumol's cost disease theory centres on the rise of automation lowering the cost of most goods (through high productivity), which inadvertently pushes up the cost of jobs with low productivity, such as teaching, science and music. In addition to this, the knock-on effect is that jobs with low productivity and high status – poet, dancer, rock musician – become *more desirable* in a traditional capitalist economy. The artists' worth becomes inflated and more symbolic the less they seem to do. They are seers, visionaries, there's a ghost in their house. Now, rock singers are still very much part of the new culture industry. They *need* Gucci waistcoats because they are signifiers, the waistcoats, of sitting on the sofa just waiting for the muse. High-cost, high-status baked beans. In the current age, a cultural product's use value has been rebranded through buzzwords such as 'community', 'artisan', 'handmade', 'limited', 'organic'. *Authenticity* defines the use value of culture.

Are the Fall authentic? Wot? Does it matter? And who sold that idea to me in Twickenham in the first place?

Buying records is never *truly* subversive; people 'wear' them as they do Supreme sneakers or those waistcoats. They are signifiers of the Real, but not actually *real* – emotions are real, gestures are real. Carrier bags from record shops are often flimsy for that reason – you can see the record sleeve through the plastic. To show what you have just bought. To show what you are *like*.

Carrier-bag man.

Taping records off the radio is subversive. Messing with the exchange value. The Fall were like the local cult selling their own jam door to door. It got big. It got heavy. *Did you hear how they sold almost a million pots of jam? That jam supported U2.*

2nd. May '88

Dear Ms. Tait.

Herewith my subscription/application to join The Arthur Machen Society.

regards –

Mark E. Smith.

Pages 260–9: Correspondence with the
Arthur Machen Society.

To. the A. M. Soc.
From the only
man banned from it!
(or can't find it, more like!
M. E. Smith —
The Fall

ROVERS BY NIGHT
© REGISTERED COPYRIGHT GRANADA TV

the **Fall**

To: Rita Tait.
19, CROSS ST.
CAERLEON
GWENT.

COG-SINISTER

Unit 39
23 New Mount Street
Manchester
M4 4DE

M.E. SMITH.
16, WINCHESTER
AVENUE
Sedgley Park
PRESTWICH.
M/CR M25

Dear Rita:

So GOOD TO HEAR FROM 28th. Sep. '95.
YOU AND YOU SOUND WELL.

AS FOR "UPDATING" COMPUTERS, I'VE
MONITORED SO MUCH CASH WASTE IN
PUBLISHERS, COLLECTION AGENCIES, RECORD
STUDIOS AND GENERAL BUSINESS — ESP.
WHERE ARTISTIC FANS LIKE YOU + I
ARE INVOLVED, I'D THINK TWICE
IF I WERE YOU!!! WATCH OUT!!

ANYTHING ME OR THE FALL CAN
DO, THOUGH, CASH-WISE FOR

264

c.c. File.
c.c. COG-SINISTER
- L. RIMMER
M. FAUX

the Fall

Unit 39
23 New Mount Street
Manchester
M4 4DE

0161 953
4028,

THE SOCIETY, JUST RING OFFICE ↗
OR ME ON ███████ (please keep no. 2 yself).

I'LL DEFINITELY RING IAIN RE. 4+5
IT'LL FIT IN WITH OUR GENE PITNEY CONCERT
VISIT IN THAT VICINITY (GOING TO WATCH HIM,
THAT IS!).

HIT ACKROYD UP FOR SOME CASH TOO -
ESP. AFTER THAT TRAVESTY BOOK ON
'OUR LORD' W. BLAKE!

A BIT OF ADVICE I'D APPRECIATE
THOUGH OFF YOU RITA. - Let Me Explain
— MY MUSIC PUBLISHERS IN CONJUNCTION W/
- funny enough - A Welsh T.V. Channel
Are seriously talking about me

3/3   28/9/95.

the Fall

c.c. File
c.c. 'COG-SINISTER'
~L.RIMMER.
m.FAUX

Unit 39
23 New Mount Street
Manchester
M4 4DE

doing six T.V. episodes in d weird vein, with total control. Me and some friends have come up with some ~~crackling~~ cracking original tales, ~~Modernish~~ "modern". Also I've done an adapt. of H.P.Lovecraft's 'THE CALL OF CTHULHU'. They want me to do a 'POE-ISH'(in their words) tale also. OBVIOUSLY, I'd rather do d Machen one – but, WHAT TO CHOOSE ???. it'd have to be d short story obviously 20 mins. in T.V.–time (I'd like 2 do the lot!) BUT I NEED OBJECTIVE VIEWPOINT! KEEP THIS UNDER YR. BELT ! YOUR FAVE. STORY! ALL THE BEST, HOPE TO HERE FROM U. Your Pal. M.E.S. X

To Rita —

From the desk
Ans SMITH
THE PRESTWICH MENTAL
HOSPITAL
m/or m23
OLJ
8th July 08.

Dear Rita:

So glad you enjoyed the book "Rubbish" hobby ment — Ghost writer. Funnily enough, six hours after I saw you I built him + poured beer over him, I'm not really keen on this literary world!

- I mean – have you seen the chapter where he involves the Trot ??? Wot my idea! Anyway, he now lives in Cheshire with all the Liverpool/Man Utd stars – I'm not kidding.

It was so shocking for me 2 meet you that day, but it made the 3 day visit worthwhile –

- Have just got back from Croatia, which was like the

- Great God P— tale. In the airport a father + son at my table looked at me and stuck out their tongues — which were Reptilian like! I'm not kidding!

  Am not a big Welsh fan — but me + Eleni do need break in August so you never know! Thanx for photos!

- An Idea — instead of GLASTO for Robin — send him to.

Croatia or Estonia – the
women + men are beautiful
+ sporty, but they to were
brought up on Dylan +
L. Cohen + they have Fang
not
like teeth! honest! 
And when you part the hair
from their faces, their ears
are like :O
Love you –
+M the boss
M.O.I xx

The Fall

FIRST RELEASE ::

IN PALACE OF SWORDS REVERSED
- THE FALL, Circa. compilation:
1980 - 83

DEAR FUTURE COGS,

This time period heralds the first L.P. release on Cog-Sinister Records Ltd.

"**In Palace of Swords Reversed**" is a collection of rare 45's, alternate takes etc. from British living legends **THE FALL**.

PRE-REJECTED Classics & Artists
- NOW under The Vendetta - Like AUSPICESS
==
OF 'COG-SINISTER' Limited -
===========================
--- THE GOLD QUALITY - STATE !!
==================================

NOT ONLY was 'Cog-Sinister" Ltd. set up to furnish frustated Fall fans with affordable past classics and alternate versions of same, but also to bring attention to other past singers and groups of note (i.e. THE HAMSTERS, The cynical, skin pop group of the early 80's, or exclusive tapes of John The Postman's legendary 'lost' 3rd l.p.). But to Recognise NEW Talent, maybe ignored by A&R's or not middle-class enough to set up their own label. (i.e. A.Berry/Obi-Men etc.).

N.B: THE GOLD 'QUALITY-STATE' will be usually Fall & Past material by others, and usually on long - player

THE 'COG-SIN RANGE' will concentrate ON ALL New Creators, regardless of location or reputation but out of necessity, solo to trio only.

SO: GEAR UP, SEMI-LIT!!!

Regards,

MARK E. SMITH
Director
COG-sinister

Further info etc SPIKE 833-2133

Pages 270–8: Cog Sinister was both the record
label and official fan club of the Fall. Correspondence
and press releases, 1988–92.

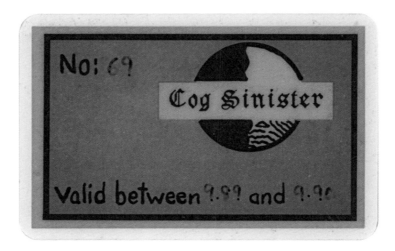

No: 69

Cog Sinister

Valid between 9.89 and 9.90

MEMBERSHIP: *209
EXPIREY DATE: OCT '91
NAME: MR.M.SLATTERY

COG SINISTER
23 NEW MOUNT ST.
MANCHESTER.
M4 4DE.

MEMBERSHIP: *209
EXPIRY DATE: Oct '92
NAME: M. Slattery.

COG SINISTER
23 NEW MOUNT ST.
MANCHESTER.
M4 4DE.

'COG-SINISTER limited

RECORDS,
32 HOLMES ROAD
London NW5
FAX: 267 1931 (London
REGISTERED:
MANCHESTER, ENGLAND.

EX DEAR MEMBER NO. 69,

LATEST BULLETIN AND UPDATE

FIRST OFF, Many many apologies for our slight delay — this is due to the continuing mental deteriation of PRES. D. LUFF(see att 'SINISTER TIMES' Example) due to his recent access to Apple computers — BUT it could well be worth sticking with him, as madness sometimes can produce off-the-wall benefits.

SO, Welcome to all new
MEMBERS _ IT IS NOT CAROLINE'S FAULT.
DO NOT ATTEMPT TO SHOOT HER.

DELAY DUE TO CHANGE OF ADDRESS —
Manchester Fan Club;
    c-o. D.LUFF 2ND.FLOOR
    48 PRINCESS STREET
    MANCHESTER M1

London; Record enquiries, mail etc;
    Caroline, C_S LTD.
    32, HOLMES ROAD
    LONDON. NW 5

the former fan club, and the address on 'In; PALACE OF SWORDS REVERSED' adressesyou should erase from your dear, dear memories.

HERE IS __THE FALL__ Y-shaped BRITISH TOUR FOR mz & non-mz MAR 88

7 th.	mar.	BIRMINGHAM	W/ 'Shack' & Andrew Berry's 'Swing'
8 th.	.	MANCHESTER Ritz Ballroom, Whitworth St.	W/ support as above
10 th.	.	EXETER U.	W/'Shack'
11 th.	.	CARDIFF	W/'Shack'
12 th.	.	OXFORD	W/'Shack'
14 th.	.	LIVERPOOL Royal Court Theatre	W/'Shack' & Andrew Berry
15 th.	.	LEEDS UNI.	W/ support as above
17 th.	.	LEICESTER	W/ 'Shack'
18 th.	.	LONDON Hammersmith Odeon	W/ 'Shack' & Andrew Berry
19th.	.	CAMBRIDGE Corn Exch.	W/ 'Shack'

SHACK Are CBS Artists

ANDREW BERRY is a 'COG_SINISTER LTD.' artist.

P.T.O.

irectors, M. E. Smith
. Smith   J. Lennard
          S. Hanley

'COG-SINISTER' feb. 88.

NEWSLETTER JAN/FEB XX 1991   FALL UPDATE

Dear Sinisters;

    A Happy new year to you all,and here's hoping you spent 'Xmas With Simon' and 1991 bears you well.

    Members will have noticed the proliferation of Beggars' Banquet compilations out recently,i.e. the 'A' side,double 'B' side(!) and video releases.Of course,if it was up to M.E.S.,none of them would've come out - but the video is well worth a look at.Of course it is not for COG-SIN to comment.

    The new 'streamlined' The Fall hit UB40's studio in Birmingham(A city definitely conducive to work,at least!) just prior to their U.K. tour-apologies to N.Ireland as usual_and are presently finishing the 6 new songs recorded there at mem.the moment.

Working titles are: 'Pittsville Direkt' ((As performed live recently)
                 'Idiot Joy Showland' ((Ditto)
             'Shift'
              'Psy-Cog Dream'
            'Edinburgh Man'
       and 'A lot Of Wind'   - two of them featuring the immortal Kenny Brady on distorted fiddle.

    As this is being written, Suzanne Vega & DNA's record is on the rad: for once I must agree with M.E.S. and say it:'Must be the most boring record in the history of mankind'

    "Most misinformed Man Of The Year" award must go to Mr.D.Jennings of the M.Maker for his review of December's London show-though favourable, he mention two songs The Fall haven't performed since 1988,and his lyric quotes are,quite frankly, barmy. M.E.S. RECKONS HE WAS still worrying about the Gulf Crisis,having met said gent in an' A interview capacity' some months ago. Talking of said Crisis,Smith laughingly claims he predicted part of it in song 'Arms Control Poseur' - 'Arms Control Poseur' being the Washington "insiders" nickname for Pres. George Bush. Anyway, give the latter half of it a listen and see who what you think.

    Tour went extremely well , especially accounting for weather etc. etc. and to bore you further,did you know electricity has to be sent out from power stations at very high voltage and then 'stepped down' to reduce voltage ? - many thanks to P.J. of Liverpool for that info.

        Anyway, onward,not inward,and no back words,

          your pal,

            MR.SMUG-INSIDER,

             COG- SINISTER.

COG-Sinister
l i m i t

COG-Sin RANGE 'COG-Sin

ANDREW BERRY

BARRY REILLY.
61, Watergate,
WHITWORTH.
ROCHDALE.

Dear Mr. Reilly,

Thank you for your letter. Unfortunately we do not no of anywhere that
is able to supply you with a lyric book. It was infact a limited
edition, and as far as we know all the stocks have sold out, the same
goes for the "Bend Sinister" T-Shirts. If you are a member of our fan-
club you could try placing an advert on our personal page. I don't think
the ballet will be available on video, though there are two promotional
videos "Big New Prinz" and "Wrong Place/Right Time" which have been
shown on T.V. and hopefully will feature again. The Christmas Tour does
not include a date in Rochdale - I'm afraid the nearest venue to you is
The Ritz in Manchester - where they will be playing 14th December. Sorry
we could not be of more help to you.

                    Your sincerely,

                    Saffron Prior

                    SAFFRON PRIOR
                for Cog Sinister Records

CoG SINISTER

TO: MEMBER NO:

FROM:THE FALL FAN CLUB
FAN CLUB ADDRESS
Upper Pittsville,
North West ECET.
P.O.BOX?⅓

DATELINE: JANUARY 192093

DEAR SINISTERITES:

As You may have heard or read,dear friends, THE FALL parted company with their Record CO,Phonogram, a month back.

SMITH thought this was for the best, as due to corporate recession panic,said Company was trying to dictate through highly ridiculous theorems, group policy.THE FALL were not prepared to hang around like so many other groups and wait for some yes/no policy around April/May.

WE think it is one in the eye for these incompetents,as,to quote:"THE FALL were one of the few groups we were considering keeping on anyway".

SO, believe it or not,much celebration in Fall-camp.

THE FALL BEGAN RECORDING THEIR NEXT WORK in November, at a spot called S.16 IN Lancs. There are no new trends,or no new financial hit-lusting cop-outs that THE FALL cannot BUCK.

WORKING titles are; 'GLAM_RACKET'/'I'M GOING TO SPAIN'/ A PAST GONE MAD/LADYBIRD(GREEN GRASS)/ THE LEAGUE OF BALD-HEADED MEN/ THIS DAY'S PORTION/ GRUDGEFUL/ IT'S A CURSE/LOST IN MUSIC/PARANOID MAN IN CHEAP_SHIT ROOM/ withxxaxxpartxxMovementxxyetxtoxbexcompleted.

In addition,there is a four part movement,half way completed,which will be the core of the record.

NO MAIN TITLE YET.

News; 1. Craig Scanlon breaks ribs on Costa Blanca
      2. Fall interest never higher,much to chagrin of SMITH,who keeps being bothered because of the daft MTV ad he did.He claims it is surprising how many fogeys and nutters watch MTV.
      3. Ex-Cog-Sinister artist, Mr. Philip Johnson of Liverpool, under a.k.a. J.S.Walker,is already ready to release the 2nd. part of his novella 'Slackhurst' on Olympia pillow Books. Congratulations.
      4.
          New trax helped by S.ROGERS,and new rising star REX SGT.

ALL THE BEST TO YOU AND YOURS:

A gibbering amorphous combination OF:
  J.OMERODTOTALELUFF,
I.E.:FAN - CLUB NEW DIRECTORATE. *

* Yeah in its
mensa-Expulsion.

NEWSLETTER JAN/FEB XX 1991   FALL UPDATE

Dear Sinisters;

    A Happy new year to you all,and here's hoping you spent 'Xmas With Simon' and 1991 bears you well.

    Members will have noticed the proliferation of Beggars' Banquet compilations out recently,i.e. the 'A' side,double 'B' side(!) and video releases.Of course,if it was up to M.E.S.,none of them would've come out - but the video is well worth a look at.Of course it is not for COG-SIN to comment.

    The new 'streamlined' The Fall hit UB40's studio in Birmingham(A city definitely conducive to work,at least!) just prior to their U.K. tour-apologies to N.Ireland as usual_and are presently finishing the 6 new songs recorded there at mmm.the moment.

Working titles are: 'Pittsville Direkt' ((As performed live recently)
                 'Idiot Joy Showland' ((Ditto)

           'Shift'
           'Psy-Cog Dream'
        'Edinburgh Man'

       and 'A lot Of Wind'   - two of them featuring the

immortal Kenny Brady on distorted fiddle.

    As this is being written, Suzanne Vega & DNA's record is on the rad: for once I must agree with M.E.S. and say it:'Must be the most boring record in the history of mankind'

    "Most misinformed Man Of The Year" award must go to Mr.D.Jennings of the M.Maker for his review of December's London show-though favourable, he mention two songs The Fall haven't performed since 1988,and his lyric quotes are,quite frankly, barmy. M.E.S. RECKONS HE WAS still worrying about the Gulf Crisis,having met said gent in an' X interview capacity' some months ago. Talking of said Crisis,Smith laughingly claims he predicted part of it in song 'Arms Control Poseur' - 'Arms Control Poseur' being the Washington "insiders" nickname for Pres. George Bush. Anyway, give the latter half of it a listen and see wh what you think.

    Tour went extremely well , especially accounting for weather etc. etc. and to bore you further,did you know electricity has to be sent out from power stations at very high voltage and then 'stepped down' to reduce voltage ? - many thanks to P.J. of Liverpool for that info.

           Anyway, onward,not inward,and no back words,

              your pal,
                 MR.SMUG-INSIDER,
                 COG- SINISTER.

'America Therein'

In the Fall's 2003 song 'Mountain Energei', Mark E. Smith claims that 'Dolly Parton and Lord Byron said that "patriotism is the last refuge", but now it's me.' Experts will note that was Samuel Johnson's line, not Dolly's and George's, but the rest is true. By the early noughties, Smith had attained 'national treasure' status in Britain. He'd become the contrary cult hero who could admire William Blake without committing the cardinal sin of being 'arty', the 'prole-art threat' who, as we liked to fantasise, consorted with avant-garde ballet dancers and still held his own in a Prestwich pub. His lyrics were English Romantic rendered caustic by post-punk, cryptic in meaning yet loaded with enough vernacular references for them to pass as whatever form of Albion-visionary-wisdom you wanted. Wisdom that could curdle from left to right and back again, like Smith's own politics occasionally did. By the new century, the singer was no longer as interview-sharp as he once was, and the Fall's shows were as unpredictably brilliant or dismal as ever, but that did not matter. Nor did Smith's ugly despotism over the Fall matter either. That was, for those who didn't have to deal with its consequences in real life, just a facet of his curmudgeonly charm. By 2006, 'Theme from Sparta F.C.' was the soundtrack to BBC Sport's *Final Score* programme, and Smith could be seen on TV reading the Saturday football results. The Fall — specifically Smith — became part of the national landscape, along with the *Shipping Forecast*, *Strictly* and seven pints of Stella before last orders on a Friday. Whether you were into punk existentialism or the footie, the Fall seemed to offer a blokeish middle ground for both. Their vast back catalogue offered whichever version of their figurehead you wanted. Smith the working-class poet-playwright, and Smith the anti-intellectual. Smith the pop star in a silk BodyMap raincoat, and Smith the ordinary bloke in slacks and a leather blouson. Smith the punk mystic separated by a thin crisp packet from Smith the pub bore.

But the Fall, like all Great British Pop Groups — indeed, like the entire history of the British Isles — would never have existed without overseas influence. Outsiders were this nation's saving grace. US bands understood that implicitly; immigration was part of their country's story. They had been telling us for years that the Fall were always part Dolly Parton, part Lord Byron. America embraced Smith and his gang early in their career. ('From the riot-torn streets of Manchester, England, to the scenic sewers of Chicago …' announces the MC at the top of the Fall's live album *A Part of America Therein, 1981*.) Big Black, Butthole Surfers, Mission of Burma and a slew of 1980s hardcore bands all worked under the Fall's influence. (Hardcore was a most American subculture, ideologically 'tied to the Puritan ethic', to borrow from the song 'Live at the Witch Trials'.) This forced US rock critics who routinely dismissed British indie groups as 'arty', out of some boorish need to defend the masculine, blue-collar credentials of their homegrown bands, to

admit the Fall's significance. And who better than the Fall to counter the facile idea that working-class bands must never jeopardise their authenticity by being artistic or cerebral, that they must stick to being voices for the disenfranchised, or sentimental rough diamonds?

Nirvana were such big fans that Kurt Cobain climbed onto their tour bus and begged to come with them. Smith refused to let him along for the ride, just as he rejected the admiration of other key players in the US indie underground. He trolled Thurston Moore of Sonic Youth by saying he should have his 'rock licence' revoked. Pavement were written off as 'just the Fall in 1985. [...] They haven't got an original idea in their heads.' (Pavement's 1992 debut LP, *Slanted and Enchanted*, is an extended love letter to the band.) Of LCD Soundsystem's James Murphy, Smith said: 'I liked him but he should stop putting on that American accent.' But Smith was no anti-American, falling in lockstep with received European ideas that the US was only good for capitalism, imperialism and MTV. Not only that, two key members of the 1980s line-up – Brix Smith and Marcia Schofield – were from Los Angeles and New York, respectively. In 1984, the Fall were briefly courted by Motown Records, who were looking to create a new UK division. (Motown. The mind boggles.) They were rejected on account of a racial epithet in a song the label's A&R man heard and knew was beyond the pale Stateside, even if Smith was quarantining it between bold air quotes. The Fall operated in a zone beyond the horizons of their most British songs, such as 'Hit the North', 'Victoria' and their take on the hymn 'Jerusalem'. Certainly beyond people's wet-eyed sentimentalism for the Manchester music scene. Smith admitted so himself in 2015: 'We've always been a multinational group. I don't like northern people, I don't like Mancunians. There's something about Manchester musicians that's particularly fucking irritating. [...] They think they're superior, but they're not. Manchester's only got Freddie and the Dreamers.'

There is a spoken-word number titled 'Dissolute Singer', written by Smith after an onstage fight with his band at Brownies club, New York, in April 1998, and his subsequent arrest the following day for assaulting keyboard player Julia Nagle. (Smith claimed to have had a vision of 9/11 while incarcerated in the NYPD Manhattan Central Booking jail that week, spitting distance from the World Trade Center site.) He maps Lower Manhattan street names onto Manchester: 'The rolling rocks you sneered at seemed like nectar at Canal Street subway / Canal sets you pining only name familiar / [...] Canal Street's near Victoria, Bridge Street connects Dalton.' Manchester's Bridge Street runs into John Dalton Street. This becomes Princess Street, from which Canal branches off along the Rochdale waterway. In Manhattan, Bridge Street leads into Battery Park, beyond which is the Upper Bay, and Ellis Island, the historic processing station for immigrants to the US. Walk north-east of Canal and you will reach Rivington Street; there's a parish of that name near Bolton, Greater Manchester, although this one was named after an English journalist who switched sides from Britain to America during the Revolutionary War. Carry on from here towards the East River and you'll cross Ludlow, Essex, Norfolk and Suffolk Streets. Here is 'Cooperative Village', a housing community originally run in strict accordance with the Rochdale Principles, the cooperative ideals devised by the Rochdale Society of Equitable Pioneers in 1844. Some fifteen miles to the east in Jamaica, Queens, is Rochdale Village, also named after the Pioneers. 'A small alteration of the past / Can turn time into space,' as the song 'Wings' goes.

   Smith understood these transatlantic links well. If you squint hard enough, you might catch a glimmer of symbolism in the fact that he once worked as a clerk at the Manchester Docks. Until the late 1970s, liners would ply routes between Manchester and the eastern Canadian seaboard. (Neighbouring Liverpool took passengers to New York.) It was through British ports in the 1950s and '60s that imports of US blues, jazz, rock and roll and soul arrived. Records which would make their way to radio stations and shops and get picked up by British youths, who would customise the sound and export their own records back to the US for further development. New sounds emerged from this musical exchange, new genres were added to the cycle, binding the two cultures tight.

   Music created elective affinities between faraway people and places. The blues brought the geography of the Deep South to Ealing, Newcastle and Glasgow. Country music, bolstered by the popularity of westerns and an abiding romance with the colonial myths of the American west, conjured a big-horizon fantasy of places that many British country fans would never get to see: Nashville, Wichita, Phoenix, Bakersfield, Austin, Denver. But country's domestic-scale dramas were relatable whether you lived in Santa Fe or Cardiff. Disaffected young people coping with the post-industrial decline of cities such as Manchester, Stoke-on-Trent, Sheffield and Wigan fell in love with the soul sounds of declining post-industrial Detroit and Philadelphia, embracing it as their own northern soul. Outdoor festivals at Glastonbury, Stonehenge and Deeply Vale (at which the Fall were regulars) were Britain's answer to Woodstock. Hip hop introduced the Bronx to British suburbia. Going the other way, the post-Beatles British Invasion made Liverpool known across the States and had US garage bands trying to imitate John Lennon's, Mick Jagger's and Van Morrison's own attempts to sing like American rhythm-and-blues singers. Elton John, from Pinner, and Brixton's David Bowie would become the first white singers to perform on the influential black TV show *Soul Train*. The American west was where British bands would meet their end. Here, they reached the country's farthest horizon, exhausted, unable to go any further. San Francisco saw the Beatles retire from live performance, and the Sex Pistols and Throbbing Gristle break up.

   The Fall paid their primary American dues to guitarist Link Wray, pioneer of the power chord and leather-clad cool. By the time they had formed in the late 1970s, it was hardly original to be influenced by Wray. Jimi Hendrix, Jimmy Page, Pete Townshend, Neil Young and other rock superstars had claimed his raw style of playing and distorted sound years before. Wray's menacing 1958 recording 'Rumble' – banned in some cities for allegedly inciting gang violence – inspired countless aspiring musicians to pick up a guitar. In the case of the Fall, perhaps Smith was specifically enamoured, for whatever complicated reasons, by Wray's Shawnee Indian heritage. 'YOU kept my head together for fuckin' years, Link, when I was a teenager and in my twenties,' gushed the singer, in a 1993 conversation between the two for the *NME*. 'You know, I like Elvis, I like Gene Vincent, but you were the one that kept me together. It is spiritual, it's that Indian thing: DAANNNG! DA-NA-NAANNGG! If ever I thought about packing the business in, I'd put on "Rumble", full fuckin' blast.' Danny Frost, the moderating journalist, noted that Smith was ranting into Wray's deaf right ear, but the American graciously accepted him as a kindred spirit: 'Who cares if we're playing the right notes or not! Who gives a shit if it's in tune!'

Smith liked to emphasise the musical importance of 'the three Rs: Repetition, Repetition, Repetition,' although the Fall's definitive instrumental sound might be characterised by the three Ts: Toms, Twangy guitar and Tinny organ. Smith reportedly fined drummers for hitting the toms during live shows, yet they're all over their recordings. The heavy pounding evoked 'Rumble''s backbeat, of course, but also Mo Tucker's drumming for the Velvet Underground. Toms were part threat, part ritual hypnotism. You can hear the Velvets' influence clearly on the Fall song 'Vixen', taken from *This Nation's Saving Grace*. It sounds like a straight nod to the Velvets' 'Run Run Run', but 'Sister Ray' might be the true touchstone. A key part of that recording's unremitting, pugilistic groove is an overdriven, tinny transistor organ that immediately evokes the Kingsmen's 'Louie Louie' and the cheap noise of 1960s garage-punk groups that Smith also loved: the Seeds, the Sonics, the Strangeloves, Count Five, the Monks, ? and the Mysterians. To my ears, it's a sound that evokes 1950s and '60s horror and sci-fi movies too. Smith was a fan of Rod Serling's TV series *The Twilight Zone*, which by the 1980s, when the series was rebooted, had formed a charming nostalgic patina that suited the decade's rockabilly revival. Retro-1950s Cold War paranoia for Reagan-era paranoiacs.

Rockabilly brings us to the twang. The Fall's sonics drew from American rockabilly, garage and surf. Early tracks especially trucked on rockabilly's up-down, two-beat rhythm. Their guitar riffs always sounded as if they had staggered – debased and detuned by speed and lager – out of a broken time machine sent from the rock-and-roll era, bypassing the 1960s and '70s altogether. Surf music made by a band who had no clue what sun, sand and sea looked like. What the Fall were mining from the genre seemed to go deeper than just its musical form. Rockabilly somehow suited Smith, with his interest in spectres and ghost stories. It is one of rock's original manifestations that never died. These days, a love of rockabilly can signal both pop connoisseurship and a yearning for youth culture's simpler past, bringing with it a faint sensation of working-class nostalgia too. To be into Carl Perkins or Gene Vincent these days is the pop equivalent of saying you prefer watching silent movies or reading classical literature over modern. If you didn't live through its first wave, then maybe it signals sentimental admiration for an older relative who did. Perhaps that's because rockabilly is, a little like the Fall, both unmistakeable yet pliant to being bent to whatever subcultural shape you want. It can fit Lana Del Rey or the Cramps. The classic rock-and-roll rebel look – blue jeans, white T-shirt and black leather jacket – can work just as well for the straight crowd as it can for Tom of Finland-inspired gay men. Rockabilly lends itself to retro-themed weekenders at British seaside resorts and to terrifying David Lynch film soundtracks.

In crate-digging for the Fall's American connections, it's easy to lose yourself in academic minutiae. Conduct a close read of 'Rollin' Dany', the Fall's 1985 cover of 'Rollin' Danny' by Gene Vincent and the Blue Caps, and report back on the title's missing 'n'. Investigate a possible encrypted nod to the Seeds' 'Mr Farmer' in the Fall's choice to cover 'Mr Pharmacist' by the Other Half. Examine the descending chord progression in 'Elves' and its relationship to the Stooges' 'I Wanna Be Your Dog'. 'Live at the Witch Trials': Pendle, Lancashire, or Salem, Massachusetts? In the song 'Wings', Smith describes finding himself 'under Ardwick Bridge with some veterans from the US Civil War / [...] under Irish patronage'. Poetic licence or legitimate historical allusion? Consider the following: the origin for the British fascination with the American west is said to be *Buffalo Bill's Wild West Show*, which first came to London in 1887. The Fall's song 'Hip Priest' was famously used in the climax to Jonathan Demme's 1991 film *The Silence of the Lambs*, as FBI agent Clarice Starling closes in on a serial killer named – wait for it – Buffalo Bill. Discuss. But the risk with concentrating on the text is that you can miss the things that really influence an artist: states of mind, friendships, love, loss and the ineffable atmospherics that draw you to a place. Focus on the Fall's external influences and you will find that all routes lead to Smith, whose cult of personality occludes the internal influences brought by other members of the band. Specifically, in the American context, Brix Smith.

The Fall produced some of their strongest work during the Brix era. She put a comb and Brylcreem through the band's unkempt surf licks. Her backing vocals – for instance, on 'Stephen Song' and 'L.A.' – evoked 1960s American girl groups, bringing the Shangri-Las alongside other all-male garage influences. Brix gave Smith a dash of personal style, encouraging him to move on from the bloody-minded anti-fashion stance he'd taken up until that point, all tank tops and polyester shirts. As his partner, she dealt with his mercurial moods and abusive behaviour too. Two songs in particular stand out, both addressing the US. 'Disney's Dream Debased' originates from a trip the couple made to Disneyland – for Brix, a locus of happy childhood memories. Brix describes in her memoir *The Rise, The Fall, and The Rise* how Smith had a powerful intuition that the Matterhorn roller-coaster ride was 'evil'. Just hours later, a woman named Dolly Regene Young fell from the Matterhorn. Her body got trapped on the tracks and she was decapitated by an oncoming roller-coaster car. The song rides on a typical Fall swing and a bed of bright, chorused guitars, which shift between cheerful major and uneasy diminished chords. Brix's voice drifts over the song like passing clouds, as Smith pulls an allegory of innocence lost from the narrative: 'And though Minnie and Mickey, and Brer and Pluto / Secretly prayed / There was no doubt at all / No two ways about it / Was the day Disney's dream debased.' By Smith's standards, the lyrics are heart-on-sleeve. His voice, glossed with a chorus effect, sounds more plaintive and tender than usual. He reaches for melody rather than snarl. Cynicism shocked by the gruesome.

If ever the Fall did a road song, 'L.A.' would be it. A shimmering electronic sequencer and *motorik* bass line are its propellants. The lyrics are unusually sparse, flashing past like landmarks glimpsed from a car window. 'Odeon,' intones Smith. The name of the British cinema chain sounds dowdy and provincial out here in Hollywood. 'Bushes are in disagreement with the heat,' he sings. It could be a deadpan vision of the city's future wildfires or simply a description of what it feels like to be a pasty-faced Brit burning up under the southern Californian sun. Brix pays tribute to Russ Meyer's Los Angeles trash masterpiece *Beyond the Valley of the Dolls*, quoting directly from the film the line 'This is my happening and it freaks me out.' Indeed, this is Brix's happening, her home. It is almost as if Smith is lost for words, deferring to Brix as his guide, a tiny figure capitulating to the vast, grotesque American landscape. This is a white-knuckle drive along the I-110 to Pasadena, not the A56 to Prestwich.

If one image sums up the Fall's relationship with the US, it's a short clip shot by artist Charles Atlas during the band's performance of the ballet *I Am Curious, Orange* with the Michael Clark Company at the Edinburgh International Festival in 1988. It might even capture something of British pop's complicated transatlanticism too. They begin the song 'Cab It Up!' The centre of the chequerboard stage is clear, save for two dancers stage-right. The Fall are pushed deep into the rear of the stage, next to a big, frowning smiley face (this was, after all, the summer that acid house hit), and a backcloth depicting Westminster Bridge, Big Ben and the Houses of Parliament. Performance artist Leigh Bowery, wearing a frightening-looking mask with light-bulb ears, helps push onstage a huge, squishy replica hamburger on wheels. Brix sits on top, dressed in a leather BodyMap leotard and ballet pumps, grinning and strumming her white Rickenbacker guitar. They spin the hamburger around, weaving Brix between the dancers and the Fall, like a UFO from Planet Pop. An alien zapping those who would, as the song 'English Scheme' puts it, 'point their fingers at America', yet cannot resist the pull of its gravity beams.

EDINBURGH INTERNATIONAL FESTIVAL 1988

I Am Curious, Orange

KING'S THEATRE

I Am Curious, Orange programme from performance
at Edinburgh International Festival, 1988.

MICHAEL CLARK
Photo credit: Dean Freeman

I AM CURIOUS, ORANGE

Choreography	MICHAEL CLARK
Music	THE FALL
Set design	MICHAEL CLARK
Costume design	BODYMAP
	LEIGH BOWERY
	MICHAEL CLARK
Additional costumes	ERIC HOLAH
	CLIVE ROSS
Lighting	CHARLES ATLAS

MICHAEL CLARK & COMPANY

LEIGH BOWERY
LESLIE BRYANT
MICHAEL CLARK
MATTHEW HAWKINS
DAVID HOLAH
JULIE HOOD
AMANDA KING
ELLEN VAN SCHUYLENBURCH

THE FALL

MARK E SMITH	(lead vocals)
STEVE HANLEY	(bass guitar)
CRAIG SCANLON	(rhythm/accoustic guitar)
MARCIA SCHOFIELD	(keyboards)
BRIX SMITH	(lead guitar/vocals)
SIMON WOLSTENCROFT	(drums)

Michael Clark & Company gratefully acknowledge the participation of the following as extras in the show: Kirstie Alexander, Winnie Armitage, Leigh Falconer, David Orgles, Maxine Railton, Alison Scott, Alison Steele.

There will be one interval of 15 minutes.

First performance: Stadsschouwburg, Amsterdam 11 June 1988 as part of the Holland Festival.

I AM CURIOUS, ORANGE

MUSIC

Overture: Theme from *I Am Curious, Orange*
Music: B Smith

Jerusalem
Words: W Blake/M E Smith
Music: M E Smith

Kurious Oranj
Words: M E Smith
Music: M E Smith/B Smith/S Hanley/ S Wolstencroft

Wrong Place, Right Time
Words & Music: M E Smith

Yes O Yes
Words:M E Smith
Music:M E Smith/B Smith

Hip Priest/Big New Prinz
Words: M E Smith
Music: S Hanley/M Riley/C Scanlon/P Hanley/M E Smith/
      M Schofield

Interval

Frenz
Words & Music: M E Smith

Bad News Girl
Words: M E Smith
Music: B Smith

Dead Beat Descendant
Words: M E Smith
Music: B Smith

The Plague
Words: M E Smith
Music:

Cab It Up
Words & Music: M E Smith

Bremen Nacht
Words: M E Smith
Music: S Rogers/M E Smith

All songs published by Warner Bros Music except *Hip Priest*
(Minder Music Ltd 1983).

MARK E SMITH
Photo credit: Steve Pyke

MICHAEL CLARK
THE BAD BOY OF BRITISH DANCE

Curiosity has always been a byword for rebellious young choreographer Michael Clark. Recently turned 26, Clark is the brightest and most notorious creative force in British dance today.

Born and raised in Scotland, Clark grew up dancing. 'Apparently,' he recalls, 'I seem to have told my mother that I wanted to be a dancer when I was only four.' That request led to Scottish dance lessons in his native Aberdeen and was followed by a move to the full-time training programme with Britain's Royal Ballet. Even when he was still a teenager Clark's exceptional dance talents were easy to spot. He was already being groomed to be a future Prince Charming for the Royal, when he suddenly rebelled and walked out. He says he loved the training but couldn't stand the way his days in the studio had to be kept separate from his nights out on the town. Only 17 at the time, he had already decided that art shouldn't be barricaded behind high walls. Clark set out to find ways of blending the rigour of dance with the vigour of real life. He spent a brief period dancing with Ballet Rambert and also went to New York to study with Merce Cunningham. By the time he returned to England at the beginning of the 1980s, he knew he wouldn't be happy unless he started creating his own choreography.

In 1983 he teamed up with the Dutch dancer Ellen van Schuylenburch. Since then his company has continued to grow. The new show features seven of Clark's regular dancers plus a host of extras. He admits that some of this year's William and Mary celebrations will end up being woven into the fabric of his new piece.

'I'm curious to find out how the ways we think and act, the way we are today, can be traced back into history. The whole Protestant and Catholic thing hasn't changed much in 300 years, has it?'

The typical Clark style is a lively mix. He infuses the formal elements of classical ballet with the stringency of Merce Cunningham and the eclectic energy of Twyla Tharp. Then, to spice things up even more, Clark tosses in subversive humour, punk glitter and a raucous sense of silliness. Clark usually choreographs his dances to rock music. *I Am Curious, Orange* has original songs by The Fall, a rough-edged band from the north of England. The band performs live on stage with the dancers. As a tribute, Clark has also choreographed sections of the new dance to both the Dutch and British national anthems.

Clark says he wants to present the kind of theatre where all sorts of styles and techniques can work together, if not in blissful harmony, then at least in joyous cacophony. Some people don't like the controversial outcome, even when it's in jest. That doesn't bother Clark much. He readily admits that some serious dance fans find his works juvenile. 'That's all right,' he says. In fact he thinks that his explosive evening-length extravaganzas are meant for people who really don't want to bother going to yet another dance concert; or, even better, for people who don't have any interest in dance at all.

'I just want people to relax and have fun,' he says. Fun is certainly one of the key elements of Clark's artistic credo. Sometimes his notions of a joke can teeter on the edge of childishness, at other times the jokes can go flying off into delirious Fellini-dreamland.

Part of the excitement comes from the way Clark enlists extras, who are usually not trained dancers. They can sometimes be distracting, but they do provide a special feeling of community. Clark feels that extras' enthusiastic amateur energy adds a real sense of variety to the choreography.

'They stop it being boring,' he says, 'and that gives the dance a raw quality that I really like. There's a certain crude way of moving that is actually very hard for trained dancers to do, so I get it by asking friends, just people I know, to come along and be in my shows.'

The fun element in Clark's dances has led him to a lot of hard work. He's been a guest choreographer for several British companies including London Festival Ballet and Ballet Rambert. Even more glamorously, Rudolf Nureyev lured him to France to choreograph for Paris Opera Ballet. After Nureyev saw Clark's troupe performing at the Edinburgh Festival three years ago, he dashed backstage and demanded Clark to come and work for him. The first piece Clark did in Paris was called *The French Revolting*. It included clever costumes that turned the dancers into apparently headless bodies topped off by miniature guillotines. Then he made *Angel Food*, a series of swank and openly sexy solos for three of the Opera's top male stars. Since then, Clark's own company has performed in New York, Los Angeles, Australia and throughout Europe.

ALLEN ROBERTSON
Dance Editor of *Time Out*

MICHAEL CLARK was born in Aberdeen in 1962. He studied at the Royal Ballet School and joined Ballet Rambert at the age of 17. He began his career as an independent choreographer/dancer in 1981 at the age of 19, and has since created over a dozen works for leading companies, including Paris Opera Ballet, London Festival Ballet, the Scottish Ballet and Rambert Dance Company. He founded Michael Clark & Company in 1984 and the company has since toured worldwide, presenting seven programmes of his choreography: *Do You Me? I Did?/New Puritans* (1984), *not H.AIR* (1985), *our caca phoney H. our caca phoney H.* (1985), *No Fire Escape in Hell* (1986), *Pure Pre-Scenes* (1987), *Because We Must* (1987) and *I Am Curious, Orange* (1988). He has appeared in numerous films and videos including Charles Atlas's *Hail The New Puritan* (1985), *No Fire Escape in Hell* (1986) and *Comrades*, directed by Bill Douglas (1987).

MICHAEL CLARK & COMPANY is now established as one of Britain's most popular contemporary dance companies. It has toured all over the world since its début season in London in August 1984, and has expanded its line-up to feature eight dancers, led by Michael Clark himself. The Company works regularly with a distinctive group of young British musicians and designers, who have contributed to their shows. These include fashion designers BodyMap and Leigh Bowery, and The Fall, whose music has been included in all the company's shows. This project marks the first time that the band have played live with the company and composed music specially for the show. *I Am Curious, Orange* was co-produced by the Holland Festival and Sadler's Wells Theatre as part of the William and Mary Tercentenary Celebrations.

MICHAEL CLARK
Photo credit: Richard Haughton

MARK E SMITH is the leader and main songwriter of The Fall group, and under his steerage they have released 14 LPs, including bootlegs. He was born in Salford in 1958 and left his job on the docks there to form The Fall at the age of 18. An eternal thorn in the side of rock music and its press, it is claimed he has single-handedly changed the course of underground music with his pen and sheer bloody mindedness. The Fall to him is life and passion through which he can filter his original words, music and ideas. There are no rules and boundaries in his group. He has had a lyric book published in Germany and in 1986 he wrote and directed the play *Hey Luciani* (The Times, Life and Codex of Albino Luciani), a music comedy which centres around the mysterious death of Pope John Paul I, a brave work relentlessly plagiarised since by scores of 'new' US novelists and moribund UK pop acts. 'Rock music is too easy for people,' he states, 'yet the possibilities are infinite.' A history buff and admirer of Michael Clark, *I Am Curious, Orange* spawned the idea of a thematic delving into the foibles and little-known psyche of William of Orange.

THE FALL released their first album in 1979. Renowned for their innovatory qualities, they still remain unique and apart, begrudgingly admired by a rapidly decomposing 'rock' world for their omnipresent influence on music plus musicians of all ranges and ages. Led since the beginning by Mark E Smith, lyricist/vocalist and feared commentator, The Fall surprisingly notched up three top 40 singles in 1987/88. Their latest line-up consists of six people, all of whom are creative composers, average age 24 years old. Personnel: Mark E Smith (lead vocal/Type FX), Stephen Hanley (bass guitar), Brix Smith (lead guitar/vocals), Craig Scanlon (rhythm/acoustic guitar), Marcia Schofield (keyboards/FX) and Simon Wolstencroft (drums). Described as the definitive British group and the only English group worth listening to, The Fall nevertheless contain two US citizens, Brix and Marcia, who in the past two years have added a unique creative angle that is fringed with a spot of glamour. Their latest release is *The Frenz Experiment* LP (February 1988). Brix also touts her own group, the Adult Net. *I Am Curious, Orange* is the first live collaboration entered into with Michael Clark & Company, and heralds yet another dynamic period in Fall history.

JOE TOTALE XV, Vancouver May 1988

THE FALL
Photo credit: Steve Pyke

KURIOUS ORANJ

Words: M E Smith

Verse:

CUR I OUS OR ANJ, I CURIOUS OR ANJ
ORANJ IM CURIOUS OR ANJ CURIOUS ORANJ

Chorus (spoken):

ANONYMOUS CURIOUS IS CURIOUS HE'S
CURIOUS, CURIOUS, CURIOUS, CURIOUS
SOME SAY WHAT A CUR AND HOW
ANONYMOUS IS HE'S
CURIOUS, CURIOUS, CURIOUS, CURIOUS
CURIOUS ORANGE CURIOUS ORANG
brrrrpa bapababa ba ba ba ba ba

THEY BUILT THE ROADS OVER DUMB FELLOWS
LIKE YOU
THEY BUILT THE WORLD AS YOU KNOW IT
ALL THE SYSTEMS YOU TRAVERSE
THEY RODE SLIPSHOD OVER ALL PEASANTS LIKE YOU
THEY WERE CURIOUS ORANGE
THEY WERE CURIOUS ORANJ
THEY DISLIKED PAPISTS
THEY RODE
AND THEIR HORSES LOVED THEM, AND THEIR
HORSES LOVED THEM TOO
THEY WERE CURIOUS ORANJ
THEY FREED THE BLACKS TOO
BUILT A CHURCH IN ONE DAY MAN-AMISH
THEIR CLOTHES WERE COOL
TURNED NAPOLEON OVER AND DIDN'T KNOW
THEY MADE HITLER LAUGH IN PAIN —
THEY WERE CURIOUS ORANJ.
THEY INVENTED BIRTH CONTROL
THEY WERE RIDICULED, INVULNERABLE TO —
COOL

Part Two

brrp ba ba ba ba ba ba ba ba ba ba ba
THEY WERE CURIOUS ORANGE
THEY WERE CURIOUS ORANJ
PAVED WAY FOR ATOM BOMB

MADE THE JEWS GO TO SCHOOL
SENT MISSIONARY GIRLS TO ARAB STATES,
AND THE SUN-BAKED MEN DID DROOL
THEY WERE CURIOUS ORANGE
THEY WERE CURIOUS ORANJ
PAINS IN THE ARSE MAN BUT THEY WERE
INQUIRIN
brrp ba ba ba ba ba ba ba ba ba ba ba
THEY WERE: ANTI SEMITIC
　　　　　 ANTI ARTIC
　　　　　 ANTI GAELIC, YOU NAME IT MAN

THEY WERE AGAINST IT
THEY WERE THE REFORMATION SPRING,
AND EVERYBODY IN THE WORLD
TURNED REFORMATION BLUE
THEY WERE POSITIVELY DERANGED,
THEY WERE CURIOUS ORANJ
STUYVESANT SMOKING.
They were beyond Ooobenblief
EFFICIENT-PRIMA TO A MAN
THEY WERE CURIOUS ORANGE.

CHARLES ATLAS has worked extensively in dance, both as a film-maker and designer, including a period between 1978 and 1983 as film-maker in residence with Merce Cunningham Dance Company. He has worked with other choreographers including Karole Armitage, Douglas Dunn and Dana Reitz and composers Rhys Chatham and Jeffrey Lohn. He began his association with Michael Clark in 1984, designing lighting for all his ballets, as well as costumes for Michael Clark's *HAIL the classical* (Scottish Ballet) and sets for *Drop Your Pearls and Hog It Girl* (London Festival Ballet LFB2). He conceived and directed the film *Hail the New Puritan*, starring Michael Clark for Channel 4 TV/WGBH TV (1985). Earlier this year, he won a 'Bessie' Award in New York, as part of the design team with BodyMap and Leigh Bowery, on Michael Clark's *No Fire Escape in Hell*. He is currently recipient of a Guggenheim Foundation Grant for video and film-making.

BODYMAP, the internationally acclaimed fashion design partnership, was formed by Stevie Stewart and David Holah in 1982. They won the Martini Award for Innovative Design in 1983, and established themselves as one of Britain's most successful young fashion teams. They have designed costumes for all Michael Clark & Company's shows and in 1987 were recipients with Charles Atlas and Leigh Bowery of a 'Bessie' Award in New York for their work on Michael Clark's *No Fire Escape in Hell*.

LEIGH BOWERY was born in Australia where he studied music and design. He came to London in 1980 and began developing his unique style of design. After successful catwalk shows in London, Vienna, Tokyo and New York, he set about creating costumes and make-up for Michael Clark. He has since designed costumes for all Michael Clark's shows along with fashion design team BodyMap. He instigated and hosted the now legendary nightclub Taboo, and most recently has concentrated on developing performance work. He joined Michael Clark & Company in March 1987.

LESLIE BRYANT studied at the Rambert School. He worked with Lindsay Kemp's company and subsequently became an independent dancer performing with numerous well-known choreographers. He has presented two programmes of his own choreography at Riverside Studios and has appeared in a number of video and film projects. He joined Michael Clark & Company in 1985.

MATTHEW HAWKINS trained at the Royal Ballet School and graduated into the Royal Ballet at the age of 17. After five years of performing at Covent Garden he began his freelance career a a dancer, working with Second Stride, Mantis Dance Company and with Michael Clark & Company from 1984-5. He has choreographed his own work since 1981, including commissions from Mantis Dance Company, English Dance Theatre and Pauline Daniels. He has formed two companies: Lurching Darts, with his colleague Ann Dickie, which performed in Britain and Europe between 1982 and 1984, and The Imminent Dancers' Group in 1986. Most recently, he has been seen in Derek Jarman's film *The Last of England*.

DAVID HOLAH studied fashion design at Middlesex Polytechnic and formed the highly successful design team Bodymap in 1982 with Stevie Stewart. He has worked with Michael Clark since 1983, and joined the company in the summer of 1986.

JULIE HOOD trained at the Rambert School and toured with Ballet Rambert before joining English Dance Theatre in 1983. She joined Michael Clark & Company as a founder member in 1984, leaving the company for a year in 1986, and rejoining for this season.

AMANDA KING studied at the Rambert School. She joined Michael Clark & Company upon graduation in the summer of 1986.

ELLEN VAN SCHUYLENBURCH was born in Holland. She trained at the Rotterdam Dance Academy and worked with Werkcentrum Dance for two years before joining the Netherlands Dance Theatre. She studied in New York and performed with leading American choreographers including David Gordon, Karole Armitage, Bill T Jones, Arnie Zane and others. She first worked with Michael Clark in 1984 on a duet programme, and she became a founder member of Michael Clark & Company in the same year.

For Michael Clark & Company:

Management	Bolton & Quinn Ltd
Production Consultant	Steven Scott
Technical Manager	Paul O'Brien
Stage Manager	Melanie Bryceland
Chief Electrician	Dick Stedman
Assistant Stage Manager	Maria Gibbons

For the Fall:

Management	JLP Concerts Ltd
Tour Manager	Trevor Long
Sound Engineers	Diane Barton, Ed Hallam
Stage Technician	Phil Ames

Luxury Complex: New Faces in Hell

Life should be full of strangeness, like a rich painting
(The Fall, 'How I Wrote "Elastic Man"')

Back in the early months of 2015, the Five Years gallery was situated in a Brutalist GLC-built block, tucked away behind the alleyways of Broadway Market in east London. The studio/gallery was based at Unit 66, on the sixth floor of the building, and was surrounded by workshops and storage units. Previously, the area had been traditionally working class, with a pie-and-mash shop serving liquor and jellied eels, and a market that sold fruit and veg, electronic devices and sportswear at knockdown prices. At the turn of the century, it had two boozers: one a spit-and-sawdust corner pub with slot machines and karaoke; the other a prototype gastropub serving Belgian Trappist beer for £7 a bottle. It was perhaps an early indication of the forthcoming gentrification that was about to infect London Fields like a contagion. By 2015, the streets below were crowded with specialist food stalls, bijoux *faux*-bohemian boutiques and swathes of hipsters drinking coffee. Like the rest of Hackney, the character and culture of the area had been radically transformed by the malevolent impulses of late-stage capitalism.

A group of four artists (and Fall fans) – Dean Kenning, Andy Sharp, Marc Hulson and Lisa Cradduck – collaborated throughout 2015 and beyond on *Luxury Complex: Remembering Satan*, a mixed-media project that explored the effect of gentrification on a former children's hospital in the area. The hospital had been boarded up for many years, and a property developer had purchased it with the intention of demolishing the interior and replacing it with elegant apartments for investors. The building was clad with advertising hoardings that were familiar to Londoners, in which young, upwardly mobile, perfectly dressed people lounged on designer sofas or rode their expensive bicycles past a 3D mock-up of sumptuous penthouse suites.

The artists believed that the development was a symbol of the erosion of London's fabric. This, however, was just the starting point for the initial conversation. There was an occult underbelly to the project, one that morphed and mutated into a series of macabre prints, paintings, performances, past-life regressions, cultivated mould spores and fake historical documents as it progressed. It was a journey into the dark recesses of the mind's swampy sewer.

The gallery space for *Luxury Complex*'s first instalment of three exhibitions featured torn flock wallpaper, golem prints constructed from letterpress blocks, film projections of slime mould, a light box with XXX and basement signage (reminiscent of old Soho), a clay sculpture on a plinth of a muppet demon named the 'grey one', site photographs, faked archival shots and structural plans of a hospital pinned to a cork board.

Prior to the exhibition, it was rumoured that locals had witnessed the desecration of architectural features at the hospital during its refurbishment; salvagers weren't allowed in to remove old fireplaces or doors. Swathes of the building were redeveloped and turned into faceless deposit boxes, earning interest for their owners of 17 per cent a year. Sadly, this was not a unique experience; London is littered with similar buildings on every street corner.

Responding to this, Cradduck created a print of dancing golems in black ink called *Holy Ground*. They were a reconfiguration of Matisse's painting *La Danse*, which was hung on the staircase of a Moscow mansion until the revolution in 1917. Matisse's original used a Fauvist colour palette, with lush green grass, fizzing cobalt and muscular reds. These frivolous naked figures dance with each other in a circle, relishing the bacchanal that surrounds them. At *Luxury Complex*, Cradduck and Hulson reproduced a version of the painting (designed by Dean Kenning) on the walls of the gallery space: faces were altered into grotesque grey masks, with haunted facial features that were both Disney-like and nightmarish. The walls at Five Years were coated in black mould that flourished on torn wallpaper, revealing the mural underneath; it even infected books and paper materials in the display cabinets. The artists cultivated the same variety that grows in bad housing, but which also forms the microbes in penicillin. The mould magically worked as a spell.

When the artists initially began their conversations for *Luxury Complex*, Operation Yewtree was prominent in the national media. The case had been triggered by the recent death of Jimmy Savile and allegations of a culture of widespread abuse among prominent political figures, which had been made by 'Nick', a man who claimed to have witnessed it first-hand.[1] The artists' research revealed that Savile was once a regular visitor to the local hospital, having walked the very corridors and wards that were now being demolished. Cradduck's *Now Then* print of Savile was included in the exhibition to reflect this connection.

The cultural theorist Mark Fisher held a belief that Savile was a pollutant from beyond the grave, that even in death he was still exuding horror — so much so that his body (and gold coffin), which had been buried at a 50° angle to face the North Sea at Scarborough, was exhumed and placed in an unmarked grave, following the revelations about his abuse of young people on an industrial scale. Responding to a conversation with Fisher about the strange power of cadavers as contagion, Cradduck's *Now Then* presents Savile as wearing a string vest; the hairs from his chest poke through the net. Resting on his nose are a pair of round spectacles; on his fingers are gold rings, including one made from a glass eye. He is chewing a cigar as smoke drifts into his perfectly rendered hair. Here, Savile is an apparition, the same ghoul who appeared on

1. Dominic Kennedy, 'Heath inquiry is "based on flawed claims of devil worship"', *The Times*, 28 November 2016.

the edge of hospital beds (out of hours) across the country for over thirty years.

Using Savile's image provided a cathartic element and evoked Marcus Harvey's *Myra* (1997), at Sensation, which used Myra Hindley's mugshot enlarged and mosaicked by casts of children's handprints. *Now Then* (and much of the work in *Luxury Complex*) follows in the tradition of what art critic Adam Gopnik noted as the 'High Morbid Manner' – 'a detached, distanced, oddly smiling presentation of violence . . . that new kind of ghostly, frozen, remote look at death and suffering'.[2] Twenty years later, Cradduck's Savile print also triggered discussion in the original gallery where it was displayed. This inky image first appeared at a folk-horror exhibition in a small Sheffield gallery, where it was turned to the wall by staff in protest, such was its assumed toxicity. This was, as Gordon Burn would describe, an example of the 'aesthetics of revulsion'.[3] Cradduck thought it ironic that contemporary horror is unacceptable, yet nostalgic folk horror is de rigueur in certain intellectual circles. Her opinion was that Savile was the closest thing to a bogeyman as we will ever experience in modern culture. Here was a celebrity who preyed upon the vulnerable, and often in hospitals, where he was given special access due to his status. This grotesque figure was so influential that his power connected him to the head of the UK government, the royal family and some of the most notorious serial killers in the country. Yet there is a curious link between the Savile case and the Satanic Panic of the 1980s, another one of the underlying themes of *Luxury Complex*.

Throughout this period, the book *Michelle Remembers* (and its exposure as fraudulent) was presented as a reason not to believe women who made allegations of sexual abuse. Beneath this media message laid a dreadful truth: that widespread abuse *was* taking place at the heart of the British Establishment by Savile, but victims were too afraid to report it. This issue provoked an investigation on recovered memory in *Luxury Complex*, and the Satanic Panic phenomenon.

Prior to 1980, the term 'Satanic Panic' didn't exist, but a Canadian psychotherapist and evangelical Christian, Lawrence Pazder, and his patient Michelle Smith (whom he eventually married)[4] recorded 600 hours of psychotherapy and 'recovered memories' under hypnosis that resulted in an account of satanic networks, blood, gore and sacrifice.[5] A media frenzy followed, and Michelle eventually appeared on *The Oprah Winfrey Show* in 1990, discussing her imagined ordeal, which was not corroborated by any other sources or witnesses. For 'survivors' like her, the emotional turmoil was convincing, and her strong belief in recovered memory and clear sincerity was enough to convince others that they were factually correct.[6] Innocent

2. Gordon Burn, *Sex & Violence, Death & Silence*, London, Faber & Faber, 2009, pp. 8–9.

3. Ibid., p. 309.

4. Douglas Todd, 'Satanism: The Other Side of the Story', *Vancouver Sun*, 9 May 1991.

5. Rachel Hoskins, 'A Satanic Injustice', *Mail on Sunday*, 27 November 2016.

6. Terence Hines, 'Satanic Panic: Creation of a Contemporary Legend', *Skeptical Enquirer*, Vol. 18, Issue 3, 22 March 1994.

people were arrested throughout America without evidence during the Satanic Panic era. It wasn't until the *Mail on Sunday* exposed the authors of *Michelle Remembers* as fraudulent that charges were dropped. By that point the panic had spread to the UK: in 1991, children from Orkney were dragged from their beds as part of the stampede, while in Hull parents believed that their teenagers, who listened to rock music, were part of a satanic cult headed by a coven leader called Scorpio. Reports were made of mutilated horses in the fields of East Riding, and beheaded rabbits were hung from trees outside a school. Local vicars urged teenagers to avoid supernatural pursuits, to steer clear of dabbling with Ouija boards and Tarot cards.[7]

As a retort to the moral panic ignited by Satanic Panic, Cradduck and Hulson took part in two past-life regressions under hypnosis to explore recovered memory (the recordings were played in the gallery space) and created a 'fake' book, E. L. Palmer's *Luxury Complex*, with Kenning and Sharp, that formed a central focus for the work. The book was so convincing to visitors that some claimed to have read it or even that they owned a copy of the first edition.

The strangest and most terrifying regressor on the internet was sourced by Cradduck and Hulson for the performative element of the exhibition. Based in north London, the therapist allowed the regressions to be audio recorded. Through hypnotic suggestion she encouraged Cradduck to believe she was a child who had died from cancer in one previous life, and a sixteenth-century witch, one who had broken the therapist's arm, in another. After the session's end, she opened the door and ordered Cradduck out of the room. Hulson, however, had a different experience. He was regressed as a Berlin prostitute, but unlike Cradduck, he wasn't made to wear a blindfold. Each session cost £100, and according to Cradduck, it was 'like being abused by a madwoman'. The finger-clicking sounds used to provoke answers under hypnosis were recorded and used as the beat for a piece of music by Sharp, which he performed live in the gallery with his band, English Heretic.

At one exhibition event, Cradduck and Hulson read extracts from Lawrence Pazder's book *Michelle Remembers*, but learned how to read it effectively by listening to their own voices under hypnotic suggestion. This provided a guide for the live readings.

Excerpt from the transcript of Marc Hulson with the regressor:

> *Up above your timeline of memories so that you are now facing your past...*
> *back to being a child... back to being a baby... back to your mother's womb...*
> *back to your conception... I want you to stop at the point in your previous*
> *life that needs to be looked at... were you male or female? (click)... female...*
> *what country were you in? (click)... Germany... what year? (click)...*

7. Mike Covell, 'When Satanic Panic Gripped the Children of the City', *Hull Daily Mail*, 31 October 2015.

1938...were you German, Jewish or something else? (click)...Jewish...what happened in 1938? (click)...in your world in 1938, obviously there was a lot of unrest...I was raped...(click) by who?...a client...and what was your job? ...a prostitute...how did it happen that he raped you, rather than the sex you were offering?...because he wanted more than he paid for, so he followed me outside... what happened after that? Did you report him?...no, he killed me...was this client Jewish, a Nazi or a normal person?...I don't know...can you see that being raped and killed in your past life has influenced your art in your current life?... yes...what happened in your childhood or early life that made you a prostitute? It's not a normal career choice...I don't know...had your parents died? Were you abused by a family member? Something must have happened because if you had a nice childhood you wouldn't have ended up a prostitute, so what happened to you as a child?...I think I was orphaned...are we talking a double orphan, both mother and father died?...yes...

Excerpt from the transcript of Lisa Cradduck with the regressor:

Are you male or female?...I'm not getting anything yet...female...what age are you when you've stopped?...six...what country are you in?...here...what year is it?...1972...what goes wrong?...I'm ill...what disease?...I don't know but my legs hurt, and I'm scared...do they do any surgery on you?...yes... does it keep you alive?...no...do you die after surgery or before?...during... I want you to drop down into being the main surgeon, read his mind and tell me what he was doing surgery on you for...I can't...get into? Well maybe you're not supposed to. Did he make a mistake or did the anaesthetist make a mistake... nah, I just died...was there anything that could have been done?...no, I was so little...if we ask your higher self, what did you actually die of...cancer... now, sometimes cancer can be in places of the body that are linked with past lives, so I'd just like to ask, is that the case for you?...(silence)...did you have cancer in a vulnerable part of the body linked to a past life? Yes or no (click)...no... was it due to any kind of magic? Yes or no (click)...no...was it due to something inherited? (click)...yes...now, between 1972 and you being born in current life, did you manage to get to the light or not?...no...do we need to comfort your parents in this lifetime? Obviously, they will be traumatised at their six-year-old daughter dying...yes...so I'd like you to go and give your parents goodbye hugs, and let them know it wasn't their fault, there was nothing they could have done. I'd like to ask for some angels around them to keep them at peace. Then I'd like to ask, if you didn't reach the light, then you keep on reliving how you died or things that happened in your life over and over again. Is that what has happened to you recently to make you keep having these dreams of surgery? Is it to do with that? That you've kept on reliving it?...I've had a lot of surgery all the way through my life...would it be appropriate to rewrite this?...no...so now you understand where it came from in the first place...

Rather than an epiphany, the resulting hypnotic regression provided Cradduck with fodder to further explore her fascination with Goya's witch prints, an artist who Robert Hughes believed had 'uncensored access to his own worst dreams [...] that will certainly never be equalled'.[8] Like Goya, her work tracks the murky waters of superstition, demons, woodcuts and psychic practice, and the regression material provided a reflection on fear and the horrors of her subconscious. For Hulson, the experience linked back to previous themes in his work: psychotherapeutic spaces (such as couches, chairs and interiors), undercurrents of sexuality and gender, perverse power dynamics and magical forms of communication. 'There was something perversely exciting about doing a regression,' he says. 'It made this vivid fiction out of something that would happen in psychoanalysis. It's role play through prompts, bullying and hypnosis.'

Hulson's 'grey ones', which featured throughout *Luxury Complex*, were a direct response to a nightmare in which a terrifying entity called 'Jimmy' (experienced pre-Savile) has an appetite for human flesh and relentless violence. Jimmy was a grey Muppet demon, with no teeth and holes for eyes. He became a series of characters that corresponded to malevolent forces in the hypothetical novel by E. L. Palmer, which grew out of Kenning's *The Dulwich Horror: H. P. Lovecraft and the Crisis in British Housing* exhibition in 2007.

As *Luxury Complex* unfolded, the material changed each day. The work was physically altered, but this development also reflected the unfolding narrative of the novel. Kenning created promotional videos to sell the flats, using the standard tropes of commercial estate agents in London, in which pictures of fruit-sellers were overlaid with shots from old documentaries about Satanic Panic. A fake archive was created of building plans, and photographs displayed shots of hospitals, and their residents, in a glass cabinet.

As part of their creative research, Cradduck and Kenning visited Hanwell Asylum on a daytime excursion. Half of the building had been turned into luxury apartments, while the other half had been left intact as the local mental-health unit. Cradduck recalls that 'One side of the fence had a Japanese water garden, and the other had people setting fire to their hair.' This was the place where Cradduck's mother had been a resident during the 1990s, and it held a powerful emotional resonance. Hanwell's flats were sold on the concept of the gated community and the security it offered; this was a discourse about not letting people in, rather than not letting them out. It was clear that the executives had finally taken over the asylum.

It is no surprise to any observer of Mark E. Smith that the various threads of *Luxury Complex*, such as H. P. Lovecraft, moral panic, hauntology, past-life regressions, contemporary horror and the supernatural, came from four artists who are long-standing Fall fans. Smith's disconnected characters

8. Robert Hughes, *Nothing If Not Critical*, Collins Harvill, 1990.

and fascinations (exemplified in tracks such as 'The N.W.R.A.', with its hospital porter, or 'Spectre vs. Rector') are present in the methodology/state of mind of this peculiar combination of artists. Collectively, their work presents a bricolage of strange associations and enigmas that show a direct lineage to the work of Smith. His work fictionalised a socio-political undercurrent by commonly using Orphic language and imagery. As a songwriter he sucked up the culture that surrounded him and vomited it back in theatrical style. He often performed whole concerts with his back to the audience, sometimes on a pulpit. This sensibility infected his fans and is clear in the concept and execution of *Luxury Complex*, which could easily have been a track or concept for a Fall album. It provided a mix of the everyday and banal, and channelled it through the terrifying imagination of four artists, transforming architecture and recovered memory into a grotesque visual fiction. Smith's shadowy influence will only continue from beyond the grave. Perhaps this is the ultimate occultist accomplishment.

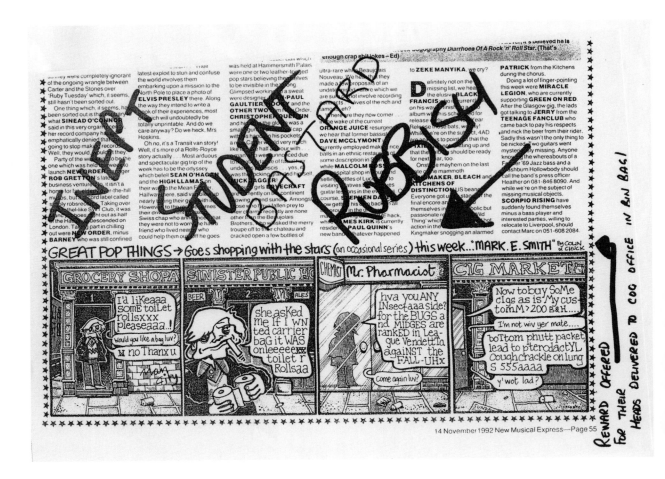

New Musical Express cartoon, defaced by MES.

LIVE at the ROADHOUSE
8/10 NEWTON STREET
PICCADILLY M/CR.

THE FALL

cerebral
CAUSTIC

The ROADHOUSE
20/21/22 MARCH 1995
Tickets £6·50 in Advance
Box Office 061 237 9789
PICCADILLY RECORDS · BOX OFFICE · HMV · ROADHOUSE

BACK BEAT

FREE LIVE MUSIC MAGAZINE

ISSUE 8

NOV-DEC '97

It's Christm-ah-s! ❄❄❄ THE FALL ❄❄❄ back in Leeds

THE BETA BAND
THE HYBIRDS
THE FLAMING STARS
EMBRACE
POLARIS
SOEZA

DUCHESS FILES • PUNK SHOWS
1 IN 12 SHOWS • HUDDERSFIELD FRINGE
LEEDS AFRICAN DRUMMING CONVENTION '97

COMMON • RAKIM • ADAM F • JONNY L • MOGWAI • CHOPPER
DARK SEASON • GRANDADDY • SOUNDTRACKS • COPING SAW
CHAPELTOWN 7 COMPILATION • CREAM ANTHEMS '97

WIN FALL TICKETS!!!
WIN HYBIRDS TICKETS!

GIGS • NEWS • REVIEWS • INTERVIEWS

Preparations for artwork for *Country on the Click* —
the original mix of the album was abandoned, remixed,
and then re-emerged six months later as *The Real New
Fall LP* (*Formerly 'Country on the Click'*). Smith described
the abandoned mix as 'sounding like *Doctor Who* meets
Posh Spice'.

Pages 310–16: Correspondence with Steve Hammonds at
Sanctuary / Cherry Red, 2003–06

310

From:

M.E. SMITH.

Sixteen .16. Winchester
Ave.

Sedgley Pk.

Prestwich.

Manchester

M25 OLJ

To:

MR. STEVE H.

SANCTUARY

. . . . . HOUSE.

43-53 Sinclair Rd.

London — W14 ONS

JAN. 05

Dearest Steveoid o.

As per phone call of 17-1 herewith
rough list tip 20 faves/worst

I am now a moron and have
a job on Metro + Big Issue compiling
"fave trdx". in no order of merit-o o.

1. PAINTER MAN — BOWEY M.

2. STRAIGHT TO I. ROY HEAD —
PRINCE JAZZBO

3. LONESOME MARY — JACK SCOTT

4. AQUALUNG — JETHRO TULL

Continued

from M.E.S.

2. S.M.

5. 'BUT IVE GOT TEXAS —
JON WAYNE.

6. FREAKS — KOOL KEITH.

7. PICK A DUB — KEITH HUDSON.

8. OMNIBUS — THE MOVE

9. I CAN'T CONTROL MYSELF —
THE TROGGS

10. TITLE TRAK OF PETER HAMMILL'S
LAST STUDIO L.P.

11. GERI TREGI — DER PLAN.

12. CUCKOO — THE MONKS

13 (I AM GUILD) — GUILDO HORN
HAT. EUCH LIEB.

312

15. BEATLE DONES + SMOKIN STONES

16. JIM SQUESHY — BIG   — CPT. BEEF
           HEART
         YOUTH.

17. RUNAWAY — TRAK 4
     WOMAN singer on
'NRTHRN SOUL ALL NITER' COMP
          on Virgin records

18. PROPOSTEROUS TALES in
the life of Ted McKenzie
     — I, ~~"Dr"~~ LUDICROUS

14 ⁰⁄₀ NEAR DISCO DAWN - ERROR

19 ⁰⁄₀ WHO MAKES THE NAZIS? smith
          THE FALL.

20 ⁰⁄₀ CHERRY RED —
     THE GROUNDHOGS.

Hope this suffice —
         all the best
         yr Pal — Mark.

"F.H.R." rel. Oct. 1st.

1) RIDE AWAY (POULOU - SMITH)

2) PACIFYING JOINT (SMITH)

3) WHAT ABOUT US? (SMITH - POULOU)

4) MIDNIGHT IN ASPEN (SMITH - TRAFFORD)

5) ASSUME (SMITH)

6) ASPEN REPRISE (SMITH - TRAFFORD)

7) BLINDNESS (SMITH - BIRTWISTLE)

8) I CAN HEAR THE GRASS GROW (ROY WOOD)

9) BO DEMMICK (SMITH)

10) YOUWANNER (SMITH - PRITCHARD - ARCHER)

11) CLASP HANDS (SMITH - TRAFFORD)

12) EARLY DAYS OF CHANNEL FÜHRER (SMITH - PRITCHARD)

✱ 13) BREAKINGTHE RULES (CROWE   - SMITH)

14) TRUST IN ME (SMITH - TRAFFORD)

PRODUCED BY _   M:E:SMITH, S.ARCHER; TIM at GRACIELANDS
PUBLISHED   by MINDER MUSIC LTD. London.

✱

CREDITS SONG 13):

CHECK WITH
PREVIOUS LIST,
WHICH YOU RECEIVED
AFTER THE MOJO AWARD.

Paul cover o.K.
inside o.K.
get rid of post office building
epic. & COURT OF ARMS
+ we're Rolling - ys. pel- Mark

314

TO: S.HAMMONDS —
SANCTUARY ETC.
COW —
w/4.ONS.

① The Best of M.E.S
M/CR.
26th. FEB 06
M.E.S.

Dear Steve —

WORDS cannot Express the
love I feel for you at
this moment.
ANYWAY. herewith front +
back 4. 12" CD single
IF Art. dept follow instructions, I think it'll be o.k.
Loved the last cut, esp. REF.

② EDIT — GO with that
last one, it's o.k. w/
me...
your pal —
Mark. for
The Fall —

CTP Template: CD_DPS1
Compact Disc Booklet: Double Page Spread
Customer
Catalogue No.
Job Title   Page Nos. 2@7

COLOURS
CYAN
MAGENTA
BLACK

FRONT:
EX-'FALL MEMBERS NEGOTIATE
(+ MANAGERS)
PATH 2 Steve's office.

To Steve + ALL AT S.
All the best.
Wishing you a
Merry Christmas + H.N.Y.
from Mark E. x 2003
"The Fall" group.

Dearest Steve, all the best
to you & family thanks
for everything this yr.
your pal –
Mark E –
+ 'THE FALL' R

To Steve and everyone at
Sanctuary Records.
wishing you a...
Merry Christmas
and a happy and
successful new year
2007!
All the best, from
elena + Mark F

FRONT: (from above)
MAIN PIC – M.E.S. new
image.
right: new slimline
Fall instruments.
drums
guitar.
bass

Dear Steve, & other Holi.
wishing you a very happy
christmas time and a
HAPPY Xmas
Season's Greetings and
Best Wishes for the New Year
lovely and successful
new year 2006
Mark E. x elena

FRONT: MARK +
STEVE'S
B RAIN
Dealing SCAN
with
Rec Co.

DEAR STEVE AND FAMILY,

WITH ALL THE VERY BEST
WISHES FOR A

Happy Christmas

AND A HAPPY NEW YEAR 2009

ALL MY LOVE STEVEOLD
+ BEST OF LUCK TO ME.
elen
> MARK - E - X -

FRONT: THE FALL'S
Attempt 'FESTIVE' IS DARK
DROP.

DEAR STEVE AND FAMILY,
WE WISH YOU A VERY
MERRY CHRISTMAS
AND A HAPPY NEW YEAR
2015!
Regards & Thanx
yr. pals -
Mark & Lthotall elen X
X

The *Goole Times* / Rabbit Hunters

Local papers. I know Mark E. Smith read his local paper, the *Prestwich Advertiser*; looked in there for stories, characters, headlines. Looked in the paper for ideas. Of course he did. Local papers are just local pubs in printed form. Every aspect of society is covered – the drink drivers, the shoplifters, the Saturday-night assaults outside the chip shop. But that's just the exciting stuff. Local papers are mainly a mirror of brilliant banality: 'Dispute Over New Roundabout: Tempers Rise'; 'Sheep Snatch: Have You Seen These Men?'; 'Police Warn of Mattress Man'.

I'm going to make a confession: when I was young, I never 'got' the Fall. In fact, when I was young, I didn't even know who they were. In Goole, where I come from, there was no 'indie scene'. There were a few goths and people who appeared briefly in the George at weekends – a civilised pub, near the clock tower. Nice young people – round glasses, tweed jackets, leggings, floppy hats and new accents; the students back from university, telling tales of Norwich and Newcastle . . . But apart from the safe haven of the George, Goole was strictly 'townie'. A white mono-class, 95 per cent working class, its micro-caste divisions evident only through ostentatious symbols of wealth. Its rulers were Friday-Night Men: Daves and Robs in chinos, short sleeves, mullets, moustaches, too many gold rings and tattoos; their female counterparts in leather trousers, hairspray, fake tan, white lipstick and XR3i's. Self-made builder men, not two but three weeks in Alicante, with speedboat ambitions, gold taps in the bathroom and hairdressers' curtains. Below them was an invisible class, the decent people whose names you could never remember: the Ordinary Mass, whose stories don't really matter here. And at the bottom, beneath the ostentatious crowd, beneath the Ordinary Mass, were the Dispossessed: the notorious, the hilarious, the rabbit killers on remand – the big stars of our local paper, the *Goole Times*. *Goole Times* celebrities whose desperate, bizarre and criminal exploits were retold weekly, fun-filled column inches about another garden-shed robbery, supermarket-steak heist or air-rifle hold-up in the sweet shop that went terribly and dramatically wrong. I didn't know about the Fall. But I did know about the Dispossessed, and one day in my early twenties I recognised them – or their Prestwich counterparts – as the actors in a song. I knew the Rabbit Hunters. I'd grown up with them.

The little port town sits on mudflats at the mouth of the River Ouse, the River Ouse flows into the River Humber, the River Humber flows into the North Sea.

It's Friday, mid-afternoon, Christmas Eve, mid-1990s. It's dark and it's snowing. There's a tinsel excitement in the air. Small-town excitement. Simple pleasures: heavy drinking and last-minute shopping. Down there, on the ground, car headlights cut through the darkness, huge snowflakes illuminated by halogen beams.

Up here, Nobby has to make a choice. Does he let go or does he hold on? If he holds on, things will probably get worse – logically, things can only get worse. But if he lets go, things are guaranteed to get worse.

Hobson's choice, they call it, don't they?

Hold on and keep holding on, and if he can hold on long enough, he might land in a soft bank of snow way out in the fields.

Let go, let go now, and he'll break both his legs, maybe even smash his spine and spend the rest of his life in a wheelchair.

There's only one choice: Nobby holds on.

The wind blows in from the docks, down Boothferry Road, and lifts him higher. He screws up his face in agony, then he swears and he roars as the steel wire tightens on his hands, but he holds on, he has to hold on.

The people below are pointing. A grandma, grandson in tow, screams – she cannot believe what she's seeing. Nobby can't hear her scream; he can't hear a thing, it's silent up here. It's the strangest thing: he *sees* Grandma scream, sees her sheepskin mitten cover the grandson's eyes, the horror of Nobby's imminent death, his huge carcass bouncing off the pavement, too much for children's eyes.

Is it snowing heavily? Yes, it's really snowing. It's dark and it's snowing – soft snow, cinematic snow, Bing Crosby snow, snow that glows as it flutters down past the council Christmas lights that hang in trails between *faux*-Victorian lamp posts. The lamp posts that leave bruises as they clip Nobby's feet.

It's Christmas, it's Friday, and people are finishing work, some already drunk from the afternoon office parties, and the factory girls from Burton's are out on the town. Suntanned women in winter, skimpy summer dresses – I think one of them is in a rah-rah skirt. They hook arms and negotiate the snow in high heels, singing and laughing.

There are so few pubs left in town now. Not like it used to be – it used to be one pub after another, all the way from the train station right down Aire Street and on to the docks. Those were the days. Goole was thriving then, before they pedestrianised Boothferry Road. What do you call a street that's been pedestrianised but has no pedestrians? They destrianised it. They closed down the pubs and turned them into chain stores. They strangled Nobby's world. They shrunk his kingdom.

Nobby holds tighter and has a fleeting clear vision of what Goole used to be like, before they sanitised it, before it died. As he floats down Boothferry Road, he remembers all of this – thirty feet and rising – he remembers Goole in the 1970s and '80s. Real characters then, not like today. People still drink, course they do, but not like they used to, not like he does. A tear wells in Nobby's eye and he can see himself – not right now, but this morning when he was Robin Hood – Errol Flynn's Robin Hood – laughing in green tights, his merry men all around him, as he orders a huge round of drinks at the NUR bar. He can see their ageing, cackling faces – he can see them in Cinemascope – they pat him on the back and raise a glass to Nobby. Folk hero, last of the boozers, who else would blow their whole giro on a single round of drinks? 'Tell us again, Nob! Tell us how you held up Yorkshire Penny Bank.' The self as Robin Hood is not without foundation, but he's going to top that today. 'The bank job was nothing,' he tells them, and he shows them the hacksaw in his pocket.

It's cold up here, freezing cold, and the wire is like a razor, cutting through his fingers. Nobby looks down the street. The Tavern is now a Dorothy Perkins, the Station Hotel a carpet shop. What have they *fucking* done? He's angry, Nobby. Where are all the characters ... what went wrong?

It's hackneyed, but true: your whole life really does flash before you when you drown – in perfect order, a mini-motion picture from infancy to death. But what happens when you float, what happens when you rise high above the ground ... what happens when you go up instead of under? Your life does not flash before you; admittedly there are racing, momentary flashes of panic, but mostly you are at ease, there is a tranquillity up here – one Nobby's never been able to find down there on the ground. It's the weirdest thing, because somehow, in some way, by some logic, you are incredibly calm. He can see more people pointing now – he can see men shouting, fingers pointed, frozen faces – all eyes on Nobby as he floats above the shops and off down the high street. The wind drops momentarily, and the balloon dips suddenly; his feet clip the top of the *Goole Times* offices, fifty yards from the clock tower. If he is going to let go, this is not the time – he'll land on the old Victorian slate roof and roll off, plummeting three storeys down to his death – so he holds on – now a gust of wind hits the huge balloon, and he's blown violently away from the rooftops and back over the pedestrianised precinct – there's a big crowd now, and he loves a big crowd – the balloon dips again and he's only twenty feet above the pavement – if he is going to let go, this definitely *is* the time – he can see every detail of their shouting faces but he cannot make out their words, the shoppers and the drinkers as stop/start images – he closes his eyes and he braces himself for the fractures, he wants to let go, but he can't let go, he meant to let go – right then, just now – his brain told his freezing, bleeding fingers to let go, but they disobeyed him – the huge balloon gently rises, then gathers speed as it barrels towards the clock tower, rising again above the rooftops.

Nobby's struck by a thought here. It's fleeting, but it's real: maybe he doesn't want to let go – maybe this is the ideal death for a drinking legend?

He's missed his chance anyway – another gust of wind and he's blown sideways with a bang – more silent screams, some people look away as the balloon lifts again: thirty feet, forty feet, fifty feet, he's now high above the rooftops and heading straight for the clock-tower roundabout.

The Christmas tree is there – on the island of snow-covered grass, in the middle of the roundabout, in the middle of the town. It's a huge tree – one of the last remnants of civic pride round here, a big tree every year – almost as tall as the clock tower, and stood right next to it – and the tree is beautiful, even Nobby can see that – it's covered in fairy lights, great big domestic bulbs in red and yellow and blue and orange, their glow magnified by the snow that has settled on the branches they sit on. It's his best chance yet. If he can just hold on till he gets to the Christmas tree, he can then let go, make a grab for the tree, maybe even land on top of it…He knows it won't take his huge weight, but it will at least break his fall.

His fingers are shredded now, he can't hold on much longer. As the balloon rises and the steel rope stretches, he can feel warm blood running down both wrists. The tree is barely twenty feet away and getting closer; he can make it, he can do this, he is fucking Robin Hood.

Strange calm, not panic – everything becomes crystal clear – not today, today is a blur. He knows he started drinking as soon as he got up, he knows he met Mickey in the Roundel – he knows they drank too much, too fast – but after that, he has no idea. The distant past *is* clear, and just for a moment – as he dangles in the now-ten-foot gap between himself and the top of the Christmas tree – the significant events of his life – just how he got here – all make sense.

He remembers the Drawing well – more than he'd ever admit – everybody in his class remembers the Drawing. *They* still talk about it when he bumps into them. It was the first and last time he'd ever been praised at school. No longer the class clown, no longer the slipper or the cane. The Drawing gave him status, there was even talk of art college and a career as a commercial artist. *They* remind him of that while they load their car boot with the weekly shop at Leo's, as he wanders past, pissed. 'You still doing drawing and that?' He tells them he isn't, never drawn since the Drawing. 'That's a shame, bloody good drawing that.' And it was. I know it was, because I saw it, pinned on his wall above his bed. I can only have been eleven or twelve, Nobby's younger brother John was my best mate then, and me and John would marvel at the Drawing: a hundred faces all crafted in great detail, every face quite different but somehow exactly the same, regimented in neat rows, all looking straight at you – it was Nobby's depiction of the crowd at Elland Road. We are looking at them as if from the pitch – we are looking at them as if we were Trevor Cherry, Tony Currie, Allan Clarke. We are looking at them through Nobby's eyes, as he stands on the pitch. They stare blankly at us – there is no emotion, they do not clap or cheer us – they just stare, a hundred faces staring at us – *us* – the star player – *us* – having reached the pinnacle of bog-standard working-class male desire – we are the superstar player in Britain's greatest league side – so why don't they cheer?

Nobby's not thought about the Drawing for years, not seriously, only in passing in the supermarket car park, only because *they* mentioned it. But the Drawing comes clearly to him now, he scans it in his mind, slowly, he wills the faces to finally come alive – and they do. They're cheering now – they're pointing at him, they're going wild, cheering him on and chanting his name – after twenty-five years of bedroom-wall immobility, the sun-faded pencil faces have finally got behind Nobby. They are on his side. The People's Prince. Robin Hood.

He's only five feet from the top of the Christmas tree now, and the balloon holds steady – if he can hold on for just one more second, and if he gets lucky, he'll reach out and grab the top of the tree, and he'll survive. It's his final chance, and he knows it – if he misses, he's had it. The balloon is heading towards Aire Street and, after that, the docks: open territory, nothing but hard concrete and acres of freezing water to break his fall. He'll never get out of the docks alive, he knows that, dozens of drunken Russian sailors have proved this over the decades; you don't fall in the docks, pissed, in winter, and come out alive. All he needs is a little bit of luck, and he gets it. The balloon bobs over the clock tower, dips, and the wire slackens – the slack in the wire swings him, pendulum-like, towards the top of the tree. The traffic is parked on the roundabout now. People are out of their cars, they point and they scream, and he still cannot hear them. The snow falls, and it is dark. A fat man in a too-small T-shirt, his arse hanging over his jeans, is dangling on a wire from a gigantic white barrage balloon, fifty feet in the air, a promotional balloon that a few minutes ago was attached to the forecourt of a newly opened discount supermarket. In big red round letters, down both sides of the balloon, is the legend 'PIONEER'.

'Tell us again!' They all do it. Every day. He's sick of telling the story – but it *does* make them laugh and *does* make them listen. When the giro has run out, as it always does in an instant, they'll buy him pints if he tells the story, then they'll buy him more pints if he sings. The story of the heist followed by a booming rendition of 'Moon River' = six pints, guaranteed. So he rolls out the story.

It's some time in the early 1980s, years ago, after a marathon all-day bender in the Tavern, Nobby has a brainwave. It's so simple, he can't believe nobody else has thought of it. He staggers out of the pub and into Woolworths. He buys a pair of American-tan tights and a red water pistol. He walks back across Boothferry Road, pulls the tights over his head and walks straight into Yorkshire Penny Bank. He marches up to the counter and says to the woman behind it: 'Hand over all your money, this is a stick-up!' The woman turns ashen with shock, then, in a moment of realisation, stands up and shouts: 'I know it's you, Robert! Just fuck off!' She points to the door; she's trying to help him get out before it's too late. The manager sees this. He's not from Goole, *he* doesn't know it's only Nobby – to the manager, this is a stick-up. He presses the panic button. The shutters roll down, inside and out, the alarm goes off, and Nobby's locked in the bank. The police arrive in two minutes flat – 'What the fuck have you done now?' says the arresting sergeant. The sergeant certainly knows Nobby, he cautions him formally for idiocy on a weekly basis. They haul Nobby away in a van. Three years in Hull prison. And everybody laughs. 'But that's nowt,' he tells them. 'Nowt compared to what I'm gonna do today.'

A lucky gust of wind, and Nobby is blown straight into the top of the Christmas tree. This is it – he has finally docked his Zeppelin. He lets go with his left hand and grabs at the big illuminated gold plastic star that perches on top of the tree. The balloon jolts, the gold plastic star instantly separates from the top of the tree, and he rises up again, his left hand still clutching the star, his right hand now slowly slipping down the steel rope. It was his last chance.

The balloon is caught by wind coming in from the river and it gains height. It drifts away from the roundabout, down Aire Street and towards the docks. Fifty feet, sixty feet, seventy feet, over the Royal, the Mac and the Lowther. His whole life now passes beneath his feet in pub form. The pub lights, the pub rooftops, the streets and, finally, the town disappear into the darkness – he's over the docks now, 100 feet, 120 feet, 130 feet and rising – the star is still shining in his bloody left hand.

The docks flow into the River Ouse, the River Ouse flows into the River Humber, the River Humber flows into the North Sea.

2008

Imperial Wax Solvent (Apr); Smith appears in BBC3 sitcom *Ideal* as Jesus; Smith's *Renegade* autobiography (May); Messing Up the Paintwork symposium, University of Salford (May); Mark E. Smith & Ed Blaney – *Smith & Blaney* LP (Nov); Smith appears in *Resistance Domination Secret: Agamemnon*, final instalment in trilogy w/ Mark Aerial Waller; *VII – THE FALL* (Lough Press, Berlin).

2009

Last Night at the Palais live CD/DVD; *Paintwork #2*, a second exhibition inspired by the group, opens at SW1 Gallery, London (May), followed by *Paintwork #3* exhibition in Hamburg (Oct); 'Slippy Floor' (Nov).

2010

Your Future Our Clutter (Apr); 'Bury' (Apr); Primavera Sound festival, Barcelona (May); Smith guests w/ Gorillaz on 'Glitter Freeze' (*Plastic Beach* LP).

2011

Ersatz GB (Nov), End of the Road festival, Dorset (Sep); *Laptop Dog* EP (Nov).

2012

'Night of the Humerons' (May).

2013

'Sir William Wray' (Apr); *Re-Mit* (May); 'The Remainderer' (Dec).

2014

Live Uurop VIII-XII Places In Sun & Winter, Son live LP (Sep); *You Can Drum But You Can't Hide* by Simon Wolstencroft (Route); *The Big Midweek: Life Inside the Fall* by Steve Hanley & Olivia Piekarski (Route).

2015

Sub-Lingual Tablet (May); Glastonbury Festival (Jun); Green Man Festival (Aug); NZ/Australia tour (Oct).

2016

'Wise Ol' Man' (Feb); *The Rise, The Fall, and The Rise* by Brix Smith Start (Faber & Faber).

2017

New Facts Emerge (Jul); 'Responding to a Rebel: Mark E. Smith Agent of Chaos', part of *Wyndham Lewis: Life, Art, War*, Imperial War Museum North, Manchester (2 Aug, cancelled); final show, Queen Margaret Union, Glasgow (4 Nov).

2018

Mark E. Smith dies at home in Prestwich (Jan 24); the Fall disband.

Imperial Wax Solvent (April 2008, Castle)

SIDE 1
Alton Towers
Wolf Kidult Man
50 Year Old Man
I've Been Duped
Strangetown

SIDE 2
Taurig
Can Can Summer
Tommy Shooter
Latch Key Kid
Is This New
Senior Twilight Stock Replacer
Exploding Chimney

Produced by:
MARK E. SMITH
GRANT SHOWBIZ
ANDI TOMA
TIM / GRACIELANDS

Engineered by:
TOM PRITCHARD
DINGO
OLLIVER GROSCHECK

Artwork: ANTHONY FROST

Recorded at St. Martin Tonstudio, Düsseldorf,
May–June 2007; Gracieland, Rochdale, late 2007.

PETER GREENWAY – Lead Guitar
KEIRON MELLING – Drums
ELENI POULOU – Keyboards, Vocals
MARK E. SMITH – Vocals
DAVID SPURR – Bass Guitar

Your Future Our Clutter (April 2010, Domino)

SIDE 1
O.F.Y.C. Showcase
Bury Pts. 1 + 3
Hot Cake

SIDE 2
Mexico Wax Solvent
Y.F.O.C. / Slippy Floor

SIDE 3
Chino
Funnel of Love
986 Generator

SIDE 4
Weather Report 2
Get a Summer Song Goin'
Cowboy George

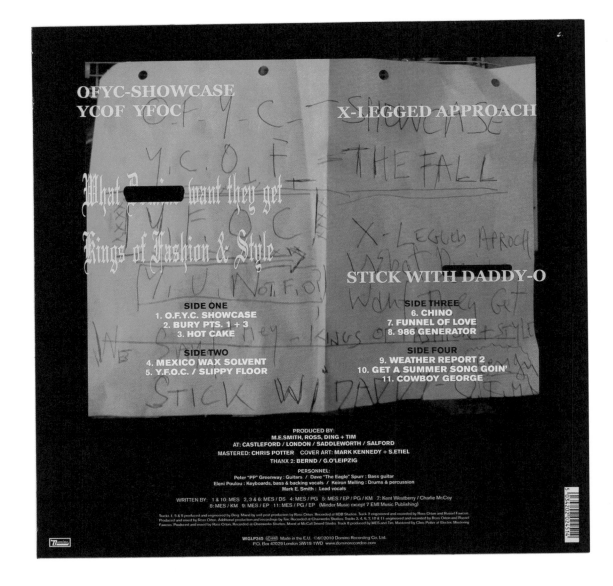

OFYC-SHOWCASE
YCOF YFOC

X-LEGGED APPROACH

What P....... want they get

Kings of Fashion & Style

STICK WITH DADDY-O

SIDE ONE
1. O.F.Y.C. SHOWCASE
2. BURY PTS. 1 + 3
3. HOT CAKE

SIDE THREE
6. CHINO
7. FUNNEL OF LOVE
8. 986 GENERATOR

SIDE TWO
4. MEXICO WAX SOLVENT
5. Y.F.O.C. / SLIPPY FLOOR

SIDE FOUR
9. WEATHER REPORT 2
10. GET A SUMMER SONG GOIN'
11. COWBOY GEORGE

PRODUCED BY:
M.E.SMITH, ROSS, DING + TIM
AT: CASTLEFORD / LONDON / SADDLEWORTH / SALFORD
MASTERED: CHRIS POTTER   COVER ART: MARK KENNEDY + S.ETIEL
THANX 2: BERND / G.O'LEIPZIG

PERSONNEL:
Peter "PP" Greenway : Guitars / Dave "The Eagle" Spurr : Bass guitar
Eleni Poulou : Keyboards, bass & backing vocals / Keiron Melling : Drums & percussion
Mark E. Smith : Lead vocals

WRITTEN BY: 1 & 10: MES 2, 3 & 6: MES / DS 4: MES / PG 5: MES / EP / PG / KM 7: Kent Westberry / Charlie McCoy
8: MES / KM 9: MES / EP 11: MES / PG / EP   (Minder Music except 7 EMI Music Publishing)

Tracks 1, 5 & 9 produced and engineered by Ding. Mixed by and post production by Ross Orton. Track 3 engineered and recorded by Ross Orton and Russel Fawcet.
Produced and mixed by Ross Orton. Additional production and recordings by Tim. Recorded at Chairworks Studios. Tracks 2, 4, 6, 7, 10 & 11 engineered and recorded by Ross Orton and Russel
Fawcet. Produced and mixed by Ross Orton. Recorded at Chairworks Studios. Mixed at McCall Sound Studio. Track 8 produced by MES and Tim. Mastered by Chris Potter at Electric Mastering

WIGLP245   Made in the E.U. ℗&©2010 Domino Recording Co. Ltd.
P.O. Box 47029 London SW18 1WD www.dominorecordco.com

Peter "PP" Greenway: Guitars
Dave "The Eagle" Spurr: Bass guitar
Eleni Poulou: Keyboards, bass & backing vocals
Keiron Melling: Drums & percussion
Mark E. Smith: Lead vocals

Recorded at Chairworks Studios, Castleford
(tracks 2, 3, 4, 5, 7, 8); 6dB Studio, Salford (tracks 1, 6, 9);
Saddleworth and London from mid- to late 2009.

Ersatz GB (November 2011, Cherry Red)

SIDE 1
Cosmos 7
Taking Off
Nate Will Not Return
Mask Search
Greenway
Happi Song

SIDE 2
Monocard
Laptop Dog
I've Seen Them Come
Age of Chang

ARTWORK: Mark Kennedy, & Mark E. Smith

PRODUCTION:
Simon Archer
Mark E. Smith

ENGINEERS:
Sam – Metropolis
Ed – Toerag

Mark E. Smith – Vocals
David Spurr – Bass
Eleni Poulou – Keyboards
Keiron Melling – Drums

Recorded at Metropolis Studios, London,
and Toerag Studio, London, mid-2011.

Re-Mit (May 2013, Cherry Red)

SIDE 1
No Respects (Intro)
Sir William Wray
Kinder of Spine
Noise
Hittite Man
Pre-MDMA Years

SIDE 2
No Respects rev.
Victrola Time
Irish
Jetplane
Jam Song
Loadstones

MARK E. SMITH
KEIRON MELLING
DAVE SPURR
PETER GREENWAY
ELENI POULOU

present:
RE-MIT

Produced by Mark E. Smith
Engineered by Ding and Grant
Mastered by Andy Pearce
Published by Minder Music Ltd.

Artwork:
Suzanne Smith
Anthony Frost
Becky Stewart

Guitar on 1, 3, 7: Tim Presley

SIDE ONE
1. No Respects (Intro) (Smith/Presley/Poulou)
2. Sir William Wray (Smith/Poulou)
3. Kinder of Spine (Smith/Presley)
4. Noise (Smith/Spurr/Greenway)
5. Hittite Man (Smith/Greenway)
6. Pre-MDMA Years (Smith)

SIDE TWO
7. No Respects rev. (Smith/Presley/Poulou)
8. Victrola Time (Smith/Melling/Poulou)
9. Irish (Smith/Spurr/Melling)
10. Jetplane (Smith/Spurr/Melling)
11. Jam Song (Smith/Spurr/Melling/Poulou)
12. Loadstones (Smith/Greenway/Poulou)

℗ & © Cherry Red Records 2013. Issued under license from Mark E. Smith

MARK E. SMITH
KEIRON MELLING
DAVE SPURR
PETER GREENWAY
ELENI POULOU

Produced by Mark E. Smith
Engineered by Ding and Grant
Artwork:
Suzanne Smith
Anthony Frost
Becky Stewart

Recorded at Konk Studios, London, and 6DB, Salford
(except Victrola Time, recorded in Chelsea),
September 2012.

THE FALL

SUB-LINGUAL TABLET

Sub-Lingual Tablet (May 2015, Cherry Red)

SIDE 1
Venice With the Girls
Black Roof
Dedication Not Medication

SIDE 2
First One Today
Junger Cloth
Stout Man

SIDE 3
Auto Chip 2014—2016
Pledge!
Snazzy

SIDE 4
Fibre Book Troll
Quit iPhone

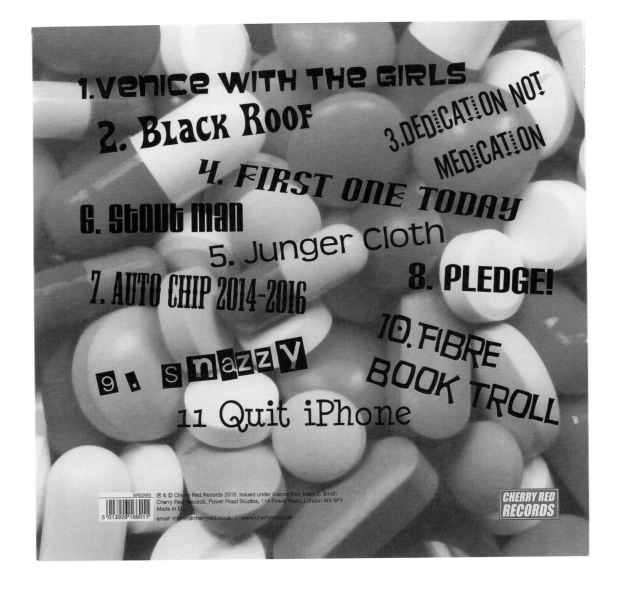

1. VENICE WITH THE GIRLS

2. Black Roof

3. DEDICATION NOT MEDICATION

4. FIRST ONE TODAY

6. Stout Man

5. Junger Cloth

7. AUTO CHIP 2014-2016

8. PLEDGE!

9. snazzy

10. FIBRE BOOK TROLL

11 Quit iPhone

BRED660 ℗ & © Cherry Red Records 2015. Issued under licence from Mark E. Smith
Cherry Red Records, Power Road Studios, 114 Power Road, London W4 5PY
Made In EU
email: infonet@cherryred.co.uk / www.cherryred.co.uk

5 013929 166011

CHERRY RED RECORDS

Bass: Dave Spurr
Guitar: Peter Greenway
Drums: Kieron Melling & Daren Garratt
Synths: Eleni Poulou
Vocals: Mark E Smith

All instruments on Track 2 Black Roof played,
recorded and mixed by Rob Barbato & Tim Presley
Produced by: Mark E Smith
Engineered by: Ding

Recorded at Chairworks, Castleford, and 6DB, Salford,
May 2014.

New Facts Emerge (July 2017, Cherry Red)

SIDE 1
Segue
Fol de Rol
Brillo de Facto

SIDE 2
Victoria Train Station Massacre
New Facts Emerge
Couples vs Jobless Mid 30's

SIDE 3
Second House Now
O! ZZTRRK Man
Gibbus Gibson

SIDE 4
Groundsboy
Nine Out of Ten

SIDE ONE
1. SEGUE 0.30
(Smith)
2. FOL DE ROL 6.34
(Smith / Spurr / Melling)
3. BRILLO DE FACTO 3.49
(Smith / Spurr / Greenway / Melling)

SIDE TWO
1. VICTORIA TRAIN STATION MASSACRE 1.14
(Smith / Spurr)
2. NEW FACTS EMERGE 4.02
(Smith / Spurr)
3. COUPLES Vs JOBLESS MID 30's 8.44
(Smith / Spurr / Melling)

SIDE THREE
1. SECOND HOUSE NOW 4.27
(Smith / Spurr / Greenway)
2. O! ZZTRRK MAN 3.50
(Smith / Melling)
3. GIBBUS GIBSON 2.37
(Smith / Spurr / Greenway)

SIDE FOUR
1. GROUNDSBOY 3.37
(Smith / Spurr / Greenway)
2. NINE OUT OF TEN 8.48
(Smith)

All tracks published by BMG Music Ltd.

M.E. SMITH – LEAD VOCALS
P. GREENWAY – GUITAR, SYNTH, BACKING VOCALS
D. SPURR – BASS, MELLOTRON, BACKING VOCALS
K. MELLING – DRUMS

PRODUCED BY MELLING / SMITH
ENGINEERED BY DING

ARTWORK BY PAMELA VANDER

℗ & © 2017 Cherry Red Records Ltd. Issued under license from Mark E. Smith
Cherry Red Records, Power Road Studios, 114 Power Road, London W4 5PY
www.cherryred.co.uk

CHERRY RED
RECORDS

BRED706

M. E. SMITH – LEAD VOCALS
P. GREENWAY – GUITAR, SYNTH,
BACKING VOCALS
D. SPURR – BASS, MELLOTRON, BACKING VOCALS
K. MELLING – DRUMS

PRODUCED BY MELLING / SMITH
ENGINEERED BY DING

ARTWORK BY PAMELA VANDER

Recorded at Chairworks, Castleford, with some vocal
tracks at 6DB, Salford, May 2016. Mixed at Hilltown
Studios, Colne, Lancashire.

The Wire 183, May 1999

The Outsider

Twelve months ago, the world of Mark E. Smith imploded. In New York he was arrested and charged with assault. Alienated by his erratic behaviour, the members of the Fall walked out on him for the final time. Now he's back, fronting a new group, and ready to carry his artistic vision forward into the next century. Interview: Tony Herrington.

The interview begins with a red herring – a lead picked up that morning, but which turns out to be another scrap of misinformation to lay on top of all the other items of hearsay and rumour that have attached themselves, like an outer, disfiguring skin, to the body of Mark E. Smith and his group the Fall over the last twenty years.

I'm told that you have just been away, I begin, to North Africa. Even as I put the question to Mark it sounds ridiculous; the kind of thing you might reasonably expect to ask one day of a subject such as Bill Laswell, Ryuichi Sakamoto, or any other member of music's intercontinental perpetual motion club. But not Mark E. Smith, a musician who makes a virtue out of the fact that he still lives within walking distance of the place of his birth in north Manchester. (As he tells me later: 'I'm near my mother now. There are no more men in the family, they all died. The family are all women, so it's handy to have somebody around, I think. And I can cadge money off them and everything,' he adds, laughing uproariously.)

Sure enough, the answer comes back in the negative.

'No, not really.'

Where then?

'Lanzarote, Tenerife. I just went up there for a bit, four or five days.'

The Canary Islands, then, located just off the coast of Morocco, but Spain rather than North Africa. I was just there myself in fact, last October.

'Was you? It's good isn't it? It's strange.'

Very. Some of it is like being on the surface of the moon.

'Iceland is a bit like that. Lanzarote was like Iceland with sun.'

The Canaries are sometimes called the Islands of Lost Souls. People travel there to escape, but often they are criminals on the run, or people who are trying to erase some traumatic past incident in their lives. In the Canary Islands there is a high suicide rate among ex-pats.

'Is there? I didn't know that . . . Just having a holiday was great. I haven't had a holiday for about two years. So that was unusual. It took me about three or four days for my body to suss out that I wasn't about to go onstage. When I've been in places like that, Greece or Spain or Portugal, it's always been to play, so it really did me a lot of good actually. For the first three days I was like this [he hunches his shoulders into a stressed-out position], because when you're in places like that you are doubly keyed-up with the group, because they're going, "Oh, isn't it lovely," and they forget that they're there to play, or they play crap. At seven o'clock I'm like, "Hurry up! Finish your dinner." No Mark, it's all right. You can do what you like tonight.'

I remember something you once wrote, in 1982, about the track 'Iceland' on *Hex Enduction Hour*, which implied that you had finally found your roots in Reykjavik but no one you were with noticed. When was the last time you were in Iceland?

'Two years ago. I've been on holiday there, worked there three or four times. That's a good holiday to go on. It's the same scene. Like Lanzarote, there's no bugger there. The beach part was rammed to the gills with Brits and Krauts, but five minutes out of there it was great, there was no bugger around.

'The thing I liked about it was, it was the first time I'd got on an aeroplane where everyone wasn't a businessman or stuck-up professional traveller. That was relaxing, to get on a plane and everybody is working class. Usually with me, when they hear your voice, it's like, "What's he doing on this plane?"; everybody watches when you go to the bog. And if you're with the group it's worse. I didn't get that this time. It was full of these people who never go away, never travel anywhere, maybe just once a year. They're asking you what to do: "Is this where we get off the plane?" Mark laughs. It was nice that, you know.'

Was the flight to Lanzarote part of Mark Smith's own process of erasure, an attempt to obliterate the traumatic events, still shrouded in mystery, that marked the Fall's 1998 North American tour? The stories emerging at that time were terrible, and salaciously reported. Perplexing bulletins of internecine fighting both on- and offstage; lacklustre or disastrous performances; Smith on a 24-7 drunk-binge, seemingly locked on a course of auto-destruction; a suicide mission designed to sabotage his group's music and future.

It all came to a head in New York City, when all but one member of the Fall walked out on the group for good, and Smith was arrested and then bailed on charges of bodily assault.

So I have to ask: how do you feel now about what happened in New York?

'I was just starting to forget about it,' he says, the reply dripping with sarcasm. 'They wrote a lot of shit about New York,' he continues, referring to a certain weekly UK music paper. 'I rang the editor up about it. They get their information off the internet. I said, "What kind of editor are you? Get a retraction printed." And it was like *that* big. It's dangerous that stuff, especially if you're still on bail. You're talking about jeopardising somebody's liberty here.

'But a lot of the time I play along with it. I mean, how many interviews have I done? They think you're that daft, but sometimes it's good to have that image of being drunk and arrogant.

'And people think it's engineered. People get very jealous. Bands, who are dead rich, I've got nothing, me, they think: how much did you pay to get that much press? People in America said to me that to get the amount of publicity I got you'd have to pay a press guy $500,000. That's what they do, you know, these actors and actresses: "My struggle with alcohol" and all that. They haven't got a cocaine problem, you must have sussed this out, they've paid the PR guy just to revive their careers. That's the rate, $250,000, if you want blanket coverage.'

Do you get frustrated by the fact that your constituency is defined by the music press, and that your peers and contemporaries are perceived to be people like ... Echo and the Bunnymen or some such. Don't you think that's ridiculous? Mark bursts out laughing.

'Very much. I did before I was in a band. You worked that out. I'm still very edgy about it, what I do, talking about it. That's my background. To my mam's mates, for instance, I'm that pop-singer fella. That's good in a way, it brings you down a peg. I do find it ... that's not what I only do. But they are my contemporaries, yes. Ian [McCulloch] out of Echo used to be our roadie ... But I don't relate to him any more. Because I don't like musicians much. I don't hate them, but I don't associate with them. Most of my mates know nothing about music. They just know I'm in a group. And I'm not what they expect of a singer. It sounds ridiculous, but if I do get a compliment it's: "You're not like what we thought you'd be like. We thought you'd be a right pain in the arse."'

At the beginning of this year Mark debuted a new version of the Fall, which retained just keyboard player Julia Nagle from the group that had come apart in New York. Performing in unlikely venues in Ashton and Whitefield, suburban areas of north Manchester, the group premiered many of the songs which now make up the new Fall album, *The Marshall Suite*. Among the record's thirteen tracks is a thundering *motorik* version of the Saints' misanthropic 1977 single 'This Perfect Day' to sit alongside extraordinary performances such as 'Shake Off' and 'Antidote'. The record is split into three sections, obliquely linked by episodes in the life of a character called the Crying Marshal.

'This new band is great,' Mark says enthusiastically. 'Tom [Head], the drummer, I'm lucky to get him, he's brilliant. His older brother is a good mate of mine. He played me this tape he'd done and it was like Zappa-esque stuff. I said, "Yeah, do you think he'd do it?" He's great because he does exactly what you want. He'd played jazz, country and western; he can play anything, I mean, really play it. It used to take days, weeks and months sometimes before the drummer got it right. He can get what you want like that [he clicks his fingers]. Touch wood. It's a pleasure to be onstage now, which is the first time it's been like that for a bit.

'It's quite weird actually,' he continues, then pauses ... 'A lot of the things that were frustrating me have disappeared. A lot of things that were put down to me rambling and all that was in fact the group, that last group. They were efficient, lazy, old fashioned, I thought, everything the Fall shouldn't be.'

Is that something that bothers you: you get all the credit for the Fall, but all the blame as well?

'For sure, course you do. I take it anyway. You've got to take it. You can't say to interviewers, "Well actually, I thought the set was rubbish last night." If people say that set was a bit long, or a bit flat, you have to say, "It was my idea." You take the rough . . . But they've got their own band now,' he says, referring to ARK, the group formed by the members of the Fall who jumped ship in New York, 'and everyone says . . . *It wasn't you* [laughs].'

Now, Mark says, 'I relate a lot to, not to DJs playing music, but a lot of these dance groups, and I think they are very much ignored, much more than we were. You never hear about them, they never get reviewed, but there are some really interesting bands in Manchester, about seventeen, eighteen years old. They've got a guy on the records, they've got a machine, something like a sampler, but they've also got a bass player and the singer looks like someone who works in a supermarket. They've got tapes going, keyboards, a lot of distortion, a lot of feedback. If they've got drums, they'll play just one drum, or a hi-hat. And the lyrics are just hitting you; stuff you can't understand.'

That will do nicely as a description of the music that Mark has been issuing over the last two years, beginning with the 'Plug Myself In' single, a collaboration with the Manchester production team DOSE, who had connections with Pete Waterman's PWL operation, and the release of the 1997 Fall LP *Levitate*, which again featured input from DOSE, and was partly recorded at the PWL studios in Manchester.

'I looked on *Levitate* as a new start,' says Mark. 'That was part of the disagreement; I think the group understood what was going on. They were even talking about going on strike if we used a DAT player. [He sounds exasperated.] You're the Fall, for Christ's sake. It's amazing how many times I've had to put up with that kind of crap. You think you're past all that; fellas with beer bellies turning everything you do into a bloody Sex Pistols track. I thought that stopped happening ages back.'

There weren't many words on *Levitate*. The texts sounded like cut-ups, like they'd been blasted into incoherent fragments. Was that deliberate?

'Yeah, very, and that was what started the rows with the group as well. I was doing that onstage, walking off. I was doing it deliberately. People would say he was too drunk to sing so he disappears for fifteen minutes, but I wasn't. What I was trying to do . . . When you've got nothing to say, don't say it, I reckon, and it was really working well. The audiences were getting younger and younger, and they were really getting into it, because if you talk to young people, that's what they listen to; they don't like a lot of lyrics. The lads who work at PWL, they don't care about lyrics; they're just another layer in the track. But the group would be saying, "You never do your job."'

Applying the Protestant work ethic.

'No, they want to be rock stars; but those days are gone in my mind, a long time ago [laughs]. And they started doing stupid things onstage. I haven't been in that situation since before I was in the Fall. You can't sing to that way of playing. I had to bring back the old Fall things, fine people for doing drum rolls [laughs]. Fined for too many solos. "What did you think of those two solos I put in?" "Did you like them?" "Yeah." "Well, it's coming out of your wages."'

What kind of response did that get?

'Not much,' he says, still laughing so hard that he almost spills his drink.

An insight into the kind of volatile relationships that exist between Smith and the musicians he works with can be heard on 'Inch', a track which came out of the collaborations with DOSE and begins with a tape of a heated phone conversation between Smith and DOSE's Simon Spencer. 'Inch' has only just been released as a single, but the relationship with DOSE was actually terminated two years ago during the sessions for *Levitate*.

'I had to fire them,' says Mark. 'Working with them was great, but the mistake I made there was asking them to work on *Levitate*. They went dead rocky. I felt like a real corrupter. They obviously read a book on how to be a rock producer, or how to behave. I said, "If I wanted a bad rock producer, I'd have got one. I want you to do what you did when I worked with you [on 'Plug Myself In')." Jason [Barron] still works with us. He was working at PWL at the time. He did a lot on *Levitate*, engineering and helping me with sounds. A lot of those funny noises, I couldn't have done that with a rock producer.

'All those lads who work at PWL, people sneer at them, they work on Steps and all that, but their own stuff is dead weird. Guitar groups sneer at Pete Waterman's, but they're pushing a few more barriers than a lot of people. They leave school at sixteen and go straight into the studio. You go into other studios, the engineer's smoking pot, he's got his own band, his own ideas. With these lads, you can say, "I want it to sound like this", and you can make the noise with your mouth. You go out for a drink, come back, and they say, "We did it, Mark, the minute you went out the door." [Laughs.] You're so used to coming back an hour later and having to say, "No, it's not like that, now do it like this."

'Triple echo. Sixties sounds. I said to them, "I want a backward noise, a bit like on *Sgt. Pepper's* but not quite." They all went, "What? A *Sgt. Pepper's* sound? What's that?" One of the older ones said, "Oh, it's an LP or something." I said, "I fucking love you lads!"

'He's been really good to me, Pete Waterman. At PWL they just have PWL artists working there, but he did it as a favour to me. He's the best record-company boss, for me. When I was working with DOSE, they'd be going, "Do this, do that"; there were all these managers, interfering buggers, from their label. Pete Waterman comes in and says, "Let Mark do what he wants, all right? He knows what he's doing." "Yes, Pete!" Stopping record labels interfering is half the job. What you hear on the record is like five per cent of the work.'

Earlier this year, the Fall's current record company, Artful, released a Mark E. Smith solo project, *The Post Nearly Man*, sections of which were recorded at PWL. Marketed as a spoken-word record, the CD was best understood if listened to as an audio scrapbook, or in the tradition of the kind of marginalised small-hours radio art discussed in Douglas Kahn and Gregory Whitehead's *Wireless Imagination: Sound, Radio, and the Avant-Garde*.

The first track on *The Post Nearly Man*, 'The Horror in Clay', opens with a quote from H. P. Lovecraft's 1926 tale 'The Call of Cthulhu'. The connection forms a link with some of Mark's earliest works. Lovecraft, who fused 'the brooding idiosyncrasies and metonymic strategies of the nineteenth-century Gothic imagination' (in the words of Joyce Carol Oates) with proto-science-fiction scenarios and his own nightmarish dreamscapes into hair-raising tales of existential terror and insight, has long been a marker for Smith's own intrepid imagination. For the Fall's genuinely spooky 1979 song 'Spectre vs. Rector', just reissued by Cog Sinister/Voiceprint as part of the *Dragnet* album, Smith invoked the terrible character of Yog-Sothoth from 'The Dunwich Horror', and many of his texts ('The Impression of J. Temperance', 'Jawbone and the Air-Rifle', 'Garden', as well as more recent songs such as 'Hurricane Edward' and 'The Horror in Clay') appear to draw on both Lovecraft's themes and techniques.

So I ask: when did you first read Lovecraft?

'When I was . . . a child really. It's funny going back to it and reading it now, which I did, with doing that record. It's very strange. It reminds you of how you were as well, what you thought . . .' Mark tails off, then continues: 'I'm one of those people who rages about the way Lovecraft is treated in the cinema.'

Hollywood does have a tendency to ruin everything it touches.

'Yeah, everything. There are not many films that are better than the books, or as good as.'

There is a lot of diverse material on *The Post Nearly Man*. Where did it come from?

'A couple of years ago I got this commission to write six episodes of what was going to be like an *X-Files* thing. I said I'll do six 25-minute stories. So I spent all this time doing it, and the music, and got all these people to help me with the scripts, got them all ready, went to the TV station, and they said, "Oh we've changed our minds", the new directors. It was like four or five months' hard work up the spout. Then the last thing I heard was *The X-Files* had been in contact with the TV station and they said to me could we have a look at your scripts again because we can't find the ones you submitted. I said, "No fucking way. You'll send them to *The X-Files*, rip all my ideas off, and then send them back and say you're not interested." So I burned half of them,' he says, laughing, 'and I used the ones that were left for bits of *Nearly Man*.'

The record features a disorientating range of characters and scenarios, which are made more oblique by the strange cuts and edits.

'I started getting deliberately obscure. That was the fun bit of it. I had people reading out parts of the script in the wrong tense [laughs], the third person. They'd say, "This can't be right, can it?", and I'd say, "No, leave it, it's great."

'I would have liked it to be about an hour and a half long, more speakers, and using these stereos you can get now where the bass is behind you and the drums are in front of you, this glorified furniture. I thought it would be good to have the voices like that, so that there's someone talking behind you.

'It was very frustrating in a lot of ways. It always happens to me; when I get the time and opportunity to do these things all these other things happen in your life. I don't know what it is with me; I've done something wrong in a past life or something. Something else will come up and it's on your mind, like that thing in New York, or I'll split up with the missus. Always.

'Another problem was, when it came time to cut it, edit it together, the guy at the cutting studio couldn't handle it, a lot of people couldn't handle it, and it became like cursed. At the record plant the lacquer went missing. They did a cut of it and it came out all hiss. There was a demo of it and it was sent to record shops and it came out backwards. You're doing it on your own and you think it's going to be totally controllable, but it wasn't, it was worse."

Because there were all these other people dealing with it down the line?

'No not really, it was just weird, It was like cursed, this bloody thing.'

The night before I am due to interview Mark, I read a short story titled 'The Misanthrope', written in the years leading up to the First World War, by the English novelist J. D. Beresford. The story is related by an anonymous narrator, who travels to an isolated rocky island in order to visit the Misanthrope of the title, who has exiled himself there from all humanity due to a terrible psychic affliction. '*When I look at people in the face,*' he explains to his horrified visitor, '*I see them as anybody else sees them. But when I look back at them over my shoulder I see [...] Oh! I see all their vices and defects. Their faces remain, in a sense the same, but distorted [...] beastly [...] I was living in a world of beasts...*'

Compared to many of the writers discussed by H. P. Lovecraft in his 1927 essay 'Supernatural Horror in Literature', among them M. R. James, Arthur Machen and Algernon Blackwood, all of whom have been cited as influential by Mark Smith, Beresford is a forgotten figure in the history of turn-of-the-century fantastical literature. But he also wrote a biography of H. G. Wells, one of the pioneers of the idea of psychic time travel; and another of his novels, written in 1911, was titled *The Hampdenshire Wonder*, the tale of a child with such an advanced hyper-intelligence that it is eventually ostracised from the working-class community of its birth.

The reason for citing Beresford here will hopefully become clear presently, but after reading 'The Misanthrope', I skim-read Philip K. Dick's 1974 novel *Flow My Tears, the Policeman Said*, trying to nail down the evidence that will lend weight to a question which I want to ask Mark the following day.

In the past, I begin, you've mentioned that you like composers such as Schoenberg and Stockhausen. I was wondering whether you picked up on that stuff from reading Philip K. Dick, who was a big fan of that kind of music, and would drop references to it into his books. Were you aware of that?

'That's interesting. No, I never knew that, but it explains a lot, because his stuff was so layered at times, like fifteen things going on at once in some books. I've seen biographies of Dick and I've had to put them away because it's horrible. It breaks your heart, the shit he had to put up with, bumming meals off students, things like that, just to live, and that was just before he died. I go on about not getting any royalties but he got nothing. They pissed around with *Blade Runner* for about five years before it came out, kept changing the script, and he's broke, health's gone, just wondering where he's going to get something to eat, and he dies like a fortnight before *Blade Runner* comes out. So, I'm not that bad off.'

Like a lot of the writers you've said you admire, Dick was interested in the notion of psychic time travel; attempting to decipher the present by intercutting it with past and future events, which has been a theme in a lot of your work.

'Pre-cog he used to call it. That's happened to me so many times. I've had a dream, or think I've seen something in the paper about an event, and six months later I'll see it. It's weird. You won't believe this, but I remember the last time we toured Yugoslavia, I said to the band, "Something's going to happen here." They said, "Why? It's lovely." But I could feel it. I could *feel* it. I could bloody ... I could virtually see it, in the audience, above the audience. I'd come offstage and say, "It's fucking weird that audience." I'd never been frightened by an audience, you know? The group go, "No, it's great, the birds are lovely" and all that. And it was ... they're better dressed than us. But every time I went out I got in trouble with the police or a soldier. Every fucking time. I got stopped. I got chased by soldiers once. I thought: there's something going on here, I don't like it, you know what I mean?' Then he says: 'I'd be talking to somebody and think they were crying. They weren't.'

Mark laughs. 'It's weird isn't it? I don't like that too much. I don't have that so much now. It used to shit me up when I was a teenager. [He shivers a little.] Some things are better you don't know; don't want to know. Don't want to forecast or hear about.'

Maybe those kinds of things only feel strange because they've been suppressed or they are not discussed, or because they have been dismissed because they are the stuff of science fiction and fantasy; weird fiction, as Lovecraft called it. Maybe they are really not that strange.

'That's right. Maybe people should be a bit more aware of it. It's like these politicians: don't they read history books? I mean, the bloody Balkans is basic History O-Level. I knew when I was fifteen that they were bloody trouble, man. They decimated the English working class, the bloody Serbians, starting that mess off, getting mad about nought again. You go to Scotland, half the bloody male population died, you know what I mean? Three quarters of the villages you go through, gone, you know, because of a bloody Serb, and taking notice of them and getting involved. I think Bismarck had the best quote. He said the whole of the Balkans is not worth the life of one single Pomeranian Grenadier [laughs]. They said he was cynical, a horrible man, Bismarck. I thought he was bloody great.

'I haven't played abroad for quite a while now, so I've had things coming back. When you think back, it's quite weird. We were in Yugoslavia about the time of . . . 'White Lightning'. I don't remember when that was. Some years are a blur.'

> 'The visionary is inevitably an Outsider.'
> Colin Wilson

Is it absurd to refer to Mark Smith as a visionary? Perhaps; and almost certainly if you subscribe to the kind of ingrained hierarchical value system imposed on our world by the likes of Roger Scruton, who might regard the likes of Smith as a mere insect, scurrying around the feet of the Great Men of art, science and literature. But many of the themes that have populated Smith's writing over the last two decades might reasonably fit the visionary-outsider identity in nineteenth-century European literature as defined by Colin Wilson in his mid-fifties tract *The Outsider*. Like both Lovecraft's and Wilson's anti-canons of Outsider authors, like Louis-Ferdinand Céline and his notorious disciple Charles Bukowski, all writers whose supernatural X-ray vision caused them to ascend/descend into misanthropic loathing and linguistic overload, Smith still conjures idiosyncratic narratives as a means of decoding and reflecting back the absurdities of his times.

The Crying Marshal is just the latest in a line of invented personae that stretches back to the late seventies and the creation of Roman Totale ('the bastard offspring of Charles I and the Great God Pan') and through which Smith projects himself and his unbidden visions.

The 'I' in your songs is very rarely you, I say.

'Right, well done, someone's got it. I find it very stimulating, writing for characters. It's a good way to filter ideas. It gives you a new slant. I feel a lot freer head-wise now, so that I have time for such thoughts, odd things. Explaining it to everybody else is a pain in the arse. But why should you have to explain it?'

It's been put about that sections of *The Marshall Suite* are based on Hardy's *The Mayor of Casterbridge*. Mark laughs dismissively.

'That got out because I was trying to explain the concept to the so-called producer, a loony, who'd get everything wrong anyway. They think: Mayor/ Marshal. I said, "Have you read *The Mayor of Casterbridge*?" No. I said, "It just goes down and down that book, which is the way you produced the record, you bastard."' [laughs]

So who, or what, is the Crying Marshal?

'He's just . . . a figure, to link it together. The idea started when I did the track 'The Crying Marshal' with these two blokes called the Filthy Three; one of them is Jason [Barron]. They had a song and they didn't have any lyrics for it. That song came from that; throwing ideas around. I thought it would be good to do it as the story of his life, a themed LP, with a thread running through it. It's such an unhip thing to do, but I do want to continue and develop it, maybe a five-sided thing next: the return of the Marshal.'

The link with the version of 'This Perfect Day' is elusive.

'There isn't one.'

So why do you do cover versions?

'It gives you a different perspective, which is good for me, and you can be a lot freer in a strange way. 'F-'Oldin' Money" [also on *The Marshall Suite*], that's half a cover; it's based on a piece of rockabilly from around 1955 [by Tommy Blake]. I can't even find the publisher or whether the bloke's alive or anything. I don't like to just lift things; I've always been against that.

'I'm still very mad that some of the mixes on the new record were pissed about with by the producer while I was away,' Mark announces suddenly. 'It's only one or two tracks, no one else will notice it, but I'm furious. I won't talk to him. And they missed a track off! "The Crying Marshal"! [He laughs hysterically.] The remix is on it, but the original song isn't, so there should be like another two and a half minutes. Not to worry. You get to a point where it's not worth putting everything back again.' Then he adds, through gritted teeth: 'It's good I can laugh about it, innit!

'I used to try and cover everything,' he continues, 'still do, but if you have your eyes everywhere and your brain everywhere it just fucks you up, take my word for it.'

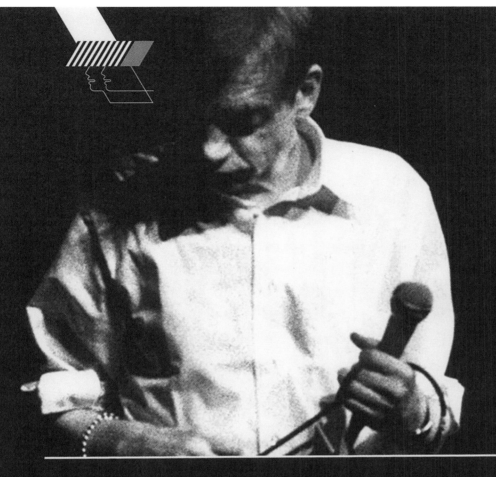

Sunday 12th November

Mark E Smith Presents

The Fall

Plus Special Guests

The Old Brewery /// Manchester

Tickets £16 /// 0161 832 1111 /// ticketline.co.uk

www.thewarehouseproject.com

346

①

B-SIDE TO 'REFORMATION!'
r — 2, 3 + 4!

In. Y   Our **O**dious o**VER**t**I**
Esti   mation + **O**vious **V**eneration of
Your   self-worth that **E**ngages in **R!**
r-r-r   ed ht. chili embracement. that
is **M**   entioned within **Y**our **D**our
Obs   session with — **O**! — all that
is —!   **R**epresenting an all time low

bench — mark **In Semi-North** U.s. +

② E̶u̶r̶o̶   p̶e̶a̶n̶ r̶o̶c̶k̶ t̶h̶a̶t̶ s̶h̶o̶u̶l̶d̶ **V̶e̶n̶e̶r̶a̶t̶**
   ̶e̶y̶o̶n̶d̶ — i̶n̶d̶e̶e̶d̶ **E̶n̶t̶r̶e̶a̶t̶**
   Euro pean rock. that surely **V**enerates
   and   **E**ntreats a. **R**eformation

③

Sketches for artwork and correspondence on
'Reformation' single, 2006.

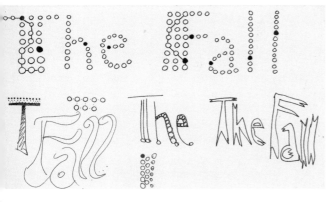

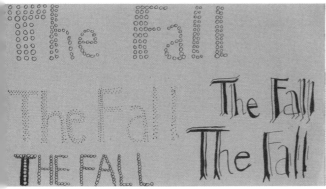

See changes,
mirror image
of left figure now
also on the right side!

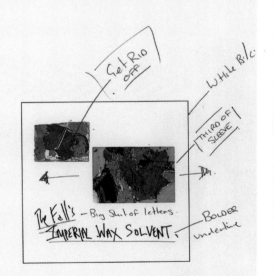

348

T:
Mr. Steve Hammonds
c/o. Sanctuary
SANCTUARY HOUSE.
45-53
Sinclair Road
LON; W14 0NS.

From:
M.E.SMITH -
16, Winchester
Avenue -
Prestwich
Manchester M25
0LT.

22ND JAN. 08

Dear Steve:
    Herewith rest of Artwork for
'IMPERIAL WAX SOLVENT'.
    If you and Becky want to
composite it up it's O.K.
by me — it'll be revenge
for Box Set 2!! ➔

Just credit Pascal le Groas +
ME + youse for it.
    Hope everything's O.K. yo-
end !!
            yo. pal.
            Mark E. Smith
            4 The Fall" + x.

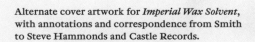

**Alternate cover artwork for *Imperial Wax Solvent*,
with annotations and correspondence from Smith
to Steve Hammonds and Castle Records.**

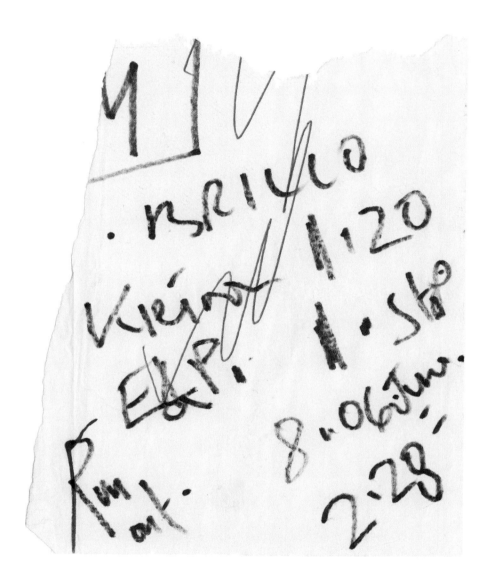

Pages 349–54: *New Facts Emerge* correspondence
and preparatory notes for songs, 2017.

Tues 25th.

F.A.O.
ANDY / MATT :

Forgot : can you
please put the 1st.
minute of this cassette
on back end of
song "OL VF ROC" ?

— Going in to —
OZZRRANC

1. NEW FACTS EMERGE
   MUST BE CD (FROGS)

2. BRILLO
   Shorter version de FATSO

3. GIBBOUS GISSUN
   USED UNISTED shorter VBS
   2-38

4. 2ND HOUSE
   move from beginning
   0-30 secs. Talking form
   NOW

5. Games 64.
   DOWNLOAD - Replace with Shadows Sent

6. FOL-DE-ROL.

7. 22V SPAZ-MAK
   From Second Joints

8. From M. House.

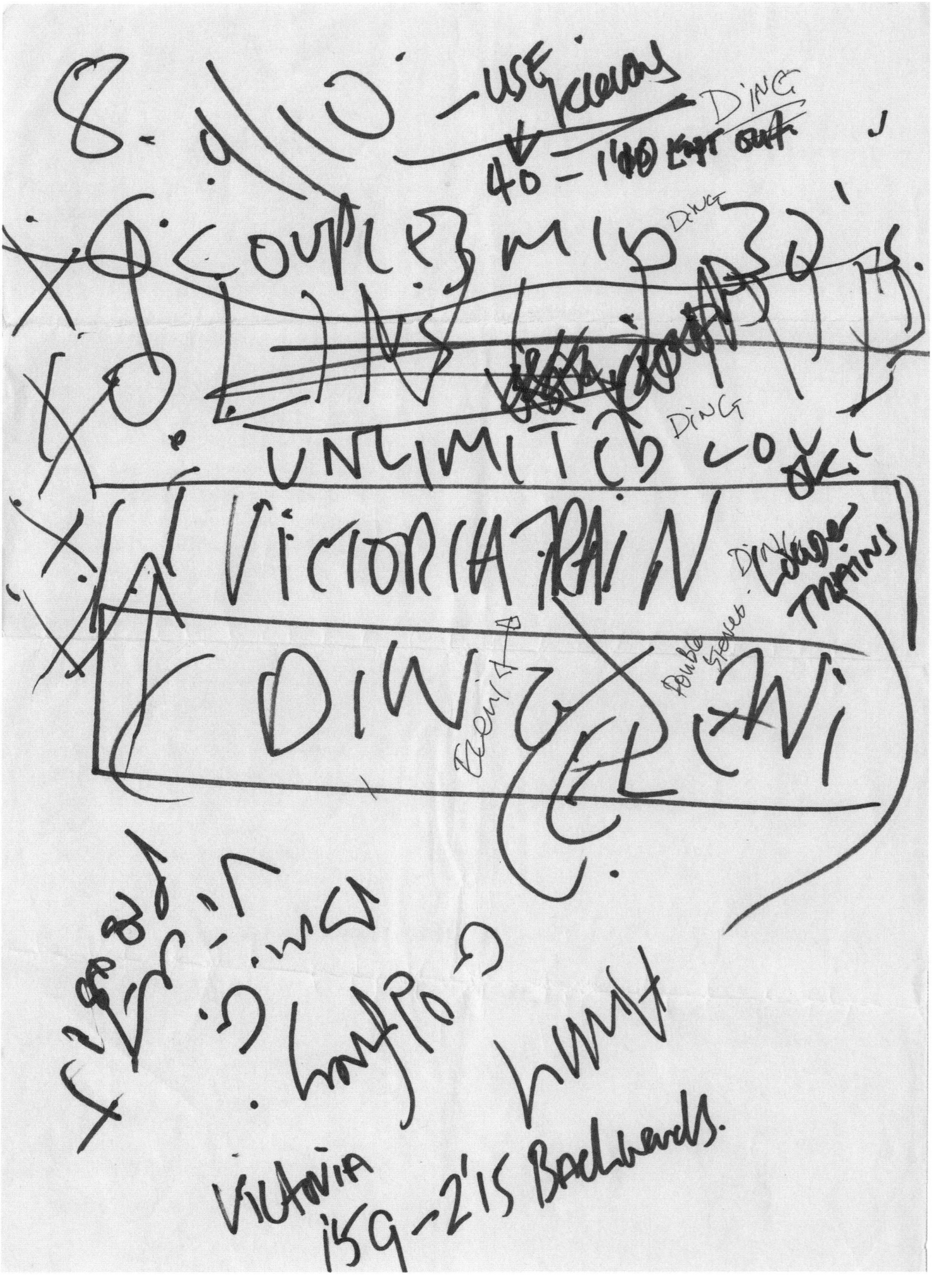

8.

10. — USE kleons

40 — 1'40 left out DING

COUPLE3 M DING 30

INS

UNLIMITED DING LOV

VICTORIA RAIN DING Longer TRAINS

DIN NI

VICTORIA
159 — 2'15 Backwards.

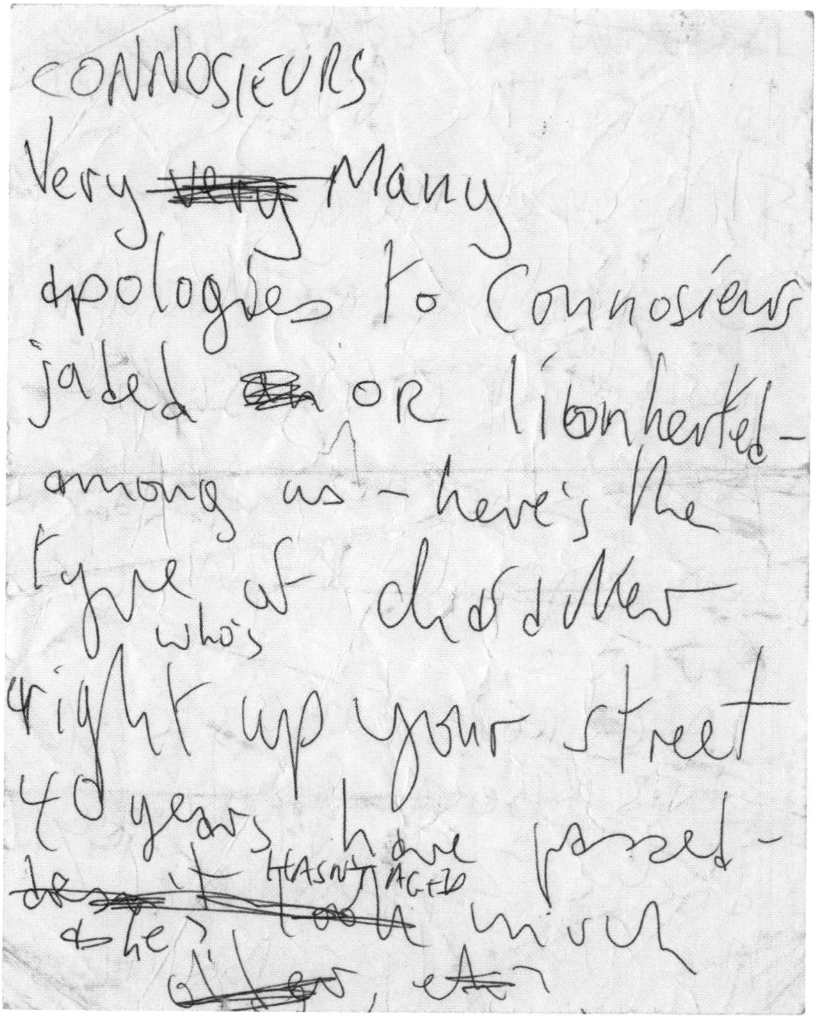

CONNOSIEURS

Very ~~Very~~ Many
apologies to Connosieurs
jaded ~~or~~ OR lionherted -
among us - here's the
tyre of chordsteer
        who's
right up your street
40 years have passed -
~~desn't~~ HASNT AGED ~~too~~ much
~~♭ he?~~ either, eh?

~~BRITAIN~~ NOW A COCKY SHROUDED MAN.
No more the budget
slit eyed mug
Decorating a Mussolini
period history shop —
— This man has Adapted
his urges to the WEST
Europe,
A EUROPE WHO'S CITIZ-
ENS Although Superficially
alike, Zipping Around
the Ucer-less, Borderless

An Episode in a Lodging House: Mark E. Smith Has Been Assigned

Mistrust all eulogies containing the words 'contrarian', 'curmudgeon' and 'national treasure': these are inevitably the work of hacks.

The north's bricks, red as meat, its tar-paper-roofed sheds, once-grand high streets grown tawdry, blackening civic buildings crumbling under the pressures of faltering socialism, burgeoning self-interest and lichen; its Roman roads, its moors – crowded with witches and freezing-cold, slow-moving trains – its murderers, its flying saucers, chantries, ginnels, fields, the simultaneous cold and heat, the overlapping historical diasporas: these are the elements constituting the map needed for a true understanding of the Fall. Other areas, regions, towns and cities possess their own stratifications too, certainly, but lack *this* particular stratification.

The north is where the modern world was, for better or worse, invented, a chance intersection of natural resources, capital, talent, geography, religion, history and greed: Manchester, Britain's true capital and hotbed of creation, and Liverpool, the great port with the world's largest hotel. Mark E. Smith, though, came not from the birthplace of capitalism but from its asymmetrical conjoined twin, Salford, and thus had three miles of distance to provide him with clarity. His relationships with Salford, Manchester, Greater Manchester, Lancashire, the north, England and, indeed, the UK itself remained ambivalent. Smith generally seemed more partial to the US, which in any case he sometimes spoke of as though it were a continuation *of* Lancashire, mentioning the 'fact' that more Lancastrians had died at the Alamo than 'Americans'. He hated the reductive paradigm of the north and its hot-blooded simpletons, though, and worked hard to personify its actual mercurial genius.

Smith had identified in the repetitive strut, clatter and heave of rock and roll a method for accelerating out of the normal: what to some extent Boards of Canada would later do with the memories of childhood, the Fall did full-on with the detritus of everyday experience and its intersection with history and the future. One of the tools Smith used was the change of mood, like a cheap New English Library horror paperback consumed in sheaves of flicked-through pages to get to the mucky bits and the nasty parts. He had a talent for never allowing comfiness, never allowing smugness. I can't call this a Mancunian mode of humour because my granddad, who was from Chorley, possessed a very similar one, albeit in an inverted version. It is certainly northern, but perhaps 'Lancastrian' is the proper definition of it, and perhaps it is indigenous to that region, with its priest holes, immigrant communities and witches: a humour of sarcasm hidden inside gentleness, and gentleness hidden inside sarcasm.

In some ways, Smith resembles a character from Liverpool's *other* modern horror great, Ramsey Campbell: a seedy journalist whose pursuit of some cursed scoop has caused him to become infected himself. MES often spoke of the psychic gifts he claimed to have drunk himself free of, and the echoes of worlds parallel to our own are there everywhere in the Fall, always ready to gnaw their way through the walls separating them from us.

Smith was a symbol of strangeness — not of eccentricity, that fundamentally harmless Victorian predilection for dressing up, but *real* strangeness: the type whose unpredictability and power to alienate never allow the spectacle to settle into place. To watch Smith in interviews — making it impossible for the practitioners of the innocuous rituals of pop and rock to practise their trade — was a thing of beauty. The brilliant anecdotes, one-liners and non sequiturs are so legion, in fact, that they threaten to colonise the character in our minds. And Smith wasn't just funny — he was fucking hilarious. In the smug haze of post-Blair British divaphilia, the music papers increasingly played up this side of MES, creating an unnuanced troll for easy laughs. In the same way, the toothless gurner he often presented to press cameras began to crowd out the memory of the young man with the feverish, oddly leonine beauty that vaguely evoked Kim Milford's performance as Billy Duncan, the youth possessed by the power of an alien weapon, in Charles Band's 1978 *Laserblast*.

Even the obtuseness and the bloody-mindedness feel like behaviours deliberately adopted to avoid being compromised, a misdirecting dazzle camouflage whose unpredictable form made it impossible to judge distance or angle, rendering appropriation and commodification impossible. Smith seemed somehow — in his art, at least — devoid of a desire to be liked, and yet also lacking in its concomitant, the desire to be hated and to provoke (though Smith *did* provoke, of course). He seemed to understand how arbitrary, instinctive dislikes provided valuable directions as to how to navigate the world. Aptly, Smith managed to personify the point at which mild drunkenness very briefly blurs into something like clairvoyance. His curse was that of being able to pick up the broadcasts of everything around him: the people, the buildings, the plague pits buried beneath the supermarket, the ley lines under the multi-storey car park.

Though most often utilised for his dissociative comedic value and genuine talent for humour on the few times he did appear on television, Smith would have been better suited to a role on *Sapphire & Steel*. Closer in spirit to the Fall than any sad-sack 'band' of clowns with guitars, *Sapphire & Steel* was a British television programme which first aired in 1979, the same year that *Live at the Witch Trials* was released. In the show, two mysterious agents of obscure higher forces attempt to resolve 'irregularities'. Though often manifesting through the most banal aspects of everyday life and history, these irregularities are described sketchily, allusively, as though their unearthly provenance makes them difficult to render in human terms. Time in *Sapphire & Steel* is treated as a dangerous and possibly hostile force with its own inscrutable agenda, capable of breaking through into the human world and wreaking immense damage.

Each *Sapphire & Steel* story was set in some unremarkable location – a farmhouse, a roadside café and garage, a station, a block of flats – and was protracted for a punishing number of episodes, until, like one of Maigret's investigations, every detail of its already-familiar setting became so intimately known to the viewer that it returned to being alien, like a word endlessly repeated. *Sapphire & Steel* was disturbing, in a way that clearly went far beyond the intentions of its creators and which impressed itself radically upon the psyches of many of those who were exposed to it in childhood. Smith, a vocal opponent of nostalgia, pretension and whimsy, would no doubt have hated the idea, but his ambiguous nature, his simultaneous avuncularity and coldness, would have sat perfectly in its world.

The cure was in no pill but in *Zeitung*, and *Zeitung* contains also that most definitive of cures: Mark E. Smith is now dead, destroyed by *Zeit* – time. It is he who is now the inanimate popular commodity disobeying its owners by refusing to perform the role foisted upon it and using its gifts for its own ends. Smith's shade wanders the chantries and shopping precincts, his placcy bag filled with ectoplasm. Unreadable, uncategorisable, shifty, an amorphous shoggoth lurking behind the bins in the alley between where Woolworths used to be and the café. Phone boxes contain unnamed threats. The bends in a stretch of provincial dual carriageway parallel an ancient curse. Or perhaps, his detective instinct posthumously vindicated, he has returned to the employ of the forces controlling this dimension and now prowls time, seeking to resolve irregularities in unloved public spaces, anonymous pubs, repurposed Victorian buildings, their fittings rendered dreamlike by a century's worth of coats of paint.

My brother commented that the loss of Smith made him feel vulnerable. At first, this statement seemed strangely mawkish. As the day wore on, however, it began to make an increasing amount of sense.

Author Biographies

Stuart Bertolotti-Bailey is a graphic designer, writer and publisher who currently works as Head of Design at the ICA in London. He co-founded the left-field arts journal *Dot Dot Dot* in 2000, is one half of artist duo Dexter Sinister and a quarter of archiving/publishing platform The Serving Library. He also designed this book.

Michael Bracewell is the author of several works of fiction and non-fiction, including *England is Mine* (HarperCollins, 1997) and *Perfect Tense* (Vintage, 2000).

Mark Fisher (1968–2017) was co-founder of Zer0 Books and, later, Repeater Books. His blog, *K-Punk*, defined critical writing for a generation, as did his books, *Capitalist Realism*, *Ghosts of My Life* and *The Weird and the Eerie*.

Dan Fox is a writer, film-maker and musician living in New York. Formerly co-editor of *Frieze* magazine, he is the author of two books – *Pretentiousness: Why It Matters* and *Limbo* (both Fitzcarraldo Editions). He co-runs the music label Junior Aspirin Records, and is co-director of the documentary *Other, Like Me: The Oral History of COUM Transmissions & Throbbing Gristle*.

Elain Harwood is an architectural historian who wrote a dissertation on Victorian asylums, including Prestwich, before specialising in Modernism, Art Deco and Brutalism. In 1979 she read a review of a Fall gig and rushed out to buy *Live at the Witch Trials*. She lost count after seeing them fifty times.

Owen Hatherley writes regularly on aesthetics and politics for various publications. He is the author of several books, including *Europe Express* (Penguin, 2018) and *Red Metropolis* (Repeater, 2020), and is the editor of *The Alternative Guide to the London Boroughs* (Open House, 2020). He is the culture editor of *Tribune*.

Scott King is an artist and graphic designer. He worked as art director for *i-D* magazine and creative director for *Sleazenation* magazine. King has also worked with Malcolm McLaren, Pet Shop Boys, Róisín Murphy, Saint Etienne and Suicide, amongst others. His work has been exhibited internationally, in both commercial galleries and institutions.

Richard McKenna grew up in the visionary utopia of 1970s South Yorkshire and now ekes out a living among crumbling Roman ruins. He's a senior editor at and co-founder of *We Are the Mutants*, an online magazine focusing on the history and analysis of Cold War-era popular and outsider culture.

Tessa Norton writes regularly about art, books and music for various publications including *The Wire*, and for exhibitions and events including Liverpool Biennial and The Tetley. She published the artists' book *The Fields Here Are Full of Ghosts* with Wysing Arts Centre in 2019, and she is a Jerwood Arts Fellow at FACT gallery for 2020–1.

Siân Pattenden is a writer and illustrator. She started at *Smash Hits* aged eighteen and has since been a features writer for titles such as *NME*, *The Face* and the *Guardian*, and is sometimes on television and radio. She has written six children's books and once acted as Young Tegan in *Doctor Who*, for about ten minutes, wearing a wig.

In 1978, Mark E. Smith and the Fall were the first people Ian Penman ever interviewed. (He was so embarrassed by the subsequent article, he tried again in 1979.) His collection of essays, *It Gets Me Home, This Curving Track*, was published in 2019. A book about Billie Holiday is forthcoming.

Mark Sinker wrote for *NME* in the 1980s and edited *The Wire* in the 1990s. In 2019, Strange Attractor published his anthology of essays and conversations, *A Hidden Landscape Once a Week*: *The Unruly Curiosity of the UK Music Press in the 1960s–80s. marksinker.co.uk*

Bob Stanley is the author of *Yeah Yeah Yeah: The Story of Modern Pop* (Faber, 2013), and *Too Darn Hot* (Faber, forthcoming), and has written for the *Guardian*, the *Times*, *NME* and *The Face*. He is also a film-maker and founding member of the group Saint Etienne. He was writer in residence at the British Library in 2017.

Adelle Stripe is the author of *Black Teeth and a Brilliant Smile*, a novel inspired by the playwright Andrea Dunbar. It was shortlisted for the Gordon Burn Prize and Portico Prize for Literature. She lives in West Yorkshire.

Between 1981 and 2017, Jon Wilde worked as a journalist, specialising in interviews with hellraisers and wild-hearted outsiders. Based in Brighton, he now works as a mindfulness teacher, mentor and recovery coach.

Paul Wilson is a researcher, designer and writer whose work explores the everyday forms, places and histories of utopian words, actions and objects. He is a lecturer at the School of Design, University of Leeds.

Acknowledgements

360

This book would not exist without the incredible generosity of Fall fans. The visual materials here are all things that were treasured and kept over the years. Huge thanks in particular to Steve Hammonds, Barrie Reilly and Martin Slattery for squirreling away so much and selflessly sharing it.

We'd also like to thank:

Kevin Eden, Paul Kelly, Christie McDonald, Rita Tait and Robin Turner, Debsey Wykes and Andy Yates for generously sharing items, Gordon and Vanessa at Action Records, Dave Simpson for tea and sympathy, Becky Stewart for rifling through her archives and pulling out plums and Dave Timperley for keeping us on top of some of the more obscure latterday records.

Pam Vander, for her time, care and her generosity in sharing her moving photos of Mark.

The collectors who have dedicated many hours to maintaining records at thefall.org, The Annotated Fall, and – previously – in *The Biggest Library Yet* fanzine. We'd like to thank, in particular, Conway Paton, Pete Conkerton, Chris Connelly, Stefan Cooke and Mark Howard.

The book's contributors who have so generously refracted their varied expertise and wisdom through the lens of the Fall, Grant Showbiz for excellent stories and sage advice, and to Elain Harwood and Ian Penman for sharing items from their own collections too. And to Darren Ambrose for all his help with Mark Fisher's essay.

Our spirit guides from the US, the redoubtable bingo master Geoffrey Weiss and the book doktor Johan Kugelberg.

Lee Brackstone for commissioning the book, David Godwin and Philippa Sitters at DGA, and the wonderful team at Faber who took it forward – Alexa von Hirschberg, Dan Papps, Kate Ward, Jack Murphy, John Grindrod and Jonny Pelham. And much love to Stuart Bertolotti-Bailey, who first contributed an essay then stuck around to design the whole book.

Andy Lyons at *When Saturday Comes* and Emily Bick and Tony Herrington at *The Wire*, who not only gave us permission to reprint their interviews but also took the time to dig through redundant technology to find the original articles – it was very much appreciated.

Everyone involved with the Manchester Digital Music Archive (MDMA), especially Matthew Norman who provided contacts to so many collections.

Our friends, for support, suggestions and kindness, Liz Buckley, Emma Cardwell, Alex Conway, Sarah Cracknell, Andy Holden, Jo Forshaw, Tariq Goddard, Martin Green, Martin Kelly, Paul Kelly, Matthew Lees, Anneliese Midgley, Sian Murphy, Pete Paphides, Andy Rossiter, James Turner, Kate Turner, Maxine Smith, Jason Steel, Pete Wiggs and Jason Wood. And thanks to all our families, and especially to Jan Norton for holding the fort while we went off scouting collections.

The community of artists who worked on artwork for the group over the years, and who have contributed to exhibitions and events inspired by them. Special thanks, for incredibly helpful conversations and advice, to Claus Castenskiold, Sebastian Cording, Anthony Frost, Bert Holterdorf and Suzanne Smith.

Chris Evans for the airbrush portraits of Mark E. Smith (p. 217) and Wyndham Lewis (p. 233), 2005.

Richard Wilson Photography, Leeds and PDQ Fotos, Shipley for photo reproduction.

And finally, thank you to all the members of the Fall, 1977–2018, and especially to Mark E. Smith.

We are grateful to the following record companies for kindly allowing us to reproduce album artwork:

Live at the Witch Trials, Dragnet, Hex Enduction Hour, Room to Live, Perverted by Language, Code Selfish, The Infotainment Scan, Cerebral Caustic, Middle Class Revolt, Levitate, Are You Are Missing Winner?, Post TLC Reformation, Imperial Wax Solvent, Ersatz GB, Re-Mit, Sub Lingual Tablet, New Facts Emerge – Courtesy of Cherry Red Records / *Your Future Our Clutter* – Courtesy of Domino Recording Company / *Totale's Turns, Grotesque, Slates, A Part Of America Therein, 1981, The Light User Syndrome* – © Sanctuary Records Group Ltd, a BMG company. Courtesy of BMG Rights Management (UK) Ltd / *The Marshall Suite* – © Cavalcade Records Ltd, a BMG Company. Courtesy of BMG Rights Management (UK) Ltd / *The Wonderful and Frightening World of the Fall, This Nation's Saving Grace, Bend Sinister, The Frenz Experiment, I Am Kurious Oranj* – Licensed Courtesy of Beggars Banquet Records Ltd, by arrangement with Beggars Group Media Ltd / *Country on the Click* – Courtesy of Action Records / *Extricate, Shift Work* – Copyright Universal Music Catalogue / *Fall Heads Roll* – Copyright Narnack Records.

PS The albums pictured in this book are all from my collection, which felt like the right thing to do for completeness' sake. This does mean the images for *Imperial Wax Solvent* are from the Cherry Red reissue as I don't own a first pressing. Also, *The Unutterable* was the only album not to be issued on vinyl when it was released in 2000 – this is the first vinyl pressing from 2014. – BS